The ROOKIE'S GUIDE TO Options

2nd Edition

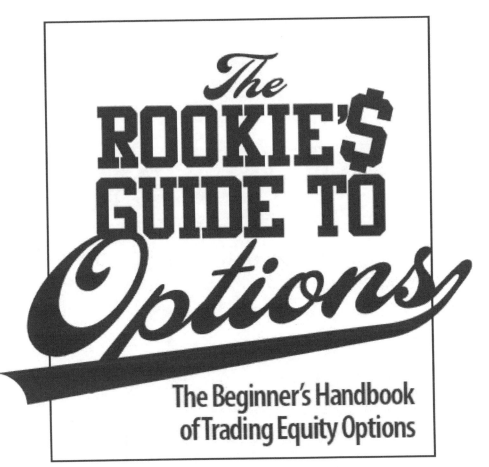

The ROOKIE'S GUIDE TO *Options*

The Beginner's Handbook of Trading Equity Options

BY MARK D WOLFINGER

Options for Rookies Books
Evanston, IL

The Rookie's Guide to Options

Published by Options for Rookies Books, Evanston IL

In the publication of this book, every effort has been made to offer the most current, correct and clearly expressed information possible. Nonetheless, inadvertent errors can occur, and rules and regulations governing personal finance and investing often change. The advice and strategies contained herein may not be suitable for your situation, and there is a risk of loss when trading options, stocks, commodity futures, and foreign exchange products. Neither the publisher nor author shall be liable for any loss of profit or any other commercial damage, including but not limited to special, incidental, consequential, or other damages, that is incurred as a consequence of the use and application, directly or indirectly, of any information presented in this book. If legal, tax advice or other expert assistance are required, the services of a professional should be sought.

ISBN: 978-0-9888439-1-2
Printed in the United States of America

To Penny

Preface to the Second Edition

Five years after publication of the first edition, it is time to revise and expand *The Rookie's Guide to Options*. I hope the revisions will make the experience of learning about options more efficient and enjoyable. Several discussions include additional clarification and detail. Some sections are brand new, offering insight into areas previously not explored.

There are two new chapters. The first (Chapter 21) introduces another useful option strategy, the calendar spread. The other (Chapter 22) provides advice on how the rookie trader can avoid mistakes when exercising options.

Even the look is new. The single column format makes the book easier to read and some material has been moved to the back of the book as Appendices.

Partnership

Your options education is a partnership. My job is to provide the necessary information and guide you through the process of learning and *understanding* the concepts. Your job is to devote the required time and effort. Your task is to be patient. Learn first—and trade later. Traders do not find success by memorizing rules. It is necessary to develop a solid understanding of how options work.

Where does a rookie's education end?

You will learn about topics such as volatility and spread trading. For reasons that are beyond my understanding, some option educators consider these to be 'advanced' topics. I consider them as necessary at *all levels*. Trading without a good understanding of these topics is similar to a jockey riding a racehorse with 20 extra pounds of dead weight in the saddlebags. Volatility plays a major role in the pricing of options in the marketplace and in strategy selection..

The discussion on 'the Greeks' is in the 'beyond the basics' section. Nevertheless, this is another so-called advanced concept that is far too basic and far too important to be ignored by newer traders. All traders—stocks, options, currencies, bonds etc. —must manage risk successfully to avoid failure. Make no mistake: trading requires skill and planning. Those who ignore risk management are likely to fail. The Greeks serve a single purpose: to measure risk. If any single risk parameter of any position makes you feel uncomfortable, it is easy to alleviate that specific risk. This ability is unique to options and it is by using the Greeks that such risk is managed. Do not be concerned if math is not your strong point because only simple arithmetic is needed when using the Greeks. By understanding how positions earn/lose money it is possible to manage risk intelligently.

Thank you to each reader who offered praise, submitted questions, or suggested changes for the first edition. Your input is always appreciated.

Send e-mail to rookies (at) OptionsForRookies (dot)com.

Welcome to the 2013 edition of The Rookie's Guide to Options.

Good trading!

Mark Wolfinger
Evanston, IL
May 2013
Updated Aug 2014

Table of Contents

Introduction

You are about to enter the exciting world of stock options. These versatile investment tools possess properties not found elsewhere in the investment universe: limited lifetimes with explicit expiration dates. Options were invented as hedging, or risk-reducing tools, allowing specific risks (described by the Greeks) associated with owning any position to be identified. Thus, each risk factor can be controlled to suit your needs.

Options allow investors to use leverage to take control of far more valuable stock positions with less cash at risk.

Options are versatile and can be used in a variety of strategies, ranging from ultra-conservative to outright gambles. I encourage readers to adopt strategies between the extremes.

It is possible to use advanced mathematics when discussing options, but in keeping with the goal of making this an enjoyable learning experience, this book uses nothing more complicated than elementary algebra. Let's leave the advanced math to the academics.

Equity options are related to stocks. The term used to describe that relationship is **derivative**. The value of an option is derived from the value of an individual stock or group of stocks (an index). If this sounds complicated, it is not. Computers and calculators do the math for us, and our job is to understand how to use the numbers — just as we learn to use any tool.

This book delivers the background information needed to understand why options do what they do. Note that key word: 'understand.' I'm not going to define a term without explaining how it relates to trading options. I'm not going to tell you how to open a trade and then leave you stranded. You will learn to open, manage and exit positions. I do not provide rules to follow. Instead, you get detailed explanations and suggestions that enable you to make your own decisions.

Many trade choices are personal, and I cannot know your specific circumstances. However, I'll help you find trades and make trade plans that suit your tolerance for risk and financial goals. In other words, we will work within *your* comfort zone.

The book contains a great deal of background information (Part I), lessons on three basic strategies (Part II), as well as explanations of how to adopt more advanced strategies (Part III).

These lessons are designed to help you use options *effectively*. That means trading with less risk, increasing the frequency of winning trades, and earning more money (when compared with trading without options). There is one important point: both the basic concepts and basic strategies are easy to understand. As with any other endeavor, the more sophisticated you become, the more you can do. Consider this book to be your college level course—perhaps even an elective course. However, it is not graduate school. Option trading can get very sophisticated and today's top experts are quants with PhDs in math or physics. The good news is that you do not have to compete directly with them. Option trading is so widespread that there is ample opportunity for everyone.

If you want to become an expert trader, this book will not get you there. However, it is an excellent starting point. And if your objective is to enhance your income by generating earnings with less chance of suffering large losses, then you have come to the right place. You do not have to compete with the professionals. Most of us can succeed by adopting the most basic strategies —if we have the discipline to manage risk. While I appreciate advanced strategies, I use only the methods discussed in this book when trading my personal money.

This guide takes you from the novice stage through the intermediate trader stage. Although intended for option rookies, there is enough meat in *The Rookie's Guide to Options* for the investor who already trades options. Re-reading these pages as you gain experience will provide insights you may have missed the first time.

My objective is for you, the reader, to gain a solid understanding of options and learn to use them to improve your investment results. You will not learn everything there is to know about options, but, you will be prepared to trade profitably. If we each do our jobs well, you will come away with a clear understanding of options—how they work and how you can make money by incorporating option strategies into your investing methods.

Be prepared for discussions on risk, including definitions (how much money can be lost vs. the probability of losing), setting risk limits (position size), using calculators to discover the odds that something specific will go wrong (stock doesn't move your way), etc. Included are ideas on how to handle risky situations. Is it better to get out of the trade or use an 'adjustment' trade that reduces risk to an acceptable level (compared with the potential reward)? These are all part of risk management, and included are my thoughts on why survival should be any trader's top priority. Earning money is important—in fact it is our reason for trading—but it ranks behind risk management, unless you plan to have a very short trading career.

Rookies

In the sports world, a rookie is someone in his/her first year of professional play. The term also refers to someone who is new to a profession. This book was written for newcomers to the world of options— not necessarily investment rookies, but option rookies. The strategies detailed are not the only ones available, but they were chosen because they can be understood and put into practice by traders who have patience and discipline. I stress discipline throughout the book because without it you have almost no chance of becoming a successful trader. Most investors who enter this realm are familiar with stock investing from the standpoint of owning individual stocks (mutual fund ownership does not count, but ETF trading does). If that is your experience, it should be a smooth transition when you add options to your arsenal of investment tools.

If you are brand new to investing, then you have more to learn. However, the good news is that you can get started without having formed any difficult-to-break bad habits.

Who can benefit from reading this book?

All investors who are interested in expanding their investing knowledge can benefit. Options are versatile investment tools that can be used in a wide variety of strategies. This book teaches you to use options intelligently—and that means using them as they were originally designed—to reduce risk.

Are you a very conservative investor who wants to protect the value of a stock market portfolio? You can use options to accomplish that. And you can obtain that insurance protection at little or no cost. Interested? Options are for you.

Are you a fairly conservative investor looking to invest in the stock market with reduced risk of loss? Options are for you. You will have fewer losing trades when you adopt any of several strategies that enhance your chances of coming out of any trade with a net profit.

Are you someone who has never used options but is familiar with the workings of the stock market? Options are for you. Depending on your investment objectives and just how much risk you are willing to assume, there are suitable option strategies that target steady income or high probability trades. There are strategies that allow you to buy stock below current market value or sell stock above current market value.

Are you an aggressive investor - someone who is much more interested in making money than in protecting current assets? Options are for you. There are strategies that provide the opportunity to make substantial returns on your investment—with limited risk.

Are you a gambler? Or do you have extra cash burning a hole in your pocket? Well, you too can use options. My purpose in writing this book is to encourage you to adopt more conservative option plays, but if you prefer to take chances, that is your decision. At least let me show you how to use options so that you have a reasonable chance of being successful. There is no need to adopt methods that offer only a small probability of working.

Whatever your investment objectives, options can help you achieve your goals

- capital preservation

- slow and steady growth with reduced risk

- aggressive growth with limited risk

- speculation

I'm sure you already understand how options work (even if you do not realize it). The concept behind options is common in our daily lives—retail store rain checks, bus transfers and insurance policies are all examples of common "options." Options can be used in very complicated strategies, but the good news is that there are enough easy-to-understand strategies that can be used to increase your chances of achieving your investing goals.

An effort will be required to absorb the material and put it into practice. The detailed examples and step-by-step guidance that accompany each strategy make this book the best available primer on the market.

Rather than just tell you what you "should" do, I'll take you through the decision-making process. When it comes to trading options, you'll discover that there are often alternatives. The early examples in the book provide a rationale for why buying or selling each option (there are often many) may be appropriate for you and your circumstances. As you experience the decision-making process, you'll begin to understand which variables are most important for meeting *your* personal goals, making it easier to make these decisions on your own.

There is more to trading than making money—it is also about satisfaction with your investment decisions. That means trading within your comfort zone. It is important to be confident that your investment choices are sound and you are satisfied with the reward potential for a given trade. But the risk required to earn the potential reward also must be considered. Too many investors do not bother to understand how much money is at risk in their attempts to earn a profit. I discuss risk management at length. It is not for the purpose of drumming an idea into your head. Investing with no consideration for risk is a foolish endeavor, and it is my job to see that you learn to pay attention to risk as an essential part of every trade. When risk is too high, then the investor is gambling. There is no need to own investments that keep you awake with worry. If the reward is too small for the risk (or the risk is too large for the possible reward), then that is a trade that is best avoided.

Options provide opportunities to trade with less money on the line. I trust that will allow you to rest easier, especially during those inevitable times when unexpected market gyrations cause many investors so much pain.

We'll talk about the risks and rewards that come with using options as we examine potential gains/losses from basic option strategies. Because this book is intended to show the average investor how to use the option markets to make money, we must start at the beginning. That requires an explanation of what an option is and how an option works—both in our everyday lives and in the stock market (Chapter 1).

Tips on Getting the Most Out of this Book:

Many chapters conclude with a brief quiz that is a helpful review for the material under discussion.

Please read the footnotes. They are not citations. They provide information that is useful to your complete understanding of the topic.

After spending more than 20 years as a market maker on the Chicago Board Options Exchange trading floor, in the year 2000, I turned my attention to educating individual investors about the benefits of using option strategies as part of their trading arsenals.

I do not promise that trading options will turn you into a money machine and that you will generate instant wealth. The hype-filled ads that you read promise much but common sense tells you they cannot deliver.

My rationale for adopting option strategies is that they provide two essential benefits when investing:

- Reduced risk. In real world terms, that means if unforeseen events occur (such as the year 2008 or the bursting of the technology bubble a decade earlier), your portfolio can be protected against significant loss. The truth is that you can use options as an insurance policy, in which you establish your own 'deductible.'

- Fewer and smaller losses. As a corollary, the specific strategies that I recommend give the trader a higher percentage of winning trades. The tradeoff is that the gains are limited.

If options provide such significant benefits, why doesn't everyone use options?

- Most traditional brokers do not promote options, and one (Raymond James) prohibits all customers from using them. Fortunately in today's world, there are several relatively new brokers who specialize in trading options.

- There is a downside. When you adopt the recommended strategies both profits and losses are limited. You can earn excellent, but limited, returns. That is not good enough for the greedy investor.

- Some investors dream of finding stocks that double (quickly) and then double again and again. Gains such as those are not possible when using the three basic conservative option strategies I advocate.

- Slightly more advanced strategies (credit spreads, iron condors, and others) are more versatile and can be used both conservatively and aggressively.

- If you seek huge and immediate profits when trading, then this book is not directed to you.

The education of investors on how to use options conservatively—and that means reducing risk and increasing the probability of earning money—when compared with buy and hold investing, is the basis for this book and blog: blog.mdwoptions.com/.

If you discovered this book after hearing the hype and unreasonable promises of promoters, you will soon discover that I offer realistic and achievable trading goals. I offer education. You learn to understand how options work and how to make intelligent trade decisions. I'll explain how to monitor positions and how to manage risk.

I'll help you recognize which personality traits add to (or reduce) your chances of becoming a winning trader. If you have the right attitude and mindset (you will learn to develop a money-making mindset), the lessons herein are for you.

Risk management is the key to your long-term success. If you trade to earn money while simultaneously reducing the odds of losing a large sum in a single trade, then your chances of success increase dramatically. Steady profits, coupled with small losses, leads to financial success.

Trade Rules

I have four rules for traders, and it is important to use them in this sequence:

- First: Do not go broke

- Next: Make money with acceptable risk

- Then: Protect your assets and earn more money

- The permanent rule: Never, never forget rule number one

My emphasis is on steady growth, with substantially less risk than comes with investing in the stock market. I trust that recent financial crises and market debacles opened your eyes to the truth: risk of loss is ever present and that owning a portfolio with less risk is prudent. It is a prudent and intelligent thing to be conservative when dealing with your life savings.

Options can help the majority of investors around the world to benefit by adopting risk-reducing strategies to manage an investment portfolio or to seek shorter-term trading profits.

You will learn to use strategies that offer better results (compared with buy and hold) when times are bad; excellent profits when the markets are calm; and good money when the markets are rallying. The drawback is that you earn less than everyone else when the markets are *surging*. That is the trade-off. If that is as appealing to you as it is to me, then the option strategies used in this book are for you.

Please understand that I cannot guarantee your results. Much depends on the individual stocks that you choose to own and trade. And because these methods are quite flexible, you may choose less protection and greater reward potential, or add additional protection against loss and accept less profit potential. In other words, a substantial portion of your results depends on how the strategies are used. Each trader makes his/her own decisions, but when you take the conservative approach, you avoid disasters and maintain an opportunity to earn returns that are well into the double digits. Isn't that good enough? Please consider if this approach appeals to you:

- Your account almost never suffers a big loss.

- Your account value is less volatile (smaller gains, smaller losses).

- Bear markets are a fact of life, and it is smart to be prepared.

- Very bullish years do occur. Will you be able to accept good, but reduced profits during those years? That is the test.

If you can pass the test, or believe you can, then using options to 'play' more safely can be a literal life-saver for you. The secret to building wealth is not making a fortune in the best of times—it is not losing a fortune in the worst of times. And remember, the recommended option strategies allow for significant profits. The profits may be limited, but you can set that limit to any level that suits your needs and tolerance for risk.

The standard disclaimer is that 'options are not for everyone.' Believe it. If you have the desire and required discipline, if you do your homework and use these lessons to learn to think for yourselves, then trading options should be a rewarding experience.

Unlike option classes you may see advertised in infomercials, or in full-page newspaper ads, the lessons contained in this book are hype-free with no unrealistic promises and no get-rich quick schemes.

Let's get started.

Part 1

Option Essentials & Background information

Chapter 1

Option Basics

Our discussion is limited to options involving stock market investments. Those include options on individual stocks, stock indexes, futures and exchange traded funds (ETFs). Many other options exist, such as options on commodities and currencies. Once you understand how stock options work, you'll also understand the principles concerning other options.

The stock options discussed here should not be confused with employee stock options (ESOP). Those are given to the employees of some companies as part of their compensation packages. Employee stock options are similar to the stock options under discussion—but are more limited because they are not traded on an exchange and cannot be bought and sold.

What is an option?

An option is a contract between two parties: the buyer and the seller. The price at which the transaction occurs is referred to as the **premium**.

That premium is quoted on a per-share basis. Because an option contract represents the right to buy or sell 100 shares of stock, the premium (paid by the buyer to the seller) is that per-share premium multiplied by 100. Thus, if you sell one option at $1.20, you receive $120.

The following description of options is not complicated. But anytime you encounter new terminology, it may not be instantly clear. Do not be concerned. You are already familiar with how options work because (as you will see shortly) they are common in our daily lives.

There are two types of options: a **call option** gives its owner the right to buy and a **put option** gives its owner the right to sell:

- A specified item (called the **underlying** asset)

- At a specified price (called the **strike price**)

- For a specified period of time (any time before the option's **expiration** date)

Thus, in return for paying a premium to purchase an option:

- The owner of a call option has the right (but not the obligation) to buy the underlying asset at the strike price any time before the expiration date.

- The owner of a put option has the right (but not the obligation) to sell the underlying asset at the strike price any time before the expiration date.

The underlying asset is almost always 100 shares of a specified stock or ETF. Options for which the underlying asset is an index are similar, but have some very important distinctions. We'll cover those differences when we discuss the trading of index options in Part III.

That is all there is to an option. Options are not complicated investment tools, despite their intimidating reputation. It is true that options can be used in complex strategies, but it is far more fun to use options in one of the many easy-to-understand strategies that provide an opportunity to make money—at the same time that your investment risk is reduced.

How does an option work?

An option grants to its owner certain rights. An option imparts certain obligations on the seller.

Rights of an option owner

If the option owner chooses to do what the contract allows, and if that decision is made before the expiration date, then the option owner is said to **exercise** the option. Once the option expires, all rights expire with it. Thus, it is crucial for option owners to make a final decision before expiration. But, do not be concerned; option expirations occur on a regularly scheduled basis—monthly for most issues, but weekly expiration dates are available for the most actively traded stocks and indexes, making it easy for everyone to know when options expire. We'll discuss expiration in greater detail later.

When an option is exercised, the option is cancelled and no longer exists. The exerciser buys (if it is a call option) or sells (if it is a put option) 100 shares of the specified stock at the strike price. Most of the time the option owner does not choose to exercise the option. As you will see later, it is often more efficient for the individual investor who owns those options to sell them, rather than exercise. But there are exceptions, so it is important to understand your rights when you own an option.

> **NOTE:** As stated above, the option owner has the right, <u>but not the obligation</u> to exercise. The term "but not the obligation" is vital in the options world. Many option novices fail to grasp the importance of this point. When you own an option, you are in control. You may choose to exercise your right to buy (call) or sell (put) the underlying asset at the strike price. But no one can force you to do so. The term "option" comes from the Greek word meaning choice. And it is strictly your choice—as long as you

make that decision before the option expires. The astute reader may wonder, "If I do not exercise the option, what else can be done with it?" Good question. The answer is discussed later in this chapter.

Obligations of an option seller

When you sell an option, you agree to accept certain standardized obligations which are defined in the contract. You are only so obligated if the option owner elects to exercise. Thus, you *may* be called upon to honor the contract, but it is also possible that the option will **expire worthless**.[1] If the option does expire worthless, your obligations are cancelled and the premium collected (when you sold the option) represents your profit.

- If you sell a call option (that you do not own) you may become obligated to sell the underlying asset at the strike price. Do not be confused. The call buyer has the right to *buy* the underlying asset. The call seller may become obligated to *sell* that asset.

- If you sell a put option (that you do not own) you may become obligated to buy the underlying asset at the strike price. For clarity: The put buyer has the right to *sell* the underlying asset. The put seller may become obligated to *buy* that asset.

- If you sell an option that you own, the slate is wiped clean and you have no remaining position. You have neither the rights of an option owner, nor the obligations of an option seller. The transaction to sell an option (when you own it) is entered as a 'sell to close' order, where the word 'close' refers to the fact that you are selling something that you own and are 'closing out' the trade.

There are two ways to cancel the option seller's obligations:

- When the option expires, the option seller is released from all obligations.

- If the option seller buys the identical option (in a closing transaction), then the position is closed, along with any obligations. The trader may have a profit or loss, depending on the transaction prices. Remember that the option owner has the right to exercise at any time. If you are notified (notifications are issued overnight and the trader is informed before the market opens for trading) that your option has been exercised by its owner (that notification is

---

[1] An option expires worthless when expiration day arrives and its owner declines to exercise.

referred to as an 'exercise notice' or an 'assignment notice'),[2] then it is too late to make a closing transaction. The exercise is final and you must honor the conditions of the contract. Many rookie traders are worried about the possibility of early assignment. It is usually not a problem.

NOTE: The owner of an option controls the situation and may decide to exercise the option any time before it expires. The option seller has no control and must wait for the option owner's decision. For clarification: when you sell an option, you may not request or demand that the option owner exercise the option. You have no say in the matter. The decision rests entirely with the option owner. You received a cash premium as payment for giving the option buyer those rights.

When the option is exercised, a randomly selected seller of that option is assigned an exercise notice and is obligated to fulfill the conditions of the contract. How the specific seller is chosen is discussed in greater detail in Appendix E. Thus, the person who receives that exercise notice must sell 100 shares of stock at the strike price (if it is a call option), or buy 100 shares at the strike price (if it is a put option). There is no escape. Once you have been assigned that exercise notice, the option is cancelled, the trade occurs and you must honor your commitment. In the real world, you do not have to do anything. Upon learning of the assignment notice, your broker takes care of the entire process. If you are assigned an exercise notice on a call option, the shares are removed from your account, and cash (100 x the strike price) is deposited. It is the same as if you sold 100 shares of stock overnight. If you are assigned on a put option, 100 shares are deposited into your account and the cash to pay for those shares is removed. It is the same as if you bought 100 shares overnight. This process occurs when the markets are closed and your broker informs you that the transaction has occurred.

One further point: when an option owner exercises an option, if you are assigned an exercise notice, you do not learn of the assignment immediately. That is not a problem because assignments occur only once per day when the markets are closed. Your broker notifies you of the assignment before the market opens for trading the following business day. Thus, you always know your positions while the markets are open. If assignment occurs on expiration Friday, that notification arrives by

---

[2] 'Assigned an exercise notice' means that someone has submitted an exercise notice and that it was assigned to your account.

Monday morning (before the opening), but your online broker should notify you by Sunday afternoon.

To give you a better understanding of the entire process that consists of buying, selling and exercising an option, let's look at some examples of how options are used in our everyday lives.

Call options in our daily lives

You may not be aware, but you probably use call options frequently. Have you ever shopped at a supermarket and tried to buy an advertised special, only to discover that the store had run out of the item? If so, did the customer service department offer to give you a rain check? That rain check is a call option, because it gives you the right (but not the obligation) to purchase the sale item (underlying asset) at the sale price (strike price) for a limited period of time (until the rain check expires, usually 30 days). You have no obligation to exercise your rights to buy the sale item, but you have the right to do so. Because you paid nothing for that rain check, the premium for your call option is zero.

If you take public transportation and buy a transfer, that transfer is a call option whose underlying asset is another ride. This time, the strike price is zero, because there is no further cost when you exercise your right to take that second ride. But, you must use the transfer before it expires. This option is not free, but the cost of the transfer (premium) is substantially less than the cost of paying a new fare.

When you take public transportation and believe you can accomplish your task in time (before the transfer expires) to use the transfer to travel to another destination (or return to your starting point), then it is probably a good investment to take the risk of paying the small premium to buy the transfer. After all, that transfer gives you the right to take that second ride at a substantial savings. If you are not ready to use the transfer before it expires, then you are not obligated to drop whatever you are doing to take that bus or train. It is your transfer (option) and you are in control. You may throw away the transfer (allow it to expire worthless) if you so choose. These are only two examples of common call options that we experience in everyday life.

Put options in our daily lives

Put options are also commonly used, and it is a safe bet that you are already familiar with them. If you own an expensive item, such as a car, a home, or perhaps some artwork or a fancy piece of jewelry, and if you own an insurance policy on that item, then you own a put option. In exchange for paying an annual premium, your policy allows you to sell that item to your insurance company if it is lost, stolen or destroyed. The insurance company pays your claim by paying cash (strike price) as a settlement that provides you (or is supposed to provide you) with enough money to replace the item.

These insurance policies are more limited than put options discussed in this book because you do not have the freedom to exercise your option at any time. Thus, you cannot force the insurance company to buy your item whenever you choose to sell. But it does allow you to sell under certain conditions (lost, stolen or damaged beyond a certain point), as outlined in the insurance policy.

What can you do with an option?

Once you buy an option (in Chapter 3 we'll discuss why anyone would want to buy or sell an option), there are three different actions you can take. Remember, if you are the seller of an option, your choices are limited. You can repurchase the option you sold and thereby cancel your obligations. If you do not repurchase, then you must wait, and there are two possible outcomes: either the option expires worthless or you are assigned an exercise notice (reminder: this notice is an alert from your broker telling you that you bought or sold stock at the strike price in accordance with the terms of the contract (the call or put option you sold). There is nothing else you can do.

The option *owner* has choices. Let's examine those choices by returning to the supermarket and continuing to discuss the rain check.

Assume this rain check is good for three one-pound cans of your favorite brand of coffee. The regular price is $5 per pound and the sale price is $4 per pound. The rain check expires in 30 days.

Choice 1: Exercise your option. One week later (or any time during the 30-day lifetime of the rain check) you return to the store and find that coffee is once again in stock and is priced at $5 per pound.

- The market price ($5) of the underlying asset is above the call's strike price ($4).

- That means the option is "**in-the-money**" and has an "**intrinsic value**." That is another way of stating that the option has real value that can be turned into cash.

- The intrinsic value is the amount by which the option is in the money, or the difference between the market price ($5) and the strike price ($4). In this example, the option to buy three cans is worth $3 ($1 per can).

You take three cans of coffee and place them into your shopping cart. When you reach the checkout line, you give your rain check to the cashier. When you do that, you are exercising your option and the cashier is being assigned an exercise notice that obligates the supermarket to deliver the coffee (the underlying asset) at the discounted price of $4 per pound (the strike price). You pay $12 for three pounds of coffee. That option no longer exists because it has been exercised.

Choice 2: Sell your option. On your next shopping trip, you notice that coffee is selling at its regular price of $5 per pound. But, you were recently introduced to another brand and are no longer interested in exercising your option. While looking at the coffee display, you notice a young woman place two cans of your former brand into her shopping cart. You tell her that you have a coupon providing a $2 discount on the coffee that she wants to buy. You inform her that you would be happy to split the savings by selling that coupon (please do not refer to it as a call option, as the other person would never understand) for $1. (In the real world you would be a Good Samaritan and give away the rain check because you have no use for it. But this is a lesson on how options work, and people do not give away their stock options.)

At first your fellow shopper is resistant to the idea, but you convince her that the coupon is genuine and she agrees to your proposal.[3] It is a good deal for both of you. She saves $1 and you make $1. The supermarket loses the $2 it would have earned if the option had expired worthless. You now have a short-term capital gain of $1. You "bought" your call option for nothing and sold it for $1.

Choice 3: Allow your option to expire worthless. You return to the supermarket, but this time you discover that your brand of coffee is on sale at $3.75 per pound! Pleasantly surprised, you pick up 3 cans. When you check out, you have a decision to make. Should you pay $3.75 per pound, or should you exercise your option and give the cashier your rain check? In other words, should you exercise the call option that allows you to pay $4 per pound? Clearly you do not want to use the rain check. You have the right to pay $4 per pound, but why would you? You can pay $3.75 per pound instead, so you keep your call option hidden and buy the underlying asset below the strike price.

Remember, you have no obligation to use your rain check. Declining to exercise your call option makes sense because:

- The market price of the underlying asset is below the call's strike price.

- That means the option is **out-of-the-money** and has no intrinsic value.

---

[3] Someone who is familiar with options could reply: "I'll give you 90 cents."

- You do not want to exercise an option that is out-of-the-money because you can buy the underlying asset for less than the strike price.

You no longer need the rain check because you have more than enough coffee to last far beyond the rain check's expiration date. Your option, the rain check, still has time remaining before it expires. It is your intention to allow it to go unused and expire worthless. But, because the supermarket may end the sale and because you may find an opportunity to sell the rain check, you keep it. You do not expect to sell it before it expires, but it costs you nothing to take it with you when you go shopping next time, just in case the underlying (coffee) is priced at $5 per pound again. If that happens, the option once again would be in the money and have a $1 intrinsic value. You may find someone to buy it.

> **NOTE:** You do not want to exercise a call option when you can buy the underlying for less than the strike price. Similarly, you do not want to exercise a put option when you can sell the underlying for more than the strike price. Option owners frequently allow their options to expire worthless.[4] It is critical to understand why an option becomes worthless: a) there is no time remaining and b) it is out of the money.

Using a put option

If your car becomes a total loss due to an accident, it is almost worthless to you. Sure, you can probably sell it to a company that salvages parts, but if you own a put option (an automobile insurance policy), it is better to sell the car to the insurance company for the car's replacement value (strike price). If you have an unusual situation in which you can sell the damaged car for more than the insurance company would pay, then you would not exercise your put option and you would not try to collect from the insurance company. Even though that option is in-the-money (it has an intrinsic value equal to the strike price) you let the option expire worthless. Why collect money on your insurance policy when you can collect a greater amount by selling the car to someone who offers a higher price? In other words, you have no obligation to exercise your option. It is your choice and if you can collect more cash elsewhere, you simply allow the option to expire worthless.[5]

Bottom Line: When you own an option, you have three choices. You can:

---

[4] It is not the hoped-for result, but the option is worthless.
[5] The option is not yet worthless, but you no longer own the car and cannot use the put option.

- Exercise the option. (You will seldom make this choice, but if you decide to do so, please be certain it is in-the-money.)

- Sell the option (as long as someone is willing to buy it, there are no restrictions on whether the option is in- or out of the money).

- Allow the option to expire worthless when you cannot sell it and expiration arrives and it is out-of-the-money.

When using exchange-traded options, you have the same three choices.

There is one more term to learn at this point: If the option's strike price equals (or nearly equals) the market price of the underlying asset, the option is **at-the-money**.

Do you agree that options are easier to understand than you expected? A short quiz follows, allowing you to discover how well you understand the basic concepts of options and how they work.

Quiz 1

Options Basics

1. The owner of a call option may be assigned an exercise notice obligating that investor to buy 100 shares of the underlying asset at the strike price. **TRUE or FALSE?**

2. QUIZ stock is trading at $34.17 per share. Which options are in-the-money? Which are out-of-the-money?

    a)   QUIZ Oct 35 call (35 is the strike price)
    b)   QUIZ Dec 30 call (30 is the strike price)
    c)   QUIZ Feb 25 call
    d)   QUIZ Oct 35 put
    e)   QUIZ Nov 40 put
    f)   QUIZ Dec 30 put

3. IBM is $104 per share. Does the Jun 100 call have any intrinsic value? If yes, how much?

4. XYZ is $49 per share. You exercise one XYZ Mar 45 call option and buy 100 shares of XYZ stock. How much cash is removed from your account to pay for the shares?

5. If you are assigned an exercise notice on 3 ABCD Oct 100 puts, is cash deposited into, or removed from, your account? How much cash?

6. What is the primary right of the writer of an XYZ Sep 70 call option?

7. What is the procedure by which the seller of a call option can request that the option owner exercise the option?

8. You sell two QUIZ Nov 40 call options (to open), @ $100 apiece. Time passes and QUIZ Nov 40 call options are trading at $0.05 ($5 per contract). What happens if you buy two QUIZ Nov 40 calls to close?

9. XYZ is trading at 41.25 per share. You sell one XYZ Dec 40 call and collect $400. What is the premium of the XYZ Dec 40 call?

10. If you buy an option and pay $200, are you allowed to sell it for $50?

11. You buy one IBM Jan 95 call, paying $3.20. Two weeks later you sell the call at $4.00. Can you be assigned an exercise notice and become obligated to deliver 100 shares of IBM at $95 per share?

12. What is your profit (or loss) in question 11?

Quiz 1 Answers

1. False. Only the seller (writer) of an option can be assigned an exercise notice.

2. In the money: Dec 30 call; Feb 25 call; Oct 35 put; Nov 40 put. Out of the money: Oct 35 call; Dec 30 put. NOTE: This is true regardless of whether expiration has passed, or is in the future.

3. Yes. $400. Stock price ($104) minus strike price ($100) is the intrinsic value.

4. $4,500. Exercise occurs at the strike price.

5. Cash is removed. You pay $100 per share for 300 shares, or $30,000.

6. The option writer (seller) has NO rights.

7. There is no such procedure. The call seller may not request that an option be exercised.

8. This purchase is called a closing transaction because you are buying options to close (exit) a position. You pay $5 per option and earned a capital gain equal to $95 per contract, or $190 less commission. Your obligation to deliver 200 shares of QUIZ @ $40 per share is cancelled and you no longer have a position in these options.

9. $400. The option price is the premium. The time premium is $275; intrinsic value is $125.

10. Yes. The answer to this question is not covered in the chapter, but I hope you know enough about buying and selling stocks to understand that if you own an asset, you are always allowed to sell. Sometimes the sale is at a higher price and you earn a profit. Sometimes you sell at a lower price and take a loss.

11. No. When you sell an option that you own, the position is eliminated and you have neither rights nor obligations.

12. $80 profit, less commission.

Chapter 2

Exchange-Traded Options

One of the great myths of the options world is that 'options are dangerous.' Once you recognize that you have been using common options for years, you understand that options are neither difficult to understand nor dangerous. How can it be dangerous to buy insurance for your car or home?

However, there is danger. It is dangerous to people's financial health when they do things they do not understand. Would you sit down to a poker table if you did not know any of the rules? I hope not. Nonetheless, some people buy and sell options without understanding the most basic concepts of options. It is not enough to 'buy call options if you think the stock is going higher.' Too many other factors should be considered before making any trade. Many of these investors buy calls, watch their stocks rally and, bewildered, discover that they lost money. I do not want that to happen to you. The better you understand what you are doing when working with options, the better your chances of being a successful investor and trader.

In this chapter we'll take a closer look at options that trade on exchanges. Options for which the underlying asset is an individual stock, stock index or an ETF (exchange traded fund) are listed for trading on a bunch of different option exchanges in the United States, plus additional exchanges all over the world. I use the inaccurate term 'bunch' because the number has been changing as new exchanges come into being and mergers eliminate others. Option trading is big business and options are tradable for other assets including currencies, bonds, and commodities.

Identifying an option by its symbol

Options are fungible, meaning they are interchangeable. Thus, whenever anyone buys or sells an option, the option must be clearly defined so everyone involved in the transaction understands which specific option is trading. Fungibility allows any trader to sell a position that was purchased earlier (this is a 'closing' transaction). For that to be possible that option must be identifiable as a unique entity.[6]

Four pieces of information are necessary to identify any option:

---

[6] In rare instances, options that 'should' be identical are not because of a stock split or merger. This is not a problem because each of those options carries a different symbol. We'll discuss this situation later in the chapter.

- Symbol of the underlying asset.

- Strike price.

- Expiration date.[7]

- Option type (put or call).

In recent times (2010) option symbology was given a facelift. (See Appendix A) That *formal method* of identifying an option is utilized by exchanges, clearing houses, and the OCC (Options Clearing Corporation). You and I, along with brokers, writers and traders, can use a simplified method.

There is no uniformity, but there is seldom any reason for a misunderstanding. Examples:

- MSFT Sep 20 '13 26 Put: a put option granting its owner the right (but not the obligation) to sell 100 shares of Microsoft at $26 per share any time before the option expires. The last day of trading for this option is Sep 20, 2013.

- IBM Oct 20 '14 195 C: a call option granting its owner the right, but not the obligation, to buy 100 shares of IBM at $195 per share any time before the option expires. The last day of trading is the traditional 3rd Friday of the month, Oct 20, 2014.

- IWM Mar 15 '13 84 call: a call option granting its owner the right to buy 100 shares of the exchange traded fund IWM (Russell 2000 index) at $84 per share any time before the option expires. The option last trades on March 15, 2013.

- BA Dec '13 90P: A put option granting its owner the right to sell 100 shares of Boeing at $90 per share any time before the option expires in December, 2013, 2013. The last day of trading is the 3rd Friday of the month, Dec 20, 2013.

NOTE: Some index options expire (their final closing price is determined) at the opening of the trading day rather than at the close. There is no designation of AM or PM settlement in the option symbol. It is something that a trader must know, but the information is readily available. I'll be sure that you never make

---

[7] European style index options are the exception. As of this writing, some are AM settled and others are PM settled.

the mistake of not knowing.[8] If you trade options on individual stocks, this is never going to be a problem.

Standardization of options

Before options were traded on exchanges, they were bought and sold in a haphazard manner. Options had random expiration dates and strike prices. Option sellers listed the contracts they had for sale in newspaper ads. In today's computer age, that seems to be an impossible situation. However, the world was very different.

If you wanted to sell an option that you had previously bought (or wanted to buy an option you had previously sold), it was a very difficult proposition. You (actually your broker) had to find someone willing to take the other side of your position, and that was a difficult task. If such a person were found, I cannot imagine that he/she would be willing to make the trade at a fair price. Basically, if you traded an option it was yours until expiration arrived.

When options began trading on an exchange (the CBOE: Chicago Board Options Exchange) in 1973 all that changed. Options became standardized. Translation: options had well-defined strike prices and expiration dates. The fact that options were now fungible (interchangeable) made it easy for buyers and sellers to trade with the confidence that comes with the knowledge that positions could be closed (by selling an option purchased earlier or buying an option previously sold) prior to expiration. Consider why this is important: If you had an option position that was performing well and you wanted to take your profit, would you be pleased if you were forced to hold that position until the option expired? If you were losing money and wanted to exit the trade to cut losses, how would you feel if you had to hold the option position and use stock to hedge the trade?

By listing options on an exchange where they can be readily bought and sold, options became available to the individual investor for the first time. On that first day (April 26, 1973), only 16 stocks had listed call options and the volume was modest: 911 contracts. In 2011, the average daily volume for equity options was almost 17 million contracts.

Strike prices

Options have standardized strike prices. Thus, when options with new strike prices are listed for trading, those strikes occur at specific intervals based on the stock price and its volatility (volatility is a major consideration in the options universe and is discussed in much greater detail in Chapter 6). More volatile stocks undergo larger and more

---

[8] Clarification comes in Part III when we talk about American and European style options.

frequent price changes than less volatile stocks and require more strike prices.

Puts and calls are listed in pairs. Thus, if the December 80 call option is available to trade, then the December 80 put is also available. Each stock has at least two different strike prices: one above the current stock price and one below.[9] That means there is always at least one out-of-the-money (OTM) call option and one OTM put option available for trading.[10] Almost all stocks have more than the minimum number of strike prices.

Let's see how this works: On the first business day (Monday, unless it is a national holiday) following expiration, the recently expired options no longer exist and to replace them, the exchanges list options with a new expiration date. For example, let's assume that June expiration has just passed. The following Monday, the exchanges list new options for each underlying asset. The expiration date is not chosen at random. There is a set protocol.

- Each underlying asset must list options that expire on the traditional 3rd Friday of each of the next two months. Thus, when Jun options expire, all equities have options that expire in July and August.

- If one of those expiration dates is not already listed, then that is the new month.

- If both are already listed for traded, then a more distant expiration date is added.

- If stock XYZ is priced at 87, then the exchanges list one strike price above and one below the current market price:

  o Aug 17 '12 85 calls and puts.

  o Aug 17 '12 90 calls and puts.

- The exchanges have discretion to add additional strike prices.

Some stocks are actively traded and generate a large interest in the options. The exchanges tend to list additional options with different strike prices to accommodate all traders. For example, AAPL (Apple Computer)

---

[9] If the underlying stock gaps significantly higher or lower when the market opens, it is possible that no out-of-the money options would be available. When that occurs, new strike prices sometimes are added immediately; at other times, new strike prices are not listed for trading until the following business day.

[10] If the stock price changes such that there are no longer any out-of-the-money options (example: the highest AAPL strike price is $650 and AAPL trades at $650 or higher) then new strike prices are added – either immediately, or more often, the following morning.

may be priced at 500 after expiration. The exchanges may list all options between 400 and 600 the following Monday.

There is no rule written in stone. The idea is to list options that attract both buyers and sellers, but not to list options that would not attract any interest from investors. There is no reason to list APPL options with 100 or 900 strikes. The newly listed strike prices are evenly clustered around the current stock price.

> **NOTE:** When the new expiration month options are listed, any strike price listed for the new month is automatically added (if it does not already exist) for each other expiration month (except for LEAPS, which are described later in this chapter). Thus if IBM Oct 100 is the lowest strike price for October, and the Aug 95s are newly listed, then the Oct 95s are also listed for trading.

Non-volatile stocks offer fewer strike prices than more volatile stocks. If it is unlikely that any specific stock will move by more than two or three points over any given one-month period, there is no reason to list more than two or three strike prices. It is the fact that a given stock (judging from its past price history) has demonstrated that it can easily undergo significant price changes that dictates the addition of extra strike prices. Look at it from the viewpoint of a potential option buyer. If IBM had little chance to increase in value from 102 to 105 over any reasonable period of time, few people would be interested in buying (or selling) options with a strike price of 110 or higher. But, if it were a more volatile stock—one with the ability to undergo significant price changes—then the exchanges list additional strike prices.

It is important to always have out-of-the-money options listed for trading (at least one call option and one put).[11] New options are added when necessary to satisfy that requirement. (See Appendix B)

Expiration dates

Options have standard expiration dates. One of the four descriptive terms for an option is its expiration month. Expiration day for these options is Saturday, following the third Friday of the specified month. Because that Friday is also the last day these options are available for trading, many people refer to that day as "expiration Friday" or "expiration day." As long as you understand that the third Friday[12] is both the last day the options

---

[11] A call is out of the money (OTM) when its strike is higher than the price of the underlying asset. A put is OTM when its strike is lower than the underlying price. More details on how new options are listed are in Appendix B.

[12] Clarification: Expiration is not the third Saturday. It is the day following the third Friday.

trade and the last day they may be exercised, the technical definition of "expiration day" is not important.

In recent times, options that expire in one week[13] have been added to the mix for actively traded stocks, indexes, and ETFs. Can options that expire daily be far behind?

NOTE: When the new expiration month options are listed, any strike price listed for the new month is automatically added (if it does not already exist) for each other expiration month (except for LEAPS, which are described later in this chapter). Thus if IBM Oct 100 is the lowest strike price for October, and the Aug 95s are newly listed, then the Oct 95s are also listed for trading.

Assume CHEM, a manufacturer of specialty chemicals used for academic research, is priced at $41 per share and has the options in Table 2.1 listed for trading. If CHEM trades as high as 45, then options with a 50-strike are added for Mar, Apr, Jun, and Sep.

NOTE: You, as an individual investor can usually fare better by selling your option rather than exercising it. But, when expiration day arrives, options that are in-the-money are not just thrown away. They are most often in the hands of market makers who accumulate them as individual investors sell out their positions. The point is that you may seldom elect to exercise an option you own, but you can count on being assigned an exercise notice when you are short an option that is in-the-money (by one penny or more) as of the close of business on expiration Friday.[14]

---

[13] 8 days. Options are listed on Thursday and trade through the following Friday (some settle at the opening Friday).

[14] Occasionally, an option that is in the money by one or two cents is allowed (by its owner) to expire worthless. That means that someone who was short that option "slides" and is not assigned an exercise notice. It is not common, but it does happen.

Table 2.1
CHEM: Listed Options

Exp	Strike
Mar	35
Mar	40
Mar	45
Apr	35
Apr	40
Apr	45
Jun	30
Jun	35
Jun	40
Jun	45
Sep	35
Sep	40
Sep	45

Adding New Strike Prices

Adding new strike prices

Each underlying asset has listed options with at least four different expiration dates. Some indexes and many individual stocks have more than four. As you may expect, the expiration months for new options are not chosen at random. There is a protocol that determines which new month is added (to replace the recently expired month) after expiration. For details, see Appendix C.

Do options provide too many options?

When trading options, you always have choices. Each underlying asset not only lists options with at least four different expiration dates, but also multiple strike prices. This may cause you to believe that making intelligent trading decisions is impossible. That belief will be short-lived, because I'll walk you slowly through the choices and carefully explain how you choose an option that is not only appropriate for the specific strategy under discussion, but also suitable for you and your style of investing.

How and when to exercise an option that you own

Most of the time you have no reason to exercise an option. One of the other two choices[15] is almost always better.

Ask your broker how they want to be notified of your intention to exercise. Each broker has a system, but the latest time that they accept instructions to exercise options is shortly after the market closes for business each day. Unless the stock is going ex-dividend (trading without

---

[15] Selling the option is best—when you no longer want to own it. The alternative is to allow it to expire worthless if you cannot find anyone willing to buy it.

the dividend) tomorrow,[16] there is no reason to exercise an option prior to expiration.[17]

When you no longer want to own any option, it is more efficient to sell, rather than exercise.[18] However, there are situations in which exercising an option may be the better choice. Thus, the question arises: how do you exercise an option? There are two methods, depending on the timing of your decision: earlier than expiration and at expiration. See Chapter 22 for complete details.

It is better not to exercise

The above section about exercising is important for those occasions when it is appropriate to exercise an option. For now, please accept the truth that you will almost never want to exercise an option. It is too soon in your education process to get into the rationale. Thus, this discussion is revived in Chapter 22, and you can refer to it when ready. I recommend doing that after learning how to write covered calls.

Stock splits and other adjustments

Sometimes companies make a corporate decision to split the shares of their common stock. The most common split is 2 for 1. Once the split is effective, twice as many shares exist and every shareholder holds twice as many shares as previously held. Is this a bonanza? Did each shareholder double the value of his or her investment? No. The efficient stock market makes sure that doesn't happen. For example, if the company was worth $5 billion before the split, it is still worth $5 billion after the split. There is no reason for the company suddenly to be worth $10 billion. Thus, the market price of each share is reduced. In effect, the share price is also split 2 for 1.

If you own 200 shares valued at $80 per share, you have $16,000 worth of stock in the company. If the stock is split 2 for 1, then you own 400 shares, valued at $40 per share, or the same $16,000. Stock splits should not make any difference in the value of your shares. In the real world, there is the perception that a stock split makes the company's shares more attractive to own, and most of the time, when a company announces a stock split, the price of the stock increases.

It is important to ask the question: If the stock splits, does that make any difference to the options? The answer is yes. Once again this is a topic best left until later. See Appendix D.

---

[16] Be careful. Even when the stock is ex-dividend, most options should not be exercised.
[17] This is an approximation. There are rare situations when a put owner may want to exercise early (put is deep in the money and interest rates are high).
[18] Again, there are rare exceptions

QUIZ 2

1. How many pieces of information are needed to describe an option?

2. Is this scenario possible? An investor wants to buy IBM Dec 120 calls, but discovers that the calls are not listed on any options exchange. The investor finds only IBM Dec 120 *puts*.

3. Oct options expired last Friday. Which two expiration months are available for all stocks?

4. It is Wed, Oct 10 and the exchanges listed XYX Oct 65 options. What are the three top reasons these options began trading today?

5. You own 2 ZZZ Aug 60 calls. ZZZ announces a 2 for 1 stock split. Does your position change?

6. You sold 10 GGG Mar 25 puts, collecting $50 for each. Subsequently GGG announced that it is being taken over by a competitor at $29.50 in cash for each outstanding share of GGG. Is this good news?

7. Today is the 3rd Friday of Dec and you own five FFF Dec 40 calls. The stock is trading near $40. You tried to sell the calls, but there is no bid. The stock closes at $40.05 and you still own the calls. Which of the choices below makes sense?
   a) Do nothing. The options will expire worthless.
   b) Do nothing. You will be assigned an exercise notice.
   c) Do nothing if you want to buy stock at $40 per share.
   d) Quickly notify broker DO NOT EXERCISE if you do not want to buy stock at $40.

8. You own 10 XYX Apr 35 call options. It is Friday, April 17 (the third Friday in April), and XYZ stock's last trade of the day is $32 per share. What happens to your options?

9. You own 5 calls and want to exercise. What action do you take?
   a) Notify your broker.
   b) Notify the OCC.
   c) Find the person who sold the options and notify him/her.
   d) None of the above.

10. You own Nov 45 calls. The stock rallies to $49. Expiration is three weeks away. Which of the following is best to lock in profits?
    a) Exercise the calls, then sell stock
    b) Buy Nov 45 puts
    c) Sell the calls
    d) Sell stock short, then exercise calls.

QUIZ 2 Answers

1. Four: Symbol, Strike, Expiration date, Option type (put or call). For specific European style options, the date is not sufficient and AM or PM is required.

2. Not possible. If the puts are listed, then the calls must be listed.

3. Nov and Dec. Options that expire on the 3rd Friday of the next 2 calendar months are always available for trading.

4. Three possibilities

    a) The stock price is rising and traded at 60 or higher yesterday.
    b) The stock price is falling and traded at 70 or lower yesterday.
    c) A customer or market maker requested Oct 65s.

5. You will own 4 ZZZ Aug 30 calls once the stock split is effective. For the moment, you still own 2 Aug 60 calls.

6. It is a great result. The put options are going to be worthless if the deal is completed. It is a good idea to repurchase those puts at $5 per contract, if possible. That is insurance against the possibility that the deal falls apart.

7. Only c and d make sense. These options do not expire worthless, but are subject to being automatically exercised. Option *owners* are never assigned an exercise notice.

8. The options expire worthless.

9. a)

10. c) is best. Under certain conditions, a) or d) may be feasible.

Chapter 3

Buying and Selling Options

Options are currently listed for trading on at least 11 different[19] options exchanges in the U.S., plus many others around the world. While trading volume in 2012 declined from 2011, over the last decade options volume has exploded (figure 3.1). At the same time, the number of equity products with listed options has grown dramatically.

Good questions are: why is this happening? Why has trading volume increased so rapidly in recent years?

Figure 3.1
Options volume exploded, with a break in 2012

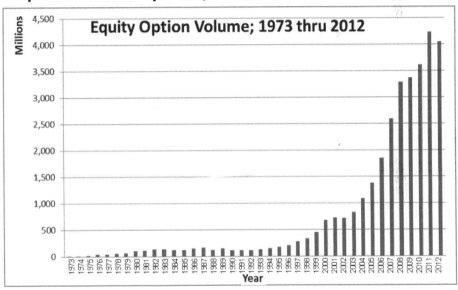

Equity Option Volume over 20 years

---

[19] New exchanges are being added as more players want a piece of the action. Number 11 (Miami) is the latest and at least two more are on the way

Figure 3.2
Number of Equities with Listed Options

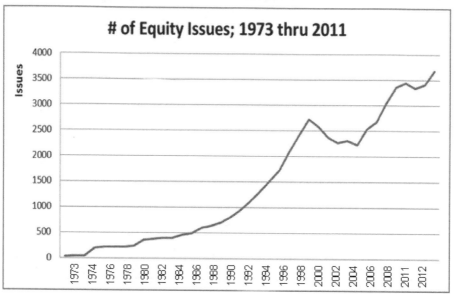

# of Equity Issues; 1973 thru 2011

Number of equity issues listed for trading

The surging volume tells us that options play an increasingly important role in the investment strategy for a great many people. Much of the new option volume must be attributed to the growth in the number and size of hedge funds. As these funds grow, the money under management constantly increases. Thus, the funds use an ever-increasing quantity of options to implement their strategies and operate their businesses. But, hedge funds are not the only contributor to the increased activity in options trading. Some traditional mutual funds have adopted an option strategy known as covered call writing. We will discuss that strategy in detail in Part II (Chapters 9 to 11).

The individual investor is also trading more options.. Several prominent online brokerage houses advertise their options expertise in an attempt to attract new customers. New discount brokers specializing in options are appearing on the scene, hoping to capture a share of the market. The International Securities Exchange (ISE) and the oldest, and largest, options exchange, the Chicago Board Options Exchange (CBOE) have already gone public. Trading options is one of the most exciting businesses in the world.

Because hedge funds do not disclose their methods, and because those methods are likely to be very sophisticated, there is no way for us to know exactly how the fund managers use options. But, I can show you how individual investors and professional traders use options. Some of these methods are appropriate for newcomers to the options world, while others require more experience and a better understanding of how options work before they can be used successfully. We'll study the most basic of these strategies in Part II and then consider a few more sophisticated, but still not-too-difficult to understand, methods in Part III.

Why would anyone buy an option?

Let's take a look at options from the perspective of an individual investor in an attempt to understand why investors want to buy or sell options.

Let's say you have an opinion on the stock market. You do not have any specific stocks in mind, but you 'just know' the overall market is headed higher (or lower). What can you do?

One obvious choice is to buy a basket of stocks, hoping to participate in the coming rally. The problem with that idea is that you do not really know which stocks to trade and, in addition, commissions can add up (even with a deep discount broker) when you trade many different stocks.

Another choice is to buy shares of a mutual fund. The problem with that choice is that so few funds outperform the market averages that you hate to pay a management fee to someone who then fails to provide above average returns. If the idea of buying shares of an exchange traded fund (ETF) or an Index Fund occurs to you, that is to your advantage. These are much more suitable for investment purposes than traditional mutual funds. And they offer a diversified portfolio with extremely low management fees.

If you invest $5,000 and the market rallies by 10%, you might make $500. Not bad, but that is not really much money for successfully predicting a sizeable market advance. It is difficult enough to predict market direction (this author firmly believes that very few people can do it on a consistent basis), and if you can do it, you want to earn a higher return than the average investor—as a reward for being so clever. To do that, an investor must use leverage.

You can always purchase your shares on 50% margin,[20] thereby increasing the number of shares that you can buy. This also doubles your earnings potential, as well as the amount you can lose. If you buy $10,000 worth of shares with your $5,000 cash, you could earn $1,000 or 20%. That is much better. But is it enough? Is there a way to gain even more leverage? Yes there is.

You can buy options. If you are right in your stock market prediction, you can make a very substantial profit. On the other hand, you may lose your entire investment—something that would never happen if you simply bought shares of that index fund. Let me repeat for emphasis: You could

---

[20] You use your own $5,000 and borrow an equal amount from your broker.

easily lose your entire $5,000 investment when you buy options. Are you willing to risk that loss? There are many investors who are not only willing, but anxious, to take that risk. And it is important for you to understand why they do so. I hope you are not among those risk-taking investors. Indeed, in this book I discourage readers from making such aggressive bets on the stock market. But it is your money and you have every right to speculate.

When buying options (calls in this situation because you are bullish) you have the opportunity to earn significantly higher returns than when buying stock. But you must also accept the increased probability of losing money when your bullish prediction fails to come true quickly enough. Remember, options have limited lifetimes—and if you own them when expiration arrives, they become worthless (unless they are in the money).

Before discussing how to adopt my recommended (especially for investors who are first learning to use options) methods, I must make one point:

> Please accept this warning: buying options is not on my list of recommended strategies. It is much too difficult for the vast majority of investors to earn money using this approach.

I know that it is very tempting to buy options and treat them as mini-lottery tickets. Speculators and outright gamblers love to buy options. And there is nothing wrong with that plan, if you understand that in return for the chance for a big payday, there is a high probability of losing money.

My goal is to introduce you to the world of options and to show you how options can enhance your income while reducing risk. If you choose to gamble, I'll try to reduce your chances of losing money.

The following is a condensed version of the option-buying strategy.

If SPX (Standard & Poor's 500 Index) is trading at 1500, and if you are correct in your prediction of a quick 10% advance, the index would move to 1650 in 4 weeks. Assume there are 36 days until the Apr options expire and you decide to buy April call options. Without going into how options are priced at this point (Chapter 5), let's just say that you decide to buy SPX Apr call options with a strike price of 1550. Those options could reasonably cost you $950 apiece.[21] Assuming you are willing to take a

---

[21] In Chapter 5, I discuss how to determine a fair value for an option.

chance with your entire bankroll, you buy 5 SPX Apr 1550 calls and pay $4,750.

Four weeks later, the index has reached 1600 (congratulations) and you decide it is time to sell your options. Sure, you predicted the index would rally to 1650, but there is no need to be that greedy.

How much should you receive when selling the calls? They are 50 points in the money and thus, the intrinsic value is $5,000 for each option. A reasonable price for these calls is $51.50, or $5,150 apiece.[22] You sell your 5 contracts and collect $25,750 for a net profit of $21,000, or a return of 442%. Pretty impressive! Many investors would never hold the position as long as you, thereby earning less money. The point is that it is possible to make outstanding returns when using leverage. And that possibility attracts too many beginners. They cannot resist the temptation. A few make substantial profits and believe it is a cinch to get rich quickly using options. Others lose their entire bankrolls – either because the rally doesn't occur, or it happens after their options expire. These investors walk away from the options world thinking that options are just too dangerous for them. It is sad. Options are versatile tools and have a place in the investment arsenal of many investors. If you chose to gamble, if you find these potential returns just too irresistible—so be it.

Figure 3.3 illustrates the profit and loss potential for those same 5 call options if the position is held through expiration.

In the example, we showed how a bullish investor might buy call options. Similarly, a bearish investor can buy put options, hoping to profit from a market decline.

Many stock market observers consider buying options to be a low risk strategy because loss is limited to the cash paid for the options. While that is true, the additional truth is that losing the entire investment occurs far too often. If you are going to buy options, it is important to understand how to limit losses. But let's not get ahead of ourselves. There is a great deal more to learn about options and how they work before you think about trading with real money.

At this point, I must re-emphasize my belief that buying options as a wager on the direction of the stock market is a very difficult path to success. There are far better plays available. But if you wish to pursue this path, please try to understand how options work first so that you fully understand the risk and rewards.

---

[22] We can only cover so much in any single chapter, and Chapter 5 is where we talk about understanding the value of an option.

Figure 3.3
Leverage

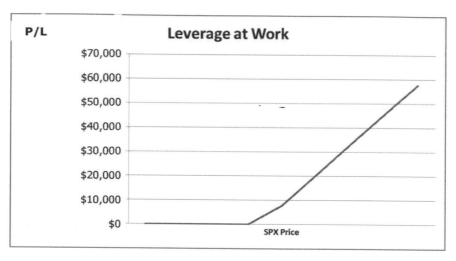

Profit/Loss when owning 5 SPX Apr 1550 call options

Why would anyone sell an option?

The option seller collects a cash premium. That cash is yours to keep no matter what else happens. Some people shudder at the thought of selling options because they believe it entails unlimited risk. And they are right when the sales are naked (unhedged). For most traders, and especially those with smaller bankrolls, the risk of selling naked options is too substantial when the potential reward is considered. Fortunately there are a variety of risk-reducing techniques that you can use to limit risk when selling options.

For readers who already understand something about options, I do not advocate the sale of naked options. However, selling an option in conjunction with the purchase of another can create an attractive risk/reward position. (An exception is described in Chapter 13). It is too early in your education to go into further details at this point. In almost all strategies discussed in this book, I'll show you how to reduce risk to manageable and acceptable levels. But for now, it is important to know that the main reason investors sell options is their ability to collect cash from those sales. When buying an option, the maximum gain is unlimited. When selling an option the maximum gain is the cash collected.

Quiz 3

1. You believe the stock market is in trouble and will undergo a severe decline shortly. Which is the most reasonable trade in that scenario?

   a) Buy calls
   b) Buy puts
   c) Sell calls
   d) Sell puts

2. You believe that XYZ is undervalued by the marketplace. It is currently trading at $42 per share. If you believe the stock will show a small price increase (to $44) over the next few weeks, which (if any) of the following trades are appropriate? It is Jul 8.

   a) Buy XYZ Jul 40 call @$2.50
   b) Buy XYZ Jul 45 call @$0.40
   c) Buy XYZ Jul 50 calls@ $0.05

3. When you anticipate that a given stock will undergo a very large price change in the near future, which of the following is appropriate when you do not know if the move will be higher or lower?

   a) Buy calls
   b) Buy puts
   c) Buy puts and calls
   d) Sell calls
   e) Sell puts
   f) Sell puts and calls

Quiz 3 Answers

1. Buying puts is the best play when anticipating a big move.

2. Buy Jul 40 calls. These may cost more, but when your target is $44 and there is little time remaining (the 3rd Friday always falls between the 15th and 21st of the month), you expect that the Jul 40 call will be worth $4 and that the other two options will expire worthless.

3. Buy puts and calls. This trade is referred to as buying a 'straddle.'

Important Note: I do NOT recommend buying straddles. It is seldom a good choice because the cost is very high and a substantial price change is required before any profit is earned. The straddle is mentioned here *only* to broaden your education.

Chapter 4

The Mechanics of Trading

Most readers are familiar with the process by which an order is entered to buy or sell stock. Options trade in similar fashion. This chapter features a brief description of the process by which traders buy and sell options.

Brokers

Before trading options, you must open an account with a broker and fill out paperwork requesting permission to trade options. Many brokers accept online applications, simplifying the process. Before your broker grants permission, they provide an excellent educational pamphlet (in digital format) entitled *Characteristics and Risks of Standardized Options.*[23] Do not ignore it. It contains useful information for the new option trader.

If you are new to the options world, your broker will place a limit on the type of orders that they accept from you. The rationale behind such limits is that riskier strategies should only be available to experienced traders. Amazingly, these limits are a hindrance and often make it impossible for an individual investor to adopt some of the more conservative strategies. These rules are designed for your own safety (as well as theirs).[24] While this policy was adopted for the right reasons, it may force investors to choose between less conservative strategies and avoiding options altogether.

If you do your homework, you may find a broker who allows customers to enter any type of order. Please be careful when using that type of broker because it is a Catch-22. More good option strategies become available to trade, but it also may lead you to enter orders for option plays without fully recognizing the risk of using such methods. If, after understanding (and practicing) the content of Chapter 7, you believe that you have the ability to manage market risk successfully, then this type of broker may be a suitable match.

I do not want to recommend one specific broker, but it is to your advantage to use a deep discount broker when possible. The good news is that there are a number of such brokerages worthy of your business. Be aware that several new brokers—offering reduced commissions for options

---

[23] Download a copy here: http://www.optionsclearing.com/about/publications/character-risks.jsp
[24] Brokers do not want their customers to go broke while owing money to the brokerage house.

traders—have appeared over the past decade. They are looking to grab market share in this lucrative business.

When opening an account consider a positive recommendation from someone you know and whose opinion you trust. If you do not know where to get started, I strongly recommend using the excellent (and free) tools provided by StockBrokers.com[25] and reading their annual broker review. There is also a yearly survey published by Barron's that rates various brokers.

The traditional method for buying and selling stocks was to telephone an order to your broker. Today, it is much more efficient—in terms of saving both time and money—to trade online. If you have the confidence to trade online, I recommend it.

Some readers may feel the need to work with a full service broker, despite the higher costs. There is nothing wrong with doing that, but be certain your individual broker understands options and that you gain something of value in exchange for paying those higher costs. Remember that you can and should negotiate commissions. There is no need to pay their published rates. And once you gain the confidence to handle option transactions on your own, it is time to move on to that deep discounter to cut expenses.

> **NOTE:** Paying low commissions are not all there is to trading. You want a broker who provides good service and good trade executions. However, one sure-fire method for earning more money is to reduce the cost of trading.

You may be surprised to discover that your full-service broker is one of those behind-the-times firms who fail to understand that options are tools to help you reduce risk. Your broker may have your best interests at heart, but unless he/she is enthusiastic about options trading, please consider moving your account elsewhere.

Several brokerage firms are option specialists. Each has something useful to offer. Learn the advantages of using a few of them by looking for broker ratings via the Internet, and choose a broker who provides something of value to you. Some have extremely low commissions, which is great if you are knowledgeable and unlikely to require too much customer service. Others offer an extremely user-friendly trading platform, making it easy to enter your option orders. And others offer outstanding software that allows you to analyze complex positions. That is appealing to many,

---

[25] http://www.stockbrokers.com/reviews/optionstrading

but if you have no intention of owning complex positions, then the software may be overkill.

Find out whether your prospective broker provides all needed information at tax time —in a format that simplifies the process of filing your tax returns. Do not overlook the time-saving importance of tax information if you are an active trader (hundreds or thousands of trades per year). There are many excellent brokers available and you can find one who allows you to trade comfortably and who fills your needs at a reasonable cost.

When your broker accepts your order and sends it to an exchange where it can be executed, the broker is obligated to attempt to fill your order at the best available price. To that end, the broker routes (sends) your sell order to the exchange displaying the highest bid price, or sends your buy order to the exchange with the lowest asking price. Most brokers use "SMART" routing that automatically sends your order to the market with the best available price. They do that by using the NBBO (National Best Bid and Offer) technology. If none of that is appealing, then some brokers allow you to send orders to the exchange of your choice.[26]

Sadly, some brokers insist on sending orders to one specific options exchange, resulting in problems for their customers. With those brokers, it is not unusual for orders to go unfilled, despite the fact that the identical option is available on another exchange at the price you are willing to trade.[27] Before opening an account, ask if they send orders to the exchange displaying the best price, or only to their preferred exchange. If they choose the latter, open an account elsewhere.

If you want to know why a broker may have a "favorite" exchange, it is because they receive a legal kickback. In the language of the business, that is called being "paid for order flow."

The option markets

For readers who are not already familiar with the language of investing, some of the important terminology is listed below.

Bid. The current highest published[28] price anyone is willing to pay for that specific option. Bid prices for options change frequently, depending on the price of the underlying asset and other market factors.

---

[26] There is seldom a good reason to do that. Be aware that there may be a fee for this service.

[27] If you do not believe this is possible, consider this: Broker A sends a buy order to one exchange, refusing to send it to another. Broker B sends a sell order to a different exchange, also refusing to send the order elsewhere. Despite the fact that one customer is willing to buy at the same price that another is willing to sell, it is possible for one of those orders to go unfilled. It is highly unlikely that both orders go unfilled because someone will eventually want to buy or sell that option at the 'locked' price.

[28] Often market makers do not display their best bids. Thus, you may sometimes sell your option at a price higher than (or buy your option at a price lower than) the best published bid (or offer).

Ask. Also referred to as the "offer." The current lowest published price anyone is willing to accept when selling the specific option. As with bid prices, the ask price changes often.

Bid-ask spread. The difference between the bid price and the ask price. Narrow, or tight, bid-ask spreads are beneficial to you, the individual investor.

NBBO. Acronym for National Best Bid or Offer. It is the highest published bid and lowest published offer on any exchange.[29] Your broker is supposed to guarantee that you never receive a fill at a price that is worse than the NBBO.

Fill. Notification that your order has been executed. It is possible to receive a *partial fill* when only a portion of your order was executed.

Market maker. A professional trader who continuously makes bids and offers and who stands by (these days that means via computer) to purchase any option you want to sell, or sell any option you want to buy. When you enter an order, it is not necessary to trade with a market maker. Many times, your order is matched with that of another individual (or professional) trader, and the market maker does not participate in the trade.

Market order. An order to be filled as quickly as possible at the best possible price at the time the order reaches the trading floor. The order is electronically transmitted and you usually receive a fill within a second or two. When trading options, it is almost always a bad idea to enter a market order because it is an open invitation to receive a fill at a very poor price. It is worth the effort to seek a better price, rather than paying the market price. Unless there is some special reason why you simply must buy or sell *this second,* no matter what the price, it is preferable to enter a limit order. And if unfilled, you can quickly change that order in an attempt to get filled. To repeat: it is not necessary to pay the ask price or sell the bid price. You can do better most of the time.

Limit order. An order that cannot be filled at a price that is worse than the limit specified by the customer. The limit price is the highest price that the customer is willing to pay when buying, or the lowest price the customer is willing to accept when selling. . Whereas a market order is always filled,[30] that is not true for a limit order. For example, when you are

---

[29] This is probably not the best 'real' bid or ask because market makers do not always publish their best. Why? Because some people foolishly insist on entering market orders.

[30] Exception: Some out of the money options are worth so little that no one is willing to pay anything.

not willing to accept less than \$1.20 per contract, enter a limit order to sell at \$1.20. Such an order always implies "or better." That means that the computer receiving your order attempts to find a higher price, but accepts \$1.20 as the minimum. If no one is willing to pay that limit price, then the order remains live where anyone may buy it (by paying \$1.20) at a later time (unless you cancel the order). Similarly, when you want to buy an option, but are unwilling to pay the ask price, enter a limit order to buy at a specific lower price.

Spread order (or combination) order. A spread consists of two or more different options—one of which is bought, and the other sold. When entering a spread order, please remember to use a limit order. Spread orders are discussed in Part III.

Order entry

When you enter an order, many brokers require specific information. I do no t understand why that requirement exists because computers can quickly and accurately determine this information. Nevertheless, here is the terminology as it is used today.

When buying an option, there are two possibilities:

- **Buy to open.** Establish a new position or add to a current position.

- **Buy to close.** Purchase an option that you sold previously. The current position is closed (buy all) or reduced (buy fewer than you sold).

When selling an option, there are two possibilities:

- **Sell to open.** Establish a new position or add to an existing short position. You are writing a new option contract—one that did not previously exist.

- **Sell to close**. Eliminate or reduce an existing position.

- Trading options is neither complex nor difficult. But it is important for you, the investor, to understand what you are trying to accomplish. That is why the individual strategies are described in great detail, beginning in Chapter 9.

QUIZ 4

1. When entering a market order to buy a put option, you expect to receive a fill at the bid price. **TRUE or FALSE**

2. Trading options online is usually less expensive than trading options via the telephone. **TRUE or FALSE**

3. Why is it best not to use market orders when trading options?

4. You enter a limit order to buy three XYX Feb 80 calls at $3 each. Your broker gives you a fill, telling you that you paid $3.20 for each option. Is that OK?

5. You decide to buy five HIJK Mar 45 calls at the market. The NBBO is $2.10 to $2.25. Your broker prefers to send all orders to the ISE, where it is immediately filled. The broker reports that you bought five calls at $2.30. Are you pleased with your fill?

6. You own three JKLM Nov 25 puts. You decide to sell them, collecting $0.50 or better. How is your order designated?

    a) Buy to open
    b) Buy to close
    c) Sell to open
    d) Sell to close

7. It is to your advantage when your broker sends all option orders to a single exchange because it is a very efficient process. **TRUE or FALSE**

QUIZ 4 Answers

1. False. You should expect to buy at the ask price.

2. True

3. You avoid getting the order filled at a horrendous price when there is a good possibility of getting filled at better price, if you only make the effort.

4. No. Someone made an error. You established $3.00 as the maximum price you are willing to pay, and your broker cannot force you to accept the fill at a higher price. You have the right to reject the trade, or tell your broker to pay the $20 per contract difference.

5. You should not be happy. Your broker is obligated to get the best available price. By directing the order to the ISE, it is *possible* that this obligation was not satisfied. Entering a market order makes it difficult to object to the execution price. Ask the broker to check "time and sales" to verify that the option was not offered at a lower price at the time your order traded.

6. d. Sell to close. (It is also a limit order). First, it is an order to sell. Second, you are eliminating a position you own, and that is the definition of a closing transaction.

7. False. It is only advantageous to your broker and is often harmful to   you.

Chapter 5

What is an Option Worth?

The purchase and sale of options takes place in an open marketplace, and, in many respects, the process is identical with the trading of individual stocks. Most people understand, in general terms, how the market price of a stock is determined. In theory, everyone can learn everything there is to know about an individual stock—as long as the information is public.[31] Taking that information into account, people who want to buy or sell the shares gather in the trading pit[32] on the floor of the stock exchange and announce[33] a price at which they are willing to trade those shares. The auction market continues until buyers and sellers agree on a price and a transaction takes place. This is a continuous process and the price at which shares change hands is constantly moving higher and lower.

The price at which trades occur is an agreement between buyers and sellers that the current price is acceptable to both, based on the available information. Buyers tend to believe they are getting bargain while sellers believe they are getting more than the stock is truly worth. Both parties are happy with the trade, but over the longer term, only one is getting the best of the deal.

At any given time, price is primarily based on supply and demand. An increasing number of buyers often push prices higher and a preponderance of sellers push prices lower.

To a point, options also trade that way.[34] But option trading involves much more. Options are derivative products and their value is derived from the value of the underlying stock, index or ETF. As the price of the stock (let's assume we are referring to stocks, but the discussion applies equally well to different underlying assets) changes, so does the price of its options.

Important **NOTE**: Supply and demand play a role in the market price of an option. However, in the options world, prices are driven by much more than the stock price. Option traders must consider more variables than do stock traders. Thus, it is

---

[31] It is clear that anyone who breaks the law and trades on insider information has a big advantage.
[32] These days, they "gather" via computers and trades are executed electronically.
[33] The broker, representing buyers and sellers, enters the pit and announce bids and offers. This is known as 'public outcry.'
[34] Option trading is almost 100% electronic and the 'old-fashioned' trading pits are a thing of the past.

important to understand how an option is valued and the factors that affect its price.

Theoretical value of an option

The value of an option can be calculated using a complex mathematical formula. The 1973 pioneering work of Fischer Black and Myron Scholes produced a formula that can be used to determine the fair market value of a European style call option when the underlying stock does not pay any dividends (European options can only be exercised at expiration).[35] Robert Merton extended the idea by allowing for dividends. The 1997 Nobel Prize in Economics was awarded to Scholes and Merton for this work. (Black died in 1995).

The Black-Scholes model has been modified many times over the years, but the basic equation is still used to determine the fair market value of an option. Most traders who calculate the fair value of an option do so without paying attention to the mathematics behind the equation.

Fortunately, there is no need to solve the Black-Scholes equation every time that you calculate fair value. Special calculators that do the math are readily available online[36] and your broker probably provides the numbers for you.

Because we are concerned with the value of an option, we must know which specific factors affect that value. They are:

- Stock price

- Strike price

- Time remaining before the option expires

- Option type (put or call)

- Interest rates

- Dividend

- Volatility

The calculators work for both American- and European-style options. Plug in the known values, such as stock price, strike price, option type (call or

---

[35] All options previously discussed can be exercised any time after they are purchased. Those are American style options. The differences between American- and European-style options are covered in Part III.

[36] There is no reason to list multiple web sites, because the Internet constantly changes. Use a search engine to find an online option calculator. I recommend www.cboe.com/LearnCenter/optioncalculator.aspx.

put), interest rates and dividend. The only unknown is the future volatility of the underlying stock,[37] and that discussion is worthy of its own chapter (Chapter 6).

Stock price

The value of an option is derived directly from the value of the underlying stock. A call option gives its owner the right to buy stock at a specified price. Regarding a call option whose strike price is $40, wouldn't you expect to pay more for that option when the stock is $39 than when it is trading at a lower price? Thus, as the stock price moves higher, the value of a call option increases.

If this is not crystal clear, consider this scenario: Your option (to buy stock at $40) expires today and the stock is $60. If you have the right to buy stock by paying $4,000 for 100 shares, and if you can sell those same shares and collect $6,000, then the option has to be worth $2,000. If the stock is above $60, then it is worth even more.

Similarly, as the stock price moves lower, the value of a put option increases. If you own a put option that gives you the right to sell shares at $75, that put is more valuable when the stock is $71 than when the stock is $74 (or *any* price above $71).

One additional consideration: You own an Aug 40 call. When a stock is trading at $39, it is far more likely that the call option will move into the money (the stock must rise another $1) and accumulate intrinsic value than when the stock is priced at $35 (stock must rise $5 before the option is ITM). That makes the call more valuable when the stock is higher. In short, the higher the stock price, the more each call option is worth; the lower the stock price, the more each put option is worth.

We'll discuss the *direct relationship* between an option's price and the stock price when we discuss "the Greeks" in Part III. For now, the important point is to understand that calls increase in value as the stock rises.

> **NOTE:** Warning. The value of a call does not *always* increase when the stock price increases. Nor does the value of a put option *always* increase when the stock declines. There are other factors that affect the option price that are in play at the same time. Time to expiration and estimates of future volatility are the most important. The very fact that several factors—often conflicting—determine an option's value makes it necessary to understand the relative importance of each of these factors. Options are not your ordinary investment tool.

---

[37] Specifically, the volatility from the present moment until the option expires.

Strike price

When you buy stock, your goal is to buy it as cheaply as possible. The lower the strike price, the less you must pay when exercising an option.[38] Thus, the lower the strike price, the more a call is worth. This should be easy to understand. The right to pay $2,000 for 100 shares of stock is more valuable than the right to pay $2,500 for those same 100 shares.[39] This is clearly visible in any set of option data. Unless the calls are so far out-of-the-money that they are worthless, as the strike price of the call decreases, the market price (premium) of the call increases. See figure 5.1 for an example.

Figure 5.1
Market Data for Call Options

Undrlyng	Description	Nt Pos	Bid	Ask	Last	Delta
		Ac Actn	TIF	Quantity	Dest	Status
AAPL	Stock (NASDAQ.NMS)		588.91	589.14	588.97	
AAPL	JAN 18 '13 570 Call		37.70	37.80	38.05	0.6354
AAPL	JAN 18 '13 575 Call		34.70	34.80	34.90	0.6070
AAPL	JAN 18 '13 580 Call		31.80	31.95	32.00	0.5780
AAPL	JAN 18 '13 585 Call		29.10	29.20	29.15	0.5486
AAPL	JAN 18 '13 590 Call		26.50	26.65	26.70	0.5194
AAPL	JAN 18 '13 595 Call		24.10	24.25	24.30	0.4899
AAPL	JAN 18 '13 600 Call		21.90	22.00	22.00	0.4600
AAPL	JAN 18 '13 605 Call		19.75	19.85	19.90	0.4303
AAPL	JAN 18 '13 610 Call		17.80	17.90	17.95	0.4013
AAPL	JAN 18 '13 615 Call		16.00	16.10	16.15	0.3734
AAPL	JAN 18 '13 620 Call		14.30	14.45	14.40	0.3454

Source: InteractiveBrokers, LLC

Calls with the lowest strike price are always priced higher than the rest of the calls.[40] Similarly, the higher the strike price of a put option, the more it is worth.[41]

You will learn how to select an appropriate strike price for your trades. This is not as difficult as it may seem right now. Be aware that there is

---

[38] Remember, you can (and probably should) sell, rather than exercise, any option that you own. Exercising is discussed here as an example, not as a recommendation.
[39] Therefore the 20-strike call costs more than the 25-strike call.
[40] With the same expiration date
[41] The right to sell at a higher price is worth more than the right to sell at a lower price.

seldom a 'best' option for everyone to trade (buy or sell) because a trade that is good for you may be a poor choice for a trader who is far more aggressive or conservative. Choosing an option that meets your needs is discussed in great detail as we study specific strategies.

The inexperienced speculator often prefers to pay a small premium and tends to buy out-of-the-money calls and puts. The speculator hopes to reap a huge bonanza—as if the option were a mini-lottery ticket. Unfortunately, that inexperienced investor usually makes two serious mistakes: buying options with little chance of becoming profitable and paying too much for those options. This important point is discussed further in the next chapter.[42]

Time

Options are a wasting asset and lose value as time passes. The loss of value is not linear.[43] Instead, time decay accelerates as expiration day approaches. See Figure 5.2.

When you own an option, you make money if the stock undergoes a favorable price change, but only if the change occurs quickly enough to offset the effects of time. The longer the lifetime of an option, the more opportunity there is for that favorable price change to occur. Thus, options with more distant expiration dates are worth more than shorter-term options.

The astute reader may ask: if more time increases the chances of the stock moving in the right direction, doesn't it also increase the chances the stock will move in the wrong direction? Yes, it does. Another reasonable question: if the stock has an increased chance to move in the wrong direction, why doesn't more time make the option worth less?

To understand why the opportunity of a favorable move is significant in determining the price of an option and the possibility of an unfavorable move is not, let's examine the rationale behind buying options.

Investors buy options to gain leverage. That means controlling 100 shares of stock for a relatively small amount of money with the hope of turning that small investment into a much larger pile of cash. If the stock moves the wrong way (down when the trader owns calls or higher when the trader owns puts), the value of the option decreases.

Consider this: if an option is worth $200 and the stock makes a winning move, the option may become worth $600 or $1,000.[44] If the stock moves in the wrong direction, the option price could drop to $100. If the stock moves

---

[42] Please do not be dismayed that much is put off for further discussion. At this stage, it is more important to introduce the basic concepts. Once you understand the bigger picture, you will be better placed to study each of the individual topics in greater detail.

[43] The value of an option does not decrease by the same amount every day.

[44] Or any value.

far enough in the wrong direction (or when enough time passes and expiration is near), the option becomes worthless, but it can never be worth less than zero. Thus, the maximum loss is known.

However, if the stock moves in the right direction, the potential gain is huge.[45] There is much more to gain than to lose. And it is *the possibility* of that substantial gain (at a low cost to play) that attracts buyers. Therefore the potential profit drives the option price, not the potential loss. Additional time provides a greater opportunity for a favorable price change and that increases the value of an option.

Figure 5.2
Decay of an at-the-money Option

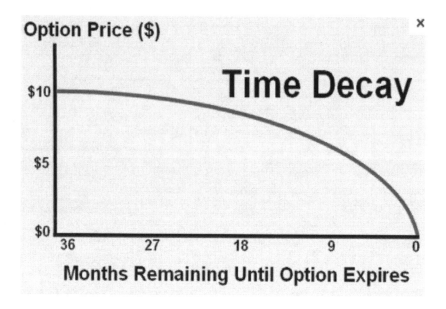

---

[45] In theory, there is no limit to how much a call can be worth because the stock price can continue to rise indefinitely. A put cannot be worth more than the strike price because the price of the stock cannot go below zero.

Option type

Calls are expected to increase in value as the price of the underlying increases and puts are expected to increase in value as the price of the underlying decreases. When buying or selling an option, it is obviously necessary to describe it as a call or put. Please avoid the habit of referring to call options as "options."

Interest rates

Buying calls requires less cash than buying stock and that cash difference can be invested to earn interest. When interest rates are higher, an investor earns more interest and can afford to pay a higher price for the call option. The call seller may choose to buy stock to hedge the option sale. When it costs more (interest) to own stock, the option seller demands a higher price for the option.

Interest rates play a minor role in determining the option premium. However when the option has a longer lifetime (LEAPS) or when interest rates are high, interest rates become a factor.

Higher interest rates reduce the value of put options.

Dividends

When a stock changes hands on the ex-dividend date, its price[46] declines by the amount of that dividend because the person who sells stock receives the dividend, not the brand-new stockholder. The stock is said to trade "ex-dividend," which means without the dividend. The larger the dividend, the greater the overnight decline in the stock price. Thus, dividends decrease the value of calls and increase the value of puts.

Those dividends are already priced into the options. If a stock closes Monday at $30 and opens the next morning at $29.60 after paying a 40-cent dividend, option prices are unchanged—except for the one day's time decay. In other words, the options "knew" the stock was going to open 40 cents lower, and as far as the options are concerned, the stock price is unchanged.

There is an exception. If a call option was deep enough in the money that its owner should have exercised to capture the dividend (more on how this works on pp. 126-7), then the value of that call is lower after the stock opens ex-dividend.

Volatility

The most important factor is saved for last. Understanding volatility is required for anyone who trades options because it is a major factor in determining the price of options in the marketplace. The discussion is so

---

[46] On the morning it first trades ex-dividend.

vital to your understanding of how options trade in the real world that the entire next chapter is devoted to the topic of volatility and its importance in the options universe. To be honest, even that chapter does not do justice to the topic.

Of the seven items listed above that play a role in determining the theoretical value of an option, six are known and only one (volatility) is unknown and must be estimated. Volatility, as defined in the options world, is an estimate of how volatile the stock *is going to be* in the future—specifically, between the current time and expiration. Because the future is unknowable, volatility can only be estimated.

When different traders use different volatility estimates, they arrive at very different estimates for the value of an option. That is why some people become aggressive option buyers when they believe the premium is low. At the same time, others are eager sellers because they believe the premium is too high. That difference of opinion is one of the factors that keep the options markets interesting.

Calculating the theoretical value of an option

It is not necessary to use a "calculator." It is not necessary to attempt to figure out how much an option is worth. Most individual investors who dabble in options do not bother. It is often (but not always) efficient to use the current market price of an option as a reasonable estimate of its true fair value. Why? Because the price is based on the current consensus value for that option, and buyers and sellers have agreed to trade at the price for that moment in time.

On the other hand, knowing the approximate fair value of an option can give you an edge. It helps you decide whether it is reasonable to trade the option or if it is prudent to allow the opportunity to slip away. Any time you can get an edge, it is to your benefit.

That said, it is extremely difficult to estimate future volatility. I do not want to discourage anyone from making the effort, but in the real world, sophisticated traders with huge computing power already estimate volatility. Over the past several years, new volatility products have become available for trading. These are bets on volatility—rather than bets on market direction. Estimating future volatility is a very sophisticated game. I do not see how we can compete with that power. For that reason, I suggest forgetting about predicting future volatility—at least until you have much more experience trading the markets.

To muddy the waters still further, there is *volatility skew* to consider. I'll have more to say on this topic in the next chapter. Volatility skew results in traders using a different volatility estimate for each strike price. Once[47] it was deemed "good enough" to use a single volatility estimate for all options on a given underlying stock. That is no longer true.

Extreme buying/selling pressure

Most of the time trading in options is a straightforward, orderly process. There are buyers and sellers of calls and puts, and option prices change only when the underlying stock changes price. But sometimes distortions occur. If there are a large number of option buyers, prices rise. And that holds true for both puts and calls.[48]

Why may there suddenly be an influx of orders to buy options? The most common reason is the company is issuing its quarterly earnings report. In the pharmaceutical industry, an FDA announcement on the success or failure of a company's new drug often generates option-trading activity. That is when people flock to buy options and prices rise. "Theoretical values" for options are no longer relevant because the normal situation does not apply. News is coming, and with it, the increased possibility of a major change in the stock price. That makes options temporarily more valuable. The big questions are: How much more valuable? Should we be buyers, sellers, or bystanders? I vote for standing on the sidelines. Playing earnings news is a higher-risk play that you can adopt *after* you have a good understanding of how to profit under ordinary market conditions.

---

[47] Prior to the stock market crash of 1987

[48] When bullish buyers pay increasingly higher prices for call options, the puts also increase in price because of arbitrage. If the puts did not increase in value, there would be players to buy those puts and also buy stock. That creates a position that is equivalent to owning a call option (More in Chapter 14). Then they would sell the high-priced call and lock in a profit with no risk. The buying pressure on the puts drives their prices higher.

QUIZ 5

Basics

1. Are the following true or false? When calculating the fair value (theoretical value) of an option:

   a) The Black-Scholes (or a modification) model is used.
   b) Interest rates are a very important factor.
   c) Most of the inputs are unknown and must be estimated.

2. How does an increase in the stock price affect the value of a call option? A put option?

3. Do you agree? When buying or selling options, the current market always represents a fair price.

4. A company unexpectedly announces a dividend increase from $0.25 to $0.50.Assuming the price of the stock is unchanged, who gains from that announcement—the put owner or the call owner?

5. All option traders must calculate the fair value of an option to make money. True or false?

6. The theoretical value of an option can be accurately calculated by using appropriate models. Thus, all traders agree on the fair value of an option. True or false?

QUIZ 5 Answers

1.

a) True. To be 100% accurate, some people use more modern models.
b) False. Interest rates are usually unimportant.
c) False. All inputs are known, other than volatility.

2. The value of a call option increases as the stock price increases. The value of a put option decreases as the stock price increases.

3. You should not agree. Sometimes the option premium is so unfavorable for your chosen strategy that it is better to avoid trading the options than accepting the current market price. In other words, if you are an option seller and the premium is far below its customary value, over the long-term you will be a more successful trader if you avoid selling those undervalued options. Similarly, if you are a buyer and prices are much higher than fair value, it is usually best not to play. NOTE: Any single play, whether it is a buy or sell, can be a winner. But, on average, you do not want to trade options when the probability of success is diminished. This is discussed further in Chapter 6.

4. Put owners. The higher the dividend, the more the stock price decreases when the stock pays that dividend.[49] As an aside, you could argue that a dividend increase is good for the longer - term, and thus, call owners benefit. But for the purposes of evaluating an option, higher dividends make calls worth less and puts worth more.

5. False. Knowing the fair value of an option is beneficial, but it is not mandatory.

6. False. The calculated value of an option depends on the numbers plugged into the Black-Scholes equation

People use different values for the estimated future volatility of the stock. That volatility difference can make a significant difference in the calculated option value.

---

[49] That is when the stock trades ex-dividend.

Chapter 6

Volatility

Volatility is the property of a stock that describes its tendency to undergo price changes. More volatile stocks undergo larger and more frequent price changes. Volatility, as it is used in the options universe, is a measure of the *absolute* volatility of each individual stock and is unrelated to the volatility of other stocks or groups of stocks.

Outside the options world, volatility is described by the term beta. Beta provides a very different measurement of volatility, and you should know its definition, because it is a term that is often misused by investors. Beta is a measure of the *relative* volatility of a specific stock when compared with the volatility of a large group of stocks (often the Standard & Poor's 500 Index, SPX).[50] A beta of 1.0 means the stock has the same volatility as the index. Stocks with beta values of less than 1.0 are less volatile than the index, while stocks with beta values greater than 1.0 are more volatile.

Beta is of interest to investors because it offers a good estimate of how far a single stock will move when the S&P 500 Index moves up or down by a given percentage. . Beta has nothing to do with the *size* of a given price change—it is used to compare the *relative* price changes of the stock and index.

When venturing into the world of stock options, the only volatility measurement that matters is that of the individual stock because our willingness to buy options is based on the probability that the stock will undergo a meaningful price change within the allotted time.

EXAMPLE

> You like the short-term prospects of Tool Works, Inc. (TOOL). The stock is currently trading at $33 per share and you want to buy the Oct 35 call, which expires in six weeks. The current bid for the TOOL Oct 35 call is $0.70 and the current offer is $0.90.
>
> Question: Is $90 per contract a reasonable price to pay for TOOL Oct 35 calls? [I know that many readers are new to trading and

---

[50] This index is frequently considered to be representative of the stock market as a whole.

have not yet made any trades or encountered a situation in which such a decision must be made. However, I am asking you to look at the question and follow the discussion to determine whether the logic behind the answer rings true.]

The correct answer to this question is: "I do not know. I need more information. How volatile has this stock been in the past and are any special announcements due during the next six weeks"

If you examined the day-to-day price changes for TOOL over the past three years and noticed that the average daily price change was 3 cents and that the largest such change was 12 cents, I hope that you would recognize that when a stock's price moves this little, there is not much of a chance that it will move $2.00 over the next six weeks. Would you be interested in paying $90 for an option when the non-volatile stock must rally (soon) by a couple of points?[51] The intuitive answer is no. And that is the correct answer. This option is priced too high.

With the stock trading at $33, it requires an increase of $2 per share for the stock to move beyond the strike price. That is a huge move for a stock that moves, on average, only 3 cents per day. If you like this stock and want to own it, it is much better to buy some shares, rather than to take the huge gamble on the Oct 35 call. It is extremely unlikely you can make any money when buying this call. (In fact, the price is so high that selling the call and collecting $70 (the bid price) per contract may appeal to you. Chapters 9 through 11 detail the strategy of buying stock and selling calls.

When examining TOOL's price history, if you discovered that the average daily price change is 25 cents and that TOOL moved more than $2 in a single day 15 times over the past three years that should grab your attention. If the stock is that volatile, then there is a reasonable chance it could trade a few dollars higher (or lower) sometime during the next six weeks. In fact, there is a reasonable chance that TOOL could jump $2 in only a few days. Under those conditions, paying $90 per contract seems much more reasonable.

---

[51] Ninety dollars per contract is the same as paying $0.90 to buy the option. Option contracts are quoted as the price per share, and each contract represents the right to buy or sell 100 shares.

The data that we considered when making the buy/sell decision (above) depended on the absolute volatility of TOOL and has nothing to do with its performance relative to a stock index. It doesn't matter if the stock is more volatile (or less volatile) than the average stock because you are buying an option based on the likelihood of this specific stock undergoing a sufficiently large price change during the option's lifetime. You are not concerned with the entire market moving higher or lower. When buying or selling options, the primary consideration is how much and how quickly the price of your individual stock (or other underlying asset) changes—and that is not what beta measures.

Volatility types

There is more than one way to talk about volatility. *Historical volatility* is calculated by measuring actual price movements made by the stock in the past. When buying or selling options, you want to know how volatile the stock is going to be from the time the option is purchased (or sold) until the option expires. That volatility can never be known because the time frame is the future. The best we can do is estimating that future volatility. Although it is never going to be a perfect estimate, the past volatility of a stock often provides a reasonable guess as to its future volatility. Please keep in mind that sometimes there are surprises in the market and stocks can become very volatile for a short time.

However, the volatility estimate used to calculate the fair value of an option is based upon more than the historical volatility of the underlying stock. It must also consider events that occur during the lifetime of the option - events that may have a significant impact on the stock price. An example of such an event is the company's quarterly earnings announcement.

General market news can also move markets. For example, when the U.S. Federal Reserve unexpectedly announces a change in interest rates, the stock market often reacts by undergoing a significant move in one direction or the other. Or, more recently,[52] any news from Europe can affect world-wide markets.

When markets are calm, volatility estimates are reduced. When markets are very volatile, all volatility estimates are raised.[53] We witnessed how this works during the October massacre of 2008 when option prices soared

---

[52] Mid-2012, the fate of the Euro and the economy of several individual countries is in doubt.

[53] That makes sense. After all, if the markets have been moving higher or lower by more than 1 % every day for the past week, investors are willing to pay more for options—hoping market volatility continues. Conversely, option sellers demand a higher premium to compensate for increased risk.

during those volatile times. Implied volatility (discussed below) reached heights not seen since the market crash of October 1987.[54]

The term used to describe the estimated *future volatility* is *forecast volatility*. Sometimes it is simply referred to as estimated volatility.

When we look at option prices, we use a different term: *implied volatility* (IV). Unlike the other types of volatility, implied volatility is a property of the option (rather than of the stock). Implied volatility is the real-world estimate of the future volatility for the stock—and that volatility determines how traders value options. In other words, when the implied volatility is used in the option pricing model, the calculator generates a theoretical option price that equals the actual price in the marketplace.

Volatility is important to option traders because it is a vital factor in determining the price of options in the marketplace. Option buyers make money when stocks undergo significant price changes (if the change is in the correct direction). Because volatile stocks are much more likely to undergo large price changes, option buyers pay a much higher premium for options of volatile stocks. As a result, the options of similarly priced stocks often have vastly different market prices.

The importance of implied volatility (IV)

To give you a much better picture of how important the volatility component of the Black-Scholes model plays in determining both the theoretical price of an option and its price in the real world, consider a call option with a lifetime of six months. The stock price is 40, the strike price is 40 and the interest rate is 2 percent:

- When implied volatility is 20, fair value is $2.43.[55]

- When implied volatility is 30, fair value is $3.54.

- When implied volatility is 50, fair value is $5.75.

- When implied volatility is 90, fair value is $10.07.

Note how different these option prices are. It is obvious that the options of volatile stocks command a much higher premium than the options of less-volatile stocks. But there is another important (and practical) lesson to be gathered from this information. When a company is about to announce its earnings for the current quarter, and especially when there is much speculation about those results ahead of the news release, it is natural for

---

[54] There was true panic in the air on that day (and the following morning) as option prices skyrocketed to levels that approximately double those of October 2008.
[55] If 20 is the estimated volatility, then the Black Scholes model tells us that $2.43 is the option's theoretical value.

speculators to buy puts and calls on that company. After all, if the company announces results that are far different from expectations—a reasonable possibility when there has been uncertainty about how the company is doing—then there is a strong possibility that the stock will gap much higher or lower.[56]

Because option rookies do not understand the fine points of buying options, they often anticipate earning a large profit when the stock undergoes a significant price change. Frequently, they are disappointed by the results. Let's consider why that happens—so that it never happens to you.

Most speculators prefer to buy out-of-the-money (OTM) options[57] because those options cost less per contract than at-the-money (or in-the-money) options.[58] The lower price allows buyers to use their investment dollars to purchase more options and gives them the theoretical opportunity to make a killing. They fail to recognize that many other investors have the same idea and are buying the same options at the same time. The increased demand for those specific options forces the market makers (or other traders) who sell those options to justifiably raise prices:

- By raising prices, they hope to attract more sellers to the marketplace. If specialists can buy at the bid price and sell at the ask price, they not only make money, but they do not accumulate positions that must be hedged.[59] The more often they can buy and sell (this is called 'scalping') the same option, the easier it is to avoid taking on risk. To achieve this objective, outside (non-market-maker) sellers are needed to offset the buying pressure.

- Supply and demand. When buyers significantly outnumber sellers, market makers cannot continue to sell options unless they are compensated for accepting more risk. They have little (or no) opportunity to buy options to offset risk (hedge).[60] Thus, they rightfully increase bids in an effort to cover their own risk and they move the ask prices higher, demanding greater compensation for taking on that risk. It is important to understand this scenario because when speculators buy options, they seldom pay attention to

---

[56] Trade at a price that is very different from the previous price

[57] Reminder: An option is OTM when it has no intrinsic value. Calls are OTM when the strike is higher than the stock price. Puts are OTM when the strike is lower than the stock price.

[58] If you do not remember why OTM options cost less, refer back to Chapter 6 and the discussion about how the strike price affects the value of an option.

[59] Hedging is the process by which risk is reduced. Professional option traders, including the market makers and specialists, do not simply take the other side of trades with individual investors and hope for the best. They buy and sell other options as well as the underlying stock with the intent of owning positions with as little risk as possible.

[60] Market makers avoid risk as much as possible, but hedging all risk is difficult

price. Most incorrectly assume that an actively-traded option is *always* reasonably priced. Because they have no idea how to determine a fair price to pay for an option, they enter the market (via orders with their brokers) and pay whatever price is asked of them. Please do not allow that to happen to you. If you decide to gamble and pay the current price[61] with no true feel for what that price would be under normal conditions, just know that your chances of earning a profit are *significantly* reduced. The problem with most under-educated option buyers is that they have no idea that the odds of success are stacked against them.

Thus, there is no reason for market makers to sell the same options (calls and puts) at the same price when there are many buyers and few sellers. Some people believe there is a conspiracy and that market makers are taking advantage of investors because option prices keep rising. But that is an unfair conclusion. No one in the investment world continues to sell a product that is in great demand at the same price. In the stock market, an increase in demand results in higher prices.

No one complains when buyers drive the price of a stock higher, but many feel that options should be treated differently. Remember, one reason for ever-increasing prices is an attempt to attract some investors to sell options to the horde of buyers. When the stock price remains essentially unchanged and option prices increase, that means the implied volatility of the options is increasing. The bottom line is that these option-buying speculators are often unaware of IV, and that leads to many unhappy speculators.

---

[61] Please remember this paragraph refers to situations when news is pending. It is quite acceptable to assume that the current market price is reasonable under 'normal' market conditions.

Trading the news

It is not only the historical volatility that determines how options are priced. When news is pending, option prices can soar—not because the stock has suddenly become more volatile—but because that news *may* result in significant volatility over the very short term.

Option prices are temporarily boosted because buyers want to own that volatility and are willing to pay for it. Once that news is released and digested and the stock begins trading, the volatility event has ended. No more news is expected, no more volatility is expected, and implied volatility gets crushed—until it reaches a level resembling its normal range.

In the above discussion we noted how the price of a six-month call option with a 40 strike price varies considerably as the volatility of the underlying stock increases. That is not only a theoretical discussion. In the real world, if the implied volatility goes from 20 to 30, the option price increases as indicated above (from $2.43 to $3.54). Let's take a look at another example to see why this is true.

EXAMPLE

Assume WOW is announcing earnings after the market closes for trading today. Because it is the last time to buy WOW options before news is announced, there is a great deal of interest in the options—again, both puts and calls. In this scenario, it is common for the options to trade with a pumped IV, as buyers, who hope to be rewarded if WOW makes a big move tomorrow, bid up[62] the prices of both calls and puts.

This stock is appropriately named because it has occasionally produced dramatic earnings surprises over the past several years—and that adds to the interest in owning options for the upcoming earnings release. WOW usually trades with an implied volatility of 40. The Nov options expire in 21 days and WOW is trading at $50 per share. Let's look at Nov OTM options because these are most attractive to speculators. The data is presented in Table 6.1.

---

[62] When buyers find that their current bids are not high enough to attract a seller, then continue to raise their bids

Late in the afternoon, Player A decides to buy some WOW Nov 55 calls. There has been a lot of interest in these options and the IV is quite high (70). Our player pays $1.65 for his calls. Player B is a bit more experienced and knows that many players tend to buy options near the close of business and that buying pressure results in higher option prices. Of course, when buying early in the day, there is always risk that the stock trades lower (decreasing the value of calls). But Player B, being bullish, is willing to take that chance and buys Nov 55 calls when the IV is "only" 60. Player B pays $1.20.

The market closes for the day and our players receive good news. WOW announces better-than-expected earnings and opens 8% higher ($54) the following morning. Our players are happy, expecting a nice payoff for that 4 point jump in the stock price. But something strange happens (from the point of view of our players). There are few option buyers. Everyone who wanted to own these options bought them yesterday. Now, most of those people are sellers, hoping to lock in their overnight profits.

Here's what happens as the markets open for trading: news has been released and no further news announcements are anticipated prior to expiration. Thus, market makers drop the volatility estimate for the underlying stock.[63] In addition, there is a preponderance of sell orders. As a result, the computers that calculate the bid and ask prices for the options[64] establish prices that are substantially lower than they were yesterday. As seen in Table 6.1, a fair price for the Nov 55 call is $1.65 when IV is 40. That means Player A is lucky to break even and, Player B, who was smart enough to shop early, has a small profit. But it is a small payoff considering the risk (possible loss of the entire $120 paid per call).[65]

---

[63] As they should with no special news anticipated. IV can readily drop to its normal level.

[64] In today's world there are so many different options to price that price changes cannot possibly be done manually. Thus, the market makers establish a set of parameters, including the crucially important volatility, and allow the computer to establish bid and ask prices as the price of the underlying stock changes. The parameters can be changed during the trading day, if conditions so warrant (and yesterday, the volatility estimate was raised repeatedly).

[65] If the stock gapped down (instead of up) by 4 points (to 46) the Nov 55 call would be worth $0.05 when IV is 40).

This is an important lesson

WOW implied volatility gets crushed (Table 6.1) after news is released. As is often the case, Player A. feeling cheated, refuses to sell the options without earning a profit. After waiting an hour, Player A finds WOW continues to trade near $54, IV has declined to 35, and there are still more sellers of call options than buyers. Just as option prices (and IV) rose when buyers predominated, so prices (and IV) decline when there are too many sellers. Player A discovers that his options are no longer trading at $1.65. Instead, the price is $1.40. Disgusted, Player A takes the loss, decides that options are a rigged game and vows to never trade another option. If you understand the nature of volatility and options pricing, you can avoid this unhappy outcome.

Table 6.1
Theoretical Value of WOW calls, when IV is as listed
Before (29 days) and after (28 days) earnings news

	Strike	IV	TV		IV	TV
Before				After		
$50				$54		
	55	40	$0.45		40	$1.65
	55	50	$0.79		35	$1.40
	55	60	$1.19			
	55	70	$1.63			
	60	40	$0.06		40	$0.36
	60	50	$0.19		35	$0.24
	60	60	$0.41			
	60	70	$0.65			

WOW implied volatility gets crushed after news is released
TV = Theoretical value

Time premium in the price of an option

You now understand that the volatility of a stock and the implied volatility of the options play a vital role in determining option premium (option price).

There are two additional terms to add to your option vocabulary. An option's premium is the sum of two parts:

- Intrinsic value

- Time value

Intrinsic value is the amount by which the option is in the money. The remainder of the option's premium is the time value. For example, if IBM is priced at $105 per share, and if the May 100 call is $9.30, then the intrinsic value is $5 ($105 minus $100) and the remaining $4.30 is the time value. Most of that time value is related to the stock's volatility and time to expiration, but a small part is associated with interest rates.[66] As we have seen, time value increases for stocks that are more volatile.

Avoiding pain

Some investors always gamble and bet that a specific company is going to announce surprising news—either good or bad. And one way to gamble is to buy calls or puts just before news is released. But, as our example (WOW Nov 55 calls) shows, it is important to pay attention to the price paid for an option. Sometimes the price is so out of line that the prudent investor chooses not to play. Of course, the prudent investor does not adopt this speculative option strategy in the first place.

Take a look at the Nov 60 calls in Table 6.1. The only way to earn a profit from the 4 point stock price increase is to buy the options when IV is near 40—and that is impossible because almost no one sells options at such low prices ($0.05 or $0.10) prior to the release of important news. But there are plenty of speculators who do pay $0.65 with high hopes. Imagine their anguish: paying $0.65 for a call option, seeing their stock gap higher by $4 (that is 8%) and discovering that the option's price falls about 45% ($0.36 theoretical value) only one day later.

Does this mean that you should never play? I cannot answer that for you, but I never buy options under these circumstances. If you choose to gamble, please do not chase options that are too far out of the money. Those are the very options that are priced unreasonably. Do not misunderstand—it is possible to have an occasional large payday when

---

[66] Call buyers save cash by buying options instead of stock. They invest that cash and the interest earned offsets part of the cost of buying the option. The more interest earned, the more buyers are willing to pay for calls.

buying such options. But the odds of making money over the long term are poor if you use this strategy. Consider buying a hedged position instead.[67]

Bottom line: Buying options when IV is much higher than its average is a poor percentage play. Use a calculator to determine the current IV of the options, and use the Internet to find historical volatility levels for each individual stock.[68]

General investment reminder

Investors usually ignore volatility when compiling a list of stocks to buy. I suggest that you take volatility into consideration, especially if you plan to adopt any of the option strategies (those described in this book) that reduce the risk of owning more volatile stocks. If you are a conservative investor whose goal is to increase annualized returns, then less volatile stocks are appropriate. If you are an aggressive investor hoping to earn substantial sums, and if you understand there is more risk involved with such investments, then you can consider more volatile stocks. I am not suggesting that you buy volatile stocks. Please continue to use the same criteria to develop your list of potential stocks to own. When you have that list, take the stock's historical volatility into consideration when ready to adopt an option strategy.

Of all the variables that go into calculating the theoretical value of an option, volatility is not only the most important factor, but also the most difficult to understand and to estimate because the time frame is the future. Use recent (past month or two) historical data as a guide if you care to estimate future volatility.[69]

Introduction to a more advanced topic: Volatility skew

Traders have come to recognize that rare events[70] occur more frequently than the statistical model suggests. Those "events" are primarily market crashes, rather than surges. Thus, OTM puts are truly more valuable than the model calculates. And even if they were not more valuable, some people learned costly lessons when their unhedged portfolios tumbled in value. Thus, they want to own these puts for protection – and that drives prices higher.

That is how supply and demand works. When there are more buyers, sellers demand higher prices. The interesting thing is that demand is asymmetric (resulting in a skewed IV picture). As the strike price gets

---

[67] Part III. You can buy a call debit spread when bullish.
[68] One site that provides free data is:
http://www.optionstrategist.com/free/analysis/data/index.html
[69] Important: You do not have to make that estimate. You can use current (or recent) implied volatility and hope that it turns out to be reasonable.
[70] Black Swan events or any large gap opening

lower, IV moves higher. Sometimes the slope of the graph is dramatic, and at other times the skew is gentle.

Ordinarily we should expect options to trade with no skew. When we talk about future volatility, it is the volatility of the *underlying asset* that matters. In fact, prior to the stock market crash of Oct 19, 1987,[71] options did not trade with much skew. The term 'volatility smile' was often used because a graph of IV vs. strike showed a smile: slightly higher volatility for both OTM puts and calls. After that frightening market collapse, puts started to carry extra premium. Too many traders refused to sell those puts at any price—as demand for these insurance policies increased. As a result OTM put premium moved higher and OTM call premium lagged.

Volatility skew is the simultaneous occurrence of multiple implied volatilities for a single stock. In other words, skew is the measure of the disparity of IV values for option contracts with different strikes but the same expiration. The levels are not random, but instead steadily increase from OTM calls to OTM puts.

- Each strike price has a slightly different implied volatility.

- For below market[72] options, IV increases as the strike price decreases.

- OTM calls often show little skew because there is much less demand for them.

If you ever decide to take shortcuts in your options education (not recommended), do not skimp on spending time with volatility. You may never do the calculations, but it is imperative to understand how volatility affects option prices.

---

[71] Black Monday when the Dow Jones Industrial Average declined by (a record at the time) 508 points (23%) to 1739
[72] Below market refers to strikes that are lower than the current underlying asset price. In other words, OTM puts or ITM calls.

QUIZ 6

Options Basics

1. A stock has a beta of 1.25. Translation: the options trade above their fair value. **TRUE or FALSE**

2. When calculating the historical volatility of a given stock, the stock's daily closing prices are used. **TRUE or FALSE**

3. Most investors who buy out-of-the-money options just prior to a news announcement pay a reasonable price for those options. **TRUE or FALSE**

4. Consider a stock whose historical volatility has been 20. How often should you expect this stock to rise or fall by more than

    a) 20% in one year?
    b) 40% in one year?

5. If all this discussion about volatility makes you uncomfortable because it is just too complex, then it is OK to ignore this topic. **TRUE or FALSE**

QUIZ 6 Answers

1. False. Beta has nothing to do with the value of an option. Options trade above fair value when the *implied volatility* of the options is higher than the recent *historical volatility* for the stock – for no good reason.

2. True.

3. False. That is when options tend to become very over-priced.

4. If the volatility is 20, then a one standard deviation move is up or down by 20%

   a) 32% of the time. A stock moves less than one standard deviation about 68% of the time.

   b) 5%. That is a 2-standard deviation move, and occurs approximately one year in 20.

5. False. You may want to avoid the details and all math, but you should understand at least this much: Volatile stocks have higher priced options. Also: options are not always priced fairly.

Chapter 7

The Importance of Risk Management

We have covered a lot of territory concerning options—far more material than most people who get involved with options ever bother to learn. That is to your advantage because understanding options and how they work puts you in a good position to begin using options successfully. It is not a guarantee of success, but it shifts the odds of success in your favor.

There is one final topic that must be discussed before moving on to trading strategies: risk. Risk is a concept that most investors tend to ignore because they are not certain how to deal with it. Here's my basic premise when trading options:[73] it is easy to make money using options when you adopt conservative strategies, such as those described in this book. The difficult part is keeping that money. If you believe that profits come with little effort, if you get overconfident, if you begin to invest ever-increasing amounts of money and trade larger positions than your financial condition warrants, if you believe the markets are always friendly, you will sadly discover the inevitability of losing money—at least part of the time.

There is nothing wrong with taking losses. It cannot be avoided. You cannot expect to earn a profit from each and every investment. That is life in the investment world. It is crucial to your long-term success as an option trader to be certain that those losses are nothing more than a sting. Do not allow them to hurt. To accomplish that, you must manage risk and keep losses under control. I'll do what I can to help you understand that point, but it is up to you to stay within your comfort zone and not to expand that zone rapidly just because you begin making money.

To trade within your comfort zone, the risk and potential reward must be acceptable for each trade. More than that, you must know that risk and reward for your entire investment portfolio is within your comfort zone. This may seem obvious, but if you are doing well and making money, it is very easy to forget.

When things are going well is the time when it is most important to pay attention to how much money you could lose if the stock market suddenly converts your positions into losers. Do not believe this cannot happen—it not only can, it will.

---

[73] Compared with buying and holding a stock portfolio

Money management is related to risk management. When I speak of risk, I'm referring to the cash that can be earned or lost from a given trade. I cannot tell you exactly how to manage your money because I cannot know how much capital you have in your trading account, nor can I know if you are averse to taking risk or if you are aggressive and willing to risk significant losses in return for the opportunity to earn large profits. Thus, I cannot recommend that if you adopt a specific strategy that it is appropriate to trade 1-lots,[74] 5-lots or any other number of contracts for a specific position. I can only tell you that the size[75] of your positions and the total money at risk is something you must decide for yourself. And that is money management.

For some investors a potential loss of $1,000 is devastating; for others, a $1,000 loss is almost insignificant. It is vital that you manage your money so that not too much of it is at risk for any individual position and that you are never in danger of losing a significant portion of your investment portfolio. There is no formula that suits everyone. Managing your money is something you must do for yourself. My objective is to be certain you understand the importance of doing so.

Investors experienced in owning stocks or mutual funds understand that a severe market correction can result in large losses. And if you didn't understand before, the 2008 stock market should be sufficient reminder. Stock investors are never concerned with losing all, or almost all, of their account value, as long as they are not trading with borrowed money (margin). It is a very different story with option trading. It is not uncommon for the careless (or unlucky) trader to lose 100% of an investment. Thus, it is absolutely essential to know how much can be lost at any given time. I shout this warning to traders who are too new to have participated in past stock market disasters.

When people begin trading options, it may be difficult to recognize that holding a position in a bunch of options that are worth only $100 or $200 (or even less) apiece can result in a significant loss. Because of that potential blind spot, it is essential to stress the importance of managing overall risk.

The methods discussed in Part II consist of three very basic option strategies. One, collars, is especially conservative and any potential loss is very limited. *If you prefer to own stocks in your portfolio*, and if you are very risk averse, collars may be the strategy for you. If you are more

---

[74] "Lot" is the term used by option traders to describe the size of the trade. A 1-lot refers to a single option or a single option spread.
[75] "Size" refers to the relative number of contracts, or lots, traded, as in "Joe trades small size because he is a novice."

aggressive, please pay close attention to the collar strategy for it reappears (in disguise) in Part III.

> **NOTE:** I DO NOT recommend trading collars as an independent strategy. But the conservative investor who owns stock may be interested in learning how to cut both potential profits and losses by converting those long stock positions into collars.

The other two strategies involve more risk than I prefer to see option rookies accept, but are popular strategies because they involve *less* risk for investors when compared with owning individual stocks or mutual funds. If you are currently a buy-and-hold investor, then adopting the methods in Part II will reduce your risk of loss.

If these strategies are riskier than others, why are they the very first methods I teach readers to use? Good question. Covered call writing is much easier to learn when the investor already has experience trading stocks. It introduces options as a modification of what you already know how to do—invest in stocks. And it does reduce risk. But this is a bullish strategy and inappropriate for bearish investors. Once you grasp how to pick individual options for a specific purpose (writing covered calls), it is easier for you to move on to the safer strategies. Thus, you may be anxious to get started and you may find the methods in Part II to be very attractive, but please take the time to read Part III to decide if those 'more advanced' methods are better suited to your investment philosophy.

The methods in Part III expand the way in which you can use options. Those are all limited-loss strategies. If you have the proper money management skills and avoid trading 100-lots when 10-lots (or even 1-lots) is the appropriate size for your comfort zone, then there is little chance that a major loss will occur. You will lose money part of the time, but if disasters are avoided, you will do fine over the long term. It is up to you to manage your money and my part is to show you how to skillfully adopt the strategies. The year 2008 was one that fully tested your ability to manage risk. If you lost more than you feel comfortable losing, perhaps the strategies described in this book, coupled with your ability to trade appropriate size, will make it easier for you to thrive when you encounter another nasty year for traditional investors.

When you begin trading with real money, it is an intelligent decision to trade only a few contracts at one time, even if you have the investing experience and the financial ability to trade larger quantities. You can easily increase the size of your positions *after* you become comfortable trading the option markets. Being aware of the amount of money at risk for a position in dollar terms is the basis of good money management. It is one thing to have a position that may, if you are very unlucky, lose $10,000 when you trade in an account worth $100,000. But, it is a far different matter to own that position when your entire account is worth only $10,000.

Some investors who have been making money trading 3-lots suddenly decide that it is time to make some real money and start trading 30-lots. All I can say is please avoid this trap.

Long-term success

Your long-term success as an option trader is not going to depend solely on how much money you make from each trade or on how much of a return you are able to generate on your investments. The fact is that it is not difficult to make money when using options, as long as you avoid risky methods. For most people, that translates into having more winning trades than losers. It also means that when you do lose, your losses tend to be smaller.

You may ask: That all sounds good, so what is the problem? The problem arises (and it is a real problem) when investors become overconfident. They believe that they are very talented traders, that they always make good money, that options really do help them make lots of money (with little effort), and that risk is under control because they are using limited-risk strategies. Do not fall into that trap. Risk is under control when you have a firm and *continuous* grasp on the potential monetary risk and reward of your entire portfolio.

You may feel that this chapter is totally unnecessary, and for the careful investor, perhaps it is. Options are fun to trade. Option strategies reduce risk. The key to success is not to trade more than your bankroll (and your trading acumen) allow. Please remain within your comfort zone.[76]

We will be talking more about risk management as we discuss individual option strategies.

---

[76] The successful and experienced trader will eventually expand that comfort zone. But when done carefully and gradually, this trader can handle it.

Part II

Three Basic Conservative Strategies

Ideal Trades for the New Options Trader

Gateway to More Advanced Methods

Chapter 8

The Basic Conservative Option Strategies

It is time to begin reaping the benefits of having a thorough understanding of what an option is and the mechanics of how to trade them. You are now far more knowledgeable than the vast majority of traditional options rookies. Too many beginners jump right in by making trades. They never really understand what they are attempting to accomplish — other than to "make money." Congratulations on avoiding that pitfall.

This section thoroughly explains basic options strategies—not because they are the best possible ways to trade options (although they are good strategies)—but because if you come away from Part II with a clear understanding of how these strategies work, then you are ready to grasp the concepts behind more advanced option strategies.

We begin from the perspective of an individual investor whose stock market experience has been limited to owning individual stocks or mutual funds. If this is your background, and if you have not previously traded options, then the three basic conservative strategies are an excellent place for you to gain your first experience with options. Why? Because these methods involve buying stock,[77] something with which you are already familiar, and that makes it easier to remain in your comfort zone while expanding your investment horizons.

For many years, mutual fund investors were unable to use options. Although that is still true for the owners of most traditional mutual funds, in today's investment world there is a new kid on the block: the exchange traded fund (ETF). Many of these ETFs, the 21st century version of the traditional mutual fund, have listed options. That means you can use the option strategies described throughout the book when the underlying asset is one of the many ETFs whose options trade on an exchange. If you are more comfortable owning a diversified portfolio rather than individual stocks, it is now possible to do just that and trade options at the same time.

The three basic conservative option strategies

These strategies are:

---

[77] In two of the three strategies, you do buy stock. In the third, you may become obligated to buy stock.

- **Covered call writing**. Using stock that you already own (or buying new stocks), hedge (reduce the risk of owning) those positions by writing (selling) one call option for each 100 shares. That means you are selling someone else the right to buy your stock at an agreed upon price for a limited time.

- **Collars**. Establish a collar position by buying stock and selling a call option, just as with covered call writing. Then buy a put option, protecting yourself against the possibility of a large loss, in case the stock undergoes a severe price decline. This is the most conservative of the basic strategies, because it has the least profit potential and offers the most safety. Collars can set up to protect almost the entire value of your investment.[78]

- **Cash secured, or naked, put writing**. Sell a put option, accepting an obligation that may require you to buy stock at a later date. It is possible that this obligation will expire and you may never buy that stock, but you must be prepared to do so. If you have cash on hand (in your account) to make that purchase, then you are "cash secured." If not, then the sale is considered naked.

These basic strategies are not only for newcomers to the options world. Many experienced investors adopt these strategies and find them so satisfactory that they never consider looking for different methods. And that may also be how you feel. I used these strategies for many years as my *only* option strategies. Later, I began using other methods which we'll discuss those in Part III. One of the basic tenets of using options (or any investing method) is that you, the individual investor, should adopt methods that make you feel comfortable with your holdings. Some investors are extremely conservative, while others are high rollers who take big chances. It is important that you sleep well at night and that means using methods that fit your comfort zone.

One of the results of a year such as 2008[79] is that many people shifted their comfort zones to one that requires taking less risk. Many investors are also less optimistic that the stock market is going to take care of them during their retirement years. If that describes you, then writing covered calls and selling cash-secured put options are somewhat less risky than owning an unhedged stock portfolio. These strategies may not provide sufficient safety to satisfy your longer-term needs. Yet, they remain excellent methods for *learning* how options can be used profitably and conservatively. Once you understand the three basic conservative option

---

[78] You can protect the entire investment, if willing to pay the higher cost.
[79] Financial crisis, housing trouble, market decline, extreme volatility

strategies, then go on to Part III. Those methods are as safe as the collar (you will understand why that is true later) and involve less risk than writing covered calls.

Choosing stocks

When choosing stocks to buy, your obvious goal is to find stocks whose value increases over time. This is not an easy task, otherwise everyone would make a fortune in the stock market. It is important not to make snap decisions when buying or selling specific stocks, especially when the decision is based upon someone else's recommendation. If some analyst upgrades or downgrades a stock, or if someone gives you a hot tip, it is prudent to conduct your own research and make your own decision whether it is reasonable for you to trade the shares before becoming a stockholder. The methods used to make stock-buying decisions are not part of our current discussion. Important point to remember: there is no reason to change your methods just because you are learning to use options.

Remember to consider the stock's volatility history when determining whether a stock qualifies as an addition to your list of potential investments (see Chapter 6). We are not too many years removed from the 2008 stock market debacle or the technology bubble of the 1990s that cost a great many investors a substantial portion of their life savings. If you are among those who were hurt during either event and if you want to return to the stock market but are afraid of sustaining significant losses, this section is for you. If preservation of capital is your top priority when investing, and if making money is a goal, but a secondary one, then the collar strategy can help you achieve your investment objectives.

Two of the methods taught in Part II provide limited insurance against loss and increase the probability of earning a profit from your investments. And more importantly, gaining a thorough understanding of how they work prepares you for Part III – more advanced, but non-complicated methods for adding much more protection against loss.

The third strategy allows you to invest in the stock market with a great deal of confidence, and depending on the deductible you choose for your "insurance policy,"[80] it can protect almost the entire value of your portfolio.

Let's take a detailed look at these investment techniques one at a time. It is my intention to leave you with an excellent understanding of each strategy, how to apply the strategy, and how to know whether the specific strategy is suitable for you and your investment philosophy. A thorough discussion of the risks and rewards associated with each strategy is included.

---

[80] The put you purchase when using collars acts as that insurance policy.

Before getting started, let's consider one basic option strategy. I must repeat the warning of Chapter 3: I do not recommend this strategy. The chances of making money on a consistent basis are very small, unless you are very talented in determining which stocks to buy and when to buy (or sell) them.

Buying options (NOT one of the recommended basic strategies)

Buying options is the single strategy that brings more new players into the options space than any other because the option occasionally produces a jackpot — similar to buying a mini-lottery ticket,[81] and the possibilities are too tempting for many to ignore. It is not that buying options is a bad strategy, but it is difficult to be successful. It requires skills that most traders lack.

There are two good features about buying options: losses are always limited to the cost of the options and there is an opportunity to earn a large profit from a small investment. Unfortunately, too many investors who buy options lose their entire investment because they are unwilling (or do not understand how) to accept a small loss and thus, they hold their options until they expire, often worthless.

In this author's opinion, it is wrong to encourage investors, especially investors with little option trading experience, to adopt a strategy with little chance of success. If you occasionally speculate, there is nothing wrong with that. But the recommendation here is that you are better served using strategies that increase your chances of making money. Isn't that the reason you picked up this book in the first place—to learn to use options to *make money*? The fact that options can be used to reduce risk (while earning that money) is a huge bonus and it is intelligent to take advantage of that risk-reducing characteristic of options.

Succeeding as an option buyer: the requirements

As an option buyer, you can expect to have more losing trades than winning trades. To succeed, the average profit must be significantly larger than the average loss.

Predicting direction

When *buying* puts or calls, you are predicting the direction that the underlying asset will move during the lifetime of the option. If you are wrong, you have no chance to earn a profit. Keep in mind that predicting direction is difficult at best. Most professional money managers do a poor

---

[81] I'll concede that you have a much better chance to make money buying options ithan lottery tickets.

job.[82] Although they are very good at collecting management fees from their customers, the majority cannot outperform the market on a consistent basis.

In contrast, option *sellers* win most of the time because they only require the stock not to move too far in the wrong direction. In other words, when selling calls, you profit when the stock declines, holds steady, or increases by a small amount. Thus, it is much easier to make money by prudently selling options. When selling options, I recommend (that word is not strong enough. I urge you) never to sell an option without buying another option[83] as insurance against a large loss. You'll see how that works in Part III.

One advantage to buying options is that profits can be unlimited. It is a popular strategy because there is always the chance to earn that large profit. Option sellers have no such paydays. When selling options (or option spreads) profits are more frequent, but limited.

Timing

If predicting direction is not difficult enough, the option buyer must also be right on timing. Options are a wasting asset and lose value day after day. Thus, it is important for the stock to make its move before the option loses too much time value or expires. Most intelligent professionals believe that it is very difficult to time the stock market correctly.

Size of move

Depending on the option you buy (OTM, ATM, ITM)[84], the underlying asset must not only move in the right direction within a limited time period, but the move must be large enough to compensate for the extrinsic value (same as time premium—it is the option premium less its intrinsic value) of the option. For example, if YYZ is trading near $29 and you decide to pay $1.00 to buy YYZ calls with a strike price of $30 and an expiration date that arrives in 30 days, you do not make any money when the stock slowly rises to $31 on expiration day.[85] If the stock reaches 31 earlier, you *may* be able to sell the call and earn a profit. Why does the time make a difference? As we learned earlier (Chapter 5), as we increase the lifetime of any option, its value increases. If the stock reaches $31 early enough, it will

---

[82] Mutual funds are run by highly paid professional managers and the majority cannot outperform the market averages. That is one reason why smart mutual fund investors have switched to buying index funds. Those investors got better performance and pay lower fees.
[83] Thereby creating an option 'spread.'
[84] Reminder: Out of the money, at the money, and in the money. Understanding these terms is essential.
[85] The option is worth $1 (its intrinsic value), and that is the price you paid. You break even, ignoring commissions.

retain significant time premium. Once expiration arrives, that time premium has declined to zero.

Unfortunately, the stock (in this scenario) takes too long to move to $31 and you do not earn money. It is very disappointing to see your stock move from 29 to 31 in a short time and discover that you didn't profit from correctly predicting the price rise. It is not easy to make money when buying options.

Premium paid

In Chapter 3 there is an example of a successful trade in which an investor buys 5 SPX call options and the market makes a favorable move. That profit potential is the lure. If you have a track record of successfully predicting whether the market is rising or falling, and if those market moves are large enough, you can do very well as an option buyer. If you have those skills, use them. Take full advantage. Most investors lack those skills, but studies show that the typical investor believes his/her track record is much better than it is.

Options can be used to gain leverage.[86] However, they can also be used to reduce risk. I believe in using options from a conservative perspective and thus, concentrate on strategies that use options as risk-reducing investment tools. But you must choose your path—the path that fits your skills and comfort zone. We will discuss how to discover where your zone is located.

We'll talk about buying options as insurance, to protect one position, or hedge an entire portfolio. When you buy options for that purpose, you are not predicting market direction. You are protecting your portfolio against an unforeseen event. One of the three basic conservative strategies involves buying put options as an insurance policy. In Part III almost all strategies involve owning that type of insurance.

A note about option strategies

Trading is a personal thing. Some readers will find that some strategies are appealing, while others strategies are not. Each investor has his/her individual comfort zone — one that differs from those of other traders. Some trading ideas are easy to understand, while others may *appear* to be complicated. If you find that you just don't "get" one specific idea, skip it for now or send questions[87] and I'll do my best to clarify. There is no urgency. Take your time. Proceed at a pace that works for you.

---

[86] Leverage represents the possibility of making a very high return on a relatively small investment.
[87] rookies@mdwoptions.com

Bottom line: Choosing one or more option strategies that is comfortable to trade is merely the first step. To play the game—i.e., attempt to make money using options, you must first make some trades that give you a position to own. That is where the specific strategy comes into play because you will trade specific options to conform to a chosen strategy. That part is important.

But, the major factor that determines your overall success as a long-term option trader is going to be how you manage risk. Exercise good judgment and do not ignore risk, and you will do well. If you open positions and then close your eyes, hoping for a favorable outcome, you are gambling. Some gamblers win, but most lose. Options are very versatile, risk-reducing investment tools. Use them wisely and there is an excellent chance that options will help you reach your financial goals.

Now let's look at specific strategies.

Chapter 9

Covered Call Writing: Preparing to Trade

By now you are more than ready to get into specific strategies for using options to make money. We've spent a great deal of time on background information. By knowing the answers to the most basic questions before committing your money, you avoid the pitfalls of many novices— and that means reducing or eliminating unnecessary losses during your first few trades.

We'll take a step-by-step approach to learning several easy-to-understand, risk-reducing option strategies. These may or may not be your strategy of choice after you complete this book, but we begin with three basic conservative option strategies, each of which is widely used by investors. Most people who learn about options already have some experience with buying and selling stock. Each of the three basic conservative option strategies is less risky than owning stock, and learning these strategies is the best way to ease into option trading. This is not the traditional path taken by most options students, but I believe it is the easiest (and by far, the most practical) way to get a firm grasp on how to use options, while at the same time reducing the risk of investing and earning money.

Traditionally, the only way to invest in the stock market was to buy stocks or mutual funds. Today, options provide an opportunity to participate in the ups and downs of the stock market without owning shares of anything. We'll begin with option strategies designed for investors who own, or are willing to own, stocks. The concept of making or losing money when owning shares is easy to understand. The owner profits if and when share prices rise and loses money when the stock price declines. But options are not stocks—they are a derivative product, and the pricing of derivatives is not as straightforward as the pricing of stocks. That is why we begin with strategies designed for stockholders, allowing you to use options under conditions that are already familiar. The best way to learn about options and understand how they work is for the investor to own a real option position.

Many people begin their trading careers by simply buying options, a strategy that has the benefit of limiting risk, but which gives that investor a very small chance of earning a profit. It is always a good idea to limit risk—a concept which is emphasized many times in these pages—but why would anyone want to begin trading options with a strategy that is likely to lose money? Instead, I'll show you how to get started with options by adopting strategies that increase your chances of earning a profit.

Once you are familiar with those basic strategies, we'll move on to methods that do not involve stock, and which reduce risk even further.

The first of the three basic conservative option strategies consists of owning stock and selling a call option. That call gives someone else the right to buy your stock. In option jargon, the strategy is known as covered call writing, or CCW. This basic strategy is very popular among individual investors, many of whom use it as their primary investment vehicle.

By adopting CCW, you, the individual investor, learn first-hand how the writing (selling) of call options makes it possible to earn extra profits from stock ownership. It doesn't always provide *optimum* results, but it does boost earnings (most of the time) or reduce losses. As you monitor your position and watch the weeks go by, you'll gain an understanding of how options are valued in the marketplace. You'll notice how option prices behave as your stock rises and falls and how the passage of time plays a vital role in the pricing of options. We discussed the theory of how options are priced earlier (Chapter 5), but it is easier to grasp the concepts as you watch your own money at work. If you have the ability to keep tabs of your positions online, rather than relying on statements from your broker, you have a great advantage. Today, few newspapers publish option prices, and often those prices are stale.[88]

> **NOTE:** Some of you have the time and desire to watch positions frequently—daily or even hourly. If it is not feasible to spend that much time on your investment portfolio, do not be concerned. For the majority of readers who are employed full time, checking an investment portfolio throughout the day is not necessary. Once per day is more than adequate to keep an eye on how option prices change over time. Even a weekly perusal— if you are an investor and not a trader—of your positions allows you to absorb important information about the pricing of options and the effect of time.

I begin with covered call writing for several reasons: It is an easy-to-understand strategy that provides an opportunity to reduce risk when owning stocks.

- CCW increases the probability that any trade will earn a profit.

---

[88] At one time, traders had to depend on newspapers to see option prices on a daily basis. Those prices were often stale. Today we all have access to live information online.

- CCW allows the investor/trader to observe how the market price of an option changes as time passes and the price of the underlying stock changes.

- Selling options (when done prudently)[89] is more likely to show a profit when compared with buying options.

Message to new option students

When learning about CCW, please be aware of your overall investment philosophy. Some investors are very conservative and want to eliminate (as much as possible) the chance of losing money when investing. Others are extremely aggressive and prefer to roll the dice and can afford to accept large losses, as long as they have the chance to make a killing (I hope you are not in this category). If you keep your goals clearly in mind, you can find at least one option strategy that makes it easier to accomplish your objectives. If you are currently an aggressive, risk-taking investor, you may be surprised to discover that the potential rewards available from adopting conservative methods are sufficiently attractive that you may elect to become more conservative. I hope to convince you to take that path because there is no good reason to accept more risk than necessary.

As you take a careful, detailed look at covered call writing, you'll discover that the risk/reward profile of the strategy varies significantly depending on the stocks you own, as well as on the specific option sold. CCW is a versatile strategy, and when it comes to selecting an option to write, there are usually enough choices to accommodate both the very conservative and very aggressive investor. Some readers may be tempted to write the call option that provides the chance (albeit a tiny chance) to maximize profits. That is understandable. You should resist that temptation. Just because a huge return is possible doesn't mean it is a likely outcome. If you write a call that offers a more modest return, the probability of earning that return increases. You'll see how that works when we look at our first example.

Bottom line: It is important to adopt trading methods that allow you to remain within your comfort zone. That means liking your positions *and* having no anxiety over your investment portfolio. You can modify your investment philosophy at any time that it becomes appropriate. As you begin to use options, reinforce your good investing habits. My job is to help you learn new strategies that help you achieve your goals—with reduced risk.

Covered call writing is not for everyone. As we discuss the strategy's benefits and risks, you can determine whether it is suitable for you. Let me

---

[89] We'll stay away from the high-risk option-selling strategies.

make this important point up front: if you are the type of investor who feels that the best possible result must be achieved with every investment, then this method will not work for you. CCW provides better results most of the time, but sometimes you can earn a larger profit by simply holding stock and not adopting any option strategy. That is the nature of the game.

With CCW, you make money more often and lose money less often, but you must give up the possibility of making a killing. If you are searching for stocks that quickly double and then double again, then this is not an appropriate strategy because CCW limits profits. Please do not skip these chapters because I show you how to think about choosing specific options to trade and how to make good decisions when selecting those options.

Covered call writing defined

The term, "write," is equivalent to the term, "sell." When you sell a call option, there are three possible phrases to describe the sale:

- **Closing**. This occurs when you sell an option that you already own.

- **Opening**. A transaction in which you are initiating a new position or adding to an existing position.

  o **Covered.** This is an opening transaction. You do not own the call option that you sell, but you do own a sufficient number of shares of the underlying security (100 shares per option) so that your broker can deliver (transfer the shares from your account in exchange for cash) the shares if you are assigned an exercise notice. Remember when you sell a call option you agree to accept an obligation to deliver 100 shares of stock per option. You may never be called upon to fulfill that obligation, but until that option expires or is repurchased, the obligation remains in effect. Thus, covered call writing is the sale of call options when your account holds sufficient shares of the underlying security to make delivery.

  o **Uncovered** (Naked). This is an opening transaction. Not only do not you own the option, but you do not own any (or you do not own enough) shares of the underlying stock to fulfill your obligation. If you are assigned an exercise notice, you sell the shares short.[90] Short selling is not something to fear, but many newcomers to the world of investing do fear it. Short selling is not allowed in an IRA or other retirement accounts. Therefore,

---

[90] The short seller borrows shares from his/her broker and sells them. At some unspecified future date, the trader buys the shares to cancel (cover) the short position.

selling naked calls is not allowed in those accounts. I do NOT recommend the sale of naked call options for any but the most experienced option traders, and is it too risky for most of them.

Why consider writing covered calls? Before adopting any strategy, it is important to understand the rationale behind it. Thus, we must ask:

- What do you have to gain?

- What do you have to lose?

- Can this simple strategy make a significant difference in the profitability of your investment portfolio?

Review: In return for paying a premium, the call buyer gets the right to buy 100 shares of your stock at the strike price, but only for a limited time. In return for receiving the premium, you accept an obligation to sell 100 shares at the strike price—but only if the call owner exercises the right to buy your stock before the option expires. You have no role in the exercise decision. The option owner determines if and when the option is exercised.

> **NOTE:** The following are crucial concepts to understand — and are worth repeating: Each person has different investment goals and a different risk tolerance. When writing covered calls, a critical decision must be made, and that is deciding which call to write. There is no "best" call to sell. Individual investors are likely to discover that more than one choice is suitable.

Our first example outlines the advantages and disadvantages of each possibility and provides insight that makes it easier to make a real-world decision—a choice that fits your investment style. For example, some investors prefer selling near-term options (options that expire within a month or two), while others prefer writing longer-term options. You will discover your own comfort zone.

Some options make better choices for conservative investors—people who prefer to concentrate on safety rather than earnings potential. Aggressive investors are willing to sacrifice some safety in exchange for the possibility of making more money, and usually choose different options to write. And there is always the middle ground for investors who are concerned with both reducing risk *and* making money. Again, there is no right or wrong decision and there is a good chance that more than one option will turn out to be appropriate for you.

Is covered call writing worth the effort?

Covered call writing is a good method for investors to learn how options work. It is a simple strategy and fits right in with their previous stock-trading experience. I consider it to be the gateway into the world of options.

But does it help your portfolio grow? Is it a good method for making money? Fortunately, statistics are available to provide an answer to those questions. The bottom line is that it is more profitable most of the time, but in wildly bullish markets you earn more money by simply owning stock.

BXM, the buy-write index

The Chicago Board Options Exchange (CBOE) publishes data for BXM, the Buy-Write[91] Index.

BXM is a benchmark index created to *compare* the performance of a hypothetical portfolio that is completely invested in covered calls with a portfolio that matches the performance of the S&P 500 Index. BXM is not an index that anyone should attempt to mimic in the real world.

Data for this index is available dating back to June 1988. BXM is based on the following investment strategy: (This description is presented to show you how the BXM works. Please do not bother to copy this investment methodology because it requires too much effort. Besides, you can invest directly in BXM if you want to do so.)[92]

- Buy and maintain ownership of a portfolio of stocks that mimics the S&P 500 Index.

- There is no need to own all 500 stocks if a portfolio has an almost 100% correlation with index. BXM is measured from a portfolio that exactly matches the index.

- Write near-term[93] S&P 500 Index (SPX) call options early in the morning[94] on the third Friday of each month.

- The strike price is always just above the current index level (the first out-of-the-money call option).

- The call is held through expiration and is settled in cash.[95]

---

[91] A buy-write is a single transaction in which you buy stock and write a covered call. The subtle difference between a buy-write and writing a covered call is that the buy-write is a single transaction. If you already own stock and then write calls, that transaction is referred to as writing a covered call, and not as a buy-write. Just know that the resulting positions are identical.

[92] BXM futures are available.

[93] Options expire in four- or five-weeks. These are NOT the Weeklys options.

[94] Options on the SPX (S&P 500 Index), unlike options on stock, settle (expire) based on the opening of the market on the third Friday of the month; not at the close. (European style options are discussed in Part III.). Exception: Options issued specifically as 'Weeklys' are based on Friday's closing prices.

- The strategy used for BXM does not allow for any adjustments. The position must remain unchanged through expiration.

- Every month, a new one-month call option is written, based on the identical strategy.

What does BXM tell us about adopting a covered call writing strategy? The comparison is illustrated in Figure 9.1.

In Figure 9.1 the performance of BXM is compared with SPTR, the Standard & Poor's Total Return Index. SPTR performance is based on periodic reinvestment of all dividends. The data shows that the option-writing strategy performed on a par with the Total Return Index during most of the 24 years for which data is available.

Figure 9.1 BXM vs. SPTR (S&P Total Return Index)
June 1988 through July 2012

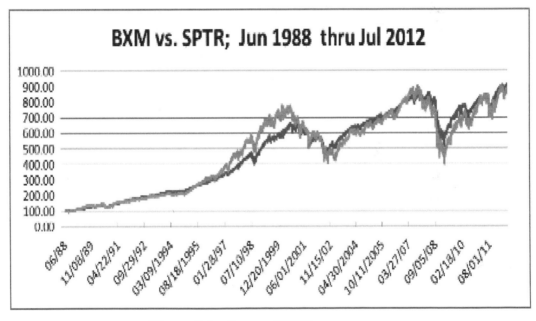

Figure 9.1   Source:CBOE

---

[95] In Part III we'll talk about cash-settled options. For now just understand that you do not have to deliver your portfolio of stocks if the option is in-the-money and you are assigned an exercise notice. You keep your stocks and deliver the cash value (intrinsic value) of the option.

Table 9.1
BXM vs. SPTR, the Bullish Years

YEAR	BXM	SPTR
1995	21%	37%
1996	16%	23%
1997	27%	33%
1998	19%	29%
Avg	21%	30%

As bubble-grew, BXM returned 21%, dwarfed by SPTR's 30% return

A closer examination of Figure 9.1 shows that SPTR performed extremely well during the four very bullish (bubble-building) years of 1995 through 1998 (see Table 9.1). BXM returned very handsome profits during those years (21 percent), but when compared with the 30 percent return of the SPTR, it pales in comparison. This illustrates that writing covered calls indeed limits profits. When the market is wildly bullish, covered call writing underperforms a simple buy and hold strategy.

However, the markets are seldom so bullish. On average, BXM outperformed SPTR during all the other years (see Table 9.2) by an average of 3% percent per year. When the markets are lower, BXM easily outperforms SPTR. This is clearly visible for the years 2000 and 2008.

When we consider that writing covered calls requires time and effort, is CCW a worthwhile strategy? The answer depends on you, your investment goals, and your outlook for the American stock market. To me, it is reasonable to conclude that writing covered calls is worthwhile because it provides better returns more often—and does so with reduced volatility, i.e., reduced fluctuation in the value of your portfolio. It is true that those who adopt this method earn less when the market is very strong, but over the long term, a string of very bullish years is a low probability event. CCW is appropriate for many investors. Unless you are wildly bullish, adopting this strategy is appropriate for a portion of your portfolio. But please do not forget the main purpose in learning about covered call writing: it is your entrance into the world of options. It is not my recommendation that it become your go-to strategy.

CCW significantly reduces portfolio volatility and, for many investors, that is important—or at least, it should be important. Large fluctuations in the value of your portfolio serve no useful purpose. If you ever have an emergency that requires removing cash from your account, it is far better not to have that occur after a large decline in your account balance. The best way to avoid that is to minimize account volatility.

BXM provides slightly superior risk-based returns. That means for a given level of risk, BXM provides higher returns than SPX (or SPTR). To earn equal returns, the investor who owns a diversified stock portfolio must take greater risk than the covered call writer.

Feldman and Roy's study showed that for the 16-year period studied, the standard deviation of the BXM portfolio was 10.99 percent and for the S&P 500 portfolio (without selling any calls) was 16.50 percent.[96] That is a significant reduction in volatility.

In 2004 Ibbotson Associates published a case study on the BXM buy-write options strategy which showed that BXM "has relatively good risk-adjusted returns. The compound annual return of the BXM Index over the almost 16-year history of this study is 12.39 percent, compared to 12.20 percent for the S&P 500. The BXM had about two-thirds the volatility of the S&P 500. The study provides credible evidence of the investment potential for the BXM Index."[97]

When adopting covered call writing for a stock portfolio, you have choices: you may write covered calls most of the time, but refrain when you believe the market is poised to run significantly higher. [98] Of course, one never knows when those strong bull markets are going to occur or when they may end. In fact, the majority of investors seem to get it wrong by jumping into the market near tops and unloading near bottoms. Unless you know (via a proven track record) that you have good market-timing skills, it is better to adopt the more conservative method of writing covered calls on most, if not your entire, portfolio—and to continue with that strategy year after year.

If picking individual stocks is not your forte, then you can use the strategy with ETFs or index options (discussed in Part III). For the vast majority of investors who cannot successfully time the market on a consistent basis, the recommendation is to maintain a consistent long-term strategy. You may even decide to write calls on only a portion of your portfolio. Or you may decide to use the strategy conservatively or aggressively. The distinction is described in Chapter 10

---

[96] Feldman, Barry, and Dhruv Roy, "Passive Options-Based Investment Strategies: The Case of the CBOE S&P 500 BuyWrite Index." The Journal of Investing (Summer 2005).
[97] Ibid.
[98] Or write calls with a higher strike price. You will understand that concept after Chapter 10.

Table 9.2 SPX vs. SPTR
The Other Years

YEAR	BXM	SPTR
1988	8%	6%
1989	25%	32%
1990	4%	-3%
1991	24%	30%
1992	12%	8%
1993	14%	10%
1994	4%	1%
1999	21%	21%
2000	7%	-9%
2001	-11%	-12%
2002	-8%	-22%
2003	19%	29%
2004	8%	11%
2005	4%	5%
2006	13%	16%
2007	7%	5%
2008	-29%	-37%
2009	26%	23%
2010	6%	14%
2011	6%	1%
2012	5%	16%
Avg	8.0%	5.0%

BXM Outperforms SPTR most of the time

Of course, it is your money and you should invest it as you think best. My job is to provide additional tools that you can put to use when you deem it appropriate. CCW outperforms a buy and hold investment strategy most of the time: in down markets, in steady markets, and in up markets—failing to outperform only during those strong upwards markets.

One further point: CCW is not recommended as the best available option strategy. Instead, I recommend it as an excellent learning tool. Once you understand how the three basic strategies work, you'll be able to move on to Part III and find strategies that provide even higher potential returns and with less risk. But please do not jump ahead. The lessons provided in Part II are necessary for understanding Part III.

Because writing covered calls provides similar returns to owning a diversified stock portfolio, but with lower volatility, it should be the preferred method for many investors. CCW is not the road to riches, but it represents an introduction into the world of options and is a perfect starting point, especially for investors who already own stocks or who like the idea of owning stock.

Calculations required for covered call writing

Before we get started, there are a few basic calculations that we use repeatedly. It is important that we agree on definitions to avoid misunderstandings:

S = Stock price. Use the current stock price when the option is sold; not the original cost.[99]

P = Option premium, the price at which you buy or sell the option.

G = Gain (profit).

DP = Downside protection.

- ROI: The return on an investment is the profit divided by the amount invested.

  ROI = G/(S-P)Call

- Amount invested: Cash required to purchase stock, but reduced by the premium collected when writing the options.

- Use the current stock price rather than original purchase price because the current price represents the value of the investment *today* and allows you to determine the current return. If you prefer to track your results using original cost, then do so. The reason for carefully defining these terms is allow us to agree on the calculated results.

- Downside Protection: The amount the stock can decline from its present value before reaching the break-even point.[100] It is equal to

---

[99] This is how the calculations are made in this book. Keep your books in any manner that suits you.

the option premium divided by the stock price. You lose no money on the trade if the stock remains above the break-even point at expiration (the close of business on the specific Friday mentioned in the option contract).

DP = P/S

- When making a trade decision, the difference between a possible profit of 15% or 16% is never going to be the deciding factor. I encourage readers to understand how to make *rough* calculations. , Please do not spend too much time on these numbers. Understanding how to get the information should serve your needs.

In this book, when considering which option to choose for any given trade, I begin by examining each possibility from the point of view of an experienced, conservative trader. That approach may not be suitable for you. If it isn't, then the discussion includes reasons why traders with a different approach can reach different (but appropriate for them) choices. Investors come with a variety of outlooks, including a different risk tolerance and different investment objectives. The purpose of this exercise (the examination of all alternatives) is to help you quickly recognize the characteristics that represent an attractive choice when writing covered calls.

As you gain experience, inappropriate choices will be eliminated quickly. You learn to make decisions on your own and in a reasonable amount of time. It is not fun to trade if it takes hours to reach decisions.

The first example is thorough and takes time to study. However, you will quickly learn to do similar analyses much more efficiently.

We take an in-depth look at covered call writing in the next chapter with our first example.

This learning method helps you develop a style of trading that suits your needs. My preferred style is to write options with 90-day expirations,[101] but the majority of traders are more comfortable using 30- to 60 day options. For CCW to be effective, the option written must provide reasonable protection against loss, as well as a reasonable (a relative term) potential profit. Your goal is to find a style that suits your psyche, your pocketbook, and your comfort zone.

---

[100] Assuming the position is held through expiration, the stock price below which your investment loses money.

[101] Weeklys are options that expire eight days after they are listed for trading. They were not available when the first edition was published in 2008. I do not recommend writing covered calls when using those very short-term options because the premium is small and there is not much downside protection.

Chapter 10

Covered Call Writing: Making the Trade

Assume that you own 500 shares of DOGS, the only publicly traded company that breeds animals for shows and state fairs. If you do not already own the shares, buy them and proceed as if you had owned them earlier. This $19 stock is reasonably volatile, and that means the option premium looks attractive to sell.[102] DOGS options currently trade with an implied volatility (IV) of 46.

To implement the covered call strategy, write (sell) five call options. The main focus of this discussion is guiding you in how to decide which calls to write. Assume the nearest expiration is 30 days from today and the stock does not pay a dividend.

As can be seen in Table 10.1, there are 16 different call options from which to choose. Sometimes you find many more choices and sometimes fewer. Exchange rules require that there always be at least one in-the-money and one out-of-the-money option available for buyers and sellers to trade. The number of options is almost always larger than that bare minimum.[103]

Let's take a detailed look at the options and discuss the pros and cons of writing each. Many times the most attractive opportunities come with writing options that expire in the *front* (next to expire) week or month. But that method assumes that a trader has the time to find new trades often. That is not a problem for active traders, but if you are an investor who wants to gain the benefits of using options and have neither the time nor inclination to trade frequently, it is more practical to choose options with longer lifetimes. And keep in mind that trading less often reduces expenses (commissions).

Reminder: each option represents 100 shares of stock, and a $1 premium ($1.00 per share) equals $100 per contract. We'll progress through these options, beginning with the near-term, and proceeding with options with sequentially longer lifetimes.

---

[102] Reminder: More volatile stocks have options with a higher premium than less volatile stocks.
[103] Volatile stocks have many more options. Every time the stock price nears the strike of the most OTM option, another group of options is listed for trading. See Appendix B for more details.

Table 10.1 DOGS call options
Stock $19; IV = 46; 30 days before August expiration

Exp	D	Strike	Bid	Ask	T Pr	ROI Un	ROI As	Ann	%DP
Aug	30	17.5	$1.90	$2.10	$0.40	2.34%	2.34%	28%	10.00
Aug		20.0	$0.55	$0.70	$0.55	2.98%	8.40%	101%	2.89
Aug		22.5	$0.10	$0.20	$0.10	0.53%	19.68%	236%	0.53
Aug		25.0	$0.00	$0.10	$0.00	0.00%	31.58%	379%	0.00
Sep	58	17.5	$2.25	$2.45	$0.75	4.48%	4.48%	28%	11.84
Sep		20.0	$0.95	$1.15	$0.95	5.26%	10.80%	67%	5.00
Sep		22.5	$0.35	$0.50	$0.35	1.88%	21.62%	134%	1.84
Sep		25.0	$0.10	$0.20	$0.10	0.53%	32.28%	200%	0.53
Nov	121	17.5	$2.90	$3.10	$1.40	8.70%	8.70%	26%	15.26
Nov		20.0	$1.65	$1.85	$1.65	9.51%	15.27%	45%	8.68
Nov		22.5	$0.85	$1.05	$0.85	4.68%	23.97%	71%	4.47
Nov		25.0	$0.45	$0.60	$0.45	2.43%	34.77%	103%	2.37
Feb	212	17.5	$3.50	$3.80	$2.00	12.90%	12.90%	22%	18.42
Feb		20.0	$2.40	$2.60	$2.40	14.46%	20.48%	35%	12.63
Feb		22.5	$1.55	$1.75	$1.55	8.88%	28.94%	49%	8.16
Feb		25.0	$0.95	$1.15	$0.95	5.26%	38.50%	65%	5.00

Exp= Month in which options expire (3rd Friday)
D = days to expiration
T Pr = Time Premium in option (Option premium minus intrinsic value)
ROI Un = ROI if DOGS is unchanged (i.e., $19 per share) at expiration
ROI As = Return on investment, if assigned an exercise notice
Ann = ROI Assigned, Annualized
DP = Downside protection. % stock can decline before break-even

NOTE: It is easy to use a calculator and produce numbers with several decimal places. Please recognize that the numbers in Table 10.1 are only a guide. Trade decisions should not be made because one trade offers a possible return on investment of 18% while another offers "only" 17%.

Taking this logical path, we begin with the Aug 17½ calls, an in-the-money option with a bid price of $1.90. For many people, rookies as well as experienced traders, it doesn't feel right to buy stock at $19 and then immediately agree to sell that stock at a lower price ($17.50). That feels like a money-losing proposition. Please be assured that this is merely an illusion and that you can write this call option and earn a nice profit when doing so.

Important **Note:** When writing in-the-money covered calls, the profit potential is the time value (option premium minus intrinsic value).

If selling your shares at $17.50 makes you uncomfortable, look at it this way: in reality, instead of buying 500 shares of DOGS at $19 per share, you are "renting" them for 30 days. You put up a deposit of $17.10 per share ($19.00 paid for the stock, less the $1.90 premium collected when selling the call options) and agree to relinquish your shares at $17.50 per share when the "lease" expires in 30 days. That produces a $0.40 per share profit.

However, there is a catch: if the other party decides not to own the shares when the lease expires, the lessor has the right to abandon those shares, making you their rightful owner. That is what happens when the option owner decides not to exercise the call options. Why would anyone fail to exercise? If DOGS is worth less than $17.50 per share when expiration arrives, the call owner would not pay $17.50 per share when anyone can buy those shares in the open market at a lower price. Thus, the calls would be allowed to expire worthless.

Do not err by believing that the original price paid by the call owner makes any difference. When the option is worthless, there is no point in exercising and increasing the loss.

This is analogous to the sad situation in which a homeowner who finds the mortgage to be greater than the value of the home, walks away, abandoning the house to the mortgage holder. Thus, if the stock is worth less than the strike price, the lessor (call owner) allows you to keep your stock. You cannot force the call owner to take your shares.

The Aug 17½ call is $1.90 bid. This call option is in-the-money by $1.50 (the stock price exceeds the strike price by $1.50) and has a time premium of $0.40 per share.[104] The good news is that this option provides excellent protection against loss. If the stock price does not decline by more than the $1.90 premium when expiration day arrives, you'll earn a profit on this trade. It is highly unlikely that the stock will drop that much[105] in 30 days, but DOGS is a volatile stock and it may happen.

If you write this call, you have an excellent chance to earn a profit equal to the time premium ($40 per contract), less commission. Of course, you forfeit any possibility of earning additional profits if the stock were to rally because you are obligated to sell the shares at the strike price—$17.50 in this example. That is the constant tradeoff—selling an option that provides excellent protection (an ITM option) means losing the chance to earn extra profit if the stock rallies.

The return on investment (ROI) for 30 days is better than 2%. Here's how to calculate ROI: the current stock value is $1,900. You collect the $190 option premium, reducing the investment cost to $1,710. If you earn $40 on that investment, that is a return of more than 2% ($40 divided by $1,710). That is a very nice return for only 30 days, especially when the risk of loss is so small. This option is definitely worth considering, especially for the conservative investor, because it offers excellent protection along with a nice profit potential. If you earn that percent every 30 days, your money doubles in 2.5 years.[106] This is an attractive choice, but we've only considered one call option and it is too early to make a final decision.

Before considering alternatives, it is important to mention (again) that commissions play a significant role in the profit picture—and this is especially true when you trade small quantities. There is no point in collecting $40 in premium when paying your broker $10 in commissions and another $10 (or more) when you are assigned an exercise notice. In that scenario, your broker earns at least half the maximum $40 profit. On the other hand, if you trade 500 shares, then the broker's share is still $20, but that represents only 10 percent of the profits. The point is that when you trade small quantities, it may be better to collect a higher premium per option and to trade less often. You can do that by writing options with longer lifetimes. We will discuss this point further when we get to Sep, Nov, and Feb options.

---

[104] Time premium is total premium ($1.90) less the intrinsic value ($1.50).
[105] The probability is 10%. We'll discuss how this number is determined in greater detail when we talk about the Greeks in Chapter 15.
[106] A $1,000 investment that compounds at 2.34% per month is worth $2,001.53 after 30 months.

The August 20 call can be sold for $55 per contract. That is not a lot of money, but it is almost 3% of your $1,845 (stock value, less premium) investment. At 3% every month, your money doubles in two years.[107] The $55 premium doesn't provide much downside protection, but because the strike price is above the current stock price (that means the call is out-of-the-money, or OTM) there is a chance to make even more (up to $1 per share) if the stock price is above $19 when the option expires. However, your highest possible selling price (for the stock) is the strike price of $20 per share.

If this stock performs well and is above the $20 strike price when expiration arrives—and you eventually are assigned an exercise notice—you sell the shares at $20. That makes the potential ROI more than 8 % (see Table 10.1). There are three factors to consider when deciding if this is an appropriate option to write.

- ROI is almost 3% for 30 days—when the stock price is unchanged. That is a good return.

- Because the option is OTM, additional profit is possible if the stock moves higher—as much as $500 ($1 on each share). That would be an annualized return of 100 percent, an excellent result.

- Downside protection is very limited, and that is the way covered call writing works. When selling lower-priced options,[108] you sacrifice some downside protection for the possibility of earning a larger profit.

Thus, the Aug 20 call is worth considering. A conservative investor may prefer the additional downside protection available from writing the Aug 17½ call because it reduces the chances of losing money. However, there are advantages to writing the Aug 20 call, especially for investors who are bullish on DOGS (and if you are not at least a little bullish, why do you own this stock?), or who prefer to write OTM options that offer a *chance* for earning additional capital gains.

> **NOTE:** Most covered call writers prefer selling OTM options because they hope to earn extra capital gains if the stock price moves to the strike. I believe more conservative investors should consider writing ITM options, as long as the option provides an adequate return. Please remember that the profit potential for ITM options is the time premium, and not the entire premium.

---

[107] A $1,000 investment that compounds at 3.00%t per month is worth $2,032.79 after 24 months

[108] Call options with a higher strike price.

Let's consider more alternatives

August 22½ and 25 calls are totally unappealing. There is not much point in selling an option for only $0.10, because it provides neither protection nor an acceptable cash premium. It is true that writing the Aug 22½ call makes it likely you'll pocket the $10, but why give up the possibility that something spectacular may happen for a measly $10? And even if nothing big happens, if the stock rises to 20 in the next few days, you could sell the Aug 22½ calls at that time, collecting a higher premium. This is an easy decision for me: I prefer to own stock without writing calls than write calls for a very small premium. However, an investor who wants to be a long-term owner of these shares may be willing to sell these calls and consider the $10 premium as equivalent to an extra $10 cash dividend. There are two points to keep in mind. First, the IRS taxes the profit as ordinary income, not as a dividend. Second, do not ignore commissions when trading low-priced options. There may be no cash remaining for you once your broker takes its share.

The August 25 call has no bid, and is totally inappropriate, even if you can collect a few pennies per share for the option.

August options offer two decent choices: one for the conservative investor (17½ calls), and another (20 calls) for the more bullish and aggressive investor. Let's see if options that expire in other months have something better to offer.

September options

Moving out one month, September expiration is 58 calendar days away. By definition, intrinsic value (if any) does not change when the number of days to expiration changes. But these options may be more attractive to sell than August options because they have a higher time premium. That time premium is important because it represents the entire profit potential for the position (when the calls are ITM or at the money (ATM)). It also represents the entire protection available if you write an OTM (out-of-the-money) call.

> **NOTE:** When you write an ITM option, there is no opportunity to earn extra profit because you are committed to selling stock at the strike price. Thus, when writing ITM calls, the entire profit comes from the time premium. When writing an OTM option, the premium is less, but in exchange for that, you gain an opportunity to sell stock at a higher price (higher strike price).

The current bid price for the September 17½ call is $2.25. If you write this call, you'd collect $225 (unless you decide to try to sell the call at a slightly better price).[109] The intrinsic value is still $1.50 per share, but the time value is now $75 per contract, and that is $35 more than the Aug 17½ call. This is a fairly attractive proposition, especially for the less aggressive investor. First, you are protected against losing money if the stock drops by as much as $2.25 because that is the amount of cash received when writing the call. That is a decline of almost 12% (Table 10.1).

As far as profits are concerned, the most you can earn by writing this call is the $75 time premium. You earn that much if you are assigned an exercise notice—and that is the most likely result.[110] That represents a return of 4.48% on a $1,675 investment ($1,900 stock value less the $225 option premium). On an annualized basis, that is more than 27%—a very nice return for an investment with a high probability of success. Sure, the stock could tumble below 17.5, but it is an unlikely occurrence over such a short period of time. Yet, as the stock market tumble of 2008 reminded us, investments such as this are not guaranteed to be profitable. Writing this call is a distinct possibility.

> **NOTE:** I mention that it is possible for the stock to be below the strike price when expiration arrives, but dismiss that possibility as 'unlikely.' You must remember this when investing in the stock market: Unlikely events do happen. Even very unlikely events happen more frequently than expected.[111] Thus, it is crucial to your long-term survival as an investor not to invest too much money in one situation. A high probability of success is not a guarantee of success. If you have the financial ability to buy 500 DOGS, do not buy 2,000 just because it looks like easy money.
>
> My trading mantra: it is easy to make money trading options, but you must be certain you do not incur large losses. It is also easy to lose money when trading options. That means risk management is important and you should never own a position that is too large, just because it looks easy to make money. If it were really that easy, everyone would be doing this. Writing Aug or Sep 17½ calls is likely to be profitable, but please do not put your trading account in jeopardy. Companies do issue

---

[109] Remember, you do not have to sell your option at the bid price. If willing to take the chance that the stock moves lower and the bid for the calls you are trying to sell decreases, you can, and should, try to collect a higher premium when selling any option.

[110] For that to not be the result, the stock must decrease to less than 17.5 in 58 days. Certainly a very real, but unlikely possibility

[111] So called 'black swan' events occurred so frequently in 2008 that they were no longer unexpected. The point is that large, sudden changes in the price of stocks should be expected from time to time.

surprise announcements that contain bad news, and that can result is a large price decline.

You can collect $95 by writing the Sep 20 call. And do not forget that it is a good idea to enter your order to sell the calls at $1.05—the midpoint between the bid and ask. If not filled quickly, you can lower the offer to $1.00 and then $0.95—if necessary.

If the stock price is unchanged when expiration arrives, the ROI (assuming a $0.95 premium) is 5%. That is a very decent return and is comparable (33 vs. 36%) to that available from writing Aug 20 calls. The Sep 20 call doesn't provide a great deal of insurance against loss, but if insurance is your primary concern, Sep 20 calls should be more attractive than Aug 20 calls (because the premium is higher and it affords better downside protection). Writing any call with a $20 strike price also allows for the chance to earn an additional $100 in capital gains per 100 shares— if the stock is above $20 when expiration arrives. This is a reasonable choice for the bullish or aggressive investor, and worth considering by the slightly conservative investor because it offers some downside protection, as well as the opportunity to earn a good annualized return. This call stays on the list of possibilities. In fact, many covered call writers would choose to write this call because it offers something for everyone—opportunity for capital gains, some downside protection and a decent time premium.

The $35 premium available by writing the Sep 22½ call is unattractive to me, but it should appeal to the long-term investor who prefers not to sell the stock—and who likes the idea of collecting time premium by writing covered calls. There is almost no downside insurance and only a small chance of being assigned an exercise notice. It comes down to these questions:

- For the conservative investor: if you do not want to sell your shares, are you willing to accept a payment of $35 in return for possibly being forced to sell those shares at 22½? Each individual investor must make that choice, but for me, this option is not a good candidate for writing because the premium is simply too small and provides almost no protection.

- For the long-term investor: the $35 "dividend" is attractive. If assigned an exercise notice, how disappointing can it be to earn $1,925 in 58 days?

- For the bullish investor: are you so bullish that writing the Sep 22½ isn't good enough? If the stock rises above $22.50, how disappointing is it to sell your shares at that price? When writing covered calls you cannot expect the best possible outcome from every trade. Even the aggressively bullish investor can find something to like about writing the Sep 22½ call. However, the total premium is small and locks the investor into holding the stock.

The Sep 25 call can be sold for $10 and is not worth the effort. If this is the call you prefer to sell, hold the stock, hoping DOGS rallies, and perhaps you will have an opportunity to sell this call at an acceptable price later. It is better not to sell any call than to settle for a premium this small. When writing covered calls, there must be some benefit. Low premium provides almost zero downside protection and little profit potential. The only investor to consider this option (and I strongly recommend against it) is someone who wants to own this stock for years and finds $10 (less commissions) to be a worthwhile dividend. But this is not an appropriate option for anyone, in my opinion—not at this price.

November and February options

Moving out to November, the 17½ call carries a premium of $290 and expires in 121 days. The intrinsic value remains at $150 and the time value is $140. By writing this call, the investment cost is reduced from $1,900 to $1,610. If you earn the time premium ($140) at expiration, it represents a nine percent return (26 percent annualized). Writing this option provides a good return that comes with excellent insurance against loss. The stock must dip under $16.10, a15% decline, before reaching the break-even point. As is typical when dealing with longer-term options, the annualized returns are less than those available from writing shorter-term options.

Writing this call does not appeal to me because the numbers do not compare favorably with those of the Sep 17½ call. If I decided to write a 17½ strike call option, I'd choose Aug or Sep because they afford a significantly higher annualized ROI. However, writing this option should appeal to a conservative investor who does not have time to devote to making frequent trade decisions.[112] If you are employed full time, or simply do not want to spend that many hours working on your investments, this may be an appropriate choice. Choosing longer-term options reduces the annualized profit potential, but it does require less work, reduces commission expenses and provides excellent downside protection. This option is worth considering for investors who prefer to trade less often.

The November 20 call is $1.65 bid. The time premium (the DOGS 20 calls are OTM and have zero intrinsic value—thus, the entire premium is

---

[112] Even when you cannot take the time to trade frequently, it is important to analyze your holdings periodically. There may have been a good reason to purchase stocks you own, but is there a good reason to continue to own them? The answer is not always yes.

time premium) provides a return of 9.5% ($165 on an investment of $1,735). If you write this call, you are protected if the stock dips to $17.35. These are attractive numbers. But the annualized return does not compare favorably with the earnings potential for writing shorter-term options. This is an attractive call for the aggressive investor and moderately conservative investor who do not want to be bothered writing options every month or two.

The November 22½ call can be sold for $85, an attractive premium for an option that is fairly far out of the money. Before writing this option, you must be convinced you want your capital tied up in this position for four months. Obviously, this is a good situation for long-term investors who want to own DOGS, collect an option premium and not be concerned with carefully monitoring their covered call portfolios. If the stock rallies beyond the strike price, and if the investor is eventually assigned an exercise notice, the profit ($435 for each 100 shares is a 24% ROI) ought to be acceptable. Because covered call writing is a very flexible strategy, and because there is no "best" call option to write, the Nov 22½ call is appealing to investors who are more interested in the opportunity to earn additional profits from an increase in the stock price than in capital preservation.

The November 25 call presents a situation similar to writing the Nov 22½ call. However, the premium ($45) is so low that I do not recommend tying up your money for four months.[113] Yet there are long-term investors who may find writing this call to be acceptable.

February calls do not expire for seven months. Too far in the future for anyone who thinks of himself as a trader. However, this is a decent choice for investors who want to benefit from writing covered calls, but who want to spend as little time as possible on the process. The $350 available from writing Feb 17½ calls represents $200 in time premium (and $150 in intrinsic value). If the stock is above the strike price seven months from now, that $200 time premium becomes profit. That is a return of 13%, or 22% annualized (Table 10.1). As is customary when dealing with longer-term options, the annualized return is less than that available from writing shorter-term options, but the higher premium provides greater downside protection. And there is nothing wrong with earning 13% every seven months. These numbers are very attractive for any conservative investor. Personally, I prefer not to lock myself into this position for seven months because of downside risk.

---

[113] When you write the covered call option, it means you cannot sell your stock unless you repurchase the call. Many brokers do not allow customers to hold a naked short call position. As discussed earlier, naked calls are very risky because any loss is theoretically unlimited!

NOTE: Do not get the impression that covered call writers always earn huge returns. Bear markets wreak havoc on portfolios that are laden with covered call positions. (Sadly, many investors learned this lesson in 2008.) The potential 21% annualized profit available when writing the Feb 17½ call is outstanding, but is not risk free. I hope this discussion does not dissuade anyone from making this choice because the potential profit is 'too small.' I'm not saying you cannot do better, but 21% is a very impressive return for almost every investor.

The February 20 calls have an attractive premium ($240), especially for an out-of-the-money option. Writing this call offers a good combination of protection (more than 12%) and profit potential (14% if the stock is unchanged and 20% if assigned an exercise notice) for anyone willing to hold this position until February.

The premium available from writing OTM Feb calls is sufficient that the idea of selling them cannot be dismissed.

Writers can collect $155 by selling the Fcb 22½ call. That is enough premium to provide decent protection against loss. The only problem for me is the annualized ROI. It is less than I want to earn, considering that simply owning this volatile stock *already carries some risk of loss.* This option is an OK choice for the long-term investor who wants to adopt a buy and hold strategy with this stock.

The Feb 25 call can be sold for $95. This call may be attractive to the long-term investor who is quite bullish and who doesn't like the idea of making frequent trading decisions. But it is not suitable for my investment philosophy. Remember: the idea is for you to write call options that suit your investment philosophy, not mine.

Style

As mentioned above, as you gain experience selecting which option to write, you eventually adopt a style of trading. You may prefer selling out-of-the-money options, hoping to make large profits as your stock increases in value. You may prefer the additional safety that comes with writing in-the-money options. Do not be surprised if you alternate between these strategies depending on market conditions. Similarly, you may decide that writing short-term options suits you best. Or perhaps mid- or even longer-term options may be more attractive. My current personal style involves writing short-term, in-the-money options. But that was not always my style. Not too many years ago, I preferred writing options that expired in six to eight months. When adopting a style, do not feel that the commitment is permanent. It is OK to alter your style when encountering different market conditions or as your investing philosophy changes over the years. Finding your investing style involves locating your current comfort zone. Many people find it psychologically satisfying to adopt CCW because it offers fewer (and smaller) losses along with more frequent profits.

If preservation of capital is important to you, then adopting one (or more) of the three basic conservative strategies allows you to invest and remain within that comfort zone. If you are a conservative investor, do not ignore other strategies that provide better protection against losses. Aggressive traders may be tempted by the higher potential profits available from adopting the most aggressive strategies. It is important to recognize that there are no guarantees and no strategy promises free money. I offer guidance on finding your individual comfort zone, a place where risk and reward are both acceptable. If you can achieve your goals by adopting a conservative style, I urge you to think carefully before taking on additional risk and perhaps failing to meet your goals.

Being aggressive doesn't mean seeking unrealistic returns, but it does require taking more risk than a conservative investor is willing to accept. One adage in the investing world is that higher returns are not given away for nothing. To earn those higher rewards, you must have extraordinary skills or accept greater risk.

Learning to use options successfully is a process—and the more you learn and understand how options work, the easier it becomes to take the next step. As you gain experience deciding which specific option series[114] to write, you begin to develop an option writing style. After the DOGS example, readers who are already familiar with option trading may recognize whether they prefer the greater profit potential available when writing near-term (or OTM) options, or the additional downside protection available from longer-term (or ITM) options. It may be too soon to recognize which covered call positions provide the secure feeling that is necessary when trading within your comfort zone. That comes later, after you trade with real money and discover your style. It may take a bunch of trades before you recognize which style suits you best.

NOTE: Profitability should not be the only basis for choosing a style. Comfort is equally important. If you were nervous about positions that ultimately turned out well, remember that nervous feeling and decide if that is how you want to feel going forward. Comfort has its own rewards.

---

[114] "Series" is the term used to describe a specific option. For example, IBM Nov 195 put is a specific option series

Looking at the data from a different perspective

Let's summarize the discussion above by rearranging the data, making it easier to reach a final decision on which call to write. This makes it easier to compare the relative merits of each option. As you gain experience, some choices jump right off the page, making the selection process much more efficient. Let's consider the data in Tables 10.2 and 10.3.

ROI vs. time to expiration

As seen in Table 10.2, for any given strike price, the annualized ROI is greatest for the front-month option and steadily decreases as the lifetime of the option increases. That should come as no surprise. Earlier, we discussed that an option's time premium erodes every day and that the rate of this time decay accelerates as expiration approaches. Thus, shorter-term options lose more of their time premium per day than longer-term options. When ROI is annualized, we prorate that rapid time decay. Thus, short-term options provide the potential[115] for the highest annualized returns.

When it comes to downside protection, the opposite is true—short-term options provide the least protection against loss. That is understandable because the more cash collected when writing a call, the greater the protection. Longer-term options trade with more time premium.

To add another factor to the discussion, longer-term options allow more time for something bad to happen. In other words, we get better downside protection, but we must hold the trade longer. Be aware that there are always tradeoffs when using options. These very versatile investment tools provide alternatives and each comes with some feature that is beneficial and another that counteracts some of that benefit.

When the covered call writer seeks better annualized returns, he chooses shorter-term options. When greater protection is more important, longer-term options are preferred. Please take both factors into consideration when making your choice.

---

[115] The word "potential" has been used many times in this book. That is all it is: potential. You do not earn this profit every time. In fact, sometimes you incur a loss because every trade cannot work as planned.

Table 10.2
How Time Affects ROI and Protection

Time	Strike	ROI	Ann ROI	DP
30	17.5	2%	28%	10%
58	17.5	4%	28%	12%
121	17.5	9%	26%	15%
212	17.5	13%	22%	18%
30	20.0	8%	101%	3%
58	20.0	11%	67%	5%
121	20.0	15%	45%	9%
212	20.0	20%	35%	13%
30	22.5	20%	236%	1%
58	22.5	22%	134%	2%
121	22.5	24%	71%	4%
212	22.5	29%	49%	8%
30	25.0	32%	379%	0%
58	25.0	32%	200%	1%
121	25.0	35%	103%	2%
212	25.0	39%	65%	5%

Options grouped by strike price. As time to expiry increases, annualized ROI declines and protection increases.

The highest returns come with an increased probability of losing money if and when the stock price crashes (a very unlikely, but possible, event). As long as you are satisfied with that protection, then writing shorter-term options may be appropriate for you.

NOTE: The above discussion is included to alert readers to the fact that there is no free money. It is not meant to be a warning of hidden danger. Trading is a constant tradeoff between risk and reward. In other words, trading is a choice between what you have to gain vs. what you have to lose. The experienced trader finds the right compromise.

ROI vs. strike price

Look again at Table 10.1. When the ROI calculation is based on the assumption that the stock rises above the strike price and the covered call writer is assigned an exercise notice, ROI increases as the strike price increases. This data is useful for bullish investors who seek maximum returns on their investment. Because we never know (at least I never know—more power to you if you do) whether the stock is going to move higher or lower over the lifetime of the option, we should consider the ROI in the event the stock price is unchanged when expiration day arrives. Unchanged is also an unlikely occurrence, but it provides a useful basis for generating information that aids in the selection process.

Do not jump to the conclusion that writing the highest possible strike price is a good idea just because it gives you the chance for a very profitable trade. First, the further OTM the strike, the less likely it is that the stock rises to that level before the option expires. Second, the higher the strike price, the less premium collected when selling the call. We not only write options to make money, but we also write call options to provide income and insurance against loss. It seldom pays to write call options that are significantly out of the money.

Time premium vs. strike price

The data in Table 10.3 show that a call option's time premium rises and then falls as the strike changes. The option with the most time premium for each expiration month is always exactly at-the-money (ATM). If it turns out that your option-writing style involves writing options with maximum time premium, then you can save research time by concentrating on only those options with strike prices that are near the stock price.

Timing your trades

Let's assume you've been writing covered calls for a while and discovered that your preferred style is to write calls that are in-the-money by 1-2%, with expiration dates 13 weeks from your trade date. If the stock is currently trading at $40 per share, it may occur to you that your preference dictates selling the covered calls when stock is priced 1-2% higher, or you may discover that there are no options expiring in 12-14 weeks. What should you do?

The answer to these questions depends on the reason that any trader adopts a covered call writing strategy. If your goal is to increase your income stream by collecting time premium or if your goal is to generate income while obtaining a modest amount of downside protection, then waiting is counterproductive. My recommendation is to write those covered calls without waiting for conditions to be perfect After all, it may be your preference to write calls that are in-the-money by a small amount (or expire in 13 weeks), but sometimes market conditions require a bit of flexibility. Once you discover your style, it is easier to select an appropriate call and choose positions that fit your comfort zone. By knowing that you prefer 13 weeks, it is not difficult to choose between options that come nearest to your preference.

Table 10.3
Time Premium vs. Strike Price

Month	Strike	Time Pr	
Aug	17.5	$0.40	
Aug	20.0	$0.55	ATM
Aug	22.5	$0.10	
Aug	25.0	$0.00	
Sep	17.5	$0.75	
Sep	20.0	$0.95	ATM
Sep	22.5	$0.35	
Sep	25.0	$0.10	
Nov	17.5	$1.40	
Nov	20.0	$1.65	ATM
Nov	22.5	$0.85	
Nov	25.0	$0.45	
Feb	17.5	$2.00	
Feb	20.0	$2.40	ATM
Feb	22.5	$1.55	
Feb	25.0	$0.95	

ATM options have the highest time premium

On the other hand, if you are an investor who believes that you are skilled at timing the market and that you just know the stock is going higher, you are in position to wait for the stock to rally. But that is not a successful plan for the vast majority of individual investors. From the options that are available to you now, it is probably best to write an option that suits your current needs and takes advantage of the ticking clock. You gain the benefit of time decay when selling options because they are a wasting asset. When possible, you want to gain the advantages of time working for you—and the sooner you get started the better. But, never force a trade. You must want to own the stock at its current price and believe that the premium is acceptable when writing the call. Otherwise do not make the trade.

As our example with DOGS shows, writers who prefer ITM calls can use any call with a 17½ strike price to obtain both time premium and downside protection. Writers who prefer OTM calls have the potential for higher profits, but in return, they have less protection. If your preferred choice is to write calls that are very close-to-the-money,[116] you prefer the stock be nearer one of the available strike prices. But as seen with the DOGS example, you are forced to choose between writing the 17½ call, writing the 20 call, or waiting for the stock price to change. The only alternative is to find a different stock to trade. If you do not own shares of DOGS, it is easy to find another place to invest your money. But if you already own these shares and if you want to write covered calls for the advantages we've discussed, waiting is not the best option.

Choosing the call to write

One of the purposes of this discussion is to allow readers an opportunity to consider the advantages and disadvantages of choosing each call option as a CCW candidate. Think about the possibilities from your own point of view. Consider risk tolerance and financial goals. You can discover how to make covered call writing a worthwhile strategy. CCW enhances your earnings (most of the time), but it is also a strategy that you may find viable for many years. Please remember that it is a bullish strategy and is not appropriate for those with bearish views.

Which option to write?

We covered a lot of territory but have not made any trades nor earned any money. It is time to make some decisions. We considered writing each of the DOGS options on its own merits. Tables 10.2 and 10.3 allow comparison of the relative merits of writing options that expire in the same month or have the same strike. There is a lot of data and it may seem difficult to reach a decision. Because there is no single "best" call to write, several options make suitable choices to help most investors meet their investment objectives.

The decision, at last

For me, a fairly conservative investor, but one who is willing to accept risk to make money, there is no clear-cut decision. Three choices are very attractive. Ultimately, I chose writing Aug 17½ calls, with Sep 17½ as a close second choice.[117] The profit potential is only $40 per option, but that provides the chance to earn an acceptable rate of return—especially when considering how much protection this call provides. It is the combination of

---

[116] "Close-to-the-money" means almost at-the-money.
[117] If the Aug call premium were 0.05 less, I'd definitely choose Sep. The decision is that close for me.

excellent protection and a fair profit potential that appeals to me. Sure, I'd like to earn a higher rate of return, but this time I'll settle for less because of the high probability of success. If the profit potential were a bit less, I'd be more aggressive and write the Aug 20 call. I'm going to enter an order to sell (to open) five DOGS Aug 17½ calls at a limit price of $1.95, or better.

When writing covered calls, compromise is the order of the day. You give up something to gain something else. What you are trying to do is adopt an investment strategy that helps achieve your investment objectives. Thus, the covered call position should:

- Provide enough profit potential to be worthwhile. If you are too concerned with limiting losses, you may not earn enough money from the trade to make it worth your time and effort.

- Provide enough insurance (some investors require very little protection) to make you comfortable with the risk and reward of the position.

In this scenario, I chose Aug 17½ call because the ROI is just too attractive, especially when bundled with such excellent downside protection. This choice is based on my conservative nature when writing covered calls. This is a prudent course to follow for readers who are gaining their first experience with options. It is a good idea to find a trade that is likely to be a winner when getting started. Once you gain experience, if it fits your trading style and personality, you may decide to accept a little more risk in an attempt to earn a larger profit.

My bottom line: do not get greedy. You can earn good profits by adopting strategies that are less risky than simple stock ownership. Gordon Gekko may have said that "Greed is good,"[118] but earning money with reduced risk is better.

> **NOTE:** The conservative Aug 17½ is not appropriate for everyone. In this example using DOGS options, there is truly something for everyone. Unfortunately, in the real world, there are usually fewer good choices, and occasionally the choices are so poor that it is best to find a different stock to trade.

Now that you entered an order, had it filled, and own a covered call position, what comes next

---

[118] In the movie "Wall Street"

Chapter 11

Covered Call Writing: After the Trade

We went through the decision-making process and made our first trade together. Now it is time to consider what to do next. Here's a summary of the initial transaction:

- You own 500 DOGS, but cannot sell them unless you repurchase the calls sold earlier.[119] If the stock pays a dividend (DOGS does not), you, the stockholder, receive it.[120]

- You collected $950 from the option sale, (5 DOGS Aug 17½ calls at $190 each), less commission. (Commissions vary. Be certain you know your broker's charges so you can accurately determine the position's potential profit.) The cash goes into your account the next business day and begins to earn interest.

What happens next?

Once in a while you may be assigned an exercise notice[121] prior to expiration. But do not expect it to happen because it is a rare occurrence. Let's assume time passes, nothing out of the ordinary happens (always a good situation for covered call writers), and there is no reason to make any adjustments to the position. When expiration arrives there are three possibilities. This discussion is from the point of view of a trader who chooses to write Aug 17½ calls.

> **NOTE:** If you did not choose Aug 17½ calls:

- If you wrote options that expire at a later date, you can ignore the fact that August options are expiring. Substitute the appropriate expiration and this discussion applies to you.

- If a different strike price was chosen, change the strike from 17½ to the appropriate number.

---

[119] If the stock were sold, the position would be naked short 5 calls. In addition to high risk, most brokers do not allow customers to sell unhedged call options.
[120] The risk of not receiving the dividend is discussed later in this chapter.
[121] This is possible only when the call is ITM

Scenario one

DOGS has not performed well and your options finished[122] out of the money. The option owner allows them to expire worthless. The call owner has no reason to exercise the options when stock is available at a price below the strike. The main point for you, the call writer, is that the options expire and you are no longer under any obligation to sell stock at the strike price. You still own both the 500 shares and the $950 premium.

If the stock is above the $17.10 break-even price, you have a small profit. Next Monday when the market opens (or any time thereafter), you may sell another five options against your 500 shares. If you decided not to wait for expiration and already rolled[123] the position to a more distant expiration date, you had to purchase the Aug calls before doing so. That precaution prevents being short naked calls.

This is not the result you expected—especially when there was only one chance in 10 that the stock would finish below $17.50, but you did fare better than other shareholders who lost $1.90 per share more than you. Thus, as a covered call writer you reduced losses by the amount of the premium. You may not have a profit, but you are definitely better off having adopted this strategy.

Scenario two

DOGS stock finishes at $17.50 and the option is at the-money. You do not know whether the option owner will exercise the options or allow them to expire. You must wait until Monday morning to find out, although brokers do make this information available Sunday via the Internet or e-mail. Please verify whether you still own your stock—preferably before the market next opens for trading.[124]

- If you were not assigned an exercise notice, you are free to write covered calls and collect more premium dollars.

- If you were assigned an exercise notice, you no longer own stock, but you have the proceeds from the sale and earned the maximum possible profit for the position. Your next decision is how and when to reinvest that money.

---

[122] Last trade before the options expire

[123] Covering an existing option position and selling another in its place

[124] It is your broker's responsibility to notify you before the market opens, but do not stand on ceremony. If you do not know whether you were assigned an exercise notice, please call your broker (before the market opens) and firmly request that information. If not assigned, you may want to write five new call options and you cannot sell those calls unless you own the shares. If you can access your account online, the needed information will be readily available.

- Occasionally you are assigned on some calls, but not all. That is OK. Proceed as above, writing the appropriate number of call options.

This is a satisfactory result. You earned the time premium in the options, still own the shares, and may write new calls, collecting another premium. Write Sep or Oct 15 (or 17 ½) calls (when October options begin trading[125] next Monday), depending on the premium that can be collected.

Scenario three

DOGS finishes above the strike price (as expected). You are assigned an exercise notice, thereby selling your stock and earning the maximum available profit. You no longer own any DOGS shares. This is a satisfactory result.

All scenarios lead to a good result. If true, why doesn't everyone write covered calls? Why haven't brokers told all their clients about this magic bullet? Why has the press not raved about covered call writing? What can go wrong? What are the risks? These questions are considered below.

What do you have to gain by writing covered calls?

What do you have to gain by writing covered call options? The short answer is to make money more consistently and with less risk, when compared with simply owning stock. The vast majority of the time that an investor adopts CCW, the goal is to earn additional profits by collecting time premium, but, as you will learn, this versatile strategy can be used to accomplish other investment objectives.

When writing a covered call, you must accept a maximum selling price (the strike price) for your shares. If that is acceptable (it is not acceptable to every investor) then you are paid a cash premium that is yours to keep no matter what else happens. That cash allows the trader to:

- Earn more frequent profits. When holding stock, the only time you earn money is when the stock price increases. When writing a covered call, you earn money (a limited amount) when the stock price rises. However, you also make money when the stock price remains essentially unchanged or decreases in value—if that decrease is less than the option premium collected. It is a comforting feeling to own stock, see it decline over the lifetime of the option, and still earn a profit!

- Insure a modest portion of the value of your investment. When owning stock, if the price drops (for example) $2 per share, your loss is $200. When writing covered calls, that loss is reduced by the

---

[125] See Appendix C for details on when new options are listed

option premium. Thus, if you write a call option with a $0.90 premium, your loss is only $1.10 per share—not a triumph, but a better result than achieved by the traditional investor who owns stock and who does not write covered call options.

NOTE: If the idea of having extra insurance to prevent a large loss is important to you, then pay special attention to the collar strategy in the next chapter.

What do you have to lose? What can go wrong?

Although covered call writing is a more conservative strategy than buying and holding a stock portfolio, it is not without risk:

- If your stock undergoes a severe downward move, you incur a loss. The premium you receive from the call may only offset a portion of the loss.

- If your main objective in writing the covered call is to sell stock at the strike price, it is possible to miss the sale. For example, if the stock price climbs above your target sale price (the strike price) during the lifetime of the option, and subsequently declines and is below the strike price at expiration, the call owner does not exercise the option —despite the fact that it reached your target sale price. If you had entered a good 'til cancelled sell order instead of writing the covered call, the stock would have been sold. If the price decline (after reaching your target) is sufficiently large, you not only miss the sale, but may incur a significant loss. The option premium reduces the loss, but that is not much consolation.

NOTE: Some beginners are under the mistaken impression that when they write covered calls and the stock subsequently rises beyond the strike price (i.e., the call is now in-the-money) the option owner immediately exercises the option. I have no idea from whence that misconception arises, but be certain you understand that it is not true. The call owner determines if and when to exercise, and it is almost always a mistake to exercise a call option before expiration.[126] Thus, it is possible to miss selling your stock at the target price when you write a covered call.

---

[126] The exception is to collect a dividend.

118

- If your stock rises through the strike price and makes a major advance, you do not participate in any profits above the strike. Because you sold the call option, your maximum selling price is established as the strike price. You earn a good profit (some investors mistakenly believe they lose money in this situation), but this profit is less than you could have earned without the option sale.

- If you own a dividend-paying stock, it is *possible* to fail to collect the dividend. The call owner has the right to exercise at any time before it expires. When the dividend is large enough, the option owner exercises (ITM options only) the day before the stock goes ex-dividend. That means someone will be assigned an exercise notice and must sell stock before ex-dividend day. If the stock pays significant dividends, and if you are counting on collecting that cash, this can be a problem. It is important to understand that not all ITM options are exercised for the dividend (see box on next page). If you do fail to receive the dividend because of an early exercise, it is not all bad news because you sell the stock at the strike price, locking in the profit. Because the stock sale occurs before expiration, you are in position to reinvest the proceeds and put the money back to work sooner than you had planned.

Keep in mind that you establish a maximum profit when writing covered calls. You do get excellent benefits in return, but there is one more risk associated with writing covered call options. It is impossible to quantify, because it is a psychological risk. If you are an investor who hates to accept anything less than the best possible result *every time*, this strategy will not work for you. Most of the time this method (compared with owning stock and not writing calls) results in additional profits. But on occasion, the stock undergoes a substantial price increase and not writing calls would have achieved a better result. That is the tradeoff, and each investor must make the decision as to whether CCW is a viable strategy.

Exercising an Option for the Dividend

"Exercising for the dividend" means exactly what it sounds like: to exercise a call option in time to collect the dividend. These examples discuss each situation from the point of view of the call owner, not the writer. Nevertheless, whether you are the owner or the writer, it is important to understand the decision that must be made by the call owner.

High-dividend stocks. HIGH pays a quarterly dividend of $0.40. The stock is trading near $22 per share and goes ex-dividend on Thursday, one day before Oct expiration. Any investor who owns the Oct 20 calls (or any lower strike) and who doesn't want to lose money must sell or exercise the call. Why? Because there is so little time remaining before expiration, there is no time premium remaining in the option (this is especially true for calls that are deeper in the money). Thus, the call is trading very near its intrinsic value, or $2.00. Thursday morning, the stock goes ex-dividend, and all things being equal, opens at $21.60 (closing price minus the dividend). The Oct 20 call trades near $1.60,[127] and has no time premium. When the option is neither exercised nor sold, the call owner loses money because the option price remains at parity (the intrinsic value), dropping from $2.00 to $1.60 when the stock price is *unchanged* (down $0.40 is considered unchanged when the stock goes ex-dividend by $0.40). If the option owner does not want to own stock, the call can be sold. But holding it overnight is a big mistake.

> **NOTE:** You may ask: What's the big deal about exercising? If I buy stock by exercising my option, don't I lose $40 when the stock price drops by $0.40? Answer: yes, $40 in market value is lost, but a $40 dividend check makes up the difference. The call owner does not receive that dividend.

Low-dividend stocks. LOWD is a stock that pays a small quarterly dividend, or two cents per share. As far as option traders are concerned, this dividend can almost be ignored. The only time it may be of concern is when the stock goes ex-dividend very near expiration Friday. There is no point exercising LOWD options for a dividend at other times. Why? There are three reasons (see Appendix E for additional discussion): first, the cost to carry (own) the stock from exercise through expiration must be

---

[127] If this is a high-volatility stock, then the option may have a bit of time premium (remember it is now expiration Friday) and trade at a higher price. But stocks that pay such high dividends are almost never volatile.

calculated and compared with the size of the dividend. Even a $20 stock costs $1.92 per week (at 5% interest) to own 100 shares. Thus, owning the stock for one week to collect a $2 dividend earns you only eight cents per option. Second, when you exercise an option, you sacrifice any remaining time premium. Thus, collecting a small dividend is almost always a losing proposition because the volatility and interest factors that make up the time value of an option (discussed in Chapter 6) are almost always greater than the small dividend. Third, and most important, is risk. When you own an option, all you can lose is the value of the option, but if you exercise the call and take ownership of the stock, it is possible to lose a great deal more money if something bad happens to the stock price. The bottom line is that calls are seldom exercised for the dividend when that dividend is small.

Non-nearest-term options are sometimes exercised for a dividend. Consider HIGH in the example above. With the stock trading at $22 per share and paying a 40-cent dividend, some Nov calls should be exercised. The cost to carry stock for four weeks at 5% interest is $5.77 for the Nov 15 call and $7.69 for the Nov 20 call.[128] Those low costs make it attractive to collect the $40 dividend and it is likely that the winning decision for the call owner is to exercise. If the stock is sufficiently volatile (not likely for a stock that pays an 8% percent dividend), the time premium in the Nov calls could make exercise the wrong decision.

A good question is: if you own this option, how do you know whether to exercise? When an option is an "exercise for the dividend" its delta is 100 and there should be zero time premium in the bid price. That means the bid is equal to, or less than, the intrinsic value of the option. When you see that, if the stock is going ex-dividend the following morning, it is almost always right to exercise the option to collect that dividend.

When the dividend is large enough and the option is deep in the money, sometimes options expiring later than the Weeklys[129] or the front month are exercised for a dividend.

For those of you who use option calculators to determine the fair value of an option, if an option is an exercise for the dividend, then the theoretical value of the option equals its intrinsic value, there is zero time premium, and the delta[130] is 100.

---

[128] The cost of carry depends on the purchase price—and that is the strike price multiplied by 100.

[129] This is the official CBOE spelling.

[130] Delta is one of the Greeks discussed in Chapter 16

Those are the major risks associated with selling covered calls. I believe these risks are small when compared with the benefits and that most investors should at least consider using options in this manner—especially as an excellent learning tool when first getting started with options. When you compare the buy and hold strategy with the covered call strategy:

- Writing the call allows you to you make **more** (or lose less) money if your stock price declines. Obviously a severe decline is not good for the covered call writer.

- Writing the call allows you to you make **more** money if your stock is unchanged.

- Writing the call allows you to make **more** money if your stock goes up by a small amount.

- Writing the call earns **less** money if your stock rises above your break-even price.[131] You still make good money, but not as much as you could have made.

There is a saying on Wall Street: "Sometimes the bulls win, sometimes the bears win, but the pigs always lose." Do not be greedy. Invest wisely, take good profits, take them often and allow the earnings to compound over time. You do very well by making good returns on many trades, even if you occasionally fail to collect a bonanza. Over the past 24-plus years, as demonstrated by BXM data (Chapter 9), buy and hold performs on a par with covered call writing. But when the market declines, this strategy significantly outperforms (see Table 9.2).

CCW gives you a more comfortable ride—i.e., less portfolio volatility and something else that is very psychologically rewarding: the possibility of earning decent profits in years when the market declines. Most of the time, when expiration rolls around (sometimes it seems like forever before it arrives), you are pleased with the results of CCW. Once in a while, you do better without the call sale. Over the long run, there are more profitable outcomes, and the value of your portfolio undergoes fewer extreme moves.

The versatile covered call

Because writing covered call options is a versatile strategy, it can be used to achieve different investment objectives. Most of the time the goal is obvious: to make money. But CCW can be used for other purposes.

---

[131] Just as we calculated a break-even price when the stock declines, there is also an upside break-even price and it is equal to the strike price plus the option premium. Above that price, you would have earned more money by not writing the covered call option.

Turning a non-performing stock into a profitable investment vehicle

When choosing which call option to write, consider the reason for owning stock. For example, suppose you own shares of DULL, a company whose stock has traded in a narrow range for the past several years and has contributed no profits to your portfolio. You do not want to sell the shares at the current price because you still have confidence in the ability of the company to increase its earning power in the coming years. But you are tired of not having DULL contribute to the growth of your investment portfolio. CCW is an excellent strategy for generating income while waiting for good things to happen.

If you find yourself in this unpleasant situation, then writing out-of-the money calls is an appropriate strategy. If the stock continues to trade within its recent narrow range, the cash premiums become your compensation for continuing to hold the stock. Keep in mind that this non-volatile stock is not going to have attractive premiums. In fact, you may find yourself writing calls for only 15 or 20 cents. I usually suggest ignoring such low-priced options, but in this situation, you can look at that option premium as if it were a dividend. If assigned an exercise notice, you'd be delighted to earn a profit for being a loyal shareholder. Remember, you are only obligated to sell your stock if DULL awakes from its lethargy and soars above the (currently out-of-the-money) strike price. Either way, this under-performing stock finally contributes to the value of your portfolio—you collect the "dividends" and sometimes you also earn your profit.

Selling stock above the current market price

You can use covered call writing to increase the chances of selling stock at a price higher than its current market price. This aspect of writing covered calls is seldom discussed, but it is an important tool to have in your investing arsenal and should be used much more often by investors and traders.

Let's look at an example to see how this works. Assume you own 200 shares of KIT, a retailer of kitchen appliances. You've owned this stock too long and are interested in selling—at the right price. This is an ideal scenario for writing covered calls.

EXAMPLE

Assume KIT is trading at $38 and you decide to sell your shares if it trades as high as $40. The traditional method for selling those shares is to enter a good 'til cancelled (GTC) order with your broker to sell 200 shares at $40. If the stock rises to that level the shares are sold. If not, then you continue to own the shares. Once you enter the order, there is nothing more to do (except remember that the order is outstanding). If your sell order is executed, your broker notifies you. If the stock doesn't reach your price, nothing happens.

Covered call writing offers a superior alternative. Instead of placing the GTC order, you can write a covered call option that gives someone else the right to buy your stock. As you know, when you write that call option, you receive an immediate cash payment. Let's look at which options you can write to increase the chances of selling stock at $40.

Consider the options listed in Table 11.1. Notice that there are no strike prices above 40. It is not that those options are not available to trade, it is because you have no reason to consider writing them. Remember, your goal is to sell stock at $40, and you are trying to use covered call writing to increase your chances of achieving that result. If you sell calls with a strike price of 40, and if you are assigned an exercise notice, you not only achieve your goal, but, as an added bonus, you keep the option premium. There is no reason to consider options with a higher strike price.

When choosing the option to write in this scenario, I look for a trade that gives me the *best chance* to unload my 200 shares of KIT and collect at least $40 per share. If I enter a GTC order to sell stock at $40, although there is always the chance of being lucky, the order probably goes unfilled because KIT has not been doing well and I see no reason for it to suddenly come to life. I can improve my chances by writing covered calls, and here's how I consider my options:

If I choose a call with a $40 strike price, and if I am lucky enough to be assigned an exercise notice, then I'll obviously accomplish my objectives. But, I do not really believe this stock has a good chance to move above 40 any time soon. (I hope I am wrong about this.) If I write the March 40 calls, collecting $100 for each option, and if they expire worthless, I can meet my target by selling the shares at $39.[132] If the stock is lower than 39, I can repeat the process by writing Apr or May 40 calls (May options are listed for trading after the March expiration).

---

[132] $1 for writing the call now plus $39 for selling the stock later gives me my $40 selling price.

Table 11.1
KIT Options; Stock $38; IV 31;
25 days to Feb expiration

Exp	T	Strike	Bid	Ask	T Pr	ROI	Ann	DP
Feb	25	35	$3.30	$3.50	$0.30	1%	12%	9%
Feb		40	$0.50	$0.60	$0.50	4%	58%	1%
Mar	53	35	$3.70	$3.90	$0.70	2%	14%	10%
Mar		40	$1.00	$1.20	$1.00	5%	37%	3%
Apr	81	35	$4.10	$4.30	$1.10	3%	14%	11%
Apr		40	$1.45	$1.65	$1.45	7%	30%	4%
Jul	172	35	$5.20	$5.40	$2.20	7%	14%	14%
Jul		40	$2.70	$2.90	$2.70	10%	22%	7%

Finding the best option to write when the goal is selling stock at $40

If I repeatedly collect a $1 premium when selling calls, sooner or later I'll collect enough premium to achieve my $40 target by simply unloading the stock.[133] But, it is not quite that simple. If the stock moves lower, the $40 strike price moves further out-of-the-money and the premium for writing calls declines. There is also risk that the stock may move substantially lower, eliminating all possibility of selling near $40. Writing covered call options again and again (as each expires worthless), looks like a great method, but in the real world stocks do decline, making the plan iffy.

To provide protection against a decline in the stock price, I can sell the Jul 40 call and collect $270. I'd have an additional $1.70 per share of downside protection, but I do not like the idea that Jul is so far in the future. But there is a tradeoff. If those calls eventually expire worthless, I meet my objective by selling 200 shares at $37.30 or higher ($2.70 now and $37.30 later is still $40.)[134]

Writing the Jul 40 call is a compromise— I receive a higher premium, but I wait longer for expiration day. I must decide which gives me the better chance to meet my goal. If I choose the Mar 40 call, I'd have to hope the stock is $39 or higher 53 days from today. And if it is not that high, I'd still be OK if the premium for the May 40 makes it attractive to write. If I choose the Jul 40 call, the stock must be $37.30 or higher. That is more

---

[133] If I write calls four times, and if I am lucky enough to collect $1 each time, I can sell stock as low as $36.

[134] I'm ignoring the additional cost of carrying the stock for such a long time because if I own stock and enter a GTC order to sell my shares at $40, I still pay the cost to carry stock.

protection to the downside, but I'd have to wait 18 additional weeks. Who knows where the stock will be trading at that time? I certainly have no idea. It is a difficult choice. But, before I reach a final decision, I must consider alternatives. Can I achieve my objective by writing any of the 35 calls?

Yes I can. The Jul 35 call can be sold with a $5.20 premium. I know July is still months in the future, but if the stock remains above 35 when July expiration arrives (and that is a reasonable hope), I achieve my goal because I collect $520 now, and another $3,500 when assigned an exercise notice in July. I'm not thrilled with the prospect of holding KIT that long, but there is an excellent chance the stock will be above $35 at that time. And I'd rather collect more cash right now just in case something bad happens to KIT shares. I do not have to consider the return on my investment because my only reason for writing this call is to find a way to unload my shares at $40, and I'm looking for the best way to accomplish that. Selling the Jul 35 call gives me the highest probability of collecting at least $40 for my shares. As with all option trades, this choice is not without risk. If the stock trades at 40 soon, I'd quickly sell the shares with a GTC order. But if I write the call, my cash is tied up in this position until Jul expiration arrives - or until I am assigned an exercise notice.[135] There is very little chance of being assigned an exercise notice before expiration, so the decision is: do I lock myself in this position for six months with an excellent chance of meeting my investment objective; do I enter a GTC sell order and hope for the best; or should I write one of the calls with a 40 strike price?

Once again, there is no "best" answer for every investor. My decision is to write those Jul 35 calls. It is tempting to write March 40s, but I'd rather make the trade that gives me the best overall chance to sell KIT at $40, because that is my investment objective. As mentioned earlier, this is a great way to use an option strategy—and most investors are not aware that this method is available to them. It also presents an opportunity to demonstrate some stock market savvy the next time someone you know is discussing plans to sell stock if and when it reaches a target price. Just ask, "Have you considered writing covered calls to give yourself a much better chance to sell your stock?"

Covered call writing is a good option strategy to get you started in your option trading career. By reducing risk, it lessens the volatility of your portfolio. It also gives you a real world opportunity to see how options

---

[135] Reminder: while the option is still outstanding, I have an obligation to deliver the shares. Thus, I cannot sell those shares unless I also buy back the call option to eliminate that obligation.

work. By writing, instead of buying options as your initial strategy, you begin with a method that has a higher probability of earning money.

Before moving on to the second of our three basic conservative strategies, let's pause for a very important discussion that is necessary to trade effectively. And that means more money in your pocket.

Risk management

Many investors who adopt covered call writing have experience owning individual stocks. For those investors, there is not much to say about risk management. We all know that stocks have a tendency to rise over time, but there are periods in which stocks go nowhere, as well as times when stock prices collapse. 2008 was a brutal reminder.

I assume that those investors have some risk management plan in place. Perhaps the plan is to sell judiciously as prices rise, and to add a small new position to their portfolio as prices decline. The point is to have a plan so that you do not get caught in a panic situation in which you dump all, or a significant portion of, your investment portfolio right near the market bottom (when the pressure of mounting losses becomes unbearable).

When you adopt CCW as an investment strategy, the good times take care of themselves. However, some attention must be paid to the possibility of a severe market correction. It usually comes when least expected and can be quite painful. When you write covered calls, you have a modicum of protection against the small losses, however you are heavily exposed to large downturns.

In the following chapter, you'll learn about the collar strategy, which goes one step further than writing covered calls and offers (for a price) some assurance that your portfolio isn't hurt in a market downturn. For now, let's look at risk management from the point of view of a covered call writer. If you already have a risk management plan from your days as a stockholder, reexamine those plans to determine whether the plan remains appropriate for a covered-call writing investor.

The major risk when writing covered calls is a severe decline in the stock price. The simplest method to cut risk is to unload the position. I'm not recommending you do that, merely mentioning that it is the simplest path. If you decide to sell stock, it is necessary to repurchase one or more call options because you must maintain ownership of 100 shares of long stock for each short call.

When venturing into the world of options, it may be comforting to know there are strategies to help minimize losses and reduce (but not eliminate) the possibility of further losses in the event the stock continues to decline. I'd like to provide one piece of advice at this point: it is acceptable to lose money on some positions.

Do not hold onto a position just because you cannot tolerate taking a loss. If specific positions make you uncomfortable or if you no longer want to own certain stocks, it best to let them go. If you do lose money on a position and decide to take that loss, the very good news is that you can reinvest that same cash into a position with better prospects. Isn't that what matters most? Do you want your money invested where you believe you can earn profits? It should not matter to you which stocks provide those profits. Your goal is to grow your portfolio. Too many investors get married to a position, vowing to stay with it until it becomes profitable. Successful traders understand how important it is to cut losses. The fact that options allow you to mitigate some of those losses by adjusting (modifying) a position, and give you a good chance to turn that loss into a profit, does not mean you must make that attempt. If your reason for owning the stock has changed, if this stock is no longer attractive to you, there is no reason to maintain ownership. I reiterate—it does not matter where profits come from—just as long as you earn them.

When you want to own shares that have moved against you, there are steps to take. The most frequently used (and abused) method is known as **rolling the position**. When you roll, you repurchase the options sold previously, and simultaneously (or very shortly thereafter) sell a different option. In the case of a covered call gone bad the roll is "up and out," which means that the new call has a lower strike price (up) with a higher premium and a more distant expiration (out). The purpose of such a roll is to take in more cash. That cash provides additional protection against a further decline. Let's look at an example to see how this works.

EXAMPLE

> You bought 1,000 shares of FIXT, a local business that provides handyman, plumbing and electrician services. You hope this chain grows into a nationwide business. You paid $32.50 for stock and sold 10 Dec 30 calls that expire in two months. You received $4.00 for each call, establishing your break-even price as $28.50.[136] You felt reasonably secure with this position, but two weeks later the company pre-announces that earnings are lower than expected. When the stock next trades, it gaps lower to $28 and quickly drifts to $27.50. This is not a total disaster, but it is certainly unpleasant. In only two weeks the stock moved below the break-even point.

---

[136] You paid $32.50 and collected $4. Your net cost is $28.50 and you lose no money if FIXT is above that price when expiration arrives in December.

You decide that this stock is worth holding,[137] but you are not going to sit still and take a further beating without protecting your position. You decide to buy back your Dec 30 call, paying $1 (which is more than you'd like to pay, but you are getting a nice price on the option you are selling) and sell the Jan 25 call at $5.20. You collect a net credit[138] of $420 for each of 10 spreads. A spread is a simultaneous transaction in which you trade two or more (different) options. In this case, you bought Dec 30 calls (to close) and sold Jan 25 calls (to open). There is a much more detailed discussion of how to trade spreads in Part III.

Because you collected $4.20 cash, the break-even price is now $24.30, excluding commission expenses. You are now obligated to sell your shares at $25, thus your profit potential is only $0.70. To earn that profit, the stock must be above 25 when January expiration arrives in seven weeks. The profit potential may be fairly small ($700 total), but the good news is that you have *any* profit potential considering that you just bought a stock that quickly tumbled more than 15%. But your immediate concern is not whether this trade ends with a profit, but how you can best preserve your assets by not taking another beating on this position.

You rolled the position from December to January and own[139] a FIXT Jan 25 covered call position. This is not a perfect position, and the stock could easily head lower. However, you made the decision (for now) to own this investment. The FIXT position is now less risky than before the roll, but is not guaranteed to generate a profit. Keep an eye on the stock price and decide whether you are comfortable with the trade, or whether additional defensive action is needed.

Rolling the position is not the only method available to mitigate risk. Another strategy used by gamblers is the martingale betting system[140]— but that is too risky for us to consider. Let's just say that the idea is to double the position at the lower price, hoping the stock recovers—and then double once again if it continues to move against you. This approach is essentially a death wish because we know that some stocks never recover.

We'll go no further at this point, except to mention that one way to be certain that further losses are small is to purchase put options for protection. One reason many investors prefer not to do that is because

---

[137] This is a difficult decision. We always want to believe that we made a good decision, and bailing out now would be admitting an error. You must learn to admit these errors to become a successful trader.

[138] The cash collected for the combination trade. If it costs cash, you pay a debit.

[139] Do not be confused. You own a covered call, and that is a position with long stock and a short call.

[140] The strategy has the gambler double the bet after each loss, so that the first win recovers all previous losses plus the original stake. Such a gambler requires infinite wealth, and thus, the method does not work in the real world.

those options are not cheap—especially after the stock (or the entire market) undergoes a sharp decline. If you do buy those puts to protect your covered call, you convert the position into a collar, and that brings us to the next basic strategy.

QUIZ 11

1. Writing covered calls is a strategy with unlimited profit potential. **TRUE or FALSE**

2. When compared with buy & hold, CCW increases a trader's chance of success. **TRUE or FALSE**

3. Covered call writing is an ideal strategy for the investor who wants to quickly double the value of an investment portfolio. **TRUE or FALSE**

4. When starting a new position by buying 300 shares and writing three call options, you are:
   a) Selling three calls to open
   b) Selling three calls to close
   c) Buying three calls to open
   d) Buying three calls to close

5. As the writer of covered calls, you:
   a) Have no control over the exercise decision
   b) Decide if and when the call option is to be exercised

6. The option with the largest time premium is:
   a) ITM (in-the-money)
   b) ATM (at-the-money)
   c) OTM (out-of-the-money)

7. From these choices (same underlying and expiration), which has the highest premium?
   a) ITM (in-the-money)
   b) ATM (at-the-money)
   c) OTM (out-of-the-money)

8. From these choices (same strike and underlying), which has the highest premium?
   a) Front month option
   b) Three months
   c) Six months

9. Rolling a position is a risk-reducing technique used when your covered call position is not working as expected. Why does it reduce the risk of losing additional money?

10. CCW increases a trader's chances of selling stock at a target price. **TRUE or FALSE**

QUIZ 11 Answers

1. False. When you sell calls, your returns are limited.

2. True. You have more frequent profits and fewer losses.

3. False. CCW is ideal for investors who want steady returns, year after year.

4. (a) Selling to open.

5. (a) No control. The option owner makes that decision.

6. (b) ATM

7. (a) ITM. True for calls and puts

8. (c) 6 months. The more time remaining, the higher the premium.

9. When rolling, the trader collects additional cash, and that cash provides a cushion when the stock continues to decline.

10. True

Chapter 12

Collars: The Ultimate Portfolio Insurance Policy

If the idea of writing covered calls appeals to you, but you are uneasy about the possibility of losing substantial sums in the event of a sudden decline in the stock market, then the strategy of using options to "collar" the value of your investment is right up your alley. When you collar an investment, a maximum value that your investment can achieve is established (identical to the covered call writing process), but you also lock in a minimum value by buying an insurance policy.

Buy-and-hold investors have neither the disadvantage of limited profits nor the advantage of limited losses, and are exposed to the risk of getting hurt when the market declines. Years such 2008 play a destructive role when investors are trying to accumulate money for long-term goals. The collar strategy could have protected millions from incurring such devastating losses, but too few were aware that options can be so useful.

If you are a conservative investor who decides that adopting the collar strategy for a portion of your investment portfolio is beneficial, then this book will have served its purpose. I believe that too many *conservative* buy-and-hold investors ignore risk when seeking large investment returns, and that collars work well as a risk-reducing strategy. More aggressive traders should *not* use collars.

Those minimum and maximum values that your portfolio can achieve are set when initiating the collar position and you can set those values wherever you prefer. As you may expect, the more profit potential allowed, or the more insurance demanded, the more collars cost. When using collars, my goal is paying no cash out of pocket for the collar. That can be done by collecting enough cash for the call you write to pay for the put you purchase. That gives the trader an opportunity to earn a profit with the guarantee that the investment is never worth less than a specified amount. Keep in mind that because collar owners are protected against a significant loss, and because that protection is not free, the profit potential is even more limited than when writing covered calls. It is a big decision. Traders/investors tend to think in terms of earning glorious profits. Some investors, who previously would never have considered accepting limited profits in exchange for limited losses, may feel different after the 2008 market crash. Bear markets can do that to you.

This conservative strategy is not appropriate for investors who seek substantial capital gains, but is better suited for conservative investors for whom preservation of capital is their primary investment objective.

I do not want to give away the ending of this book, but you will discover that collars are far more versatile than they appear at this point in your learning experience. Collars 'in disguise' play a vital role in Part III. The point of mentioning this now is to encourage you to pay attention to this chapter because if decent profit potential with limited risk appeals to you (as I hope it does), then you will find other ways to use positions that work *just like collars* to provide substantial opportunity for profits along with limited risk.

One other advantage of owning collars is that these positions significantly reduce your portfolio volatility. If you prefer not to see large swings in the market value of your holdings, then owning collars limits those swings. Traditional stockholders always see their stocks rise and fall in value as the market moves higher and lower. If you are one of the very few who have the skills to select stocks that continue to rise as time passes, or if you have the ability to sell some of your holdings near market tops and reinvest your cash near market bottoms, then there is little need for you to use collars. However, if your stocks regularly rise and fall, and if you prefer to limit the peaks and valleys in your net worth, then collars represent a strategy that dampens those ups and downs. Although the primary purpose for most readers is probably learning to use options to generate additional profits, the very important secondary purpose is to reduce risk and protect the value of your portfolio. The collar strategy places emphasis on the protective properties of options and is underutilized because it appears to be so conservative. Those who adopt the collar strategy to secure the value of an investment portfolio also have the opportunity to earn decent profits. And that possibility is often overlooked by today's investors. Learning how collars work is an important part of an options education because it provides an opportunity to see how put options can be used as an insurance policy.

Another reason relatively few people adopt collars is that most investors simply are unaware that this strategy exists. This unfortunate situation is one of the results when brokers, as well as financial planners and advisors, fail to educate investors about the benefits of using options. And that is a shame because understanding how to protect one's assets would have helped a great many investors fare better during 2008-9 (or any other down market). Bear markets are a fact of life. They will occur again and again.

Collars represent an ideal investing method for obtaining an insurance policy to protect your portfolio against a large loss. People buy insurance for their homes, cars and other valuable assets, but few understand that collars can be used as insurance protection for their life savings.[141] And the best part is that the collar can be structured so that this insurance policy costs nothing (but it does limit profit potential). If this sounds too good to be true, it is not. But there is a tradeoff. Any investor willing to accept a cap on his/her potential profits can gain the benefits of using collars.

The collar defined

A collar is a position consisting of three parts, or legs:

- Long stock

- Short call

- Long put

The term, "collar," is derived from the fact that a collar, or limit, is placed on the maximum profit or loss that can be attained from the position. What makes owning a collar so different from a traditional investment is that the investor owns insurance against the possibility of incurring large losses. When you own stock, it is unlikely, but as we have recently seen, possible, that something bad can happen and the stock's value could be cut in half (or even worse). When you own a collar, you are protected against that possibility. Because of this insurance feature, collars are an attractive investment choice for the conservative investor.

If you are not a conservative investor, it still pays to understand how collars work because in Part III you will learn how to adopt a strategy that provides the same safety features as the collar, but which can be used by very aggressive investors trying to earn much higher returns from their investments. These are the "collars in disguise" mentioned earlier.

Dissecting the collar

Let's look at the three legs that constitute a collar more closely. The first two legs, long stock plus a short call should be familiar. It is a covered call position, the first of our three basic conservative option strategies. As you already know, when using the covered call, upside profit potential is limited, but the strategy is attractive because it allows you to make money as the value of the call option erodes over time.

The third leg, or the purchase of a put option, converts a covered call into a collar. Owning the put protects the value of your investment against a catastrophe because that put grants you the right to sell your stock at the strike price, no matter how low the stock price may go. On the other hand,

---

[141] I believe this is so because salespeople cannot generate huge commissions by encouraging the use of collars. My conclusion is that if huge profits cannot be earned by the sales force, there is no interest in accepting reasonable fees in return for providing a service that benefits customers.

the put must be purchased, and most of the time it loses value as time passes,[142] and thus reduces profits when the stock price increases. Is it worth a significant reduction in your potential profit to have an insurance policy? That is the decision you must make for yourself. But for many, it is the insurance policy that makes this investment method so attractive.

When establishing a collar position, both the put you purchase and the call you sell are out-of-the-money options (most of the time).

First, the bad news:

The put option is not free, and when the markets are nervous about the possibility of a steep decline, puts can be very costly. Buying the put cuts profit potential.

Next, the (very) good news:

When the collar is established, losses are limited. No matter how far the stock market, or any individual stock, tumbles, the collar owner always has the right to sell that stock at a predetermined price—the put's strike price. This provides peace of mind and true security.

As an aside, it amazes me that this investment methodology is not taught to every novice investor by the brokerage houses. Brokers provide seminars on the basic (and advanced) use of options, but teaching option rookies how to insure the value of a portfolio ought to be something that brokers *want* to do for their customers. It is an especially valuable concept for beginners because they lack the experience needed to recognize that bear markets can wipe out a substantial portion of every investor's net worth. Unfortunately, we recently witnessed such an occurrence, and nowhere did I see any broker boasting about how much money they saved their customers.

Collars can be structured so that profit potential is substantial. By choosing appropriate strike prices for the put and call, you can always generate cash when establishing your collar.[143] And that cash represents an important part of your profit potential.

What do you want to happen when you own a collar?

When opening the position, it is usually best to collect cash by selling the call at a higher premium than you pay for the put, although you may not always choose to do so. If the underlying stock remains essentially unchanged over the lifetime of the options, then both options expire worthless and the initial cash you collected becomes your profit. This profit

---

[142] It loses value most of the time because it only gains value when the stock price drops sufficiently.

[143] By collecting more for the call option than you pay for the put option.

is not available to the stockholder who simply owns the shares without bothering to establish a collar position.

You also earn a profit whenever the stock trends higher or declines by a small amount. The only time you lose money (a limited amount) when you own a collar occurs if the cash collected from the options is insufficient to offset a loss resulting from a small decline in the stock price. We are referring to those situations in which the decline is relatively small and the stock remains above the put's strike price. The value of the collar becomes apparent when the stock plunges below the put's strike and losses were limited by put ownership.

> **NOTE:** In Chapter 2, I discussed reasons why you would seldom exercise an option. One of the exceptions occurs when you own both a put and stock, and the stock is trading far below the strike price. By exercising, both the put and stock positions are removed from your portfolio, allowing the cash to earn interest. But, please do not exercise a put option just because the stock is a few dollars below the strike.

The collar strategy is profitable most of the time, yet few investors find it attractive because profits tend to be small. But, the insurance aspect should encourage more conservative investors to adopt collars.[144] Insurance is generally an expensive proposition, yet the value of your most valuable assets can be protected for no more than the cost associated with limiting profits. That has to be one of the best deals around. Why is it that so few investors know about it? Are you one of them? To get a better idea of how all this works, let's consider some examples.

EXAMPLE

A basic collar

You own 500 shares of DECK, a company that manufactures playing cards and accessories. DECK last traded at $33 per share. You decide to establish a collar for your 500 shares by selling five call options and buying five put options. Assuming the third Friday of October (expiration) is six weeks from today, you decide to:

- Sell 5DECK Oct 35 calls

---

[144] Repeat: 'collars in disguise' makes this strategy appealing to a wide variety of investors and traders, but that discussion must be postponed until Part III.

- Buy 5 DECK Oct 30 puts

If the implied volatility (IV) of DECK October options is 35, (assuming interest rates are 5% and the stock pays no dividend), you can expect to receive approximately $60 for each call and pay $30 for each put.[145] If you require a refresher about how options are priced, refer to Chapter 5. Thus, the net credit (cash collected) for each combination (buy put, sell call) is $30 and you collect a total of $150 for your 5-lot.

What happens next?

Let's assume you hold this position through expiration.

Scenario one. DECK finishes between the strike prices (30 and 35). Both options expire worthless. You collected $150 in option premium, and you keep that cash with no further obligations. This is a good result for you. Compared with an investor who owns 500 shares but doesn't establish a collar, you earn an additional $150.

Scenario two. DECK is above the higher (call) strike price. The puts are out-of-the-money and expire worthless. The calls are in-the-money and you are assigned an exercise notice, thereby selling 500 DECK at the strike price of $35 per share. This is a good result. You not only keep the $150 in option premium, but you also sell shares at $35. Over the six-week lifetime of the options, you earned $2 per share on $500 shares ($1,000) plus the $150 in option premium. Your net profit is $1,150, less commission. This represents the maximum profit available from this collar position.

It is possible that this is not the *optimal* result. If DECK shares last traded above $35.30 (the price at which you earn the same $1,150 profit without having a collar position), then those investors who own stock without a collar earn more money by simply holding the shares. That is OK. First, you cannot expect to make the maximum possible profit on every trade. Second, without the collar you would not own an insurance policy, and owning that policy is worth something to you, even when you do not collect on the policy.

You opened the collar position for two reasons. First, to prevent a big loss. Mission accomplished. Second, to have an opportunity to make a decent profit. Mission accomplished once again. To gain these benefits, something must be sacrificed. That sacrifice is accepting a limited profit.

---

[145] You are not expected to determine these prices in your head. I used an online calculator.

This time, the collar did limit your gain. If you find that upsetting, if you feel that you must always make the maximum on any trade, then you are going to have a difficult time accepting any strategies recommended in this book. Options are used for hedging purposes—and although that reduces potential losses, you must accept the fact that it also reduces potential profits.

My objective in writing this book is to help readers find and adopt methods that allow an investment portfolio to grow consistently and to reduce the chances of large losses. If your goal is to ignore risk in an attempt to maximize profits, none of the basic conservative strategies suits that investment style. In fact, if you choose to ignore risk, I think that you are making a big mistake. But it is your right to invest as you see fit. The purpose of this book is to increase your chances of success, regardless of the strategy chosen. Be patient, because the needs of more aggressive traders are addressed in Part III.[146]

This is the opportune time to reiterate a point made earlier. Some brokers charge a high fee for an exercise or assignment, while others charge nothing. Some brokers charge much higher commissions to buy or sell stocks and options than others. If you are not using a discount broker for these collar trades, then your profits are less than they should be. If you believe it is in your best interests to use a full service broker, please be certain that your broker provides services that warrant those higher fees. If not, it is OK to maintain an account with that broker, but you can also open another account with a discount broker for your option-related trading.

Scenario three. DECK is below the lower (put) strike price. (Bummer!) The calls are OTM and expire worthless. Your puts are ITM and you may exercise them, thereby selling your shares at the strike price ($30). If you prefer to keep the stock, it is okay to sell the puts instead of exercising, because they served their purpose by providing complete protection below $30 per share.

This is not the result you wanted. Yet, by establishing a collar, you saved some cash. First you keep the $150 in option premium, reducing your loss by $150. Second, by selling shares at $30, you escaped an even larger loss because DECK is currently trading lower than $30 (how much lower is not an important part of this discussion, but if it is significantly lower, the collar saved a bundle).

You opened the collar position to protect against a big loss. This time the collar served its purpose. It is unfortunate that you suffered any loss, but as is true whenever you collect on an insurance policy, the loss is limited to

---

[146] Gains are still limited but can be substantial.

the deductible.[147] Instead of the relatively small loss incurred, would you have preferred an even smaller loss? You can meet that objective by buying a put with a higher strike price. When you do that, it is more difficult to earn any profit because the cost of the put is so high. I do not recommend paying so much for insurance that there is no room for profits.[148] Extra insurance always costs more money. As we consider additional examples, you will get a better feel for choosing strike prices.

When playing with the numbers, you will learn to make decisions that offer the best compromise between risk/reward and your personal comfort zone.

Warning: do not be tempted to skip the call sale. The call is sold to collect premium to pay for the puts. If you do not bother to sell calls, upside profits become unlimited. That is an acceptable strategy, but I do not recommend it because those puts can cost plenty! If you pay 20% of your portfolio's value every year for insurance, how can you expect to earn a profit?

Let's take a look at another example. This time we'll carefully examine each decision made by the investor.

EXAMPLE

A hot stock

You decide that biotechnology represents the wave of the future, and after careful research, buy 400 shares of WDRG (WonderDrug Inc.), paying $31 per share. You anticipate making a good-sized profit, but because this stock has a history of being extremely volatile, you elect to swap some upside profitability for downside protection, and thus, initiate the trade as a collar.

Let's look at the available call and put options and decide which are best suited for your purposes. In this case, you are willing to lose some (but not too much) money if your hunch on this company doesn't prove to be successful, but you insist on allowing for a good-sized profit. After all, you are buying the shares for their upside potential.

The option data is presented in Tables 12.1 through 12.4. Note that option prices are much higher for WDRG options than they are for DECK because WDRG is much more volatile. The current implied volatility of WDRG options is 50.

---

[147] The lower the put strike price, the larger the "deductible" because stock is sold at a lower price (with a larger loss).
[148] If an investor is so concerned about owning the shares that a ton of insurance is deemed necessary, perhaps it would be wiser to find an alternative investment.

Trading the collar: detailed thoughts of the experienced trader

I'd like to collect a large premium for the calls, but I also believe in the future of this company. There is a distinct possibility that WDRG has an edge when it comes to finding the next big drug in the fight against cancer. The option prices are listed in Tables 12.1 and 12.2.

There is no reason to write in-the-money calls when I am so bullish. I'm planning to write OTM calls: either the 35 or 40 strike price (stock is currently $31). But before I make the final decision, I'll consider other options just in case one of them offers an excellent combination of time premium and downside protection.

Deep in-the-money call options are bid no higher than *parity* (the option's intrinsic value) for July and barely above parity for August. When selling an ITM call, the time premium represents the profit potential, and these options have none. Thus, selling in-the-money options is inappropriate.

What about selling an at-the-money call, such as the Jul 30 or Aug 30? The Jul 30 call can be sold for approximately $2.40. That is $1 in intrinsic value (the stock is $31) and $1.40 in time value. The $1.40 is attractive, but I'm too bullish on this stock to accept this premium. The Aug 30 call doesn't do it for me either, as an additional $70 in time premium is not good enough to make me change my mind. I'll stick with my original plan and look at the OTM calls. If I had a more neutral outlook on this stock, these ATM calls would be much more appealing.

Table 12.1 WDRG call options
Stock @ $31.00; 35 days before expiration; IV 50

Exp	Strike	Bid	Ask	T Pr	M Gain
Jul	17.5	$13.50	$13.80	$0.00	$0.00
Jul	20.0	$11.00	$11.30	$0.00	$0.00
Jul	22.5	$8.50	$8.80	$0.00	$0.00
Jul	25.0	$6.20	$6.50	$0.20	$0.20
Jul	27.5	$4.00	$4.30	$0.50	$0.50
Jul	30.0	$2.40	$2.60	$1.40	$1.40
Jul	35.0	$0.55	$0.75	$0.55	$4.55
Jul	40.0	$0.10	$0.20	$0.10	$9.10

Jul Calls for WDRG

T Pr = Time Premium; M Gain = Max profit per share, if assigned an exercise notice

Table 12.2 WDRG call options
Stock @ $31.00; 63 days before expiration; IV 50

Exp	Strike	Bid	Ask	T Pr	M Gain
Aug	17.5	$13.50	$13.80	$0.00	$0.00
Aug	20.0	13,1	$11.40	$0.10	$0.10
Aug	22.5	$8.60	$8.90	$0.10	$0.10
Aug	25.0	$6.50	$6.80	$0.50	$0.50
Aug	27.5	$4.60	$4.90	$1.10	$1.10
Aug	30.0	$3.10	$3.40	$2.10	$2.10
Aug	35.0	$1.20	$1.40	$1.20	$5.20
Aug	40.0	$0.35	$0.55	$0.35	$9.35

Aug Calls for WDRG

I can sell calls that expire in either five or nine weeks. The Jul 40 only pays a dime (i.e., 10 cents per share or $10 per contract) and for that price, I'm not going to sell calls. I can get $35 for the Aug 40 call, and I can probably get $40 or $45 if there is trading volume in these options. I note that the open interest is over 500 contracts, so there is a chance I can split the market[149] and sell my calls above the bid price. If the stock zooms above 40, I'd have a great profit, but I do not expect to be that lucky, especially before expiration (although I have high hopes that it happens later).

Perhaps it is wiser to write the 35 call. It has a much higher premium, and if the stock rallies that far, I'll earn $4 per share profit, in addition to the option premium. That is pretty good for just a few weeks. I prefer selling the near-term option, as it usually generates the highest annualized bang for the buck. But this time, I can get $55 or $60 for the five-week option (Table 12.1), and I can get at least double that for the nine-week option (Table 12.2). Thus, in this situation, the nine-week option offers a higher annualized return.[150]

That feels right. I'll try to sell Aug 35 calls. But I'll offer four calls at $1.30, trying to collect a few extra dollars. But, I will not be stubborn. I already own the stock and I'd like to get the calls sold as quickly as possible. If I cannot get a fill within a half hour, I'll reconsider my price.

---

[149] Enter an offer (or a bid) that is between the current bid and ask. In other words, I can try to receive a higher price by offering my calls below the current ask price, but above the current bid.

[150] Earning $60 in five weeks is clearly less, when annualized, than earning twice as much ($120) in less than twice as much time (nine weeks vs. five weeks).

Put option (Tables 12 .3 and 12 .4)

There are not many good choices where the puts are concerned. I do not want to buy a deep in-the-money put option because I'm too bullish on this stock and these puts cost far more than I'm willing to spend.

Because I'm selling Aug calls, I'm buying Aug puts. If I buy a put that expires in July, after July expiration I would be long stock and short Aug calls (a covered call position). I would be forced to buy Aug puts to maintain the collar on my investment. It is almost always more convenient to establish the collar in which both options expire at the same time.

The 17.5s, 20s, 22.5s and 25s are all inexpensive options, but I'd hate to sell my stock at 25 (or lower). That potential loss represents a greater risk than I want accept. If I buy the Aug 25 puts at $50 and sell the Aug 35 calls at my price of $130, I'll net $80 cash. That means in the worst-case scenario, I'll be forced to sell my shares at 25, losing $6 per share ($2,400 loss; I'm buying stock at 31). The $320 ($80 for each collar) reduces the loss to $2,080, but that is not much consolation. Those puts do not feel right because I want better protection.

Let's see what happens if I buy the 27.5 puts. I'll have to pay $1.10, or perhaps $1.05. That results in a small credit because I'm selling calls at approximately $1.30. If forced to sell my shares at 27.5, I'd lose $3.50 per share. That is a good-sized, but acceptable loss under these conditions. I really like the prospects of this company. If I were a more conservative investor, I would not settle for these numbers. Of course, a much more conservative investor would never buy WDRG, so there is no reason to dwell on that.

My mind is made up. I'll bid $1.05 for the WDRG Aug 27.5 puts and try to sell the WDRG Aug 35 calls at $1.30. If I cannot get my orders filled at my prices within a few (5 to 15) minutes, I'll change my limit and hope I didn't miss my chance to get filled at the current price of $1.10 and $1.20.

Bottom line: The collar was established by buying stock at $31, selling Aug 35 calls at $1.30 (my price) and buying Aug 27.5 puts at $1.10 (a nickel higher than I had hoped to pay). I collected a total of $80 ($20 per collar) for the option trades, reducing the net cost for the stock to $30.80.

- Maximum possible profit occurs if I sell stock at $35 (a profit of $1,680).

- Maximum possible loss occurs if forced to sell stock at $27.50 (a loss of $1,320).

Table 12.3 WDRG put options
Stock @ $31.00; IV 50
35 days before expiration

Exp	Strike	Bid	Ask
Jul	17.5	0.00	0.10
Jul	20.0	0.00	0.10
Jul	22.5	0.00	0.20
Jul	25.0	0.10	0.25
Jul	27.5	0.45	0.65
Jul	30.0	1.35	1.55
Jul	35.0	4.40	4.70
Jul	40.0	8.90	9.20

Jul puts for WDRG

Table 12.4 WDRG put options
Stock @ $31.00; IV 50
63 days before expiration

Exp	Strike	Bid	Ask
Aug	17.5	0.00	0.20
Aug	20.0	0.00	0.20
Aug	22.5	0.10	0.30
Aug	25.0	0.30	0.50
Aug	27.5	0.90	1.10
Aug	30.0	1.90	2.10
Aug	35.0	4.90	5.20
Aug	40.0	9.00	9.30

Aug puts for WDRG

Post-expiration decisions

As expiration day approaches, it is important to have a basic plan. When I anticipate losing my stock (I'll exercise ITM calls or be assigned on ITM puts), it is a good idea to plan ahead and know whether I want to reestablish my position with a later expiry. Once expiration has come and gone, if I no longer own the shares, my choices are:

- Reinvest the proceeds in shares of the same stock.[151]

- Keep the cash until I find a suitable investment. It is wise to keep an updated list of new investment ideas for times when you have cash to invest.

- Invest the proceeds in a different stock.

NOTE: If I exercised my puts, there are two ways to look at the situation. The stock has performed badly and some investors are thankful they owned puts and have no further interest in the stock. Others feel that the stock has dropped to such a low level that they want to repurchase the shares. This is a decision each investor must make on his/her own.

The most likely outcome: The options expire worthless

Depending on a trader's style and the strike prices chosen, much of the time the calls and puts expire worthless. As a result, the investor/trader continues to own the shares, probably requiring the building of a new collar. The usual procedure is to place that order Monday morning following expiration. Adopting that policy requires taking a very small, but real, risk that bad news may be announced before the market opens Monday. If that happens, the stock could open significantly lower and all the effort made to maintain a collar position would be for naught. Of course, there is also an equal chance that good news is released, resulting in a higher stock price. I recommend not taking this tiny risk by rolling the position (see Chapter 11) Thursday or Friday of expiration week. Rolling involves trading both puts and calls. (To keep this discussion about collars, and not about rolling, let's continue as if the options expired worthless.)

Let's assume that WDRG performed well and closed last Friday at 33.50 per share. The puts and calls expired. It is now Monday, following August expiration, and it is time to set up a new collar.

EXAMPLE

Shifting strike prices

You still own 400 shares of WDRG, but the company has issued a news release that may play a significant role in the company's future. WonderDrug has been testing a promising, new medicine

---

[151] If I sold my shares by exercising puts, and if and only if I want to retain ownership, an efficient alternative is to SELL, rather than EXERCISE, those puts. I keep the stock, save on commissions, and still collect the full value of those puts.

and is announcing the results of phase I trials within two or three weeks.

This important news is pending and there is a strong probability that it will have a major impact on the stock price. There has been a great deal of interest in the options and trading volume has quadrupled. The demand for both puts and calls has driven the price of all options higher. As is typical in such situations, the near-term options—the ones speculators want to trade—are in greatest demand. Some players, expecting good news, have bid the calls significantly higher, which means the implied volatility (IV) is above its normal range. The out-of-the-money call options are trading with an IV above 80 (a typical level is 50). That is excellent news because those are the calls you plan to write.[152]

Similarly, put buyers abound. It is common for the stock price of biotech companies to tumble by more than 50% when bad news is released. WDRG has a promising future, but only if they make money before consuming all their cash on hand. If this company is forced to abandon the new drug because of unsatisfactory phase I results, it will be bad news for shareholders. The puts are trading with an even higher implied volatility (90), and that means there are no cheap puts to buy.

September expiration is 32 days in the future. The markets for the Sep options are listed in Table 12.5.

Making the decision

I still refuse to sell ITM calls to collect the small profit potential available because the news may be excellent and I remain bullish. On the other hand, I must buy puts that are not too far OTM because the news could be dreadful.

This time the stock is priced at $33.50 and Sep 40 calls are worth considering. That is especially true because I can buy the Sep 27.5 puts for approximately the same price. I'm really hopeful that the news is good, but recognize that I'm taking a significant risk with that position.

---

[152] Option premium increases significantly when IV increases (Chapter 6). In fact, IV can more than double in this 'news pending' situation for biotech companies.

Table 12.5 WDRG Call options
Stock @$33.50; 32 days before expiration
Call IV = 80; Put IV = 90

Exp	Strike	Bid	Ask	Time Pr	M Gain
Aug	17.5	$13.50	$13.80	$0.00	$0.00
Aug	20.0	13,1	$11.40	$0.10	$0.10
Aug	22.5	$8.60	$8.90	$0.10	$0.10
Aug	25.0	$6.50	$6.80	$0.50	$0.50
Aug	27.5	$4.60	$4.90	$1.10	$1.10
Aug	30.0	$3.10	$3.40	$2.10	$2.10
Aug	35.0	$1.20	$1.40	$1.20	$5.20
Aug	40.0	$0.35	$0.55	$0.35	$9.35

September puts and calls for WonderDrug, Inc.
T Pr = time premium
M Gain = maximum profit per share, if assigned an exercise notice

I'll enter a spread order[153] to buy the Sep 27.5 puts and sell the Sep 40 calls for even money (meaning the call premium equals the put premium). I'm not concerned about not collecting extra cash to own this collar because all I want is protection against a disaster. Normally, it is important to generate cash from the option trades (of a collar)[154], but with a big news event in the works, that importance is dwarfed by the likelihood of a huge price change for the stock. I do not expect both options to expire worthless and I want the chance to make money if the news is good, while not losing too much (a relative term) if the news is bad.

> **NOTE:** If you are not familiar with the concept of entering a spread order, here's how it works: The broker (electronic or live) is instructed to buy one option and sell another. However, there are conditions. First, both parts of the order must be filled. It is not acceptable for the broker to fill one part (leg) but not the other. Although the transactions can occur at any price within the current bid/ask range, the order is not filled at any random price that suits the market makers (unless you are foolish

---

[153] An order to fill two different trades simultaneously or neither. In other words, there is no danger of selling calls without buying puts and vice versa.
[154] DO NOT generalize this statement. It is NOT necessary to generate cash from all option trades.

enough to enter a market order). Instead it must conform to the limits indicated when the order is placed. In this case, the order tells the broker to buy the puts and sell the calls, but only when the transactions can be completed at a next cash debit of zero or less.[155] If both options are priced at $1.15, or $1.10, or any other price, I'd be satisfied with the fill.

Results

This time, the outcome of the investment is expected to be known before the options expire. When the news is released, the stock will probably[156] undergo a large price change. The problem is, no one knows just how large or in which direction. For example, if I *knew* the stock was going to gap up to 50 or down to 15, I'd be buying calls and puts, not holding onto my collar.[157]

Let's make the assumption that something favorable happens (for a change). In the world of biotechnology, the news is often disappointing, but sometimes the bulls are rewarded. The company reports that the trial shows promising results and that phase II trials are already underway. The stock gaps one morning (at a price that is significantly different from the prior day's closing price) to $42 per share and there are still three days remaining before Sep options expire.

Now that the news has been released, IV collapses (because *another* significant price change is very unlikely) and the options are trading with an IV (50), near its customary level. This is a great result. If the stock remains above $40, the puts expire worthless and you are assigned an exercise notice on the calls, thereby selling stock at $40. The stock was $33.50 when you opened this month's collar, resulting in a tidy profit of $6.50 per share, or $2,600. And that is just the profit for the past month. You also earned additional money earlier.

A word of caution: this outstanding result is possible when owning collars, but it is very unusual. Most investors who use collars play far more conservatively and earn much less money than illustrated in the example.

---

[155] Less than zero means that I collected more for the call than I paid for the put.
[156] Sometimes the news can be insignificant. However, with phase I trials that would be unusual.
[157] Because I do not know, I'm not going to gamble by buying options. But, for the purposes of discussion, if I did want to bet that the stock is trading at 15 or 50 after news is released, I'd be buying a combination of puts and calls (known as a strangle). If I bought the Sep 27.5 put and the Sep 40 call, I'd be investing about $250 for each strangle. If the stock drops to $15, then the put is in-the-money by 12.50 points, allowing me to (at least) quintuple my investment. If the stock moves to $50, then the call is worth at least $1,000 (its intrinsic value) and my investment quadruples. Those are the possibilities that make investors want to buy options. If the idea of buying options sounds attractive, refer to the discussion in Chapter 9.

Rolling the position

Let's assume you are thrilled with your success and want to own WDRG through one more expiration cycle. Because you expect to be assigned an exercise notice on the Sep 40 calls, to maintain ownership of the stock, you must buy back those calls (to prevent being assigned an exercise notice). Doing so cancels your obligation to deliver the shares to the call owner. The puts are going to expire in three days, and your plan has been to own WDRG only with an insurance policy in place. Thus, at the same time that you repurchase those Sep 40 calls, you plan to sell new call options and buy new put options. Selling the Sep 27.5 puts is probably out of the question because they are so far out-of-the-money there are not likely to be any bids for them.

First you must decide which options (Oct or Nov) to trade. Then you must construct a spread order that eliminates the September position at the same time that it establishes a new, longer-dated position. Let's see how this works.

Keeping the profit train moving

It is Wednesday, three days before Sep expiration, and four weeks, or 31 days, before the October options expire. The options data are in Tables 12.6 and 12.7.

Thought process

I do not like the idea of paying $2.30, or 30 cents over parity to buy Sep 40 calls, but if I enter a spread order, I may be able to pay a little less.[158] Looking at the October option prices, I do not like what I see. There is too little premium in the Oct 50 calls, so selling that option is out of the question. Similarly, the deep in-the-money Oct 30 and 35 calls also have too little time premium. (The 30s are $12.00 bid and every penny of that represents intrinsic value, with $0 time value.)

The 35s are not much better, with $7 in intrinsic value and only 30 cents in time value. It looks like my choice is between the 40s and 45s. I can sell the Oct 40 calls and collect a premium of $3.50. That is $2 in intrinsic value and $1.50 in time value. I've already made a bundle on this stock, so if I can eke out another $1.50 (less the cost of the put), that is good enough. After all, this stock cannot rise forever. (Yes, I know it may rise significantly from here, but I do not want to be too greedy.)

---

[158] $0.30 over parity seems like a lot of money with only three days to go, but this stock was recently much lower and who knows—profit takers may appear out of the blue and drive the stock price below 40. I have a very nice profit to protect. It is worthwhile to pay those 30 cents as insurance. Besides, I need this trade (the plan is to do the call spread AND buy Sep puts) because my current puts are essentially worthless.

If I sell Oct 45 calls, I'd collect $1.25 in time premium. Not bad. But I must take into consideration that it is going to cost more than $2 to buy the Sep 40 calls and I'd like to collect net cash, just in case the stock moves lower. That means I'm going to sell the Oct 40 call.

The put is a much easier choice. The 30s are too far out-of-the-money and the others are too costly. The 35 put is all I need. I recognize that this is 7 points below the current price, but with the good news already known, I'm willing to take the chance that the stock is not going to plunge from today's level. In addition, by selling the Oct 40 call, I will not begin to lose any of the profit I already earned unless the stock dips below 40.

Table 12.6 WDRG options
Stock @$42; 3 days before expiration; IV 50

Exp	Strike	C Bid	C Ask	Strike	P Bid	P Ask
Sep	40.0	$2.10	$2.30	27.5	$0.00	$0.05

Covering the short Sep 40 call

I'm now ready to roll this position. I'll enter two separate orders—one for the call spread and one for the put. I'll enter the call spread first, but entering both simultaneously is viable. Thus, I'll enter the following limit spread order:

- Buy to close 4 WDRG Sep 40 calls

- Sell to open 4 WDGD Oct 40 calls

- Net credit $1.30 ($3.50 minus $2.20[159]) or better

Table 12.7 WDRG Options;
Stock @ $42; 3 days before expiration; IV 50

Exp	Strike	Calls		Puts	
		Bid	Ask	Bid	Ask
Oct	30.0	$12.00	$12.30	0.00	0.20
Oct	35.0	$7.30	$7.60	0.15	0.35
Oct	40.0	$3.50	$3.80	1.35	1.60
Oct	45.0	$1.25	$1.50	4.10	4.40
Oct	50.0	$0.30	$0.50	8.10	8.40

Oct Puts and Calls for WDRG

---

[159] Or any other equivalent prices

By entering the order as a spread, I'll get both legs filled or neither. And if I do get filled, then I'd be buying the Sep 40 calls at $2.20 and selling the Oct 40 calls at $3.50 (or equivalent prices). As soon as I get that fill, I'll place an order to buy to open 4-lots of WDRG Oct 35 puts at 30 cents. I doubt that I'd be forced to pay 35 cents, but I will if I must. There is no reason to take any chances here, especially for only $20 ($5 x 4 puts). I want to own those puts.

If I get my prices on both orders, I roll the position and collect another $1 in credit per collar, or $400 total. If the stock remains above 40 when October expiration arrives, that $400 represents an additional profit for holding the position (and taking downside risk) one extra month.

The worst-case scenario occurs when WDRG drops below 35 and I am forced to exercise my puts. If that happens, holding for the extra month costs $4 per share, or $1,600. How did I get that number? My position is currently worth $40 (if I do not roll, I'll be assigned an exercise notice and will sell the position, collecting $40 per share). If I sell at $35 later, I'll lose $5 per share. But, I am taking in another $1.00 in cash by rolling the position. Thus, I'd be worse off by $4 per share if forced to sell my shares at $35. That is $1,600. Generally, it is not a great idea to risk $1,600 to make $400, but this stock has behaved well and the company has no announcements expected over the next month. I think it is a reasonable investment.

Collars: What Investors Need to Know, but no one is telling them.

The collar strategy is unexciting. To many, it can be boring. But investing in the stock market is not supposed to be fun (although I love making trade decisions). It is a serious business whose purpose is to help people accumulate enough assets to provide for their financial needs—whether it is a college education for children (grandchildren?) or a comfortable retirement for themselves. Investing is considered to be the most efficient method for building long-term wealth. If you prefer to spend investing profits as they accumulate, that is your right, even though it is economically foolish.

The reality is that every so often, a bear market arrives on the scene, destroys wealth, and scares a significant portion of investors sufficiently that they choose to sell their holdings (near the market bottom) and escape from the stock market. Many remain out of the market for a long time and re-enter only as the market is approaching another bull market peak. It is not bad enough to have already been burned, then miss the subsequent rally, but by getting back into the market as prices are soaring and yet another bear market is about to begin, these unfortunate investors wind up getting hurt a second time. It is a financial tragedy, but it is human nature to run away when the world is tumbling around you and to come back to play when euphoria reigns.

There must be a better way. I'm not advocating that anyone adopt a frugal lifestyle (but it does have its benefits) or telling you that your money isn't to be used to enjoy yourselves, but unless you are already wealthy beyond your needs, investing is a business that should be taken seriously. Because you are reading this book about using options, then you probably already know that.

When an investor is willing to accept smaller (but not small) profits when the bulls are in charge, in return for much better results (than others can achieve) the rest of the time—including when markets are stagnant— and small losses when those around them are seeing their assets disappear, then a boring investment method is appropriate. The conservative collar strategy is at the top of my list for how investors can earn money while protecting their assets. Reminder: in Part III we will examine ways to expand the possibilities when using collars ("collars in disguise").

The general investing public is not aware that collars are available. In fact, most have no idea that options are conservative investing tools that can be used in a variety of ways to preserve wealth and limit risk when investing. To me, it is the fault of the traditional stockbrokers who refuse to encourage clients to learn how options work. I also blame financial planners and advisors who, thus far, have failed to adopt option strategies for their clients. Fortunately, the trend is changing. New brokers exist who specialize in option trading and they educate clients on how options can be used. They do what seems obvious to me—they make an effort to *help* their clients succeed. How quaint! If this book encourages you to consider trading options, I urge you to find one of the many brokers who offer options education to their clients.[160]

It is easy to look back and say what could have been done, but it is my contention that investors should always protect at least a portion of their assets with positions similar to collars. Older or more conservative investors may prefer to protect all their assets. But the common practice of protecting nothing—simply because investors are unaware such protection is available—is unacceptable to me. And it is time for it to end.

Here's an example of how an investor could have used collars to protect a portfolio during the 2008 stock market meltdown. The same method can be used today.

---

[160] When opening an account, consider a positive recommendation from someone you know and whose opinion you trust. If you do not know where to get started, consider using the free tools provided by StockBrokers.com and reading their annual broker review. There is also a yearly survey published by Barron's that rates various brokers.

Let's say you prefer to own index funds, rather than individual stocks, and that you chose to invest in SPY, the ETF that tracks the performance of SPX, the S & P 500 Index. Let's look back to the spring of 2008, when SPY was trading near 130 and you owned 1,000 shares worth $130,000.[161] If you held those shares without hedging, as most investors worldwide did, you watched those shares fall lower and lower, eventually trading below 70 just one year later. That is a substantial loss by anyone's definition. Remember this is merely an example. Perhaps you would have reacted differently and not watch helplessly from the sidelines.

ETF portfolios can be protected with collars, but you must be willing to forego a potential windfall if the market soars higher. This is unacceptable to many because they tend to think of potential gains and ignore risk. If going for the pot of gold is your game plan, then boring collars are inappropriate. But it is still a good idea to find *some* method for hedging risk and avoiding the large losses.

Looking back at that 2008 position, one reasonable collar position would have been to buy 10 SPY Jun (2008) 120 puts and sell 10 SPY Jun (2008) 140 calls. Even though the puts and calls are equally out of the money, the puts cost more because of the way implied volatility is skewed.[162] It may have cost about $1,000 to own that collar. This position has a potential upside gain of only $9,000 ($10k less the $1k collar cost) and a maximum loss of $10,000 plus the collar cost. These numbers do not look attractive, but collars are very flexible. To save a bit of cash, the collar trader could buy the Jun 129 put or even the 128 put, paying less for a bit less safety. Or additional cash could have been generated on the call portion of the collar by selling the Jun 138 or 139 call. That reduces profit potential, but reduces cost. Similarly, if you prefer to pay more for the collar in exchange for the chance to earn more money if the market moves higher, writing a call with a strike above 140 makes sense. This is a flexible strategy.

With the collar in place, the portfolio is protected against a catastrophe. While bear markets are not the norm, it is an individual decision as to whether you want to protect your portfolio against bad times. The bottom line remains: can you accumulate enough money to meet your needs with slow and steady growth, or must you be positioned for that seldom occurring, but richly rewarding, bull market run? If the answer is 'slow growth,' why would you take the chance of losing a nest egg, in return for having more assets than you'll ever need?

---

[161] If you own as little as 100 shares of a specific stock or ETF, you can adopt these methods. Never believe your portfolio is too small to protect. You are learning how to make that portfolio grow.

[162] Skew is a topic too advanced for this book. But it refers to the fact that implied volatility increases as the strike price of an option moves lower. The idea is that investors pay more for puts than calls because the sudden and major market moves have been to the downside.

I know how it is. In the aftermath of any market decline, people are afraid and want protection. After all, we always insure our homes and possessions, so why not our investments? That is the correct attitude from this writer's viewpoint. And when times get good, we tend to forget about the possibilities and get overly optimistic. Ask yourself: do you cancel your homeowner's (or renter's) insurance policy when times are good? If not, why would you cancel portfolio insurance? The flexibility of collars allows for tweaking. You can give yourself a bit more room for profits and accept a little less insurance. You can choose your own strike prices for collar positions, but do not get too greedy. The bear will return someday.

When the options used to build the collar are about to expire, you can roll the collar to a new position. Depending on how often you want to be bothered making the trades, the options can expire at any expiration. I'd suggest 3- or 6-month options, but one-year (LEAPS) options are also acceptable.

The questions are: Would millions have protected their assets had they known about the availability of collars? Would they have considered it too much trouble or too difficult to understand? I must confess that I do not know the answers. Many would never sacrifice the upside possibilities and believe a bear market is never possible. But investors ought to have the option of using options. And that is one reason behind the existence of this book.

Managing the collar

Collars require less management than almost any other option position because the trade was made with profit and loss parameters that were acceptable to the trader. That minimizes the need to adjust the position. If the stock is declining, you may choose to find a way to reduce the potential loss, but if you own a put option, that provides all the protection required. You can sit tight, hoping the stock rebounds. I do not recommend trading on hope, nut when you own the put and your maximum loss *is not much larger* than the current loss, it pays to hold the position.

When trading collars, the major decisions are:

- Once the options expire worthless, should I reestablish the collar?

    o If yes, which options do I buy and sell?

    o If no, should I own the stock without the protection of a collar?

- If one of the options is in-the-money, should I allow the position to go away[163] or should I roll it?

These examples illustrate how to initiate a collar position and some of the choices you have as expiration nears. We discussed two different ways to change the option strike prices. You can open a new collar (after expiration) with different strike prices; or you can roll the position prior to expiration—preferring not to be assigned an exercise notice.

When advantageous, you may want to roll a position before expiration. It is not necessary for the calls to be in-the-money. A discussion of how and why you may want to roll a position was covered in Chapter 11.

Collars represent an excellent strategy for the conservative investor. Limiting the potential loss, coupled with the opportunity to earn a decent profit, makes this an ideal strategy. Later, in Part III, we'll examine how more aggressive traders use collars (in disguise).

Bottom line: As you progress through this book, you may be adding new strategies to your trading arsenal. A top priority is protecting yourself by owning limited-loss positions. One of the strongest arguments for option trading is that it increases your chances of making money. But the crucial factor in determining your long-term success is the ability to keep that money by limiting losses. You never want to be in position to incur a huge loss that wipes out months or years of profits.

NOTE: The collar is not "THE ANSWER" for most traders. Collared portfolios seriously underperform market averages over time and are for very conservative traders or special situations when you want to maintain ownership of a specific stock, but are concerned about the downside.

---

[163] Whether I am assigned on the calls or exercise the puts, there is no residual position.

QUIZ 12

1. How does a collar differ from a covered call?

TRUE or FALSE (Questions 2 through 8)

2. Collars are risky positions, suitable for very aggressive investors.

3. Collars must be closely monitored to protect against the possibility of a significant price change that places traders in jeopardy of a significant loss.

4. Collars can be used to insure the value of a stock portfolio in a manner similar to insuring the value of your home or other valuable possessions.

5. When you own a collar position, most of the time the put option that you bought expires worthless. Therefore buying the put option is a bad idea and owning a collar position is also a poor choice.

6. When you own a collar, the put limits your losses, but you have unlimited potential profits.

7. If you believe in buying homeowners insurance, then owning a collar is a similar way to protect your stock market investment portfolio.

8. Collars provide some protection against loss, but if the market declines by 50%, you out of luck and are going to lose a large sum, even when owning a collar.

9. You own 300 shares of ZXY, currently priced at $105 and buy 3 Aug 95P @ $600. You sell 3 Aug 100C, @ $600. What is the maximum loss if ZXY is trading at $85 when the options expire in August?

Quiz 12 Answers

1. A collar is a covered call with the addition of a long put option.

2. False. Collars are very conservative positions.

3. False. Losses are limited to a pre-determined level. Collars require less maintenance than the vast majority of option positions.

4. True.

5. False It does mean that you may earn more money by not buying the put option. But it also means you may lose substantially more. *The put option was not bought to "make money."* Instead, it was bought as an insurance policy, and insurance is not free. In this case it reduces potential profits.

6. False. The call limits your profits.

7. True

8. False

9. $3,000. The stock is $105 now and you sell the shares @ $95 per share. That is a loss of $10 per share.

Chapter 13

Writing Cash-Secured Puts

Writing cash-secured or naked puts is the last of the three basic conservative option strategies. Some professional advisors steer their clients away from writing naked puts because they claim it is too risky. Sure, there is downside risk, but owning stocks is even riskier.[164] Those professionals do their customers a major disservice. Many individual investors never bother to learn about options once they hear any negative statements from their brokers.

Except for extremely bearish prognosticators, no one suggests that owning stock is anything but the most prudent of investment strategies. It is touted far and wide as sage advice that investors must invest in the stock market to maintain spending power and keep up with long-term inflation. Yet, writing naked put options is more conservative and less risky than buying stock and deserves consideration as an investment alternative. Buy and hold investors would fare better if they incorporated put writing into their arsenal of investing ideas.

Why is selling naked puts less risky than owning stock? When buying stock, you pay for the shares now. When selling puts, you receive a cash payment in return for accepting an obligation that *may* require you to buy stock later. It is the same stock, and the only difference between buying it now and buying it later is that it costs more[165] to buy it now. When selling puts, the premium effectively reduces the price paid for stock (assuming you eventually arc assigned an exercise notice). If the price declines and stockholders lose money, the put writer loses less. Part of the time that a stock declines, the put writer earns a profit,[166] whereas the stockholder never earns a profit when the stock price moves lower. When writing puts, profits are limited and that is the tradeoff. If the stock soars, the stockholder fares better than the put seller.

Options are inherently neither risky nor dangerous. Investors trading options before understanding how they work is what is certainly dangerous. While it is OK to occasionally use options to speculate, options were invented as risk-reducing investment tools—and I hope to convince

---

[164] If the stock falls to zero, the put seller loses less money (the cash premium collected) than the stockholder. Why this is considered to be very risky compared with stock ownership is incomprehensible.

[165] When buying stock, cash is used—cash that could be sitting in the account earning interest. When buying stock later, you not only earn interest while waiting, you collect the option premium.

[166] When the decline is less than the premium collected.

159

you to use options primarily as a hedging tool that reduces risk. If you are someone who owns a stock portfolio, you can earn profits even when the stock fails to rally and reduce losses when stocks decline by writing puts instead of owning stock—but only if you are willing to accept the whole package which includes limited profits.

Definitions

Assume you find a stock in which you want to take a bullish position. If you decide to sell puts instead of buying shares, you become naked short the puts. This is far from risk free, but it is not the same as selling naked calls (because potential losses are limited with puts. A stock can only fall to zero, capping losses, but a stock can theoretically rise indefinitely). The put has less risk than the investor who buys stock.

When selling puts, your broker requires sufficient assets (in your account) to meet margin requirements.[167]If you have enough cash to pay for the shares (if eventually assigned an exercise notice), then the puts are considered to be 'cash-secured'.

EXAMPLE

When selling five XYZ Jan 50 puts, there is the possibility that you become obligated to purchase 500 shares of XYZ at $50 each. Thus, if you have $25,000 cash in your account, the put sale is "cash secured." Although naked call selling is not allowed in some types of retirement accounts, sell cash-secured puts in an IRA is permitted.

A simple strategy to execute

Covered call writing involves two transactions—buying stock and selling calls. The collar strategy involves three transactions—buying stock, selling calls, and buying puts. Naked put writing is the simplest of all, involving only the sale of put options, and requires paying the fewest commission dollars.

For each put sold, the premium is collected and you accept an obligation to buy 100 shares of stock at the strike price. That obligation is in effect until the option expires (or until you repurchase the same option in a closing transaction).

---

[167] Details of that requirement are discussed later in this chapter. When buying stock, a 50% (or higher) deposit is required. The margin requirement for writing puts is less.

When adopting covered call writing, you have a bullish position: long stock and short calls. You benefit as the option decays over time. If the stock goes higher, you always earn a (limited) profit. If the underlying declines, you may earn a profit, depending on how far the stock declines.

Each of those characteristics is present when selling naked (or cash-secured) puts. Selling puts is a bullish position and you benefit as time passes. If the stock rises, you always make money—either by allowing the put to expire worthless or by buying the put at a lower price. If the underlying asset declines, you may have either a profit or loss.

These two strategies appear to be very similar, and we will discuss just how similar they are in the next chapter.

EXAMPLE

A new retail store opened recently in your neighborhood and it is always crowded. You investigate and like what you see. The merchandise is neatly displayed, the employees are polite and knowledgeable and there are enough cashiers to keep the lines moving. After completing additional research on the company that owns the stores (RETS), you decide to establish a bullish position by selling put options. The stock is currently trading at 21. It is Monday morning (December options expired last Friday). RETS options currently trade with an implied volatility of 36. Let's consider which option (if any) to sell. All data refers to Table 13.1.

RETS has 12 puts listed for trading. We'll consider each in turn. For the purposes of this discussion, assume you are willing to own 500 shares. Thus, you plan to write five put options.[168]

> It is <u>important</u> not to fall into a common trap—and it is a treacherous trap.

When an investor decides to buy 500 shares of stock @ $21 per share, it is understood that the investment is approximately $10,000. If $10,000 is an appropriate amount to invest in this stock at this time, there is seldom any temptation to buy more than 500 shares.

---

[168] Reminder: If you are assigned an exercise notice, you are obligated to purchase 100 shares at the strike price for each put sold.

However, when the put writer sells five puts at a low price—perhaps $50 to $200 per option—unless that investor truly recognizes that each put comes with *an obligation* to purchase 100 shares of stock at a later date — it is easy to conclude that five puts, worth only several hundred dollars , is a tiny trade. Surely (thinks our misguided investor) it is OK to sell 10 or 20 of these puts—after all 20 puts at $50 each is only $1,000 and if buying stock, I'd be investing $10,000. *You must avoid this trap.*

Table 13.1
RETS Puts; Stock 21; IV 36

Month	T	Strike	Bid	Ask	Time Pr	ROI	Ann ROI	DP
Jan	25	17.5	$0.00	$0.10	$0.00	0%	0%	17%
Jan		20.0	$0.35	$0.45	$0.35	2%	24%	6%
Jan		22.5	$1.65	$1.90	$0.15	9%	123%	1%
Feb	53	17.5	$0.05	$0.15	$0.05	0%	2%	17%
Feb		20.0	$0.60	$0.75	$0.60	3%	20%	8%
Feb		22.5	$1.90	$2.15	$0.40	10%	68%	2%
May	116	17.5	$0.30	$0.40	$0.30	1%	4%	18%
May		20.0	$1.00	$1.20	$1.00	5%	16%	10%
May		22.5	$2.35	$2.60	$0.85	13%	39%	4%
Aug	144	17.5	$0.40	$0.50	$0.40	2%	5%	19%
Aug		20.0	$1.15	$1.35	$1.15	6%	14%	10%
Aug		22.5	$2.50	$2.75	$1.00	14%	34%	5%

ROI = Based on the assumption that the put is secured with cash
DP = Downside protection

Please, do not allow this to happen to you. It may be tempting to seek $1,000 by selling 20 puts at $50 each rather than $250 by selling "only" five puts. But you must understand that the market does not always behave as we want it to behave. If the stock suddenly drops below the strike price you may be assigned an exercise notice earlier than expected.[169] If that misguided investor suddenly finds 2,000 shares in the account, $40,000 is required to buy those shares. That is four times as much as the investor wanted to invest in this company—an inefficient way to trade. Imagine how much worse it becomes if a margin call[170] is created because of that involuntary $40,000 stock purchase. If buying 500 shares is the correct position size, then write only five puts.

Selecting the put

Once again, this discussion is from the perspective of an experienced option trader. Jan 17½ put is not a consideration. First, there is no bid. Second, even if you were able to sell this put for $0.05 it is not a good idea to write options for such a low price. It is not worthwhile to tie up your assets[171] with so little to gain.

I can sell the Jan 20 put and collect $0.35 per share. If the option expires worthless, the $35 profit represents a 1.8% (23% annualized) ROI.[172] This is nothing spectacular, but it is a reasonable return for a four-week investment.

The Jan 22½ put is in-the-money by 1.50 points. Thus the $1.65 option premium represents $1.50 in intrinsic value but *only $0.15 in time value*. The time value represents the profit potential for this trade if the option remains ITM when expiration arrives. Selling this option offers little downside protection because the break-even price ($20.85) is only $0.15 lower than when owning stock. That is not an attractive proposition. In fact, it is not much better than buying stock. But it is enough better (I collect $15 time premium per option and avoid paying interest to carry the stock) to consider as an alternative to buying stock. I am not primarily interested in buying stock and this is the wrong put to write. I prefer a chance to earn a profit even when the stock does not rally. Writing ITM puts is strictly a one-way bullish play, and not for me. The general plan

---

[169] When a put becomes deep in-the-money (stock significantly below the strike price), there is an incentive for the put owner to exercise (this is very different from calls, where there is no incentive to exercise early). Why? Many times a put owner also owns stock. By exercising, the put owner releases the cash tied up in the position (long stock + long put) and interest can be earned on that cash. When the put is deep ITM, there is little to be gained from owning the put and stock. The put served its purpose in preventing a huge loss, and can be exercised (one of the rare times you may want to exercise an option) because it is no longer needed.

[170] If you receive a margin call, you must make a rapid deposit of funds into your account. Some brokers give you 10 minutes; others give you a full week. If unable to meet the margin call, your broker closes positions until your margin requirement is small enough that you can meet it. Avoid margin calls.

[171] When selling cash-secured puts, cash is tied up in the position. Even using margin, there is too little to gain for this trade to make sense. Do not sell options for nickels and dimes ($0.05 or $0.10).

[172] For each option sold, $2,000 cash is required to make the sale cash secured. But the $35 premium can be used, making the net investment $1,965.

when selling option premium is to earn a profit most of the time, without predicting market direction.

When writing covered calls, we considered the maximum possible profit, even when it is an unlikely occurrence. We'll do the same here. If the stock rises above the strike price and the option expires worthless, I keep the entire $165 per option, or 9% ROI, as profit. And that is an attractive prospect for the aggressively bullish investor, not for the market-neutral trader.

Writing in-the-money (ITM) puts with little time premium is seldom attractive to the naked put seller. Stocks do not move higher just because you are bullish. To increase the probability of making money, write options that are ATM or OTM. Do you prefer the higher probability of a winning trade or the higher profit potential of correctly predicting stock direction? That is the choice being made with every put written.

I believe in making money steadily over time and prefer to write OTM puts rather than ITM puts. But, the purpose of this discussion is to demonstrate the pros and cons of each potential candidate and to enable you to think through the process logically and choose an option that is appropriate for your investment style.

The Feb 17½ put has far too little premium (Table 13.1). The Feb 20 put can be sold for $0.60. For traders who find this to be an attractive candidate, I suggest entering the sell order, asking $0.65. Those extra nickels add up—when you can get them. If this put eventually expires worthless, ROI is almost 3% (20% annualized). When compared with writing the Jan 20 put, the Feb 20 put provides a bit more downside protection, and a bit less annualized ROI.

The Feb 22½ put has more time premium ($40 vs. $15) than Jan, but it is still an ITM put option, which does not fit my investment objective: a higher probability of earning a profit with a non-directional play. For an investor who loves this stock, this option is a reasonable choice.

May and Aug options expire in four and seven months, respectively. As is always the case, a longer option lifetime provides a greater time premium. That higher time premium affords additional downside protection, a reduced annualized return, and the ability to spend less time with your option-writing program.[173]

Take a look at the May 17½ put. That is a very safe put to sell. By that I mean there is little chance the stock will fall below the break-even point (17.20). The probability of keeping the $30 (for each put) is high. So is this

---

[173] Trading less often saves time and commission dollars, but that does not give you permission to get lazy. Do not ignore your positions. Monitor at least weekly to verify that no adjustments are necessary—and that includes closing the position to lock in a nice profit or prevent further losses.

a good put to sell? No. If you look at the annualized return, it is only 4.5%—less than you can earn from Treasury bills[174], certificates of deposit and even many savings accounts. This may be a relatively safe investment, but there is a chance of losing money and you could get the same return (in the world of 2008) with no risk. Do not consider selling this put. The same is true for the Aug 17½ put. The only way this put becomes a satisfactory trade occurs when the put can be repurchased for a quick profit. If you hold through expiration, the less-than-Treasury-bill profit is simply not worth the risk. If you get a chance to repurchase quickly then the annualized return becomes acceptable.[175]

In this scenario, most put writers opt for a put with a 20 strike. My choice is to sell the Jan or Feb. Others may prefer to trade less frequently and opt for the May or Aug 20 put. Those who are more bullish and less concerned with downside protection may choose a put with a 22½ strike.

Bottom line: None of these puts makes an outstanding choice, but for an investor interested in owning this stock, these are acceptable puts to write. Why use this as an example? Because some stocks do not offer good put-writing opportunities—and you should be aware of that.

Why write naked puts?

Writing puts is a bullish strategy for both long-term investors and short-term traders. It can be used to achieve either of two very different investment objectives:

- Profit. You have a bullish outlook for a stock or index and expect the price of put options to decline as the stock rises (or time passes). Your plan is to buy (to close) the put option at a much lower price or perhaps allow it to expire worthless. When this plan works, the reward is a nice, but limited profit. Traders or investors who hold positions for a short time can benefit by adopting this strategy.

- Buy stock at a discount. If the put option is in-the-money when expiration arrives, you are assigned an exercise notice and become obligated to buy a stock you want to own[176] at a discount to today's price. This is an intelligent method by which an investor gradually adds positions to a long-term portfolio. Of course, you do not always

---

[174] This is no longer true. In 2013, interest rates are near zero. However, they will not always be low, and this is a reminder to consider alternative investments when looking at low rates of return.
[175] There is no way to know if you will be able to do that. This trade is not recommended.
[176] If you are a long-term investor who does not want to own this stock at the strike price (minus the put premium), recognize selling puts is most efficient for traders who want to accumulate stock over time.

buy the stock. That is just fine. If the option expires worthless, you keep the option premium as a consolation prize. Remember: it is normal to want to pay $46 for stock when it is trading at $50. If you sell a put you may find yourself paying that $46 when the stock has declined all the way to $40.

EXAMPLE

WXY is trading at $30 and you want to pay no more than $27 per share. If you collect $3 in premium when writing a put struck at[177] 30, you buy at your target price—if you are eventually assigned an exercise notice. The shares are bought at the strike ($30), but you collected $3 in premium, and the net cost is $27. If not assigned an exercise notice, then the $300 premium is your consolation prize profit.

If you want to buy shares at $27 after expenses, then collect an extra 5 or 10 cents when selling the put. Be sure you understand that if you try to get that additional premium, you may miss the trade—and a profitable opportunity.

Knowing you require a premium of $3 or more, you must decide which expiration months are acceptable. Obviously, it is best to sell the near term put for $3, but when the put premium is too low, you have some choices: 1) wait for the stock to decline and the put premium to reach your price; or 2) choose a longer-term put. That is a personal trade decision.

Some investors are willing to write a put with a six-month (or longer) lifetime if it allows them an opportunity to purchase stock at their price, while others patiently wait for the stock to come in (trade lower). Do the math and decide if any puts are appropriate to write.

If willing to buy stock but prefer to earn a trading profit, write a put that meets your requirements for profit potential—both in dollars and ROI. In this scenario you prefer not to be assigned and not to buy stock. But, if you are assigned an exercise notice, it is an acceptable result. Note that the trader can always buy the option that was sold earlier, canceling the obligation to purchase shares. The point of being willing to buy stock is to allow for the possibility of being assigned. If you seek a trading

---

[177] 'Struck at' is the same as saying 'with a strike price that equals

profit, it becomes acceptable to collect less than $3 per option.

Bottom line: When selling a put option, the cash is yours to keep, no matter what else happens. However, you accept obligations; specifically the put owner has the right to force you to buy 100 shares of stock at a specific price for a limited time. As is the case when you sell call options, you have no say as to whether you are eventually assigned an exercise notice—that decision, and the timing of that decision, rests entirely with the option owner.

When the position is held through expiration, there are only two possible outcomes, depending on the price of the underlying stock. Each of those outcomes accomplishes one of your original goals (you earn a profit or you buy stock at a discount).

> **NOTE:** If you buy stock at the strike price, you own the shares at a price that looked attractive at the time the puts were sold. However, if assigned an exercise notice, the stock is obviously priced below the strike price and the premium earned may not be sufficient to prevent a loss.[178]

Making trading decisions

Before trading, certain decisions must be made. First and foremost is choosing the underlying asset. Remember, put writing is a bullish strategy. A decision to sell cash-secured puts should be based on these criteria:

- A stock (or index) on which you are bullish. If you are investor, it must also be a stock you are willing (or eager) to own. It is not smart to write puts on some random stock just because you find the option premium attractive.

  > **NOTE:** Traditional buy and hold investors make money when their stocks increase in value. You, the uncovered put writer, also make money any time the stock goes higher. However, you earn a profit when the stock remains relatively unchanged or decreases by a small amount—and the buy and hold investor cannot do that. It is far easier to find a stock that 'doesn't decline' than it is to find a stock that 'must go higher'. But do not choose stocks randomly because profitably selling puts is not that easy.

- The price you want to pay for stock, if assigned.

---

[178] If stock is priced below [strike minus premium], then the trade is losing money

Next step: deciding which put option to write

- Choosing the put strike price

  o How much profit potential to seek. The higher the premium, the greater the profit potential.

  o How much risk to take? That determines how many puts can be sold.

  o How badly do you want to buy stock? Farther out-of-the-money puts are more likely to expire worthless.

  o Choosing the expiration date. How long do you want to own the position?

  o Options with shorter lifetimes give the seller less potential profit *per trade*. However a higher annualized return is possible along with less protection against a market decline.

Bottom line: There is no "best" put to write. Each investor has a different investment objective, risk tolerance and comfort zone. Choose a put that provides an opportunity to earn a return that meets or exceeds your minimum objective. It may seem obvious, but there is no reason to own any position when the potential reward does not justify the risk. I've been asked many times to tell a trader what constitutes a 'reasonable' profit expectation when writing naked puts (or covered calls). I suggest that the average investor should consider 2-3% per month as a reasonable *target* when writing ITM calls or OTM puts. Do not expect to meet that target every time.

When trading options on more conservative stocks, 1.5% per month is an appropriate target. Aggressive investors may decide to aim higher, but when targeting 4-5% per month,[179] you will find yourself trading volatile stocks and thus accepting additional risk.

Some option choices (writing an OTM covered call or selling an ITM cash-secured put) allow for the possibility of earning capital gains if the stock rallies. However, when looking at profit potential, I suggest that a

---

[179] Keep this in mind. While a 2 percent monthly return is fine when markets are calm, you may find yourself aiming for higher returns when markets are more volatile. That is OK. The warning is not to trade high-volatility stocks just because they are high volatility stocks. Do research and only adopt bullish positions for stocks that give you a good reason to be bullish.

favorable price movement should be considered a bonus profit, rather than part of your target.[180]

Calculations

The maximum profit (equal to the put premium collected) is earned when the put expires worthless. When discussing covered call writing, the profit calculation is straightforward. You have a profit when the current position value exceeds the cost (cost of stock minus option premium). When writing uncovered puts, nothing is bought and determining the position cost is far less obvious. I consider the cash put aside to purchase stock (if assigned an exercise notice) as "the investment cost." That equals the strike minus the option premium.

EXAMPLE

WXY is trading at $31 and you sell four WXY Dec 30 puts described above and collect $320 for each, making your break-even point $26.80. To be cash-secured, you must set aside $12,000 to pay for 400 shares of WXY at $30 per share. But you can use the premium ($320 x 4) and thus the investment is the $10,720 cash set aside. And there is a small bonus: when selling puts, cash is deposited into your account and your broker sometimes pays a reasonable rate of interest on that cash.[181]

Assume expiration day arrives, the option is out-of-the-money and expires worthless. Your profit is $1,280 (plus earned interest, less commissions) divided by the investment ($10,720). If commissions and interest cancel each other, then the profit is 11.9%. In this example, there is no annualized ROI to calculate because the time to expiration was not relevant.

If you decide to be more aggressive and write puts on margin, then you are using leverage and have the potential to earn (or lose) a much higher return on your investment.

Assume the margin requirement for the above trade is $3,280, and your profit is $1,280. Your investment is the $3,280 you put up to meet the margin requirement, and the ROI is 39%. This is an outstanding rate of return. But keep in mind that using leverage is a two-way street and it is possible to lose more than

---

[180] Example: Stock is $33 and you write a call struck at 35. If the stock rises above $35 and you are assigned, look at that $200 gain from $33 to $35 as a bonus profit. The 'target' profit should equal the option premium.
[181] Not in the world of 2013. But one day they will once again pay interest.

your original margin requirement of $3,280. Trading with leverage increases both risk and reward and it is not for everyone. That is why I recommend selling puts only when secured with cash.

Margin

Although I recommend that option beginners avoid using margin,[182] once you gain experience and have confidence that options can be used conservatively to generate profits, you may become more comfortable using margin. And more experienced traders may already use margin. It is relatively simple to calculate the current margin requirements (though some brokers have different requirements and margin requirements change over time).

When writing naked puts, if you choose *not* to be cash backed, your broker requires a deposit as collateral for the position. The *initial* margin requirement is determined in the following manner (with a minimum of $250):

- 20% of the price of the underlying stock[183] plus

- The premium collected from the option sale minus

- The amount the put option is out-of-the money.

EXAMPLE

Stock price is 28. Sell 10 Nov 25 puts at $1.00. Note that the options are out of the money by 3 points. The margin requirement for selling each put is:

20% of stock price = $2,800 x 0.2 ($560) plus the premium collected ($100) minus the out-of-the-money amount ($300)

Margin requirement = 560 + 100 − 300 = $360 per put, or $3,600 total.

To be cash secured, $24,000 cash is required.[184]

Tips for investors (people with a long-term approach to investing)

- Maintain an updated stocks-to-buy list and the target buying price.

---

[182] Many option transactions require opening a margin account. However, you are not obligated to 'use' margin.
[183] The requirement is less (15 instead of 20%) for certain broad-based indexes.
[184] $25,000 to buy 1,000 shares at 25, less $1,000 collected in option premium.

- Know which strike prices are candidates for put selling.

- Determine the minimum premium to buy stock at the target price, if assigned. For example, if a 25-strike put is $2, the potential stock purchase price is $23.

- If you are a proponent of technical analysis (and even if you are not) be aware of support and resistance levels for stocks on your list. Consider writing a put option when the stock price is just above support.[185]

- Monitor market prices of put options under consideration. To avoid missing a buying opportunity, and especially if you do not have time to constantly monitor the market, enter an order[186] to sell specific puts at a limit price.

  NOTE: Do not enter too many such orders at one time because a severe market sell-off may result in too many filled orders.[187]

Tips for traders (people who hold positions for a relatively short time)

- Maintain a list of stocks on which you are considering making a bullish trade.

- When timing is right, sell an appropriately priced put (strike price suits your needs).

- Pay attention to support levels and be prepared to write put options when the stock is just above support. If the stock breaks support, be ready to close the position.

- Monitor put prices. When profit potential and risk/reward profile look attractive, enter an order to sell puts.

Other considerations when entering a trade

EXAMPLE

---

[185] If the stock breaks support, you may decide to take a quick, small loss and close the position. Better yet, if support holds, the premium is earned as the profit.
[186] An order good for one day is best, but if you lack the time, make each order good for one week and reevaluate the situation over the weekend. GTC (good 'til cancelled) orders are inappropriate for opening option trades because conditions change and you may no longer want to buy stock. This also eliminates the need to remember to cancel some orders.
[187] In a declining market, by not entering all orders at one time, a trader can scale into his/her positions at lower prices— if the decline continues.

YXW, a reasonably volatile stock, is currently trading near $30 per share. Accept the following four statements as a given:

1. You are an investor interested in buying YXW at $27 or a trader who is bullish on YXW and interested in opening a long position near current levels.

2. It is Monday immediately following March expiration. April expiration is four weeks away and May expiration is an additional five weeks in the future.

3. Apr 30 put is $1.25 bid. Apr 27½ put is $0.55 bid

4. May 30 put is $2.00 bid. May 27½ put is $0.95 bid

Investors

Sell the Apr 27½ put at $55 per contract.

If the stock is above the strike price when expiration day arrives, you earn a profit of $55, or approximately 2% (of the $2,695 investment[188] when the put is cash backed).

If the stock is below the strike price when the market closes on expiration day, you are assigned an exercise notice, obligating you to buy stock. The net cost is $26.95 per share, which is below your target price.

Either result is acceptable.

Traders

Sell either the Apr 30 put or the Apr 27½ put.

Choose the Apr 30 put if confident the stock is moving higher. You may earn $125 (4.34% ROI)[189] if the stock remains above the strike price.

Choose the less risky (and less rewarding) Apr 27½ put when mildly bullish. The maximum profit potential is not exciting ($55), but there is an excellent chance to earn that profit.

May puts are reasonable candidates for writing, when additional protection is more important than ROI. Most traders reject this choice.

Selling an April put provides the opportunity to earn a quick profit if the stock performs as predicted.[190]

---

[188] Strike price ($2,750) less the $55 premium
[189] $125 profit, $2,875 investment
[190] Most traders go long and short based on their market expectations, and options can support a trader's needs. Long-term investors make fewer predictions, although everyone likes to buy stock (or sell puts) when they believe the stock is going higher.

Disadvantages of put writing

From a trader's point of view, profit potential is limited. By accepting much greater downside risk, stock buyers may earn a very substantial profit.

Advantages of put writing

Profits can be earned even when the stock price does not increase. Time is the ally of the put writer, especially when the stock remains near its current price level. When choosing a lower strike price (an OTM put), money may be earned even when the stock declines below the strike price (by less than the premium). That is a new experience for a bullish trader and should more than compensate for limiting profit potential—unless the trader is a gifted stock picker.

> **NOTE:** As a trader looking to earn a profit as quickly as possible, there is no reason to hold a position until expiration. You may elect to buy the put any time you are satisfied with the profit or are no longer bullish on the stock. Investors can also take advantage of the early exit strategy, but for a different reason. The two main reasons for closing the trade are a) when the option price is so low that there is little to be gained by holding, or b) the option you plan to write next (after expiration) is attractively priced now and it makes sense to pay a small price to buy the option previously sold, freeing yourself to sell the new option (This combination of trades is 'rolling the position', previously discussed in Chapter 11). Of course, you can always sell the new, attractively priced put option first,[191] but that involves extra risk.

Exiting the trade

Knowing when to exit a trade is often as crucial as knowing when to enter, but it deserves less emphasis when adopting the strategy of writing naked put options.

Investors seldom close these positions before expiration because being assigned an exercise notice is a viable alternative for them. I recommend that investors consider closing a position that has worked well and the put can be bought at a low price. Of course, "low price" is a relative term. I suggest $0.15 to $0.20 for options with less than one month of remaining

---

[191] This is NOT the same situation as with a covered call in which selling the new option leaves you with a naked call position, which is forbidden by many brokers. When the new put is sold without buying back the old put, position size (and risk) is doubled. Not covering those inexpensive, soon-to-expire options is a losing strategy over the long term, (unfortunately, I know that from experience) but it is allowed.

lifetime.[192] I seldom allow an option to decline to $0.10 without covering. But that is my comfort zone and I urge each reader to find his own. There is little profit potential in waiting to collect the last few nickels on the trade.[193] I'm happy to take profits and reduce risk. Do not pay a price when it seems too high, but do not be greedy.

Traders close their profitable positions more frequently. The decision is often based on a trader's outlook for the stock in the immediate future. When considering whether a specific set of conditions is suitable for writing naked put options, each individual must make the final trade/no trade decision. The following discussion is designed to give investors from different backgrounds a better feel for how to think about the writing of naked put options.

Because each reader enters the options world from a different place with different levels of experience, it is worthwhile to consider how to approach a trade—taking that experience into consideration. Let's consider how writing naked put options fits into individual investment styles.

Stock UVW is trading at $41. It is shortly after the July expiration and the Aug 40 put can be sold for $1.00.

Thoughts of the experienced put-selling investor

I've been watching UVW and it is approaching my target purchase price ($39). I'm going to write the front month puts for a buck ($1.00). I will have a good trade. I'll own 400 shares at $39, or I'll keep the premium and walk away with $400.

Thoughts of the first-time seller of naked put options

I'd like to own 400 shares of UVW stock. I'm a bit nervous about selling put options because my broker doesn't think it is a good idea. But I've been reading an excellent options book and I'm convinced the strategy is much more conservative (and profitable) than my broker realizes. If I proceed with my plan to sell four of these puts, it is going to be a nervous four weeks as I wait for expiration. But, I must remember that only two things can happen. In four weeks I'll either own 400 shares at $39 per share, or I'll have a profit of $400 (less commissions). Both of these alternatives appeal to me.

Of course, I could simply bid $39 for the stock, and there is a chance I'll buy it. But if the stock rallies, as I believe it will, I will not be able to get the stock at my price. If I sell the put option, at least I'll have $400 as a consolation prize if I'm right about the stock.

---

[192] If you sell low-priced options, then this cannot apply to you.
[193] It is prudent and good risk management to cover (repurchase) your short puts when selling new puts.

I'm going to make this trade tomorrow morning!

Thoughts of the experienced trader, but 1st time naked put seller

UVW is $41 and approaching support at 40.50. I'm convinced that taking a long position in the stock is the right move. I believe the stock moves higher within several months. Of course, I can simply buy stock, but if I understand correctly, there are advantages to selling put options. I know my profit is limited to $100 (the premium) for each put. But in return for limiting my profit, my breakeven point drops from the current price of $41 to $39. I like the idea of having that extra cushion.

Because I'm not sure the stock will run higher immediately, by selling the puts, the passage of time becomes my friend. If I buy stock now, I must use cash. If UVW remains locked in a narrow range near its support level, I'll gain nothing. But, if I sell the put option, I not only collect time premium, but I can keep my cash and earn interest on that.

Yes, put selling seems to be a good idea in this scenario and I'm going to jump into this strategy first thing tomorrow morning. I intend to make a bit extra and will offer to sell those puts at $1.05 because the market is $1.00 to $1.20.

Thoughts of the trader with experience as a put-writer

The UVW chart looks good here, but the stock may stay in a trading range before breaking out to the upside. I've seen this happen too many times. Instead of buying stock, I'll write these August 40 puts for $1. Sure, it limits my profit potential, but I want to make money if the stock trades in a narrow range.

If the stock has not moved much in a month, I'll decide whether to sell the September 40 puts or buy the stock. But for now, I'm writing the August puts. I'll sacrifice the chance to make a large profit in return for a better chance to make some profit.

What can go wrong when you sell naked puts?

Like any stock market investment, an investor with a long position runs the risk of seeing the stock price decline. Writing puts gives the trader a long delta position.[194] The discussion of delta is postponed until Chapter 15). Thus, a significant decline usually results in a loss.

What can be done to minimize losses if the stock moves against you (lower)? Owning a hedged (reduced risk) position (sell put spreads instead of naked puts; these spreads are described in Chapter 17) limits losses and prevents a disaster.

---

[194] Long delta is similar to owning shares and often results in profits when the stock rises and losses when it declines.

Let's consider repairing a position that is not working.

Repair strategies (risk management)

In the example above, assume you decided to write the YXW Apr 27½ put at $0.55. Within two weeks, YXW has declined to $24 per share. You have several choices, depending on your priorities:

- If content to own the stock at $26.95, risking a further decline, do nothing because no repair is necessary.

- Most traders understand that holding losing positions with the hope of recovering losses is not intelligent. To cut losses now, buy back the put and accept a loss on this trade, acknowledging that every trade cannot be a winner.

- To own a position in YXW, but with less the risk of additional losses, buy back the Apr 27½ put and simultaneously[195] (or immediately thereafter) sell a new put with a lower strike price. Most of the time the new put comes with a more distant expiration.

EXAMPLE

Let's say you decide to buy four Apr 27½ puts (to close) and sell four Jul 25 puts—or perhaps Oct 25 or Oct 22½ puts—to open. Now that you own a position in YXW, there are two paths to consider. Decide which is more important for you:

a) Gain protection against further loss. Bring in as much cash as possible by selling an option with a higher premium. This may lock in a loss, but that should not be a deterrent.[196]

b) Give yourself the best chance to turn the position profitable over time, consistent with accepting reasonable risk. This entails greater downside risk, but may be a suitable choice when you retain a bullish outlook on YXW. Unfortunately, too many investors automatically make this choice. *It is not a good idea* to try to convert every losing trade into a winner. Pick your spots carefully and decide if this stock is one you still want to own today. Sometimes it is best to salvage what you can and find a better place to invest money.

Two weeks passed since the put sale and the YXW is $24 per share.

---

[195] By entering a spread order (to buy one option and sell another)
[196] Taking care of risk comes first. Earning profits is second.

176

- Apr 27½ put is offered at $4

- Jul 25 put is $2.25 bid

- Oct 22½ put is $2.00 bid

- Oct 25 put is $3.10 bid

What should you do? There is no "right" choice when rolling the position. It is reasonable to buy the April 27 ½ put to close and to sell (to open) any of the three puts listed (or others expiring in January).

Choose the option that fits your comfort zone. Be certain you want to own the new position and do not force the trade just to do something. Repeat: do not believe it is necessary to force a trade. Exiting with a loss is often the best possible decision. If you do not know which position you prefer to own (i.e., which put to sell), then it is probably best to get out of the trade and move on to another.

If you are more concerned with limiting losses if the stock continues to decline, then writing the Oct 22½ put makes sense. On the negative side, you own a position with more than five months remaining before expiration day. On the other hand, the Oct 22½ put is out-of-the-money (currently) with *a chance* to expire worthless. This provides an increased possibility for recovering some of your loss.

Let's look at the numbers when October expiration arrives:

- If YXW is above $22.50, the put expires worthless. You collected $55 for the initial sale, paid $400 to repurchase the put and collected $200 for selling the Oct put. All in all, you paid $145 to establish the position. You have no remaining position (the puts expired), and the loss is $580 ($145 x 4). That is not too bad, considering you went long YXW when it was near $30 and watched it drop to $24. You managed risk well and cut those losses by rolling the position to October.

- If YXW is below $22.50, you are assigned an exercise notice and buy shares at $22.50 (the strike). Subtract from that price the amount collected for selling the put (negative $1.45 in this instance),[197] and the shares cost $23.95 each. This is considerably better than the $26.95 the shares would have cost if you held and did nothing.

You own the shares. What next? You have three choices. Sell stock and eliminate this loser from your portfolio; hold stock and hope it recovers; or write covered calls. The third choice is recommended, but only if willing to

---

[197] Collected $55, paid $200. Net cost, $145.

own stock. Covered call writing was discussed at length in Chapters 9 through 11.

If you are still bullish, but prefer to hedge the position to reduce the chances of further losses, consider selling the Oct 25 put (instead of the Oct 22 ½ put) at $3.10. It costs $90 to roll the position.[198] Because you collected $55 for the initial sale, the total debit is $35 cash (plus commissions).

When October expiration arrives:

- If YXW is above $25, the put expires worthless and the loss is only $35 per 100 shares. That is an excellent result, considering that YXW declined so rapidly.

- IF YXW is below $25 you are assigned an exercise notice and pay $25 for stock. The cost basis is now $25.35 per share.

- Because the stock was trading at $24 when rolled, it was reasonable to expect to be assigned when expiration day arrived. As mentioned above, when assigned, writing covered calls is the recommended course for traders who want to own stock at its current price.

- Another alternative is to roll the Oct 25 put to a Nov or Dec position. Again, this is recommended only when you want to maintain a bullish position in the stock.

What to do when expiration day arrives

If the puts are safely out-of-the-money (and you have not previously covered by paying $0.05), do nothing. Allow them to expire worthless. That cancels all obligations and the next day the market is open for business (or any time thereafter) you may reinvest the cash kept in reserve.[199]

> **NOTE:** When the put you plan to write next is attractively priced today, consider buying the worthless put, paying $0.05 or less,[200] to take advantage of the attractively priced put. If the put you sold appears to be worthless,[201] it is not necessary to wait until expiration Friday. Any time your short put can be bought cheaply it is a good idea to close that position. It is not necessary to collect that final 5 or 10 cents on each option

---

[198] Pay $4 for the Apr put and sell the Oct put @ $3.10. Cost $90.
[199] The cash you were going to use to buy stock if assigned an exercise notice.
[200] Options trade in penny increments.
[201] Stocks do make unexpected moves and waiting for expiration to collect the last few pennies occasionally backfires.

written. You are then ready to sell a new put, if an opportunity presents itself.

When maintaining a list of potential investments, the weekend after expiration is the ideal time to select top candidates in preparation for trading the following Monday morning.

If the puts sold earlier are in-the-money, you have three reasonable alternatives:

a) Buy the puts and exit the trade. It can be either a profit or loss, depending on the price paid for the puts.

b) Do nothing and be assigned an exercise notice. You now own stock and may decide to write covered calls.

c) Roll the position. Buy the put sold earlier and write a put option expiring on a later date. In the repair strategy described above, the roll was initiated to reduce risk. In this scenario, the position is rolled to maintain a position going forward.

NOTE: Do not roll the position just to have something to do. If you are not satisfied with the premium available, close the position. Forcing a trade is not a good strategy. Roll a position only when the profit potential is satisfactory when compared with risk.

Writing covered calls after being assigned an exercise notice:

If the put is in-the-money at expiration, you can expect to be assigned an exercise notice. If the option is ITM by only a penny or two, there is a tiny chance you will not be assigned. Be aware of the possibility, but be surprised if it happens to you. Maintaining ownership of the stock is acceptable, but unless very bullish, it is usually more profitable to write covered calls (Chapters 9 through 11).

In the examples above, October expiration arrived and 400 shares of YXW stock were put to you.[202] Your cost is $23.95 in the first scenario or $25.35 in the second. You can write YXW Nov 25 or Dec 25 calls, collect a premium, and perhaps the whole trade will turn out to be profitable. But that requires holding stock that has performed poorly. If that makes you uncomfortable, there is no need to invest in this company. Sell the stock and move on. Not every position has to be profitable.

Most traders believe their primary concern is to make money. I do not. If you follow the strategies in this book (especially Part III in which all losses

---

[202] You were assigned an exercise notice.

are limited and the probability of profitable trades is high) you earn profits frequently. The primary consideration should be to avoid large losses. If successful in achieving that, you will be a successful trader.

The method taught so far increases the probability of having winning trades, but they are basically bullish strategies. If the market tumbles or if you find stock selection to be challenging (as I do), then you may do better trading a diversified portfolio. That can be accomplished by owning exchange traded funds (ETFs) rather than individual stocks. Or, you can trade options on indexes, such as the Standard & Poor's 500, the Dow Jones Industrial Average or the Russell 2000.

If you are eager to learn more, then the material in Part III will be of interest. Before moving on, the next chapter provides a much clearer picture of options and how they work. It contains information that every option trader ought to fully understand, but few bother. The knowledge gained may not increase profits on every trade. However, the material is necessary for anyone who wants to understand how options work.

Writing naked puts is a strategy suitable for most investors, even though many investment professionals consider it risky. It is more conservative than owning stocks—and almost all professionals consider it a prudent strategy.

One of the great advantages of writing puts for bullish investors and traders is the increased likelihood of earning a profit, compared with buying stock. Even though potential profit is limited, the fact that there are many winning trades compensates.

One word of caution: naked put writing is a bullish strategy and does not do well in bear markets. Never sell too many puts. Remember: if assigned an exercise notice, you will buy 100 shares for each put sold.

Happy put writing!

QUIZ 13

1. When writing naked puts, the potential loss is unlimited. **TRUE or FALSE**

2. What makes a put sale "cash-secured"?

3. It is much easier to close (hopefully for a nice profit) a naked put position than a covered call position. **TRUE or FALSE**

4. You are considering buying 400 shares of stock at $50 per share, investing $20,000. If you sell 10 puts instead of buying those 400 shares, and if you collect $100 for each put, you have far less risk because the investment is worth only $1,000. **TRUE or FALSE**

5. When it comes to selling naked puts, it doesn't matter which stock you choose. If the market rises, you do well; if it sinks, you fare poorly. **TRUE or FALSE**

QUIZ 13 Answers

1. **False.** The loss may be large, but it is limited. The stock can fall no lower than zero, and, if forced to buy stock at the strike price, the most you can lose is the strike price x 100 less premium collected.

2. Having enough cash in your account to buy the shares, if and when assigned an exercise notice.

3. **True.** To close, you merely purchase the put. To close the covered call position, you must buy the call and sell the stock, and that involves twice as many transactions.

4. **False.** By selling 10 puts, it is possible that you find yourself owning 1,000 shares (instead of 400) — and that $50,000 worth of risk.

5. **False.** Volatile stocks are much riskier than others. Some stocks have news pending and that news may result in the stock gapping much lower. Pay close attention to the underlying. It is important and you must choose carefully.

Chapter 14

Equivalent Positions

This chapter provides tools to help traders gain both a trading edge and significantly more important—a knowledge edge. There is nothing in this chapter that is absolutely essential when learning to trade options. However this information will put money in your pocket and provide a better understanding of the versatility of options. If you decide to skip this chapter now because you are in a hurry to read about specific strategies that can be used immediately, please return to this chapter later.

> **NOTE:** Trading without this knowledge is inefficient. Your ability to use options effectively will be significantly hindered. Your education will lack cohesiveness—that 'something' that ties it all together.

There are two very practical reasons why this chapter should be of interest:

- Trading equivalent positions occasionally provides an opportunity to make more profitable trades.

- Trading equivalent positions provides frequent opportunity to reduce commissions. That alone makes it worthwhile.

When trading equity options, there are always choices. You can trade calls, puts and/or the underlying asset. When building a specific position to trade, most of the time, the straightforward path is best: buy what you want to own and sell what you want to be short. If you want a specific option position (such as a covered call), then go ahead and buy stock and write the specific calls you have in mind. There is nothing complicated about that. But sometimes it is possible—and advantageous—to construct an equivalent position that uses different options, but provides the same profit/loss. In the case of covered calls, selling a put option with the same strike price and expiration date as the call is equivalent to the covered call (details below). There is no reason to buy or sell stock.

For our purposes, when two positions are equivalent, it means that each position makes or loses the same dollar amount at every possible price for the underlying.

By taking the time to understand the ideas described below, you discover that any position involving options can be transformed into a different, equivalent position. Such positions are called synthetic equivalents, or synthetics, for short. You may not trade synthetics often, but some of the more popular option strategies (covered call writing and collars) have synthetic alternatives that are more efficient to trade. That means it is easier to adopt those strategies when using synthetics. As a bonus, commissions can be reduced by trading synthetically equivalent positions, and those savings go directly to your bottom line.[203]

Learning about equivalent positions is NOT too sophisticated. Nor does it require too much effort. There is nothing complicated about choosing to own a position that is essentially the same as your desired position, but *appears* to differ. All that is required is for a trader to recognize that the alternative trade is available.

> **NOTE:** If you have difficulty with algebra, do not be intimidated. Beneath each equation is an explanation in easy-to-understand language of the argument behind the formula. Readers who prefer to understand why certain things are true can follow the logic and find proof that supports the conclusions.

Abbreviations

S = number of shares (in round lots, or multiples of 100) of stock
C = quantity or call options
P = quantity of put options
P_{50} or C_{15} = a put struck at 50 or a call struck at 15
P_H or P_L = a put with higher (H) or lower (L) strike price
R = collar position
B = box spread (described later in this chapter)

The basic equation: S = C - P

This single equation represents the foundation of option theory.[204] Let's look at this equation from three perspectives:

When P and C represent the same underlying asset and have the same expiration date and strike price, then the three basic synthetic equivalents are:

---

[203] I often encourage traders not to worry about commission expenses when first getting started. However, there is no reason to waste money.

[204] This is a simplification. There is another factor involved (cost of money and interest rates). There is no reason to add that complication. For our purposes (as a retail trader), this factor can be ignored. The information is widely available, if you are interested.

1) S = C − P

Buying 100 shares of stock is equivalent to buying one call and selling one put. For example, if you buy five XYX Apr 60 calls and sell five XYX Apr 60 puts, your position behaves exactly as if you own 500 shares of XYX stock.

Proof

Assume you buy one XYX Apr 60 call and sell one XYZ Apr 60 put and hold this position until the options expire. When the market closes for trading on expiration day, if XYX last trades above 60, the put expires worthless and the calls are exercised. Thus, the position is long 100 shares. If the stock last trades below 60, the call expires worthless and when assigned an exercise notice on the ITM put, the position is again long 100 shares.

Thus, at any stock price, the position is equivalent to owning 100 shares. But, there is a risk (see sidebar describing pin risk).

2) C = S + P

Buying one call option is equivalent to buying 100 shares of stock and buying one put. Some investors who own stock choose to purchase put options as insurance against a catastrophic decline in the price of the shares. These investors can accomplish the same investment objectives by owning the equivalent position. That means there is no need to own the stock *and* the put. Instead, owning *only* the call option with the same expiration and strike price as the put is the equivalent position.

That position (long put, long stock) is a synthetic call and is often referred to as a "married put."

Proof

Assume you own one ABC Nov 40 call. If the shares last traded above 40 when expiration arrived, exercise the call to buy 100 shares at the strike price. If the stock last traded below 40, allow the call to expire worthless and there is no position.

If instead, you own 100 shares plus one Nov 40 put, consider what happens when expiration arrives. If the stock last traded above 40, allow the put option to expire worthless and you still own 100 shares. If the stock last traded below 40, exercise the Nov 40 put, thereby selling 100 shares. That leaves no remaining position.

Thus, at any stock price you have the same position. There is no pin risk when you *own* the options and have control over the exercise decision.

3) P = C – S

Buying one put option is equivalent to buying one call and selling 100 shares.[205]

If $-P = S - C$.
Then $+P = C - S$.

A covered call is $S - C$ (long stock, short call) and is also called a "short synthetic put." Therefore, a covered call is the same as $-P$. Instead of owning a covered call, you can own the equivalent position by selling one put with the same strike and expiration as the call. These are equivalent strategies, but the minor advantages of selling naked puts (reduced commissions, ease of closing the position)[206] makes that method the better choice most of the time.

Proof

Assume you own one JKL Feb 20 put. When expiration arrives, you are short 100 shares of stock below 20 (because the put is exercised) and no position above 20 (put expires worthless).

If you are short 100 shares of stock and own one Feb 20 call, when expiration arrives you exercise the call when the stock is above 20, leaving you with no position. Below 20, the call expires worthless and your position is short 100 shares of stock.

Again, at any stock price the positions are the same, and because you own either the put or call, there is no pin risk

Bottom line: A covered call position is equivalent to a short put position when the put and call have the same strike price and expiration date. It is important to be familiar with this equivalent position, in particular, because writing covered calls and selling naked puts are popular strategies frequently used by individual investors.

The astute reader may recognize that:

- Stock ownership allows for collecting a dividend (if the stock pays one), whereas the investor who sells puts receives no dividends.

- Stock ownership requires cash to pay for the shares, and interest to pay for the cash. Put sellers pay no interest.

---

[205] If you do not own the shares, that is OK. You can borrow the shares from your broker and sell the stock short.

[206] Buying the put to exit the trade is one simple transaction. To close a covered call, you must buy the call and sell stock—and be certain the prices are acceptable. That is more difficult to accomplish.

When the markets are efficient, the pricing of options in the marketplace takes these factors into consideration. For example, we discussed that buying 100 shares of stock is equivalent to buying one call and selling one put. When you buy stock, there is an interest cost. That cost is factored into the price of the options when buying calls and selling puts. If it weren't, everyone would save the cost of carrying (paying interest to own) stock and purchase the synthetic position instead—and the only people owning stock would be those who do not understand options. But, options are almost always priced so that there is no advantage to buying the call and selling the put. Here is an example:

EXAMPLE

Let's assume you want to buy 100 shares of XYZ at $80 per share. You use cash that is currently earning 5% interest.[207] Holding stock for six months costs $200 in lost interest. XYZ does not pay a dividend.

Consider buying synthetic stock instead. Buy one XYZ Nov 80 call (Nov options expire exactly six months from today) and sell one XYZ Nov 80 put. How much should this position cost?

If you can buy the call and sell the put at equal prices, then you own a position that is equivalent to owning 100 shares and you save the $200 in interest—interest that the investor who owns stock must pay. That is not possible because the markets are too efficient. Instead, when buying synthetic stock, it costs roughly $200 to buy the call and sell the put. That is the same $200 in interest that it costs to carry the shares for six months. Thus, when options are priced correctly, there is no monetary advantage to owning real shares vs. owning the synthetic equivalent.[208]

---

[207] That is an incredibly high rate in 2013. However, interest rates were once that high and will be again.

[208] But options are not always priced correctly and on occasion it may be possible to buy the call and sell the put at a slightly better price than it costs to own stock.

Pin Risk

The astute reader may ask what happens when the stock closes exactly at the strike price. That possibility represents a risk when owning synthetic stock instead of real shares. "Pin risk," refers to the risk that results when, at expiration, the stock last trades at the strike price. When that happens the stock is said to be "pinned" to the strike. If the stock closes exactly at (and occasionally within a penny or two of) the strike price on expiration day, you never know in advance whether you will be assigned an exercise notice or if the options expire worthless. The decision to exercise an option rests with the option owner. Thus, when you own synthetic stock, you do not know whether to exercise your long calls. You want to exercise calls if you are not assigned an exercise notice on the puts, but you do not want to exercise if those puts are assigned.[209] This is a true quandary.

Most of the time when the stock is pinned to the strike, the person who owns the option chooses not to exercise and the option expires worthless. However, having chosen to own an equivalent stock position instead of the "real" position, then you probably want to own that stock. Intelligent investors do not to take the risk of finding a surprise in their account on Monday morning following expiration. It is not an enjoyable experience to discover that you are assigned an exercise notice on an option that you thought expired worthless. It may be fun to find that you were not assigned on an option that was in-the-money by one or two cents (a rare event), but not when you were counting on being assigned that exercise notice. Owning synthetic stock requires paying attention. You do not want to discover that you have no position when you thought you owned stock.

There is a solution. The simplest path to eliminating pin risk is to exercise the call option and buy the put option, paying $0.05, or $5 per contract. Being forced to spend that $5 plus commissions is a nuisance, but it does avoid the risk of an unpleasant surprise.

Be aware that sometimes the stock opens at a price that differs significantly from its previous closing price. Thus, discovering no remaining stock position on some after-expiration Monday can be expensive (or rewarding. But why gamble?) When the stock price opens lower, you come out ahead. When it gaps higher, you lost a profitable opportunity. Why take the chance? One reason for using options is to reduce risk and it is best not to play with risk. Do not wait until Monday morning to learn your fate.

---

[209] If you fail to exercise calls, and the puts expire worthless, you have no stock position, but if you exercise calls to get long stock and if you are also assigned on the puts, you find yourself owning twice as many shares as planned.

188

NOTE: Obviously the interest cost used in this example is a variable and depends on the stock price, interest rates and time to expiration. If the stock is above $80, or if interest rates are higher, or if more time remains before the options expire, then the position costs more than $200

Using equivalent positions

Recognize that one position is equivalent to another, may allow for more efficient trading. In the discussion above, we concluded that there is no cost advantage to owning synthetic stock instead of real shares. But there are situations in which a synthetic option position presents an advantage. Let's look at a simple collar to see one example when a synthetic position is worthwhile.

If we let R = collar position (collars are discussed in detail in Chapter 12), then:

$$R = S - C_H + P_L$$

Collar = long stock, short call (with a higher strike price, H), long put (with a lower strike price, L). All options have the same expiration date.

Because we know that S - C_H (the covered call portion of the collar) is equivalent to a short put position (same strike price and expiration date), we can rewrite the equation:

$$R = (S - C_H) + PL \text{ becomes } R = -P_H + P_L$$

In other words, the collar is equivalent to a position in which one put (with a higher strike price) is sold and another put (with a lower strike price) is bought. This is a spread position. Here's a bit of option jargon:

- When you buy one put and sell another, the position is a "put spread."

- When long[210] one call and short another, the position is a "call spread."

- By definition, when you own the more expensive option and sell the less expensive option, you "buy the spread."

- When buying the put spread and both options have the same expiration date, it is called a "bear spread" because the position makes money when the underlying declines.

---

[210] 'Long' and 'short' are common investing terms. An owner is long. A seller is short.

- When buying the call spread and both options have the same expiration date, it is called a "bull spread" because the position makes money when the underlying increases in value.

- When selling the more expensive option, you "sell the spread."

Instead of owning a collar position, you can choose to own the equivalent position. To accomplish that:

- Instead of initiating the covered call portion of the collar (long stock, short call), sell the put (P_H or same strike as the call).

- Buy the same put (P_L) as when buying the collar.

- By making those two trades at the same time (via a spread order), you sell the put spread. Because you sell the put spread, the position is bullish, and is 'long delta' (more on delta in next chapter).

Why bother with the collar equivalent?

Any time the stock does not pay a dividend (and many times when it does) you may prefer to sell the equivalent put spread, rather than establish a collar position. When options are priced correctly (as they are most of the time), there is no difference in profit potential or risk. Remember—when you own the collar, you collect dividends. However, you also must pay interest to carry stock. Unless the dividend is large enough to offset the cost to carry or you have a tax situation that favors collecting dividends, the put spread is a better choice for most investors.[211]

Several reasons to choose the equivalent, or "collars in disguise":

- There are two commissions (put and put) required to open a put spread. The collar requires three (put, call and stock).

- It is more efficient to trade the put spread. Market makers almost always quote spreads at a discount to the individual market for each option. Thus, entering an order to sell a put spread often provides a better fill. By that I mean you seldom are required to pay the ask price on one leg and sell the bid price on the other.

  NOTE: You are not forced to sell the spread at the price quoted by market makers. You may attempt to sell the spread at any price, knowing there is a chance your order will not be

---

[211] Truly it should not matter because the dividend is priced into the options.

executed. It is more difficult to get a good quote for a collar position—simply because it has three legs. You can readily trade the put spread in a single transaction, but you may be forced to "leg"[212] into the collar trade.

- The same situation occurs when it is time to close the position. The advantages of trading two items, rather than three, remain. And that includes lower commissions.

Bottom line: Selling the put spread, the synthetic equivalent of the collar, is easier to trade and requires paying fewer commission dollars. Investors who are unaware of equivalent positions never consider selling the put spread. And many investors who do sell put spreads are unaware they are trading collars. If the conservative collar strategy (Chapter 12) suits your investment objectives, then you can make things easier for yourself by selling put spreads.[213]

This is an important lesson. Understanding that a collar is a relatively conservative option strategy and that selling a put spread is its equivalent, you are better placed to recognize the advantages of selling put spreads. It is one of the least risky methods available for the individual investor who wants to take a mildly bullish stance on the stock market. Further discussion of this strategy is postponed until Chapter 17.

Let's look an example demonstrating that a collar is the synthetic equivalent to a put spread.

EXAMPLE

Collar

- Buy 500 PQR at 50

- Sell 5 PQR Aug 55 call

- Buy 5 PQR Aug 50 put

Equivalent put spread

- Sell 5 PQR Aug 55 put

- Buy 5 PQR Aug 50 put

---

[212] In this context, "leg" is a verb. It refers to trading one part of the desired position first, then the other(s). It is less risky to trade all parts of any position simultaneously.
[213] Just be careful when choosing the strike prices. If you are looking to replace the collar, then choose an equivalent, and not random, put spread.

These are equivalent positions because the first two legs of the collar (long stock, short call) are equivalent to selling the put (same strike). Let's take a detailed look the possibilities to see if these positions really are equivalent.

Position at expiration
Collar

- If stock is below 50, exercise Aug 50 puts. No remaining position.

- If stock is between 50 and 55, call and put expire worthless. Long 500 shares.

- If stock is above 55, you are assigned an exercise notice on the calls. No remaining position.

Put spread

- If stock is below 50, exercise Aug 50 puts. You are assigned an exercise notice on Aug 55 puts. No remaining position.

- If stock is between 50 and 55, you are assigned on the Aug 55 puts. The Aug 50 puts expire worthless. Long 500 shares.

- If stock is above 55, both options expire worthless. No remaining position.

Thus, at any stock price, the positions are the same. Note that pin risk is present at the higher (call) strike price with either position. At the lower strike, you own the puts and have no pin risk.

Profit and loss at expiration
Let's consider the P/L for the trade. Both positions includes the purchase of Aug 50 puts. Thus, our task is to show that P/L for the covered call portion of the collar (long 500 shares and short five Aug 55 calls) is identical with that of the corresponding short put position (short five Aug 55 puts).

This proof is similar to that presented earlier in this chapter when we discussed buying XYZ Nov 80 calls and selling Nov 80 puts instead of buying stock:

1. When the options are priced correctly, the time premium collected when writing Aug 55 covered calls is greater than the time premium collected for writing the naked Aug 55 put. That appears to favor selling the call. However, the difference in those time premiums is identical (when the markets are operating efficiently) with the cost of carrying the stock. In other words, the covered call writer collects extra time premium in the option, but pays that amount in interest. Thus, there is no monetary advantage to owning either position.

2. We showed that -P = S − C. That is the situation here: selling the Aug 55P is equivalent to owning stock (S) and selling the Aug 55C. Many times there is no advantage to trading the synthetic equivalent. That is not true for collars where the trading advantages are clear. Opening and closing spreads with two legs is far easier and less costly, than positions with three legs.

It never hurts to consider alternatives when trading options.

Box spread

The box is another spread to help educate traders. This is not a spread you will trade, but understanding boxes adds to your arsenal of useful information.

The box is a riskless (and rewardless) position. It consists of one call spread and one put spread, with each spread having the same strike prices. The options expire at the same time and have the same underlying asset. When buying both the call spread and put spread, you buy the box. When selling both spreads, you sell the box. The description of a box spread includes the underlying and both strike prices, e.g., ABC Apr 60/65 box.

$$B = (C_L − C_H) + (P_H − P_L),$$
where B = box spread, L = lower strike price, and H = higher strike price.

When expiration arrives, the box is worth exactly the difference between the strike prices. For example, the FGH Jul 30/35 box owner is:

- Long Jul 30 calls

- Short Jul 35 calls

- Long Jul 35 puts

- Short Jul 30 puts

If the stock is above 35 (the higher strike) when expiration arrives, both puts expire worthless. The calls are both ITM and are exercised. The box owner pays $3,000 for 100 shares and sells those 100 shares, collecting $3,500. Net proceeds: $500.[214]

If the stock is below $30 per share (the lower strike), both calls expire worthless. You exercise your Jul 35 put, selling 100 shares and collecting $3,500. You are assigned an exercise notice on the Jul 30 put and pay $3,000 for 100 shares. Net proceeds: $500.

If the stock is priced between the strikes (30 and 35 in this example) then the short options (Jul 30 put and Jul 35 call) expire worthless. Exercise Jul 30 call, paying $3,000 for 100 shares. Exercise Jul 35 put, selling 100 shares and collecting $3,500. Net proceeds: $500.

Thus, at any stock price, the box spread is worth the difference between the strikes, or $500 in this example. In the strikes are 10 points apart, the box is worth $1,000 at expiration.[215]

As a trader, you never want to trade the box spread as an entity. However, just knowing about the box spread adds flexibility to your ability to know which of several choices represents the best trade.

Why not trade the box? First, it involves four commissions to open the position and then you must pay either four commissions or two exercise/assignment fees to exit. Second, there is no one to sell you this spread for less than $5.[216] And if you want to sell, there is never a bid high enough to leave a profit for you. (Yes, there are situations in which professionals trade box spreads with each other, but as an individual investor, ignore boxes as trading vehicles). Boxes are subject to pin risk at either strike price—just one more complication.

Why care about box spreads?

Let's say you decide that BCD is a good, conservative investment and that you want to collar the position. Because you are aware of synthetics, you decide to sell a put spread, rather than trading the shares. Thus, you plan to buy BCD Dec 45 put and sell BCD Dec 50 put. Looking at the markets, you believe you can collect $150 for this spread. You can go ahead and sell

---

[214] This is the cash. It is NOT the profit.
[215] This basic fact is vital. I once heard of a new market maker who learned that a box is always worth $10. He went onto the trading floor and bought a boatload of boxes at $6 each. Unfortunately for that market maker, those were $5 boxes.
[216] You can buy it for a bit less than $5, but it is not going to be a profitable trade. When buying a box spread, approximately $500 (or $1,000 if the strike prices are 10 points apart) cash is used. The interest not earned on that cash is always (when the markets operate efficiently) greater than the discount you can receive on the box. In other words, if the cost to carry (own) the box from the time you buy it until expiration is $15, then buying the box for anything under $485 is not possible—and that ignores the extra expense of commissions.

the spread, establishing the position you want to own. Let's look at alternatives.

Assume you own one BCD Dec 45/50 box (please do not buy the box). The position is:

- Long Dec 45 call

- Short Dec 50 call

- Long Dec 50 put

- Short Dec 45 put

We know the box is a riskless spread, and we can combine it with the position you want to own, which is:

- Long Dec 45 put

- Short Dec 50 put

When we combine (add together) these positions, the puts cancel each other and we get:

- Long Dec 45 call

- Short Dec 50 call

It is definitely inefficient to make all these trades, but if you make them in your mind, sometimes an equivalent position can be found *at a better price*—and that means more money in *your* pocket. For example, one way to sell the put spread described above is to buy the corresponding (same strikes and expiration) call spread.

Buying a call spread is now shown to be equivalent to selling a put spread with the same strike prices and expiration date. That put spread is equivalent to owning the collar position.

Thus, instead of buying a collar, a trader can sell a put spread or buy a call spread because each position is equivalent to the others. However, it is essential to remember that the strikes and expiration must be identical.

EXAMPLE

Above, we considered selling the BCD Dec 45/50 put spread @ $1.50. Before entering the order, take a look at the Dec 45/50 call spread. If it can be bought for less than $3.50, then buying the call spread is a better deal.

Here's some practical advice: do not bother if the difference is only $0.01 or $0.02 because there is a small interest cost involved when owning the call spread. Buy the call spread when you can save enough to make it worth your time, and that is probably $0.05. This opportunity is not available often,[217] but unless you have an extreme urgency to complete the trade, it is worth the time to check the market for the call spread and determine whether one spread is priced better than the other.

NOTE: Comparing the price of the call spread with that of the put spread is a method that saves money on occasion. If you feel it is not worth the effort that is fine. But just knowing about these possibilities makes you a much smarter option trader than the vast majority who simply shoot from the hip and do not understand how options work.

If the stock pays a dividend, the situation becomes more complicated because it is sometimes a good idea to exercise a call option before expiration—just to collect the dividend. To keep it simple, make the trade you prefer to own, and avoid the equivalent position when there is a dividend involved.

Let's consider how you can benefit from this information:

1. Determine the price at which you can sell the put spread.

---

[217] The market makers never offer this opportunity. But sometimes, an individual investor offers to sell the call spread (in this example) at a lower price than the market makers. If you find that offer, then buy the call spread instead of selling the put spread.

2. Subtract that price from the expiration value of the box (the difference between the strike prices, multiplied by 100). In our example, the put spread is $150. Subtracting that from $500 yields $350. That is the break-even (no benefit to be gained by trading calls instead of puts) price. The goal is to buy the call spread for $345 or less. (Now that options trade in pennies, you can get more sophisticated and calculate the exact difference required for additional profits.)

3. If the corresponding call spread is less than the target, then it is more profitable to buy the call spread. It should not make any difference which of two equivalent positions a trader has in a portfolio.

4. When selling the put spread, your hope is that the stock rises above the higher strike and for the spread to be worth $0. In that scenario, the call spread is worth $500 (box is worth $500 and puts are worth zero). The profit potential from the put spread is $150 and from the call spread it is $155 (less cost to carry, assuming you can get if by paying $345).

5. These spreads can never be worth more than the difference between the strikes, or $500 in this example. Thus, the maximum loss for the put spread is $350.[218] (Chapter 17 contains much more information on spreads.

Any time you can earn a larger profit by buying the call spread[219] it pays to buy it, rather than selling the put spread. When ready to sell the put spread, take a look at the corresponding call spread to determine which spread to trade. Most of the time an opportunity to earn an extra nickel or two will not available. However, any time you can make a few extra dollars—with no added risk—it is a good idea to do it.

Conclusion

- If the box is worth $500 (strikes five points apart), then the call spread and the put spread together are worth $500, less the cost to carry.

---

[218] Trader collected $150 and maximum value is $500
[219] Be careful. It must be the spread with the same strike prices and expiration date as the put spread.

- If you can buy the call spread for less than it is worth,[220] it is a smart way to play.

- Sell the put and you collect interest. Buy the spread and pay interest. Do not ignore that interest.

Bottom line:

- Selling a put spread is equivalent to buying the call spread with the same strike prices and expiration date.

- Selling a call spread is equivalent to buying the put spread with the same strike prices and expiration date.

- Selling the put spread or buying the call spread is equivalent to owning the corresponding collar (same strike prices and expiration).

You can get the advantages of owning a specific position by owning another (equivalent) position—while earning a few extra dollars. But the real benefit derived from understanding the material in this chapter is that it gives you a significant advantage over the vast majority of individual investors who trade options without making an effort to thoroughly understand how they work.

As you become more familiar with options, return to this chapter to reinforce what you already know and add to your knowledge base.

---

[220] In this scenario, it is worth $500 less the price of the put spread.

QUIZ 14

1. If you buy three HHH Nov 40 puts and sell three Nov 40 calls, what is the equivalent position?

2. You are considering selling the YYY Feb 50/60 put spread and collecting $400. You can buy the YYY Feb 50/60 call spread for $620 instead. Should you do that?

3. How much is the GOOG Jun 610/670 box worth at expiration?

4. Trading box spreads is a money making strategy. **TRUE or FALSE**

5. You own the IBM Oct 110/120 call spread. On expiration day,
   a) IBM closed at $110.00 Do you have pin risk?
   b) IBM closed at $115. Do you have pin risk?
   c) IBM closed at $120. Do you have pin risk?

6. You plan to sell the ABCD Jun 35/40 put spread for $1.25. You notice that the ABCD Sep 35/40 call spread is offered at $3.60. Should you buy it instead of selling the put spread?

Quiz 14 Answers

1. Short 300 HHH shares. This requires some thinking on your part, but if long calls and short puts equals long stock, then long puts and short calls equals short stock.

2. No. You must pay less than $600 for the trade to be worthwhile. Sell the put spread instead.

3. $6,000. The difference between the strike prices, multiplied by 100: (100 x $60)

4. False. It is a futile endeavor for the individual investor.

5.

   a) No. You own the ATM (at the money) option and control the exercise decision.
   b) No. None of your options is pinned to the strike
   c) Yes. The owner of the 120 call may decide to exercise. The safest course of action is to sell the call spread to close your position. You will have to accept a little less than $10.

   NOTE: In practical terms, you would not be holding this trade this long. There is too much downside risk. The point for this quiz question is that you should plan to trade out of the spread (sell it), rather than face this pin risk. Do not wait too long. The options stop trading before you see the final closing price for the stock.

6. No. The plan is to trade June, not September options. These are not equivalent.

Part III

Beyond the Basics

The Adventure Continues

Chapter 15

The Greeks

The importance of risk management has been mentioned repeatedly. When you correctly use the strategies outlined in this book, you earn profits on most trades. But losses are inevitable. It is crucial to your long-term success as an option trader that those losses are not large enough to hurt. In other words, if you establish positions that earn $500 per trade, you cannot afford to occasionally lose $10,000. The best way to prevent large losses is to recognize the potential risk of owning each position. If that risk is too large compared with your average profit per trade, you have alternatives: avoid the trade, reduce trade size (number of contracts), or buy insurance.[221] But if you are unaware of the the size of a potential loss, or the probability of incurring that loss, it is difficult to take appropriate risk management steps.

One way that option traders measure risk is by considering a set of mathematical parameters identified by Greek letters,[222] and known collectively as "the Greeks." When risk (exposure to loss), is quantified it is easier to decide when a specific position, or an entire portfolio, is within your comfort zone. I am not suggesting that you can trade without risk. However profit potential is limited when adopting the recommended methods and you must not allow losses to overpower those gains.

Once again, no mathematical skills (beyond simple arithmetic)[223] are required to use the Greeks. The term, "delta" was introduced earlier. In this chapter, delta and four other Greeks are described.

Each Greek measures the *sensitivity* of option prices (i.e., how much change to expect in the option price) when something changes in the marketplace. By understanding why option prices move higher and lower you learn how various market actions affect the value of individual options. By now you understand that calls increase in value as the

---

[221] We have not previously discussed the idea of buying separate insurance. All recommended trades in Part III have limited risk because the methodology includes buying one option for each option sold. Sometimes it is a good idea to own additional insurance, although it is seldom cheap. See Chapter 19.

[222] With one exception: "Vega" is often used as one of the Greeks, even though vega is NOT a Greek letter.

[223] The calculations are not simple, but fortunately, you do not have to calculate the Greeks. The data is readily obtainable by using calculators and supplied by your broker.

underlying moves higher or as the implied volatility increases, but by using the Greeks you can make a good estimate of just how much the option price is expected to change. Estimating exposure to loss (as well as having a better understanding of potential gains) allows a trader to intelligently adjust (hedge) any risk factor that is threatening to move beyond his comfort level.

You may even decide to pre-hedge, protecting against the unlikely possibility of losing money if some external event causes a significant market move. And sometimes that insurance policy not only prevents large losses, it turns what would have been a losing trade into a good-sized winner.

There are two sides to this insurance issue. If your portfolio leaves you within your comfort zone, then you probably do not have a reason to pre-hedge. On the other hand, if your positions make you worry about losses, insurance is probably a good idea. A bit of clarification is needed here. When each position feels OK on its own, it is still possible that the aggregate portfolio may become uncomfortable to own because all positions run into trouble at the same time. That is when portfolio insurance can come to the rescue.

- If you pre-hedge a specific risk factor before being threatened, it is much less costly to buy insurance. For example, you can buy a few calls and/or puts[224] to protect your portfolio against a rare overnight market surge or collapse. This idea is discussed in Chapter 19.

- If you buy insurance only when it is needed—when you require protection— it will be expensive. For example, buying a few puts *after* a substantial market decline is costly because the puts now have a higher delta and lower market prices usually result in an the increase in implied volatility[225]

Calculating the Greeks

The obvious question: how are the Greeks calculated? Luckily, it is not a problem. The calculator used in Chapter 5 to determine the theoretical value of an option does all the work and provides all Greeks discussed in this chapter. Such a calculator can be found at the CBOE website: www.cboe.com/LearnCenter/ OptionCalculator.aspx.

When the underlying stock undergoes a significant move, you already know if the position is profitable. It will be very helpful with the

---

[224] Buy useful options. Do not randomly buy options for protection. First, study Chapter 19.
[225] IV increases substantially when the market declines because nervous investors buy puts for protection—just as you want to do. This IV increase almost never occurs when the market rallies strongly, although it was not always this way. Through the 1970s and most of the 1980s, substantial rallies were accompanied by a large increase in the IV of call options.

hold/close/adjust decision to pay close attention to the Greeks after such a move because it becomes apparent whether the position is now at imminent risk for additional losses.

'Imminent' risk differs from ordinary risk. It is one thing to be concerned about losing a given sum when the underlying moves 5% (ordinary risk). However, that is very different from a situation in which an additional 1% move would result in losing much more than you are willing to accept. That threat represents imminent risk and it is wise to take defensive action before that threat becomes reality.

Investors usually think of risk in negative terms—as something that measures potential loss. Risk also plays a role in deciding when to take profits. For example, there will be residual profit potential in a position (such as a credit spread, see Chapter 17), but if you already made 80-90% of the maximum possible profit and there is still one month remaining before the options expire, do give serious consideration to taking that profit. The decision is whether to risk that profit to earn the last 10-20%. When holding a position with little to gain, please recognize the possibility of sacrificing the large[226] profit already in hand.

When buying options (they come with positive gamma), profits come from major market moves and losses occur when time passes and nothing good happens. Use a calculator and the Greeks to estimate potential gains as well as the cost of waiting. Greeks help every option trader get a handle on how much money is likely to be won or lost under various market conditions.

> **NOTE:** You can get along without using Greeks. If you choose that route, you will be flying blind part of the time and have difficulty estimating current risk. You'll probably survive, but you are at a disadvantage compared with investors who have a better understanding of potential losses. It is worth the effort to learn to use the Greeks to make intelligent trading decisions. Your broker provides the Greeks for every option in your portfolio. That saves time and removes any excuse for ignoring the friendly Greeks.

---

[226] Do not take small profits in this scenario because there is still much to gain by holding.

Individual Greeks (delta, gamma, vega, theta, rho)

Delta

Delta measures the expected change in the price of an option (or group of options) as the price of the underlying asset changes by $1. Keep in mind that delta never gives the *exact* change in the price of an option because:

- Delta itself is not constant, but changes as the stock price changes. The rate at which delta changes is measured by *gamma*.

- Delta represents the *theoretical* change in the option's price. Most of the time the *observed* change in the option price differs because other factors (including other Greeks) are in play.

- Market factors may result in an implied volatility (IV) change. A news event, or an influx of buy (or sell) orders can trigger such a change. *Vega* describes the sensitivity of the option price when there is a one-point change in the implied volatility.

Delta is important. It may not predict the exact price change for the option, but it provides a very good estimate that can be used to gauge profit/loss resulting in a change in the stock price. That is the information needed to estimate risk and reward for a specific position.

Although not part of the official definition of delta, it is a good estimate of the probability that the option finishes[227] in the money. In other words, when an option has a 36 delta (or -36 for a put), statistically[228] it finishes ITM 36% of the time. Obviously that means it finishes OTM (expires worthless) about 64% of the time. NOTE: This is not the percentage of the time that trading the option will be 'profitable.' Delta only compares the price of the underlying asset with the strike price <u>at expiration</u>. Profitability depends on much more, including how the position is managed, whether it is hedged or naked, etc.

> **NOTE:** An option with a 36 delta may expire worthless 64% of the time, but it does not mean the option remains OTM 64% of the time. Stocks move up and down—and occasionally the option expires worthless—but only after it goes ITM for an unspecified period of time. Thus, when you sell options (hoping they expire worthless), it may feel comfortable to sell options with a high

---

[227] Remember, "finish" refers to the stock's closing price on expiration Friday.
[228] If you take this exact situation an infinite number of times, probability tells us that these percentages will reflect reality

probability of expiring worthless,[229] but the probability that the option remains OTM for its entire lifetime is not as high as the probability that it expires worthless. In practical terms, this means you should not sell options, close your eyes, and hope for the best. Low probability events do occur and it is important to manage risk so that those events do not cause too much harm.

EXAMPLE

You sell 10 HUGS (a manufacturer of stuffed toy animals) Jul 40 puts at $0.60 each when the stock is trading near 44. Two weeks later, the stock rallies to 47.25 and Jul expiration does not arrive for another 50 days. The market in these puts is $0.10 (bid) to $0.15 (ask).

The delta was -17[230] when the ten puts were sold, and you were +170 delta, the equivalent of 170 shares. The current delta is -5 and the position is +50 delta. Here are your choices: If you pay $0.15 for the puts, you lock in 75% of the maximum profit ($45 out of a possible $60) for each option. You can try to buy the puts for less than $0.15 to lock in a higher profit. Or you can hold and try to earn the full $60 per option. How do you decide?

Each investor must choose the appropriate action for his/ her comfort zone, and thus, as with most option decisions, there is no perfect action to take. Because the delta is currently -5, there is approximately a 5% chance that these options finish in-the-money[231] (stock lower than 40). It feels pretty good when the odds of making money are 19:1 in your favor, but all you have to gain is that last 10 or 15 cents, and there is still substantial time remaining. I recommend taking profits and finding another investment. This idea is not universally accepted and some prefer to hold out for every last penny and prefer to wait for the options to expire (hopefully worthless). Based on more than 38 years of option-trading experience, I cannot recommend holding out until the end. First, there is too little to gain and you can do better investing your money in a new position. Second, unexpected market-moving events do occur. It would be sad to turn this sure winner into a loser if something unexpected

---

[229] The probability that the underlying will touch the strike price during an option's lifetime can be calculated, and calculators that determine the probability that an option will touch the strike price—at some time during its lifetime—are available.
[230] Use the CBOE calculator. Volatility =30.
[231] Remember, delta represents approximate probability of finishing in-the-money.

happened. This is not to suggest that you take quick profits as a general rule. This suggestion only applies when there is little to gain by holding.

In this scenario, you can enter an $0.11 to $0.14 bid and hope to buy the puts at less than the current asking price (but there is nothing wrong with paying the offer, $0.15, if that feels right). The rationale is this: you quickly lock in most of the profit and there is not much profit potential remaining. If only seven days remained in the lifetime of the options, I would not consider paying more than $0.05 (and for most traders, waiting one week to earn the last nickel is the norm).[232]

Delta can be considered as "equivalent number of shares." Thus, if you own a position that is long 87 deltas, the position performs as if you own 87 shares of stock. It is a simple process to determine profit and loss when we own a stock that undergoes a price change. By knowing position delta for an option position, we can make a good estimate for how much money is gained or lost as the stock price changes. That is why we pay attention to the Greeks—it allows traders to quantify and manage risk.

Additional details about delta:

- Call options have a delta that ranges from 0 to 100 while the delta of a put option is between 0 and -100. Some traders prefer to define delta as being between 0 and 1 (or 0 and -1 for puts). This distinction is unimportant. Thus, if you come across a delta of 12 or 0.12, know that these numbers represent the same thing.

- The value of a put option decreases as the underlying price increases. Thus, puts have *negative delta*. The value of a call option increases as the underlying price increases, and calls have *positive delta*.

- For example, if a call option has a 30 delta and the stock increases by $1, the price of the call is expected to increase by $.30.

- If a put option has a -60 delta and the stock moves higher by $1, the price of the put is expected to *decrease* by $0.60. If a put option has

---

[232] Waiting one week is not the same as waiting one month. It is extremely conservative to pay that $0.05, and there are good arguments against wasting nickels to close options that are obviously worthless. But, there is no such thing as "obviously" worthless. Markets can do very unexpected things every once in a while. Holding out for the last nickel or dime is something I no longer do. Many years ago, I refused to buy in these "worthless" options. Of course, I won the bet most of the time, but every few years or so, it was a costly mistake. I no longer play the final nickel game and suggest you decide for yourselves whether it is worthwhile to play.

a delta of -45 and the stock declines by $2, the price of the put option *increases* by approximately $0.90.[233]

- The delta of the underlying asset is constant (100).

Deltas are additive. To determine the delta for a position, add deltas for options owned and subtract deltas for options sold.

- Positive deltas come from calls owned and puts sold.

- Negative delta comes from calls sold and puts owned.

EXAMPLE

If you own a collar, the position delta is:

- + 100 (for stock)

- Subtract call delta (because call was sold)

- Add the put delta (remember, the put delta is negative).[234]

Using delta

Deciding to take a bullish position in ARTS with the stock trading at $22.35, you sell eight ARTS Nov 20 puts at $0.50.[235] ARTS owns a series of galleries specializing in works by early twentieth century artists. Using the calculator, you find the implied volatility is 50 and each put has a -22 delta. The delta of your position is +176 (-8 x -22).

Writing puts is a bullish strategy, and if there are doubts about that, the +176 deltas is confirmation. What can you do with this information? If ARTS moves higher by one point, you expect the position to earn $176. All by itself, this doesn't tell you much more than you already knew.

But, what happens if two days pass and you find the stock trading $2.00 lower at $20.25? How concerned should you be? Is position risk still within your comfort zone? Should you do anything with this position?

The calculator (or data provided by your broker) shows that these options are worth $1.13 with a -43 delta. Because you sold this put for 50 cents[236] and it is now worth $1.13, you have an unrealized loss of

---

[233] There are other Greeks that affect the price of an option. Therefore the delta contribution to an option's price change may be offset (or increased) by the effect of other Greeks.
[234] Subtracting a negative number gives a positive number. Thus, selling puts adds positive deltas to a position and buying puts adds negative deltas.
[235] 40 days before November options expire.
[236] That is 50 cents per share, or $50 per contract.

approximately \$63 per contract.[237] There is not much you can do about that now, but by knowing position delta (+344 deltas[238]) it is understood that if the stock continues to decline, the immediate exposure is \$344 for the first point.[239] It is necessary to make a risk management decision: do you leave this position as it is, or is it too risky to hold?

If you are an investor willing to accumulate shares, the position is acceptable and there is no action to take. When expiration arrives, you will buy shares (+800 deltas) or collect a profit when the option expires worthless.

For the trader who has no interest in owning stock, a decision must be made: are you within your comfort zone knowing your current exposure? If the stock declines further, the loss is ~\$344 for the first point (and increases after that). Is that uncomfortable—are potential losses greater than you are willing to accept? I cannot answer for you, but by knowing the position delta, you can gauge immediate risk and decide if this position must be managed to reduce that risk.

Perhaps other positions in your portfolio offset some risk. That may help you decide whether to hold or adjust. If you have a good balance of long and short deltas, then you may feel better about doing nothing with your ARTS position right now. On the other hand, if most of your positions are delta long, you may not be comfortable with the position. Bottom line: knowing delta helps a trader estimate risk associated with any position and allows you to make informed decisions. Remember these are not always winning decisions, but do not let that concern you. Part of the time when making an adjustment the stock reverses direction, making that adjustment appear to have been unnecessary. That is the cost of doing business—and your primary business is protecting your assets by managing risk.

We have not discussed specific adjustments to make, if you decide that a position's risk should be reduced, but the simplest path is to reduce your current position by buying back all or some of the puts sold earlier. There are other choices, some of which are discussed below and in greater detail in Chapter 17.

> **NOTE:** Some investors initiate positions and consider only expiration possibilities. They hope to make money over the long term and are not concerned with risk, do not adjust positions and ignore Greeks. This is not the path to success. Being aware of risk and reward potential for any position leaves the trader in

---

[237] The actual loss is determined by the market price of the option, not its theoretical price.
[238] (-8 x -43).
[239] How delta changes is better understood after the discussion on gamma

control and frees him from depending on good luck. It is not necessary to make adjustments every time a position moves against you, but it is also foolish to always ignore these events. Understanding risk enables traders to significantly reduce or eliminate the occurrence of career-destroying, large losses.

Gamma

Gamma measures the rate at which delta changes when the underlying asset moves \$1. It is always a positive number.[240] Because of gamma, delta is not constant and declines to zero when options are far out of the money and increases to 100 (or -100 for puts) when options are deep in the money. Gamma is additive, meaning that for a given position, total gamma is the sum of the individual gammas (add gamma for options owned and subtract gamma for options sold).

When investors buy options, gamma is their friend. This is especially true for OTM options. The lure of owning an option with a 20 (or -20) delta, watching the stock move in the right direction and seeing the option's delta increase (because of positive gamma) to 80 (or -80) is irresistible to some. These "exploding deltas" can produce large profits.

For example, if you buy 10 puts with a -20 delta, your position is short 200 deltas. If the stock moves quickly in your favor, you may find yourself with a large profit and a position that is short 800 deltas.

When selling options, gamma is the enemy and it must be paid proper respect. That means avoiding the sale of naked options.[241] When short any option, if the underlying moves in the wrong direction for the option-selling strategy, the value of those options rises at an ever-increasing rate—until delta reaches 100 and the option price moves point-for-point with the stock price. That is gamma at work.

Returning to our example, did you notice that delta was -22 when the ARTS puts were written and increased[242] to -43 after the stock declined? That is the effect of gamma. Thus, current delta provides a good estimate of how the value of a single option (or option position) changes as the price of the underlying moves one point and gamma provides information on how delta changes. Positive gamma causes profits to accelerate when the stock continues to move in the same direction. Conversely, negative

---

[240] If an option has a gamma equal to 10, then delta changes by ~10 regardless of whether the stock moves higher or lower. Gamma itself is not constant, but changes as the stock price changes.

[241] Selling naked puts because you want to accumulate stock is an exception. The strategies discussed in Part III do not involve the sale of naked options. We always buy one option for every option sold.

[242] Technically, when a number grows more negative, that number is decreasing. But, let's not nitpick. For our purposes, when the delta of a put option changes from -20 to -50, the delta is said to increase.

gamma results in increasing losses when the stock moves in the same direction.

Gamma is the property of an option that makes it painful to be wrong when selling options or joyful to be correct when owning options. Gamma is the driving force that suggests adopting option strategies that limit losses.

Gamma is not constant; it changes as the price of the underlying stock changes. '**Speed**' is the Greek that measures the rate at which gamma changes.

> **NOTE:** Gamma is always a positive number. Because call options have positive gamma, they increase in value as the stock price increases. Because puts have positive gamma, they increase in value as the stock price decreases. Gamma for puts and calls (same underlying asset, same expiration, same strike) are equal.[243]

Vega

Vega measures the sensitivity of an option price to a one point change in volatility. Vega is always positive because the value of both puts and calls increase as volatility increases. Vega is additive.

When accumulating several positions, a trader may not be aware that the portfolio has become subject to vega risk. In other words, a substantial change in implied volatility can significantly alter your account value. When a broker provides the Greeks, it is a simple matter to look at total vega and decide whether you are long or short too much vega. This is not something to be learned overnight, but a little trading experience makes this far easier to know when you have too much exposure to a change in volatility.

Some positions are associated with positive vega and others with negative vega. When it is desirable to neutralize portfolio vega, use this quick guide:

- Longer-term options have more vega than nearer-term options.

- OTM[244] options have the most vega, followed by ATM and then ITM.

---

[243] I hope this feels right to readers. Calls and puts have different deltas, but when the call delta increases, the put delta decreases by the same amount.

[244] If too far OTM, all Greeks become zero. Thus in this context OTM means not far out-of-the-money.

Theta

Theta measures the sensitivity of an option's value as one day passes. Option owners have negative theta because an option is a wasting asset and its value decreases every day. The option seller owns a position with positive theta.

The option strategies recommended in this book have positive theta and the passage of time is beneficial to our positions. Do not allow this short discussion to minimize that fact. These strategies all benefit from the passage of time.

Rho

Rho measures the sensitivity of an option's value to a change in interest rates. Because interest rates tend to change slowly (if at all), a change in the current interest rate is not that important to the value of an option (unless it is a very long-term option), and thus, rho is the least important of the Greeks.

Using the information

How does all this help the trader? What are you supposed to do with the information? If you adopt the basic conservative strategies, then your portfolio is always bullish—and bullish is the traditional way that the vast majority of investors (they own stock and mutual funds) look at the stock market. Assuming you are comfortable with that, the Greeks do not provide a great deal of useful information.

Traders who are in and out of positions more often must manage risk carefully. Options were designed as risk-reducing investment tools, but many traders adopt high-risk strategies. Monitoring the Greeks allows a trader to understand when danger lurks.

EXAMPLE

Assume it is Jun 1, interest rates are 5%, and ABCD pays no dividend. There are 50 days remaining to July expiration. You own 1,000 ABCD (currently trading at $21.87) and wrote 10 Jul 20 calls (IV = 35). Stock has a delta of 100 (by definition) and you are long 1,000 shares. That is equivalent to 1,000 delta.[245] The Jul 20 call has a 79 delta. You sold 10 calls, and that contributes 790 negative delta. Net: long 210 delta. Thus, the current profit/loss expectation is approximately the same as if you own 210 shares of ABCD outright, instead of the covered call position.

---

[245] Delta is share equivalent. Thus, one share equals one delta.

Other Greeks are: -85 gamma (-8.5 * 10) and theta for seven days is $.076 per share (or $7.60 per option contract).

To the investor who plans to hold this position, Greeks are less important. They provide a reasonable estimate of potential gains/losses over the near term, but because their intention is to hold and profit from theta, they have no plans to close this position and expect to collect $76 from theta over the next week. That is not very much money, but the position is working—as long as nothing bad happens to the ABCD share price. This position has negative gamma and delta of the short calls increases (it approaches 100) as the stock price increases. Thus, if the stock rises one point, the 8.5 gamma means that delta changes from 79 to approximately 87.

Sample analysis

Assume you sold puts on XYZ and that the stock quickly dropped from $53 to $48. As a result of negative gamma, the position is losing money and your position is long (+ delta). Assume you are long 500 delta with negative 100 gamma. The first decision must be whether you are comfortable with this position, knowing that if the stock declines another point you will lose $550 as your delta increases to +600.[246] If the decision is to reduce risk, there are two issues to address. First you need negative delta to make the position less long. You can sell stock, buy puts or sell calls. (For now, let's ignore alternatives.) Second, the position can use positive gamma. Of the adjustment choices, only put buying accomplishes both the need for negative delta and positive gamma.

You are not forced to buy puts—it is merely one choice. But you are already short puts and buying back some of those puts is the simplest adjustment. Alternatively, you can buy a different put and convert the current put position into a put spread (more on put spreads in Chapter 17).

NOTE: Be careful. When the stock is falling, it may seem that the best strategy is to sell call options or call spreads (it is far from best (and not recommended) to gain negative delta. Please do not sell naked calls.[247] It is easy to fall into the trap of believing that the sale of OTM call options is safe. It does provide some positive delta and does add positive theta, but it adds very little downside protection (and that is what you need

---

[246] Because your gamma is -100, if the stock moves one point lower, you gain 100 additional delta. To calculate a P/L on such a move, assume you were long an average of 550 delta (500 to begin; 600 at end) for the one point move.

[247] It is OK to sell calls you own, as long as it does not leave short any naked calls.

now) and introduces upside risk. While it is true that being short both puts and calls is a viable option strategy, it is far too risky for a less-experienced options trader. In fact, it is an unsuitable strategy for most traders and I suggest not selling naked straddles (call and put with same strike price and expiration date) or strangles (different strikes with same expiration date).

If you are long 500 deltas, that is the equivalent of owning 500 shares. The question to ask is: are you comfortable holding that position in the current environment? If the potential loss from such a position is outside your comfort zone, then the answer is 'no' and you should adjust the position by adding short delta.[248]

If you prefer to have a more market-neutral[249] portfolio, then it is mandatory to be aware of portfolio delta, and more importantly, gamma. Some professional traders are quite risk averse and manage their portfolios by keeping delta, gamma, vega and theta as near zero as possible. There is no need to go that far, but unless you are always bullish, or want to place a bet on market direction, there is no reason to be long or short many deltas. My (current) favorite market-neutral strategy is covered in detail in Chapter 19.

Market exposure

Not all deltas are created equal. This becomes obvious if you consider this scenario: you own 100 GOOG (Google) shares (equal to 100 delta), a stock trading above $1,000 per share. If the stock moves 2% (20 points), your position makes or loses $2,000.

Compare that with being short 100 MSFT (Microsoft) shares (also 100 delta). This stock trades near $41. If MSFT changes price by 2%, the gain or loss is $82. Thus, long 100 GOOG and short 100 MSFT, is NOT market neutral, even though it is delta neutral.

While it is correct to sum deltas for options of a specific underlying asset to determine a position delta, simply adding deltas for individual positions does not offer a true measure of market risk. A portfolio may have zero net delta, but if it is long 100 GOOG deltas and short 100 MSFT deltas, it is a bullish portfolio due to the nature of those deltas.

A better method for determining exposure to a market move—in either direction—is to determine the "dollar delta." That means summing the

---

[248] Add short delta by closing part of the position. You may also buy puts, sell calls or sell stock.

[249] A market-neutral portfolio has neither a bullish nor bearish bias.

delta for each individual underlying asset and then multiplying that delta by the share price. You then add together those dollar deltas to give a clearer picture of where the portfolio stands. Doing that with the GOOG/MSFT portfolio, we get:

GOOG: $1,000 x 100 delta = long 100,000 $delta
MSFT: $41 x (-100) delta = short 4,100 $delta
Sum: +95,900 $delta. This portfolio is long, not market neutral.

Bottom Line: The Greeks help traders manage risk of a specific position or an entire portfolio. It is not necessary to live or die by the numbers, but it is also not in your best interest to ignore them.

Monitoring risk and doing your best to minimize large losses is the path to success as an option trader. The practical importance of the Greeks becomes more apparent in Chapters 17 through 19.

If you are trading options for the first time, you may not feel ready to use the Greeks. That is a mistake, but acceptable when it is a temporary situation. Get used to trading. That comes first. Gain experience opening and closing positions (hopefully for profits). Observe how options expire worthless or move into the money. Roll positions (only if necessary). Return to this chapter later because this information is necessary to developing good risk-management skills. The Greeks help traders decide if position reward is worth taking the required risk. When wild things happen, profits or losses can exceed reasonable expectations. The Greeks are guidelines, not mathematical certainties, but they can be used to decide how much reward to target and the risk involved in seeking that reward. Use good judgment when opening positions and use the Greeks as instruments to help manage your portfolio.

Remember that Greeks help quantify potential gains and losses. If you follow the advice in this book, all trades have *limited* losses, and that is the best way to control ultimate risk.

Delta and Time

The passage of time affects delta.

When expiration arrives:

If the option is in-the-money, it becomes equivalent to stock (100 delta). This must be true because ITM options are exercised at expiration and become (long or short) stock.

An out-of-the-money option expires worthless and its delta is 0.

As expiration approaches:

The delta of an ITM option moves toward 100. The further ITM, or as time passes, the more rapidly delta becomes 100.
The delta of an OTM option moves toward 0. The further OTM, or as time passes, the more rapidly delta becomes 0.

Quiz 15

1. You own a covered call position. You are long 200 shares and short two Oct 50 calls. Each call has a 65 delta. What is the position delta?

2. In the above example, if the stock moves from 51 to 52 today, do you expect to make or lose money? How much?

3. You own 10 put options. Are you long or short: gamma, vega, theta and delta?

4. A specific call option, whose vega is $0.040, is trading at $3.00. A sudden influx of buy orders drives the implied volatility from 35 to 40. What is the new price of this call option?

5. You sold 10 put options at $1.00 apiece. When the underlying stock declined by $1, you lost $200 (the option price became $1.20). If the stock declines another point tomorrow, do you expect to lose:

   a) Less than $200
   b) $200
   c) More than $200

Chapter 15 Answers

1. +70. You are long 200 shares of stock and that is always 200 deltas. You are short two options, each with a 65 delta, and that is -130 deltas (minus because you are short calls). Total is +70.

2. Make money. You are long and the stock moved higher. Approximately $70 because you have + 70 deltas and the stock moved one point. Reminder: delta measures the change in the option (or entire position) price as the stock price changes by one point.

3. You own options. Thus, you are long gamma and vega. You are also short theta. Because you own puts, you are short delta.

4. $3.20. When the option's vega is 0.040 (per share, or 4.0 per contract), it means the option's value increases by approximately $4 for each one point increase in implied volatility. The 5point increase corresponds to $20 per contract.

5. More than $200. Because of gamma, put delta has increased as the stock declined. A further decrease in the price of the underlying results in additional losses. Another way to look at his is to say the delta was approximately -20 when you sold the puts (because you lost $20 per put when the stock declined one point) and because of gamma, the delta is larger (more negative) now.

Chapter 16

European-Style Index Options

The strategies discussed in Part III are especially appropriate for index options, and unless you have a strong preference for trading options on individual stocks, many of you will ultimately trade European-style options.

Trading European options differs from trading American options and this chapter explains what a trader must know before using index options. This is not an idle warning. The differences may change how a trader chooses his/her trades.

Most traders prefer using actively traded options because they are very liquid. Some European-style index options trade huge volume every day. That means the chances of buying well below the ask price and selling significantly above the bid price are excellent. Most high volume index options traded in the U.S. are European style (the notable exception is OEX).

All individual stocks use American-style options. Thus far, the discussion and examples used in this book focused on American-style options because most investors own stocks, and thus, it is natural to use options on those stocks when beginning to trade options. However, there are advantages to adopting option strategies when the underlying asset is a diversified stock portfolio[250] rather than an individual stock. You may discover that you are more comfortable trading options on exchange traded funds (ETFs; American style) and indexes (European style).

Your full service broker may be one of the few brokers that provide helpful information, but they tend to assume that traders know what they are doing and are not likely to offer sufficient guidance—unless you ask the right questions. Too many investors who use European-style options are not aware of the 'fine print' and take unnecessary losses.[251] Before trading European-style options, please understand the pros and cons.

---

[250] For readers who adopt strategies recommended in this book, it is best when the underlying asset does not undergo large moves. Because individual stocks are prone to surprise announcements, it is not unusual for individual stocks to gap higher or lower when news is announced. Although this occurs with diversified stock portfolios (when the entire market makes a big move), it happens far less often. For that reason, trading index options is often a wise choice.

[251] Yes, some are fortunate enough to collect unexpected profits.

219

Difference one: settlement price

The first major difference between American- and European-style options is the manner in which the settlement price of the underlying index is determined. The settlement price is the official closing price for the index and is the basis for determining which options are in the money and the intrinsic value of those options. If you are considering trading index options, it is necessary to understand the process. Many a newcomer to index options has incurred a substantial loss because of his or her failure to understand this basic information:

When a stock closes for trading on the third Friday of the month,[252] the last trade determines the settlement price. It is obvious which options finish in- or out-of-the money and which options will be exercised by their owners.[253] As anyone would reasonably anticipate, the last price is the final price. However, the rules are *completely different* with European-style index options. To complicate matters further, different index options (with different settlement times) became available in recent years.[254] Be sure to become familiar with 'difference four' on p 229.

- European options cease trading at the close of business on Thursday, one day prior to the third Friday of the expiration month. Note, they stop trading, but they have not yet expired. These options do not trade on expiration Friday, but their value is determined by the market's opening prices on that day.

- The closing price of the underlying index on that Thursday is *irrelevant*. Difficult as it may be to believe, this is not the closing index price for the expiration cycle. In fact, the settlement price, the official terminology for the 'final' expiration price of the index, can be very different than Thursday's closing price.

- Many an investor who believed that his short index options expired worthless on Thursday afternoon were shocked to discover that the value of those options soared the next morning and that those "worthless" options were now in-the-money and worth many hundred (or even a couple thousand) dollars each. Investors who owned those options were thrilled, while those who were short these

---

[252] Some options use different expiration dates. For example, some SPX options expire on the last business day of the calendar quarter.

[253] Be aware that options that are barely in the money occasionally expire worthless when their owner elects not to exercise. That decision is made by the option owner and never by the seller.

[254] See 'Difference four' below (page 229).

options were filled with other emotions, including bewilderment and outrage.

- The closing price of the index (settlement price) is *calculated* based on the market opening on the third Friday. If you do not exit positions by the close of business on Thursday, then the final value of any options in your portfolio is determined by how strong or weak the market opens on expiration Friday.

- Above, note the word "calculated." *The settlement price is not a real-world index price.* In fact, the settlement price is often significantly higher than the official daily high price or significantly lower than the official daily low price for the specific index. Too many option traders have no idea how that is possible, but you are not going to be one of them.

- The settlement price is a *theoretical* price. It is calculated by determining the *opening price* of each component of the index (and that means all 500 stocks in the S&P 500 Index or all 2,000 stocks in the Russell 2000 Index, etc.) Then a theoretical price for the index is calculated *as if all components of the index were trading at their opening price at the same time.* It is important to understand that this settlement price is not a real-time price. It is likely that the index never traded at the official settlement price at any time during the trading day. Some stocks open at the opening bell, others shortly thereafter and some may not open until much later. In addition, stocks change price—some rise above the opening price and some fall below. The settlement price is based *only* on the opening price of each individual component of the index. Thus, traders who keep an eye on the actual price of the underlying index, expecting the first published index price for the day to be near the settlement price, are often dismayed at how different those prices can be.

- The value of all outstanding options expiring on that Friday depends on the settlement price.

- It takes several hours before the settlement price for SPX) is calculated and published. The settlement price is not published until the end of the trading day (Friday) for some indexes (RUT, for example).

- The settlement price has its own ticker symbol. SPX is the symbol for the S&P 500 Index, but SET is the symbol for the settlement price for that index. Other sample settlement symbols are:

- o RUT (Russell 2000): RLS

- o NDX (NASDAQ 100): NDS

- o DJX (Dow Jones Industrials): DJS

My two cents: when adopting a strategy that involves the sale of European-style index options, give serious consideration to closing the position no later than Thursday afternoon (of expiration week). It is seldom worth the risk to maintain a short position, hoping it expires worthless.[255] This is known as "settlement risk."

Difference two: cash-settled

European options are cash-settled. If an option is ITM when the settlement price is determined, the exercise/assignment process involves transferring the intrinsic value of the option, in cash, from the account of the person who is short the option to the option owner's account. When using American options, shares of the underlying asset (not cash) exchange hands via exercise and assignment.

EXAMPLE #1

You bought four NDX Jun 1950 calls @ $450 (options on the NASDAQ 100 Index) on a day when you felt bullish. At expiration, the settlement price of NDX is 1950.97. Your options are ITM, but this is not a victory. The intrinsic value of each call is $97. $388 (4 x $97) is transferred into your account and the long call options are removed. It is as if you sold the calls @ $97.

No shares were bought or sold. There is no concern with buying or selling a bunch of different stocks to rid your portfolio of any unwanted positions—because there is only cash.

EXAMPLE #2

You sold 10 SPX May 1500 calls (This is not a naked short, but the other parts of your position are not relevant to this discussion). At expiration, the index settlement price is 1508.73.

---

[255] This advice does not mean you must close all positions without thought. If you are short an option that is trading near $0.50 (for example), even if appears to be far out-of-the-money, it pays to cover. Every once in a while this option can become worth many hundreds of dollars because of a significant market move at the opening on expiration Friday. On the other hand, if you are short a spread that can never be worth more than $10 (discussed in Chapter 17), it is foolish to repurchase on Thursday afternoon and pay $9.80. The most you can lose by holding is the last $0.20. But, a significant market move can make this spread worthless, presenting you with a $980 gift per spread. If you own such a spread, rather than wait for that last $0.20, please consider selling and being satisfied to collect approximately $9.80.

That means the 1500 call is ITM by 8.73 points and has an intrinsic value of $873. Because you are short 10 of these calls, $8,730 is removed from your account and the SPX May 1500 calls disappear. This is the same as if you repurchased those May 1500 calls at $8.73. Nothing bad appears to have happened.[256] The bottom line is that expiration arrived, the calls sold earlier were covered, and you no longer have a position in these options.[257]

This cash settlement feature of European-style options is efficient. However, the method used to determine the final price of the index introduces a new risk factor. Settlement risk is real, and often unexpected. I urge you avoid being exposed to that risk. An index can easily move more than 2% on expiration morning.

EXAMPLE #3

SPX is trading near 1540 late in the afternoon, one day before expiration Friday.

a) You are long an SPX 1520 call option. The option is trading near $21 and you decide to hold it overnight. Friday morning, the market opens substantially lower and the settlement price is only 1525.50. You collect $550 per option. True, the market could have opened higher, but why take that chance?

b) You are short five SPX 1530 puts. The market makers are asking $0.60 apiece for those puts. You are not going to let them take advantage of you. After all, the options expire tomorrow morning and they are 10 points out-of-the-money. So, you decide you'll teach them a lesson and refuse to pay that ridiculous price. The next morning there is bad news overseas and the nervous market opens lower. You note that the opening SPX print is near 1529, You are disappointed that your puts are in-the-money, but it is only $1 and that is not much worse than if you had bought those puts last night @ $0.60. The rest of the day is better for the market. The opening price was the low for the day, and by day's end the market has recovered almost all of its losses

---

[256] But something very bad may have happened. If this option was OTM at last night's close and you failed to cover, you must now pay $873 apiece for these options.
[257] Consider it to be a regular expiration in which you were assigned an exercise notice, delivered shares of the underlying and repurchased those shares. Of course, the sale and repurchase of the underlying are imaginary and because no commissions are involved, it costs nothing. Settling options in cash is very convenient for all involved.

You think no more about your expired puts, but in the afternoon you notice that SET, the official settlement price, is 1525.50. That means you will pay $450 for each of those puts. Investors in this situation often feel cheated. Some are outraged. Those investors ignored settlement risk and probably have no idea how settlement price is calculated.[258] Please do not let this happen to you. If you choose not to cover short option positions, understand that most of the time that is the winning decision, but part of the time it is going be an expensive decision: paying $0.60 for those options doesn't seem like such a bad idea in retrospect. One way to avoid settlement risk is roll front-month options (before they expire) to a different expiration.

EXAMPLE #4

You are long six NDX Jun 2025 calls and short six NDX May 1975 calls. It is expiration week (May) and NDX is currently 1960. Deciding it is too risky to hold the May short,[259] you enter a spread order to buy six May 1975 calls (to close) and sell six Jun 2000 calls (to open). You collect a cash credit of $400 for the spread (that means 4 points for each spread, or $2,400 total). Your new position is long six NDX Jun 2025 calls and short six NDX Jun 2000 calls. If you prefer to close, it is important to understand the choices.

One obvious choice is to exit by covering the May calls and selling the long June via entering a spread order. Another choice is to wait for the opening Friday morning. At that time, sell the June calls and allow your Mays to disappear via settlement. (This is the high risk play that I hope you will avoid.) The May options expire worthless when they are OTM. If they are ITM, the intrinsic value is removed from your account.

---

[258] Because the market was headed lower at the opening, investors sold stocks "at the market." When that happens, there are more sellers than buyers and stocks often open at depressed prices. Because the settlement price is determined by those individual opening prices, and because those stocks open at various times, the settlement price is often lower than the actual index price posted. Here's why: while some stocks are already rebounding after the opening (and SPX is moving higher), other stocks are not yet open. These stocks may also open at depressed prices—and the settlement price depends only on those opening prices.

[259] The May position is not a naked short and you do own calls to limit upside risk. If the market rallies, the May calls will increase in value much faster than the Jun (they have a higher delta and an exploding gamma), and if the move is large enough, it results in a large loss. Many investors (including this author) feel it is better to eliminate that risk. On the other hand, if the market holds steady and if the May option expires worthless, you can make a very tidy profit by holding this position. As always, it is another risk vs. reward decision.

A reasonable question is: is that a good idea? The answer is no. If the market gaps higher, the June calls are sold at a nice price (if IV does not collapse), but the settlement price is often so high that you get punished when forced to cover May calls at the settlement price. Often, this is an unprofitable situation. When talking about risk, there are winners. Sometimes taking extra risk pays off. If the market opens relatively unchanged—and that does happen often—then it would better to exit Friday morning when the May options expire worthless. Take your choice, but it is safer and more profitable over the long term to get out of these positions before settlement.

Cash settlement is a mixed blessing for index traders. Without this feature, index options would not be so popular. Imagine owning a portfolio of hundreds of stocks (in an attempt to mimic the performance of the S&P 500, or any other index) and delivering all those shares when assigned an exercise notice. What a nightmare. Cash settlement simplifies the process for everyone, but the fact that the process is simplified does not eliminate that Friday morning settlement risk.

Difference three: exercise rights

The owner of an American-style option has the right to exercise *any time* before it expires. European-style options cannot be exercised before expiration. Thus, owners of European-style options who do not want to hold a position have no choice but to sell their options. This represents a small inconvenience for the option buyer and a nice bonus for the option seller who never has to be concerned with being assigned an exercise notice early.

Being assigned early represents significant risk when dealing with American-style cash-settled index options. Options on the S&P 100 Index (OEX)[260] present extra difficulties to anyone who sells them, as the following demonstrates.[261]

Clarification: Trading American-style options on stocks or ETFs is acceptable. The warning applies to *Index* options: avoid OEX.

EXAMPLE #5

Assume you sell two OEX Dec 650 puts and that your timing is unfortunate. The market declines for several days and falls

---

[260] These American-style options expire Friday afternoon, not Friday morning.
[261] It doesn't matter if naked short the options, or if they are part of a spread. When short OEX options, the threat of early assignment is real

especially hard one afternoon. OEX closes at 620, at the low price of the day. Let's ignore why you may still be holding this position.

Immediately after the close, IBM (or AAPL or GOOG) announces spectacular earnings and SPX futures trade much higher,[262] indicating that the market is likely to gap open significantly higher tomorrow morning. That is good news for you because the anticipated rally presents an opportunity to recover some of the losses. With OEX at 620, the Dec 650 puts now have 30 points of intrinsic value. You are not pleased with how much money has been lost, but tomorrow's rally will help.

The next morning, two things happen:

- Futures indicate that the Dow Jones Industrial Average will open + 200.

- You are notified that you were assigned an exercise notice on two OEX Dec 650 puts. These options are cash settled based on yesterday's closing OEX price. You paid the intrinsic value, or $3,000 each.

Sure enough, the markets open strongly higher and the OEX Dec 650 put is trading at $13, or 17 points better than last night's close! But, for you, it is too late. You were forced out of the position and paid $30.

This is a very real phenomenon. When it appears that the market is about to change direction immediately because of some news item, it is common for traders who are short deep in-the-money OEX options to be assigned an exercise notice. It does not matter whether they are calls or puts. It does not matter if the options are hedged. When OEX options are deep in-the-money, there is a significant chance of being assigned an exercise notice. Why exercise? Shouldn't the option owner sell the options? The question is: who's going to buy them? The put bids disappear as soon as news hits and options are bid far under intrinsic value. Similarly, calls are bid far above intrinsic value.[263] The only way to collect anything near $30 for the Dec 650 put option (in this example) is to exercise.

If you think the loss just described is bad, imagine how much worse it is when you own long puts as a hedge against those short puts *and fail to*

---

[262] Futures contracts on the indexes trade after the market closes and before it opens
[263] The option prices reflect the current best guess as to where the index will open on the next trading day.

exercise your long puts. Not only would you repurchase your shorts at the worst possible time (because of the assignment notice), but you now have additional losses because you still own the (now unhedged) other part of what used to be a spread position.

Any trader who sells options as part of a strategy should avoid trading OEX in favor of one of the European-style index options. This is mandatory.

Difference Four: AM and PM Settlement and Weeklys

At one time, all European-style index options were exactly as defined above. In more recent times, there have been changes. They are still European style options, but some characteristics are different. Traders must be certain they know which options they are trading. It can be confusing.

- PM settlement. SPX options are now primarily PM settled. That means the settlement price is determined by the final closing prices for each component in the index. There are no surprises.

- Just to keep things complicated, there is an exception. The regular 'monthly' SPX options—those which expire on the 3rd Friday of the month[264]—are still AM settled.

There is also a separate group of options that trade with the ticker: SPXpm. These are identical to 'regular' SPX options with one exception: the settlement price is based on the closing prices of the day. That means the confusing, awkward method of calculating AM settlement prices is gone. The final closing tick of the day for SPX is the settlement price. In other words, SPXpm options are similar to individual stock options in that respect. They remain cash settled.

- AM settlement. RUT, NDX, and DJX options remain as they were. Settlement is based on Friday morning opening prices and is calculated as described earlier in this chapter.

- Weeklys.[265] New options that expire in one week[266] are now listed for trading, but only for the most actively traded issues. The CBOE provides a link[267] to the latest list (revised every week).

- More Weeklys. If 'regular' Weeklys are not enough, the CBOE also offers options that expire in one, two, three, four, and five weeks for

---

[264] Keep reading. The alternative expiration dates are described immediately below.
[265] That is the official CBOE spelling: Weeklys
[266] Listed on Thursday and expire after the market closes on Friday, 8 days later.
[267] http://www.cboe.com/micro/weeklys/availableweeklys.aspx

a select group of stocks and indexes. RUT and SPX are included. Find the list at the same link.[268]

The European-Style Indexes

Not all indexes are European style. Although we have not yet addressed the specific strategies that allow you to best take advantage of index options, traders who adopt the strategies recommended in Part III are often better served by trading European-style, rather than American-style index options. The elimination of early exercise risk is sufficient reason.

The most actively traded options are easier to trade[269] than options with little investor interest. Among the European indexes, consider trading any of these broad-based indexes:

- SPX. S&P 500 Index. This index has more trading volume than any other, which is advantageous to the trader. However, as of this writing, this index trades on a single exchange and there is not as much competitive market making as in other index options that are listed on multiple exchanges. The bid/ask differential for SPX options is so wide that I no longer make any attempt to trade them. My advice is to try SPX options to see if you can accept the conditions. As an alternative, consider using SPXpm[270] options.

- NDX. NASDAQ 100 Index. A good portion of this index is comprised of technology stocks.[271]

- RUT. Russell 2000 Index. This index consists of stocks in the small-cap universe and is comprised of the smallest 2000 companies in the Russell 3000 Index.[272] It is significantly more volatile than SPX.

- DJX. Dow Jones Industrial Average (stock of 30 large companies).

- SML. S&P 600 Small Cap Index, which consists of 600 small stocks.

If you prefer to trade the stocks of a specific market sector (biotech, banks, heath care etc.), funds or indexes are available.[273] These are standard

---

[268] http://www.cboe.com/micro/weeklys/availableweeklys.aspx

[269] Extra volume provides more opportunity to trade with orders from other individual investors—and that means better trade executions for everyone.

[270] These options settle at the close of trading on the 3rd Friday. The underlying asset is the S&P 500 Index (same as SPX options).

[271] AAPL is the largest component (even after declining from the 700s to the mid-400s (as of Jan 2013)

[272] An index composed of the 3,000 largest (by capitalization—the market value of all outstanding shares of a company) stocks. This index is also divided into two other indexes: the Russell 1000 Index, which consists of the largest 1,000 stocks, and the Russell 2000 Index, which consists of the other 2,000 stocks.

[273] A partial list can be found here:

American options—if assigned an exercise notice, the deliverable is shares of the underlying sector fund.

Bottom line: To successfully trade European-style options, be aware of how they differ from American options. There is also a tax advantage for trading European-style options (for U.S. taxpayers) because profits are taxed as 60% long-term and 40% short-term capital gains. You can get more information from the IRS (publication 550).[274]

---

http://www.nasdaq.com/markets/indices/sector-indices.aspx
[274] http://www.irs.gov/pub/irs-pdf/p550.pdf

QUIZ 16

1. American-style options trade in the U.S. and European-style options trade overseas. **TRUE or FALSE**

2. If you are short an American-style option on ABCD stock, the settlement price is determined by its opening price on expiration Friday. **TRUE or FALSE**

3. Which option owner has more extensive rights regarding exercise: the owner of the American-style option or the owner of the European-style option?

4. What's the major reason for not holding a short position in an AM-settled, European-style option later than Thursday of expiration week?

5. The settlement price of European-style options is almost identical with the opening price for the specific index on expiration Friday. **TRUE or FALSE**

6. You own six European-style cash-settled SPX options.
   a) Are you allowed to exercise them before expiration?
   b) Are you allowed to sell them any time before expiration?
   c) If the options finish in-the-money, what must a trader do to get the cash value?

QUIZ 16 ANSWERS

1. False. There are no geographic restrictions.

2. False. The settlement price for American-style options is the closing price Friday afternoon.

3. American. They may exercise any time, whereas European option owners may exercise only at expiration.

4. The danger of a large adverse gap opening on Friday. The way settlement prices are calculated, those gaps are almost always exaggerated when the settlement price is calculated. i.e., the settlement price is much higher (gap up) or lower (gap down) than expected.

5. False. It is often substantially different.

6.

a) No
b) Yes
c) Nothing. Your broker and the OCC see that cash is automatically transferred to your account.

Chapter 17

Credit Spreads

A credit spread is an option position consisting of two legs—both calls or both puts. In addition, both options expire at the same time and have the same underlying asset. When initiating (opening) this position, it is more efficient and far less risky[275] to enter the order as a spread[276] instead of two separate orders—one for each leg in the spread. The discussion here includes specific instructions on how to do that. When selling the spread,[277] cash is collected. Hence, it is referred to as a credit spread. When buying the spread, cash is spent and it is called a debit spread.

Do not allow others to confuse you. You can use the terms bull and bear spread, but all they do is lead to confusion. The definition of a credit spread is simple:

- All vertical spreads[278] are defined from the buyer's point of view: The more expensive option is bought and the less expensive option is sold.

- When buying (paying cash) a spread, it is always a debit spread

- When selling (collecting cash) a spread, it is always a credit spread

EXAMPLE

Credit Spread (selling a spread, puts in this example)

Buy 10 IBM Oct 90 puts; Sell 10 IBM Oct 95 puts

Debit Spread (buying a spread, calls in this example)

Buy 8 MSFT Dec 30 calls; Sell 8 MSFT Dec 35 calls

Earlier we showed that selling a put spread is equivalent (Chapter 14) to owning a collar—a conservative strategy that allows an investor to protect a position against significant loss.

---

[275] The price of the option may change before you get a chance to enter the second order.
[276] All options in the spread order are bought/sold—or none. There is no chance to getting an unwanted trade.
[277] Selling a spread means selling the higher priced option and buying the lower priced option.
[278] Two calls or two puts with same expiration and same underlying, but different strike prices

Let's take a closer look at the put credit spread to see why this conservative strategy is appropriate for many investors.

Put credit spreads

If you have a neutral to bullish opinion on a stock (or the entire stock market), you can sell naked puts in an attempt to profit when your forecast comes true. That method is suitable for investors who prefer to accumulate stock when their short-term opinion is wrong and the stock is below the strike price when expiration arrives (as described in Chapter 13).

There is a better (less risky) put-selling strategy you can use. When adopting this strategy, buy one (less expensive, i.e., lower strike price) put for each put sold. When both options expire at the same time, the position is a vertical put spread.[279] If buying the spread, you have a bear put spread. If selling, you have a bull put spread.

> **NOTE:** In an effort to keep things simple, but 100% understandable, I prefer to refer to these trades as buying or selling a put spread (or call spread). Most others refer to buying and selling bear put spreads, bull put spreads, bear call spreads and bull call spreads. In my opinion that is unnecessarily complicated. When we buy a spread, we pay cash and own the more expensive option. It is obvious which are bullish and bearish without having to so state.

When selling put spreads, the goal is similar to selling naked puts: allowing the spread to expire worthless, or be repurchased at a profit. That is how these spreads are used to generate profits. As with any position that you sell, the objective is to pay a lower price later, when exiting the trade. With options, there is also the possibility of having the position expire worthless. That means the position just 'goes away' without a need to actually buy the position.

Some stocks offer a significant number of spread choices because they have numerous strike prices. Others offer a more limited choice. We'll look at a real-world example, using the Russell 2000 Index (RUT), and consider how to decide which options to trade. As is always true, there is no single "best" answer.

The numbers presented in Table 17.1 were collected during market hours on September 21, 2007. Four weeks remain before the October

---

[279] If they do not have the same expiration, the position is referred to as a diagonal put spread.

options stop trading (Thursday, October 18). The final settlement price (see Chapter 16) is calculated from the opening prices on Friday, October 19.

Today, index options are offered at intervals of five points. However this data was collected when options were only available with 10-point intervals. Options are listed for trading with strikes 550 through 980, but the table only includes Oct 660 through 810 for two reasons:

- This strategy is almost always implemented using out-of-the-money (OTM) options and ITM options need not be considered.

- Options that are too far OTM cannot be used because they don't meet the suggested minimum requirements (described below).

The table shows the bid/ask quotes and delta for 16 different options. When selling a credit spread, you can trade any pair of those options. That means there are 120 possible credit spreads. In reality, far fewer choices are practical. When selling credit spreads, there is room for individuality. My personal preference is to sell spreads in which the strike prices are as near each other as possible. For me, that means selling 10-point spreads[280] (spread nomenclature defines a spread by the difference between the strike prices.) for RUT options. But it is perfectly reasonable to sell 20- and 30-point RUT put spreads. And some investors sell spreads that are wider.

Choosing the underlying

If selling put spreads on individual stocks, trade options on stocks you have been following. That is wiser than randomly choosing stocks. Do not have a list of stocks? No problem. This strategy may be used with index options. Many indexes have listed options, but if you prefer to trade cash-settled options (Chapter 16), be certain to choose an appropriate index. If you cannot find which indexes qualify, ask the OCC (Options Clearing Corporation).[281]

The most popular European-style, cash-settled index options are SPX, NDX and RUT (Standard & Poor's 500 Index, Nasdaq 100 Index and Russell 2000 Index, respectively). It is important to be comfortable trading the stock portfolio represented by the index, because this method involves market risk, and traders do not take bullish positions at random. They prefer a portfolio they believe has a small probability of falling. If you are more comfortable trading larger stocks, then SPX or DJX (Dow Jones Industrials) may be a better choice. If you prefer smaller companies, the Russell 2000 (RUT) is appropriate. Sector indexes are also available (with American-style options). Stay within your comfort zone.

---

[280] Even with 5-point intervals now available, I prefer to use 10-point spreads. Later in this chapter, we will talk about how a specific spread width is chosen.
[281] Send e-mail to options@theocc.com

Table 17.1
RUT Put Options; RUT $815.55
28 Days before Expiration

Strike	Bid	Ask	Delta
660	$0.60	$0.75	-2
670	$0.75	$0.85	-2
680	$0.95	$1.05	-3
690	$1.20	$1.30	-4
700	$1.55	$1.75	-5
710	$1.95	$2.05	-6
720	$2.45	$2.60	-7
730	$2.95	$3.20	-8
740	$3.80	$4.00	-11
750	$4.70	$4.90	-13
760	$5.60	$5.90	-16
770	$7.10	$7.50	-20
780	$8.90	$9.10	-24
790	$10.90	$11.20	-29
800	$13.40	$13.80	-35
810	$16.60	$16.90	-42

Choosing RUT options for trading

Choosing the strikes

There are several items to consider when choosing the specific strikes for the spread. With individual stocks, there are often few choices. But when trading indexes, there are more than enough possibilities. When first learning this strategy, I recommend always selecting the specific option to be sold first and then finding the appropriate option to buy

There are two main schools of thought on which option to sell. There is the OTM school and the CTM[282] school. The most popular strategy (and the one I prefer) is to sell options that are reasonably far out-of-the-money (OTM). The idea is to sell option spreads that have a high probability of

---

[282] Close-to-the-money. I loosely define that term as closer to the money than your 'regular' credit spreads. This concept is far easier to understand after making your first trade or two.

expiring worthless, but which have enough premium to make them worth selling. The good news for OTM supporters: the probability of earning a profit is excellent. That is inferred from the low delta of these options (Table 17.1) because the delta represents a fairly good estimate of how often an option will be ITM when expiration arrives (assuming all market conditions are unchanged). The bad news: the maximum possible loss is far greater than the potential reward, and the risk/reward ratio is unattractive.

- Maximum gain when selling a credit spread: the cash credit collected. Thus, when selling a spread for $1.00, the maximum gain is $100. To earn that amount, the options must expire worthless.

- Maximum loss when selling a credit spread: if both options in the spread are in-the-money at expiration, then the spread is worth the difference between the strike prices (multiplied by $100). That loss is the maximum possible, after deducting the premium collected. When selling a 10-point spread for $1.00, the maximum loss is $9.00 per spread or $900. Why is this true? Whenever the put option you own finishes in-the-money, then the option you sold also finishes in-the-money because it has a higher strike price. Similarly when the long call (in a call credit spread) is ITM, the call you sold must also be ITM because the strike price is lower. Whatever your option is worth, the sold option is always worth 10 points (for a 10-point spread), or $1,000 more. The loss is that $1,000 minus the $100 premium collected earlier.

The other school of thought supports the idea of selling options that are closer-to-the-money (CTM).[283] There are several benefits to adopting this method:

- A larger premium is collected, allowing for a higher potential profit per spread.

- The maximum loss per spread is reduced,[284] making the risk/reward ratio more attractive.

- The same profit potential is available by selling fewer spreads, significantly reducing risk (the amount of money that can be lost).

Along with the benefits, there are also disadvantages:

---

[283] CTM options are also OTM, but they are OTM by less.
[284] If selling an OTM 10-point spread for $1.00, the maximum loss is $9.00. When selling a CTM spread for $4.00, the maximum loss is $6.00.

- The options sold have a higher delta, and thus, a lower probability of expiring worthless.

- The options of CTM credit spreads move ITM far more often. That necessitates additional risk management decisions.

NOTE: It is true that selling a put credit spread is equivalent to owning a collar position, when the strike prices and expiration date are identical. It is also true that when discussing the collar (Chapter 13), I always used strike prices that were fairly close to at the money because traditional collar buyers prefer to use those strikes.

In this chapter, I'm recommending the use of options that are farther OTM. There are two basic reasons for this difference. One: the collar examples use individual stocks and most collar owners have a bullish bias, but want a small-deductible insurance policy (a put that is not too far OTM)—so they have good protection against loss. If you own a 30-strike put on a $50 stock that is not going to be very helpful if the stock declines. Two: selling put spreads is used by investors who do not own stock. They seek a trading profit. Thus, there is no reason to prefer any specific strike prices

For the CTM school, there is less overall risk with at least as much overall profit potential.

There is a third school (FOTM, or far out-of- the-money), but it is best ignored. These spreads have a high probability of being profitable. But, the premium is small and you cannot collect enough cash to provide a worthwhile return. Selling index spreads @ $0.10 or $0.20, earns a profit almost all the time. That is not good enough because those premiums are reduced by commissions. More importantly, the market undergoes major moves every so often, and one of these spreads could easily result in a loss that wipes out years of profits. Do not do it. The odds of long-term success are very much against this style of trading. I suggest never selling a credit spread for less than a certain minimum. Each investor can determine a suitable minimum.[285] Do not accept less than $0.40 or $0.50 for 10-point index spreads.[286] This is not a rule, just a guideline.

If you begin the search for a good spread with an idea of which strike price to sell, there are few alternatives to consider. Begin with 5- or 10-

---

[285] For indexes, 50 cents is my minimum. However, I almost never accept that little, unless it is a one-week option.

[286] My personal minimum is higher. Double those amounts for 20-point spreads

point spreads if trading RUT (or any high-priced index). If you prefer NDX, many times the most narrow spread width is 25 points.

With so many choices, the obvious question is: how are you supposed to make an intelligent decision? Let's look at one example and discuss the possibilities. But first, some notes about entering orders:

Entering the order

I anticipate that the majority of readers have little experience trading options, and even less trading index options. The first thing you need to know is that *the published bid and ask prices do not represent the true state of the market*. You can almost always buy below the offer and sell above the bid. Thus, it is important to NEVER enter market orders and to use limit orders. When entering those limit orders, unless you must make a trade this very second, do not pay the ask price for the option you want to buy and do not sell the bid price for the option you want to sell. Most index options are published with notoriously wide markets, and it requires some trading experience before you know at what price you can get an order filled. I suggest beginning by entering orders near the midpoint between the bid and ask.[287] If there is no trade execution, you can raise the bid (or lower the offer). But please have a true limit in mind. Do not trade at any price just to get some action.

When trading credit spreads, always[288] use spread orders. The order stipulates:

- The broker must trade both options or neither.

- The broker must fill the order at your specified (limit) price or better.[289]

Repeating: enter a *limit* order, not a *market* order. If filled, you sell the spread at your price (or better). If the order is not filled, the limit price can be changed. Or you can try again the next day.

EXAMPLE

Choosing credit spread width

For the moment, let's not choose the "school" and assume the Oct 740 put is a suitable option to sell. The current bid is $3.80 and

---

[287] Five or ten cents above the midpoint if you are buying and the same below when selling
[288] Unless you have a *very* good reason
[289] "Or better" means the order is filled at an even higher price when selling or a lower price when buying.

the delta is -11. Let's consider three different credit spreads in which we buy the Oct 730, 720 or 710 puts.[290]

There is one important point that cannot be ignored. The bid-ask spreads in Table 17.1 are excellent. By that I mean they are very tight and it is not painful to pay the ask price when it is only 10 or 20 cents above the bid. But, as this book is being updated (2013) current bid-ask spreads are *much* wider. The volatile market of 2008-9 has left one semi-permanent scar: wide markets. Thus, it is more important than ever to use limit orders and avoid (avoid doesn't mean 'never') paying the ask price when buying, or accepting the bid price when selling.

10-point spread

The RUT Oct 730 put is offered at $3.20 and its delta is -8. Thus, the spread delta is -3 (-11 minus -8).[291] If you pay the offer and sell the bid, you collect $0.60 for the 10-point spread. The "outside market" for this spread is $0.45 wide. That means if you use the individual quotes to determine the market for the RUT Oct 740/730 put spread, the bid is $0.60 and the offer is $1.05. The "outside market" is the price seen on your computer screen[292] when you agree to pay the offer for one option and sell the bid for the other. (Again, I must emphasize that you can get better prices when trading).

Here are some important things to know:

- There is always an "inside market." That means the specific spread you want to trade almost certainly has a bid price (using our example) that is higher than $0.60 and an offer price that is less than $1.05. Most brokers provide no help in obtaining that inside market quote and their customers are left to their own devices. That is unfortunate, but it is the way the world operates. Some brokers (for an additional commission if the order is filled) have a way to get a live quote from the trading floor or from off-the-floor market makers. But, this service is usually reserved for customers

---

[290] And sell the Oct 740 put

[291] Clarification: The spread has -3 delta. But we are <u>selling the spread</u>, so we add +3 delta for each spread sold.

[292] Assuming you trade online. If not, it is the market your broker supplies when you request a quote.

who trade larger orders.[293] In this specific example, it is likely that the inside market is tighter, perhaps $0.70 to $0.95.[294]

- When you do not know the inside market, you must guess a price when entering orders. Once you have some experience you will have a sense of how far you have to go to get orders filled. Here's my suggestion: use the midpoint between the bid and ask prices as your starting point. In this case, that is $0.825 (halfway between the bid of $60 and the offer of $1.05). Shave something off that midpoint and enter your limit sell order, asking 80 cents credit. After 10 seconds (longer if you are patient), lower your price to 75 cents. Then 70 cents. DO NOT do this indefinitely. There has to be some limit. There is a price at which the trade is no longer desirable.

- If you enter orders online, become very familiar with your broker's trading software. Do not be afraid to ask customer service for help if you are unable to figure it out for yourself. If uncertain, try entering orders in a play money account (called paper trading) to be certain you do not buy when you intend to sell or make other mistakes due to unfamiliarity with the software.

- When using a live broker and you want to sell five of the spreads described above, tell the broker: "I want to enter an order to sell five lots of the RUT Oct 740/730 put spread at a limit price of seventy-five (or eighty) cents or better." Obviously this statement is for this specific example and you must substitute the correct quantity, underlying stock, premium and strike prices.

- Markets and market conditions change over the years. Sometimes you can receive a quick execution near the midpoint, and at other times it is more difficult to trade. You are probably anxious to get started trading, and may be willing to sacrifice a little cash to get started. But (important) to repeat, there must some minimum price for the trade. Do not reduce the price until someone buys the spread. Have a little patience.

- When entering an order that is not filled immediately, that order remains visible to market participants and can be filled at any time. If the underlying moves lower, it becomes more attractive for someone to buy your put spread. If the underlying moves higher, it reduces your chances of getting filled. Why? Because the put credit

---

[293] It varies by broker. The order does not have to be large, but do not expect this service for fewer than 100 contracts or 50 to 100 spreads.
[294] "Tighter" means the bid and ask prices are closer to each other.

spread increases in value as the underlying moves lower—and the lower it moves the more likely it is that some market participant buys your spread.

- Once you determine (from experience) how much to shave off the midpoint price, you have a better idea where to start the next time you trade. It is a cat and mouse game and there is no substitute for experience in discovering at which price to try to sell (or buy) your spreads. There is nothing wrong with always starting at the midpoint.

- If happy to sell the spread at $0.70, you are not obligated to try for a better price. You may offer at $0.70 right away. However, extra nickels and dimes add up over the years (it is a way to pay commissions, for example), so do not give them away without at least a minimal effort to get a better price on every trade. A difference of $0.05 on a 10-lot[295] is $50.

- When selling the 10-point spread @ $0.75, your maximum gain is $75 per spread (less commission). What are the chances of earning that maximum? The best way to get a good handle on that probability is to look at the delta of the put sold. Remember, the absolute value of the delta is roughly the same as the probability the option finishes in the money. Using the calculator (or referring to Table 17.1), you find the put has a delta of -10.9. Thus, the chance that this option finishes ITM is approximately 11%, or 1 in 9. Using the same volatility for the Oct 730 put, the calculator returns a delta of -8.2. This means both options finish ITM more than 8% of the time, and if no adjustments are made, you can expect to lose the maximum, or $925 per spread, approximately one time in 12, or once per year, assuming one trade per month.

NOTE: The $925 loss is more than you earn, even if you make the $75 maximum, during the other 11 months. Those numbers suggest two obvious conclusions: Either it is a poor strategy to sell this spread at any price below $1.00[296] or you must prevent losing the maximum by taking appropriate defensive action.

---

[295] Ten option contracts or 10 spreads.
[296] When collecting $1.00 every month for one year, you earn $1,100 (100 * 11) and lose $900 once for a net annual gain of $200. This is not a very good return, but it is not a loss.

- Do not begin trading options with too little capital, despite the fact that you are anxious to get started. Each broker establishes a minimum monetary requirement to open an account, but these requirements are too low in my opinion. If you begin trading with a small number of contracts and have the patience to learn more before trading larger size (more contracts), you may survive. When using the suggested strategies skillfully, your chances of making money increase. That is the reason each strategy is covered in detail. The better you understand what you are doing, the better results you can expect. But the primary factors that determine your long-term success are your risk and money-management skills, along with the ability to trade with discipline. It is not the chosen strategy that makes the difference.

The margin requirement to open a 10-point spread is $1,000, less the premium collected. How is that determined? The broker requires that the maximum possible loss be deposited into the account ($925 in this example). Once the margin requirement is met, the trader cannot receive a margin call.[297] The maximum profit is $75 and the maximum return on investment (ROI) is $75/$925 or 8.1%. That is very good for a one-month investment. That return makes these spreads attractive, despite the large possible loss.

20-point spread

The RUT Oct 720 put is offered at $2.60. The outside market for the RUT Oct 740/720 put spread is $1.20 to $1.55. The midpoint is $1.375. Enter an order to sell this spread at $1.35, knowing you probably must accept $1.30 or $1.25.

If selling this spread at $130, the maximum loss is $1,870 (this is a 20-point spread). The Oct 720 put has a -7 delta, and the maximum loss occurs about one time in 14. The margin requirement is $1,870. The maximum return is $130, and the maximum ROI is $130/$1,870 or 7.0%.

30-point spread

The RUT Oct 710 put is offered at $2.05 (Table 17.1). The market for the RUT Oct 740/710 put spread is $1.75 to $2.05. With the midpoint being $1.90, enter an order to sell this spread at $1.80 or $1.85.

Assuming $180, the maximum loss is $2,820 (30-point spread). The delta of the Oct 710 put is -6 and this spread loses the maximum when RUT finishes at 710 or lower. That is one time in 16. The margin requirement is $2,820 and the maximum gain is $180 or 6.4%.

---

[297] Some other positions may result in a margin call, but not the sale of credit spreads.

Deciding how wide the spread should be is an important decision, and it is OK to be flexible. I suggest starting with the narrowest possible spread for your first trades and deciding if that style works. The narrower spreads are, the easier to handle because maximum losses are smaller, the position has fewer negative delta and rolling (if necessary) is easier for most traders to handle. The goal is to become comfortable with risk/reward parameters of the chosen spread. If you have a strong feeling that 20-, 30- (or wider) point spreads are best for your comfort zone, you can go with that feeling and see how it works. However, to repeat, I believe you will fare better by beginning with narrow spreads. This is another of those situations in which there is no 'wrong' method. But please recognize that a 30-point spread is equivalent to three consecutive 10-point spreads. In other words, if your correct position size is fifteen 10-point spreads, then do not sell fifteen 30-point spreads. The correct number of spreads is five.

Summary on spread width for the more advanced trader

We know that the 20-point spread is equivalent to two 10-point spreads (proof below). Thus, instead of choosing the 20-point spread because it 'feels' right, make a more intelligent choice. Choose the 10-point spread that you prefer. When there truly is no preference, the 20-point spread is appropriate.

Proof:
    a)   Sell 5 Oct 220 calls
    b)   Buy 5 Oct 230 calls

    c)   Sell 5 Oct 230 calls
    d)   Buy 5 Oct 240 calls

If we trade spreads a) and b) then we can add the positions to get:
    Long 5 Oct 240 calls
    Short 5 Oct 220 calls

Thus, buying two adjacent 10-point spreads is the same as buying the 20-point spread. Notice that we bought five of each spread for a total of 10 spreads. The equivalent position is to own only five of the 20-point spreads. That should make sense because the 10-point spreads can reach a maximum value of $1,000 and the 20-point spread can reach a maximum value of $2,000. To trade with essentially equal risk, the double-width spread is traded in half the size.

When pondering the idea of trading a wider credit spread, examine each of the 'inner' spreads to determine whether there is one you prefer to own. When there a preferred choice, there is no advantage to the double-width.

Choosing the strike to sell

This is an important decision. When trading individual stocks, your choices are usually limited.[298] But with high-priced indexes, there are more than enough strike prices for everyone.

When selling your first credit spread, choose a narrow spread with lower delta options (8 to 12 for an index). It is not that this is the best money-making choice, but it is likely to provide a more comfortable experience. It is easier to learn when there are few risk management decisions. Those decisions are easier to handle after you have some trading experience.[299]

There are two important requirements. First, the option sold must have sufficient premium to make the trade worthwhile. Very low priced options are inappropriate, primarily because the second condition cannot be satisfied. Second, when choosing an option to buy (this option is always further OTM than the option sold) the difference in premium between the two options must provide an acceptable potential profit. Using very low-priced options makes it difficult to collect more than a few nickels in premium—and that is not something you want to do.

Referring to Table 17.1, take a look at the markets for the first two puts listed: the Oct 660 and Oct 670 puts. The bid/ask for this spread is zero to $0.25. How much can you expect to collect for this spread when the market makers are willing to sell it for twenty-five cents? Answer: too little. And it is not much better with the next possible spread, the Oct 670/680. The bottom line is that you cannot go too far OTM because the very low price of the options makes trading a put credit spread undesirable.[300] If you truly want to trade options this far (or further) OTM, you can do so by going out another month to November options (see Table 17.2).

Again, referring to Table 17.1, the Oct 740 put is as far as my comfort zone allows me to go. You may feel comfortable selling the 730 or 720 instead, but the reason I choose not to do that is that the spread premium becomes too small. The outside market for the RUT Oct 720/730 spread is $0.35 to $0.75, and it is unlikely you can collect more than $0.50 for the spread. If $0.50 appeals to you, then go for it. There are no rules, just guidelines. I'd provide a list of conditions that must be met for optimum results, but no such conditions exist. You're on your own in deciding how much profit potential and how much risk to take. That is yet another reason for beginning with paper-trades.

---

[298] When trading high-priced or volatile stocks, such as GOOG (Google) or AAPL (Apple Computer), there are many strikes from which to choose.

[299] If you are not sure what to about a position that becomes uncomfortable, it may be best to simply exit and take the loss. But please do not panic. Have a trade plan that specifies a target profit and maximum loss.

[300] Do not forget, this is not the entire list of October RUT options. This inability to trade gets even worse as you move further OTM.

If one trader opens a trade with four weeks remaining to expiration and another makes the same trade one week later, prices and premium levels are going to be different. When all else remains unchanged, the passage of time reduces the premium available when selling OTM credit spreads.

If you attend the CTM school, there are several acceptable choices when choosing options to trade. Decide how far out-of-the-money the short option should be. I suggest making this decision based on the option delta. For example, if very bullish on the underlying, then it may be better to sell a put spread that is almost at the money. That offers the chance to earn a higher reward. The Oct 800/810 put spread is $2.80 to $3.50 (Table 17.1) and you have a decent chance to collect $3.10. DO NOT sell the 790/810 put spread (20-points wide) in an effort to earn even more profit. That would double risk. If you prefer that 20-point spread, cut position size in half.

Other CTM traders would be comfortable selling the 770 or 780 put. There is no best choice. This truly is a question of being comfortable with the risk required to collect the reward. Let's look at one CTM spread and compare the risk and reward with that of the OTM chosen in the previous example.

EXAMPLE

The RUT Oct 770 put market is $7.10 to $7.50 and that of the 780 put is $8.90 to $9.10. Notice that the market in the latter put is only twenty cents wide—a rarity for index options priced over $1. The outside market for the Oct 780/770 put spread is $1.40 to $2.00. You can probably collect $1.60, and perhaps $1.65 for the spread (these actively traded index options trade in penny increments).[301] If the price is $1.65, then the maximum loss is $8.35. Notice that risk is five times the profit potential, whereas it was more than 12 times greater ($925/$75) for the 740/730 put spread. That improved risk/reward ratio provides a feeling of security. However, the delta of the Oct 770 put is -20.1,[302] reducing the likelihood that this option finishes out-of-the-money to 80% compared with 89% for the Oct 740 put. By adopting the CTM methodology, you get something, but you give up something else.

---

[301] Thus, you may enter an order to sell at $1.62, for example.
[302] A put value of $7.30 tells us the IV is 27.7. Using that IV, the calculator produces -20.1 as the put delta. In the text, I've repeated the data from the tables, but the numbers are not that accurate, and we refer to the delta of this option as 'minus 20' and ignore any decimal places.

The objective in discussing these spreads is to find the right combination for your comfort zone. There is no substitute for trading with real money to get a sense of which strike prices appeal. Make your best judgment when starting to trade and you will know which positions feel 'right' to manage. You never want to feel fear, and you never want to believe that your position can never lose.

Do not trade too many of these put spreads at one time until you are comfortable with how they work.

Choosing the expiration month

Front-month options are the most popular choice among those who sell credit spreads. In fact, in more recent times, the Weeklys (when offered) have taken over the most-active spot. The primary reason is that option buyers prefer paying less for options and want the biggest bang (positive gamma) for the buck. Premium sellers are attracted to options with rapid time decay. Both buyers and sellers take substantial risk for their potential rewards.

By moving the expiration date out one month (or two), several important parameters of the credit spread position change:

- Because there is more time before expiration, more bad things can happen[303] and there is an increased chance for the underlying to move against the position.

- Option prices are higher (see Table 17.2 to compare), allowing a trader to sell further OTM options and still meet minimum premium requirements.

- Gamma is reduced. If the underlying moves lower after you sell put spreads (or higher after you sell call spreads) gamma is less and changes more slowly for longer-dated options. And that results in position delta changing more slowly. Translation: If the underlying drops significantly, position delta grows quickly[304] when there is little time before expiration.

- When collecting more cash to open a position, the trader may be more inclined to exit early to lock in a profit. It is easier to pay that last 20 cents to close a spread when it was sold for $1.50 than when the premium was $0.75. The advantage to this type early exit is

---

[303] When buying options time is the enemy because things must happen 'soon.' When selling options or spreads, time passing is our friend. More time is thought of as when something bad can happen.

[304] Unless it is still far out-of-the-money

that risk is eliminated at the maximum cost of a small additional profit.

EXAMPLE

The data in Table 17.2 represents midpoint prices (the average between the bid and ask prices) for specific NDX put credit spreads. Traders should not anticipate receiving these prices when selling the spreads,[305] but the comparisons are still valid.

With the index trading near 2092, the front-month NDX 1800/1825 spread is unappealing because the credit is $0.35 or less. By moving out one month, the ~$1.30 premium is far more attractive, even though the spread has a 4-week longer lifetime. The same combination (higher premium coupled with longer lifetime) is available for the OTM spreads listed in Table 17.2.

FOTM adherents may consider trading options with a later expiration date as a way to boost the premium to an acceptable minimum.

When actively managing risk, it is not always necessary to make adjustments. Much of the time all goes well and the credit spreads peacefully decrease in value and are covered at some low price. "Low" does not refer to a specific price. If your style calls for selling spreads @ $1.25 or higher, then paying $0.15 to $0.25 (depending on circumstances) is reasonable. If selling spreads @ $0.50 or less, it is difficult for some traders to pay anything to exit. I'm a believer in sacrificing a small portion of my potential profit in return for complete safety.[306] As you gain experience and discover a comfort zone, you will know whether holding or closing early better suits your risk management needs. Remember, when the spread premium is small, there is little to gain (and a great deal to lose) by holding.

For starters, it is fine to reduce position size. As you learn about alternatives, they can be considered. Keep written records for later review. This is a wonderful method for being able to look back and discover what you were thinking.

Keep in mind that the results from the first few trades do not represent a true picture of what lies ahead. Your ultimate goal is to build a portfolio of one or more positions that allows you to trade in the stock market—but with less risk than that of a buy and hold stock investor.

---

[305] It is rare when a market maker is willing to pay the midpoint to trade with a customer. However, there is always the chance of trading with another individual investor—and that leads to better trade execution for both parties.

[306] Time is a vital element of the decision. I love paying 15 cents to exit any trade when it has a greater than a 4-week lifetime. However, I would not pay more than 5 cents to cover a 'safe-looking' position when less than one week remains.

**Table 17.2; Time vs. Spread Value
Midpoint; NDX Put Spreads;
NDX = $2,091.85**

Spread	24 days	52 days
1800/1825	$0.35	$1.30
1825/1850	$0.48	$1.60
1850/1875	$0.58	$1.65
1875/1900	$0.83	$2.15
1900/1925	$1.15	$2.60
1925/1950	$1.50	$3.10
1950/1975	$2.10	$3.65
1975/2000	$2.85	$4.45
2000/2025	$3.40	$5.10

Time affects the value of NDX put spreads;
Days = days to expiration

This thorough discussion of put credit spreads does not replace hands-on experience. If you have the patience, open a paper-trading account and play with a few different credit spreads. If trading an index, consider CTM and OTM spreads that expire in the front month (with at least a 3-week lifetime). I encourage selling more than one-lot of the spread because it allows some versatility when managing risk.[307]

After doing that two or three times, next open positions (paper-trading account) in both the front- and 2nd-months. The reason for not following multiple positions for the first few trades is that it can easily overwhelm any trader. Do not try to manage more positions that you can comfortably follow. This is a learning experience and following trades that do not involve real money takes patience and a commitment to learning. As time passes, watch the positions. Notice the conditions under which the positions make and lose money. When you are comfortable with the decisions (reducing risk, taking profits, exiting with a loss) that must be made during the lifetime of a trade, it is time to move on and initiate one-lot positions with real money.

As a new risk manager, decide if any adjustments are necessary and which spreads make you feel more comfortable to own. When necessary make a risk-reducing trade. Do not immediately be concerned with making the best choice, but get in the habit of reducing risk when uncomfortable.

---

[307] With only one-lot, the most obvious adjustment—reducing position size—is unavailable.

When selling put credit spreads, the goal is to cover those spreads when they are no longer appropriate to hold—hopefully at a profit. When the underlying moves too far or too quickly in the wrong direction, money is lost. If you find yourself in that unfortunate situation (and you will), it is important to know when to adjust (or exit) the position. That is the reason for practicing before getting started. Closing your eyes and hoping for the best is not a winning strategy.

Risk management

The discussion that follows presents some ideas on managing risk. There is no simple, easy-to-follow formula for deciding when a position should be adjusted. Nor are there specific trades to make. There are always alternatives. Your goal, as risk manager and money manager for your portfolio, is to make those difficult decisions. You must decide whether to "hold 'em or fold 'em."

> **NOTE:** For emphasis: managing positions is difficult. The goal is to own positions that earn profits and to know when to take those profits. The problem is that we also have a goal to exit positions that are too risky to hold, especially when they are losing money. It takes experience to recognize when a good position has crossed the line (or is about to cross the line) from good to bad (too risky).
>
> Much of risk management is 'art' rather than 'science.' Thus, do not expect specific rules to follow. However, the best guideline is your comfort zone. When a position makes you queasy or disturbs your sleep, that position has clearly crossed over to the dark side. In general, we do not hold positions until that happens. We want to cut risk (even when it means locking in a loss) before we reach that stage. On the other hand, we cannot cut risk every time the underlying stock or index makes a small move against the position. There is a compromise, and it is my job to help you discover where that compromise lies and it is your job to pay attention to risk. I cannot repeat it too many times: ignore risk at your peril. The chances of surviving are small when a trader (investor) becomes a gambler.

Neither every trade nor every risk-management decision results in the best possible outcome. Part of the time you would have been better off not making the adjustment. Another part of the time those adjustments save a bundle of cash. Do not be harsh on yourself. Remember, when trading credit spreads or iron condors (Chapter 19) or any option strategy, you will probably make money most of the time. Your goal as risk manager is to be certain that losses do not hurt. They are never pleasant, but if you maintain good discipline, losses do not be large enough to threaten overall profitability.

When to adjust a credit spread

The term, "adjustment," refers to making one or more trades that changes a current position. The most common reason for taking this action is to reduce risk, but locking in a profit also falls under the adjustment umbrella. This discussion covers some of the general concepts of adjusting. A whole book can be written on the details.

Knowing when to adjust a position to reduce or eliminate risk is more art than science. There is no single set of rules to cover all contingencies. My goal is to provide a pathway for the rookie trader to understand the importance of managing risk and to learn a sampling of suitable strategies.[308] Once more, experience is the best teacher, but traders want a place to begin and the goal is to help you find that place. With experience comes confidence. Obviously it is easier to ignore risk and hope all goes well. I've been there, and take my word for it—ignoring risk does not work well over the long term.

Table 17.3 Value vs. Time
NDX 1925/1900 P Spread;
NDX = $1925; IV = 22

Time	Value
52 days	$11.20
38 days	$11.15
24 days	$11.02
17 days	$10.86
10 days	$10.53
3 days	$9.25
2 days	$8.64
1 day	$7.34

Time affects spread value

When I was a market maker on the CBOE trading floor and held positions with outrageous risk,[309] the results were as expected: I won most of the time, but the occasional losses were horrendous. Why did I allow that to

---

[308] No list can be complete. When it comes to modifying a position, there are many alternatives. However, if you understand the rationale behind the adjustment process, you will be able to discover reasonable adjustment trades.
[309] That is what some less experienced, over-confident, traders did.

happen? Sometimes I was stubborn and "just knew" the market could not go any higher. Or perhaps I decided there was no reason to cover short positions that were available @ 1/16 (options traded in fractions, not too many years ago). I mention these painful stories with the hope readers take my advice: do not allow your portfolio to carry more risk than is reasonable for your circumstances. Do not be greedy over that last nickel or dime. Have patience and discipline and you should be well rewarded.

Adherents to selling OTM credit spreads collect less premium than those who believe in selling CTM spreads, and thus, their maximum losses are larger. While CTM believers do not lose as much money per spread when disaster strikes, they begin with a short option that has a higher probability of requiring an adjustment (because it begins life when not too far out of the money).

Table 17.4
NDX 1925/1900 Put Spread vs. Time
One-day Plunge from $1925 to $1900

Days	NDX 1925	NDX 1900	Loss
52	$11.20	$12.75	$1.55
38	$11.15	$12.97	$1.82
24	$11.02	$13.31	$2.29
17	$10.86	$13.58	$2.72
10	$10.53	$14.07	$3.54
3	$9.25	$15.56	$6.31
2	$8.64	$16.23	$7.59
1	$7.34	$17.58	$10.24
0	$0.00	$25.00	$25.00

Time affects loss when NDX dives in one day
Zero days: Fri AM settlement price

One popular method for managing risk is to make an adjustment when the short[310] option moves into-the-money. The major advantage of this method is that few adjustments are necessary. The major disadvantage (and it is a

---

[310] The short put option is the one with the higher delta, i.e., the option you sold. The long option is the one you own and has a lower delta.

large disadvantage) is that by the time an adjustment is necessary, the position has already lost a substantial sum. This method does not suit everyone, nor should it. And I do not recommend it. However, let's look at it in more detail for those who may prefer to consider this method.

The passage of time is beneficial to the credit spread seller. The data in Table 17.3 show the value of the NDX 1925/1900 put spread when NDX is 1925 and expiration approaches. This is an at-the-money (ATM) spread.[311] As expected, the spread decreases in value as time passes. There is nothing surprising about that, and it suggests that holding onto the position may be viable. However, once the short option moves ITM, the effect of additional time is minimal—and the effect of delta and gamma dominate, especially when expiration is nigh. In Table 17.4, the numbers illustrate how time affects the money lost when an ATM spread becomes a deep ITM spread (as NDX moves from 1925 to 1950).

Why is this information important?

a)   To demonstrate that holding the position is a gamble. The short option is ATM, and if NDX drops another point or two, it is not too significant. But a larger drop is costly (Table 17.4). This data should be an eye-opener for most option rookies. A decrease from 1925 to 1900 is not what you want to see when short the 1900/1925 put spread. But, with several weeks remaining, the one-day loss is a manageable few points, and there is time to adjust the position. Contrast that with the $2,500 loss (per spread) with no more chances to adjust—that can occur when the index opens 2% lower on settlement Friday.

By the time the 1925 put option becomes ATM, NDX has already declined from 2092 (167 points!), and unless there is some compelling reason to believe the decline is over, there is no reason why another substantial decline is not imminent. How bad can it be if NDX declines another 10 points? Assuming there are 10 days before the options stop trading,[312] if NDX declines from 1925 to 1915, the spread moves from $10.53 to $13.92.[313] That is a significant loss *on top of previous losses*. I believe preventing such losses is vital for success and that taking defensive action is the long-term winning strategy. Again—no one enjoys taking losses. But remember that selling credit spreads is a profitable strategy most of the time, but not every time.

b)   To convince traders that holding is not viable. Making an adjustment may mean locking in a loss, but holding has become too risky. Not only is the potential loss large, but the probability of

---

[311] The short option is ATM.

[312] Do not forget settlement risk the following morning (discussed in Chapter 16).

[313] The calculator gives these values for the options with NDX at 1915 (IV 22, time 10 days): $31.70 and $17.78

incurring that loss is much higher. Even the passage of a few days doesn't help enough to take the risk (see Table 17.3 and 17.4).[314] Why? Because negative gamma explodes as expiration nears. Options quickly move from 0 to 100 delta, and the option value changes dramatically when markets move. The data in Table 17.4 illustrate this important fact.

Notice that the size of the loss increases from about $3 when 52 days remain before the options expire to more than twice that amount with only 10 days remaining. And as more days pass, the potential loss increases dramatically. In fact, sometimes the spread could appear to be worthless one day and move to its maximum value the next. This is something to avoid! Hence, I suggest covering that risky position, rather than holding.

This situation catches too many investors by surprise. The uncertainty of where the market opens Friday morning when settlement prices are calculated (Chapter 16) makes holding the position through morning settlement a huge risk. By buying back short positions[315] before expiration, this risk is avoided. When to buy back the spread and how much to pay are individual decisions. It is tempting to wait just one more day again and again, but the bottom line is that going home with this position on Thursday, one day before settlement[316] is just not worthwhile in the long run. The potential for disaster should not fit within anyone's comfort zone. I'm not suggesting paying $24 for a 25-point spread (let's ignore why you are still holding the short spread when it is priced at $24), but I am suggesting you sell that spread if you own it. With $2,400 invested per spread, it is prudent to sacrifice that last $1 than to risk losing all or part of that $2,400.

c) Yes, the market may reverse direction and head higher, rewarding those who held onto the position. This should not make any difference in your approach. First, the market has been moving lower and there is no reason to expect it to stop right here and reverse. Second, the risk of being wrong is greater than the reward that comes from being correct. Third, I guarantee that part of the time, after an adjustment, the market goes the way you wanted it to go, and the adjustment is regretted. Do not fall into the trap of believing this is relevant. The most likely event does not happen all the time and underdogs can win part of the time.

---

[314] This statement is obviously an opinion, not a fact. You must handle your positions to satisfy your personal situation. As you gain experience, feel free to override these suggestions.
[315] Buy back (cover) the whole spread, not only the short option!
[316] European-style, cash-settled index options cease trading on Thursday (before the third Friday, see Chapter 16)

Make the best available decision you can make at the time the decision must be made. Then sleep well.

This discussion leads to an important risk-management concept:

> When holding a risky position and the time to adjust has arrived, it is a poor idea to hope that the ticking clock or a favorable stock market move will save you from a large loss.[317]

More on when to adjust

For many investors, waiting until the short option goes in-the-money is not an acceptable strategy because too much money has already been lost. I agree that a more reasonable plan (for most) is to adjust earlier. The bottom line is:

- More frequent adjusting results in losing out on some trades that would have been profitable.

- When adjusting early, losses are smaller and disasters are eliminated.

- It is a compromise. Trading experience makes the decision process easier.

    NOTE: When selling put spreads, it is easy to get spooked the first time the market moves lower. If selling an option that is 75 points out-of-the-money, it is not a good thing when it is only 65 points OTM a day later. But it is not so terrible. Do not rush to make an adjustment. Instead, be prepared. When making the opening trade, decide (and write it in a trade plan) at what point you will seriously consider adjusting. With that decision behind you, the 10-point decline will not feel as frightening. As important as it is to avoid being stubborn when it comes time to reduce risk, it is equally important not to panic.

Another idea is to consider position delta when adjusting. You may decide no position (or entire portfolio) ever should be positive or negative[318] more

---

[317] The passage of time helps, but it is not enough to compensate for the risk of holding. It is true that credit spread sellers make their money from the passage of time (or a favorable stock price change), but that does not translate into holding positions just to collect theta. When the chances of losing money are high and when the amount at risk is high, that is no time to play macho. It is time to protect your assets.

than a specific number of deltas. By following the Greeks, you can determine when that point is reached and make an appropriate adjustment. If the underlying continues to decline, your put spread continues to accumulate positive deltas, and it may become time to adjust again.

There is only one rule concerning adjustments: do not ignore them. If there is no other guideline, it is essential to pay attention to your body. It may alert you to the fact that a trade has moved beyond the borders of your comfort zone. As you gain more experience, that comfort zone widens (slowly). That is good for your longer-term growth as a trader, but do not allow it to widen so far that you never adjust bad positions.

How to adjust a position

When considering a position adjustment, the position is probably underwater.[319] Do not let that alarm you. Just as they do when trading stocks, too many novices hold losing positions (and quickly take profits on winners), hoping (in reality, praying) that everything turns out all right in the end. A happy outcome is possible, but the current loss can easily become a much larger loss. Holding a position, planning to make no adjustment, is gambling, pure and simple. If that suits your investing style, then by all means, gamble to your heart's content. But, if your goal is to invest with limited risk, then gambling is not for you. Let's consider possible methods for adjusting a put credit spread.

Assume you sold ($310 credit) 10 NDX 1950/1925 put credit spreads with expiration arriving in 52 days. NDX was near 2092 when you made this trade, but the market has declined and there is a significant chance of losing more than you are willing to lose. The good news is that 42 days have passed, but the bad news is that NDX has declined to 1970. There are 10 days remaining before the options expire, but the short option is now only 20 points out-of-the-money. Is this a dangerous situation, and if so, what are your choices?

If implied volatility is unchanged (22), then the spread is worth $7.93.[320] Assuming this spread can be bought or sold near its theoretical price (a good assumption for a discussion, but unrealistic in the real world).[321] You are currently losing $483 per spread, or $4,830.

---

[318] When a put credit spread goes bad, the position continues to gain positive deltas as the underlying declines. When short call spreads misbehave, the position picks up negative delta as the market rises.

[319] Losing money

[320] Once again, our trusty calculator (or your broker's software) is used to determine all values for specific spreads and individual options.

[321] The bid/ask spread tends to be wide and it is difficult to trade at the midpoint.

- If this loss is now too large for your comfort zone, consider this trade to be a learning experience. You could have

  o Taken action sooner.

  o Traded fewer than 10 spreads.[322]

- The easiest adjustment is to exit a portion of the position. Many investors prefer to cover all 10 spreads when fixing a losing position. Others prefer cover part of the position to reduce current risk.

  o When reducing size, additional losses are possible.

  o The opportunity to recover some of the recent loss is also possible. One caution: do not hold onto a position with the goal of getting back to even. Hold only when the position meets all criteria for a trade you want to own.

- Another adjustment involves buying options. If short 10 1950/1925 put spreads, buying one or two NDX (same expiration) 1975 puts provides some insurance. Only buy puts with a higher strike price[323] than the puts you sold. Why? Because the longer this position is held, the less protection the newly bought options provide. Puts with a 1975 strike always have more value than the 1950 put (the option you are short), and provide solid protection. The quantity purchased (and they are expensive) determines just how much protection.

- Another option is to "roll" the position. Rolling consists of two separate decisions. First, cover all the spreads sold earlier, locking in the loss. Second, find a new position that meets your needs. **Do not roll to open a new position just to reduce risk. If the new position is not good enough to own, then do not own it**

Rolling is an acceptable, but over-used, risk management tool. Investors who are desperate to find a way to eventually salvage a profit and unwilling to accept a loss often roll the position just to buy more time. They hope the underlying will reverse direction and turn a losing position into a winner. That occasionally works, but it means opening an unattractive position—and there is no reason to do that. When an acceptable position cannot be found, forget about rolling and exit the risky position.

---

[322] There is nothing wrong with trading 1- or 2-lots if that is appropriate.
[323] Or, when trading call credit spreads, buy calls with a lower strike price.

- When you do roll a position, a new put credit spread with lower strike prices is sold. In addition, the new spread is often moved 'out' to a more distant expiration date.[324]

Choose any spread (and any expiration date) that is acceptable. Select the new spread as you do when opening a new trade. It may be psychologically satisfying to 'roll for a credit' (collecting more cash for the new spread than is paid to cover the old spread), but that is neither desirable nor always possible. The main consideration is that it is unwise to open a position that does not fit within your comfort zone. Collecting that cash credit may feel good, but **when adjusting, the primary (but not the only) goal is to reduce risk**.

> **NOTE:** Risk management is a topic that can fill a huge volume, and still be incomplete. Thus, ideas are mentioned above, without elaboration. Please pay special attention to the words in bold. They represent key risk-management ideas.

EXAMPLE

> Deciding to roll a position down and out,[325] you cover the 10 NDX 1950/1925 spreads and sell 10 new NDX spreads that expire in the following month. You choose lower strike prices hoping NDX doesn't decline enough to threaten that new strike price during the remaining 38 days.[326]
>
> When selling the 38-day NDX 1900/1875 spread, expect to receive about $550. In this example, you cannot roll to a significantly lower strike and still collect a cash credit (the cost is $2.43[327] to make this roll). There is nothing wrong with paying cash to roll the position. The market moved too far and you lost money. You can hold the current position, hoping the loss goes away, or you can act prudently and reduce risk by closing this position and substituting one with much less current risk. The main concern must be to protect your assets. You may prefer to sell the 73-day NDX 1875/1850 spread[328] @ ~$6.60. The good news is that it costs less to roll ($1.33 vs. $2.43) and the strike

---

[324] I do not recommend changing the date. However, the reality is that most traders prefer moving the position 'out' to a later expiration date.
[325] Farther OTM strike prices with a more distant expiration
[326] The current position expires in 10 days. The next month's options expire 28 or 35 days later.
[327] You pay approximately $7.93 for the near-term spread and sell the new spread at approximately $5.50.
[328] Two months is either 56 or 63 days.

price is 50 points lower. But the position does not expire for another *two* months.

There is no specific formula to determine which spread to sell. There are usually several reasonable choices. The major requirements for the new spread are:

- The new position must place you within your comfort zone, and that includes position delta, and the other Greeks. If there is no suitable spread, then close. Exit the bad positions and accept that this trade was a loser. You are not forced to roll.

- The new spread must[329] meet the same requirements as when initiating a new stand-alone trade that is not part of a roll.

- It is not necessary to roll. Do not force the trade. If a new position is one you want to own, then rolling makes sense. If unable to find a suitable position, do not feel obligated to roll. Do not try to salvage some profit from a bad position. The goal is to grow assets over time, and is NOT to profit from each trade.

Another method for adjusting involves buying insurance before it is needed. That discussion is postponed until Chapter 19.

When all goes well

Positions can be adjusted to lock in profits. When the profit meets your pre-trade target, exit and bank the gains. When the word "adjustment" is used, most investors think about a losing situation in which reducing risk is the primary consideration. Closing a profitable position is also a good method for reducing risk.

Conclusion

Selling put credit spreads is equivalent to buying call debit spreads (same strike and expiration) or owning collars. It is a bullish strategy and profits are earned when the underlying doesn't decline below the strike price (or threaten to do so). Because this strategy involves limited risk, margin requirements are lenient. When selling a 10-point spread, the maximum loss is $1,000 (minus premium collected) and the margin requirement is that maximum loss. When selling naked put options, the margin requirement is higher. Suggestions: begin selling credit spreads with the minimum possible distance between the strikes (i.e., 25 points for NDX, 5- or 10-points for RUT and SPX). If this strategy is too bullish and you

---

[329] This is my strong opinion, not a rule.

prefer to be more market neutral, then consider selling call spreads in addition to put spreads. This idea is covered in detail in the next chapter.

WARNING

There is one additional risk when selling credit spreads. It is not a risk associated with the strategy *per se*. It is a risk that results from a poor decision on the part of an inexperienced trader.

When selling a 10-point credit spread @ $100, you may notice that the margin requirement is "only" $900 and conclude that such a low margin requirement translates into low risk and that you can sell many such spreads. Please do not allow think that way.

When investing $5,000 by buying 100 shares of a $50 stock, there is almost no chance of losing the entire $5,000. However, when selling a 10-point put spread, the probability of losing the maximum may not be high,[330] but it is far greater than when owning 100 shares. Thus, be careful with position size. If you would buy 300 shares of a given stock, then sell ONLY three put credit spreads. Just as it is up to you not to buy too much stock when investing in the stock market, it is equally important not to buy or sell too many spreads when trading options.

---

[330] If you make the poor risk-management decision to hold all the way to expiration, and if the underlying asset finishes below the strike of BOTH options in the spread, then the maximum is lost. The chances of that happening are the same as the delta of the option bought.

QUIZ 17

1. Credit spreads are only for bullish investors. **TRUE or FALSE**

2. It is a good idea to initiate your credit spread by first buying the option you want to own and then selling the option you want to sell. **TRUE or FALSE**

3. You decide to sell a 20-point put credit spread. You buy SPX Mar 1520 put. Which put do you sell?

4. You sold the RUT Aug 800/790 put credit spread. It is Thursday afternoon during expiration week and RUT is trading near 810. What, if anything, are you thinking about this position?

5. When the short option in your credit spread becomes an option that is at-the-money, each day that passes makes the position less risky. **TRUE or FALSE**

6. When entering a spread order, it is reasonable to expect to sell the spread at a price nearer the bid price or the ask price?

7. Which of the following is a credit spread?
   a) Buy Nov 60 put, sell Nov 65 put
   b) Buy Apr 100 call, sell Apr 90 call
   c) Buy Feb 750 call, sell Feb 750 put

QUIZ 17 Answers

1. False. Put credit spreads are for bullish investors. Call credit spreads are for bearish investors.

2. False. It is far better to enter both orders simultaneously via a 'spread order.'

3. The SPX Mar 1540 put. The puts are 20 points apart and expire in the same month. Sell the higher strike price.

4. The spread appears to be expiring worthless. But, anything can happen tomorrow morning when the settlement price is determined. I intend to buy back this spread later today. **NOTE**: You may not be able to sell the 790 put because there may be no bids. Do not let that bother you. The key to eliminating risk is covering the 800 put. Forget the put you own when there are no bids.

5. False. This is a difficult concept to grasp and may not be suitable for rookies. However the intention of this book is to help readers truly understand how options work.

   The passage of time generally is your ally and reduces the value of credit spreads. This situation is the one exception. The position may earn a small additional profit every day, as risk increases.

   Once the short option is almost ATM, negative gamma becomes a bigger threat. The fewer days remaining before expiration, the larger the value of the credit spread (if it moves into the money. See Table 17.4). That is why holding a spread when the index has moved near the strike price is not a long-term winning strategy.

6. True

7. a and b.
   c is equivalent to owning 100 synthetic share

Chapter 18

Iron Condors

The iron condor represents an option strategy for investors who have a neutral opinion on the market, i.e., neither strongly bullish nor strongly bearish. It is also suitable for investors who seldom, if ever, have an opinion on market direction. Iron condors represent an opportunity to earn money when the markets are range-bound, and are very popular among individual and professional traders. At least one major brokerage firm recommends this strategy to its clients. In addition, there are numerous advisory services and hedge funds who charge high fees[331] to trade this strategy for clients.

> **NOTE:** To readers who jumped ahead when reading this book: please do not skip Chapter 17 on Credit Spreads. This chapter is a natural extension of the material covered in the previous chapter.

An iron condor consists of two credit spreads—one call spread and one put spread—on the same underlying security. All four options expire at the same time. When buying iron condors, the investor's objective is to profit as time passes and the options decrease in value. Profit is limited to the premium collected, and the maximum profit—the total premium collected—is earned when all four options expire worthless Losses are limited to the maximum value of the call or put spread, reduced by the premium collected.

> **NOTE:** In theory, more than the maximum just described can be lost,[332] but prudent risk management (discussed below) eliminates that possibility.

> **NOTE:** Very Important. When trading iron condors, the calls act as a hedge against being short the puts. The puts act as a hedge against being short the calls. In other words, we do not sell the call spreads to 'make money'; we do not sell the put

---

[331] 20% of profits in addition to 2% of assets under management

[332] This unhappy event can occur if the market moves sharply lower and the trader covers the put spread at a large loss and the market then reverses direction, resulting in a large loss on the call spread.

spreads to make money. We sell both spreads, looking to make money from the whole position. If you understand this concept you will avoid some the common traps.

Terminology (nomenclature)[333]

The options world does not use consistent language. The definition for *buying* used in this book is not universal, but neither is the alternative definition. Most brokerage houses and Wikipedia refer to buying an iron condor as I do.

When BUYING an iron condor one call spread and one put spread are *sold*. Thus, when buying an iron condor, a cash credit is collected. The condor is equivalent[334] to the iron condor.

Buying an iron condor is similar to selling a put spread, but it also includes the sale of a call spread. That introduces the possibility of losing money when the market rallies. In exchange for additional risk, profit potential increases because more total premium dollars are collected by selling two credit spreads instead of one. There is no need to repeat details already covered in Chapter 17. This chapter primarily emphasizes situations that are specific to trading iron condors. A good understanding of credit spreads is necessary to get the most out of this chapter.

The maximum profit occurs when each spread expires worthless. However, investors who understand how to manage risk do not try to collect the last few nickels. Over the longer term it is prudent to buy back (cover) individual spreads if they become available at a low price.

A call **condor** is an option spread in which one call spread (with lower strike prices) is bought and another call spread (with higher strike prices) is sold, with the stipulation that the underlying asset, expiration, and spread width are identical. For example:

Condor: Buy 12 XXX May 400 calls
Sell 12 XXX May 410 calls

Sell 12 XXX May 470 calls
Buy 12 XXX May 480 calls

In this example, buy 12 XXX May 400/410 call spreads and sell May 470/480 call spreads. When expiration arrives, this condor is worth its maximum value ($10, or $1,000 per spread) when XXX is between 410 and

---

[333] Wikipedia is a good neutral authority: http://en.wikipedia.org/wiki/Iron_condor
[334] Chapter 14 describes equivalent positions.

470. The profit is $1,000, less the premium paid. Because the more expensive (higher delta) call spread is owned, this is *buying* the condor.

A put **condor** is a spread in which one put spread (with higher strike prices and higher delta) is bought and another put spread (with lower strike prices) is sold, with the stipulation that the underlying asset, expiration, and spread width are identical.

An **iron condor** is an equivalent position which has the same profit/loss potential. If buying the condor, then to be consistent, we also 'buy' the equivalent iron condor. For example:

Iron Condor: Buy 9 XXX May 400 puts
Sell 9 XXX May 410 puts

Sell 9 XXX May 470 calls
Buy 9 XXX May 480 calls

In this example, nine (the quantity is immaterial to this discussion) iron condors are bought. As with the condor, the maximum profit is earned when XXX is between 410 and 470 when expiration arrives. The spread would be worth zero and the premium collected represents the profit.

When examining these spreads, notice that both include selling the OTM call spread (the one with the higher strike prices). With the condor a lower-strike call spread is bought. In the iron variety, a put spread with the same lower strike prices is sold. Take another look at chapter 14 (if necessary) to verify that these are equivalent positions with equivalent profit /loss potential.[335]

If we 'buy' the iron condor, then we 'buy the equivalent iron condor.'

A personal note

It is often difficult for newcomers to the world of options to know where to begin. As far as deciding which strategies to learn, my recommendation is to work through the strategies in the order presented in this book because we move from simple to more complex in a logical order. If you lack option-trading experience, I suggest practice trading[336] without using real money in a paper-trading account.

At the iron-condor-trading stage, there is a similar setup. Even though all iron condors look alike, in my opinion the 'iron condor strategy' can be subdivided. There are several different types of iron condor. The factor that

---

[335] Assuming the puts and calls are priced efficiently, the condor and iron condor have the same potential profit.
[336] Most brokers allow customers to open a practice, or paper trading account. Many traders prefer to begin with real money. No objections, but keep position size small when getting started.

separates them is apparent when we look at the details for managing risk. For that reason, a trader must choose a style that fits into a comfort zone. The following discussion assumes that most readers are interested in 'traditional' iron condors. The other two types (my terminology) are

- Very-short term iron condor. Options that expire in ~one week.

- CTM (close-to-the money) iron condors. Constructed with higher delta options.

My goal is to teach readers how to build, manage, and exit iron condor positions and that is the reason for concentrating on the more traditional iron condors. In Chapter 19, there is some discussion about managing other IC types.

When getting started, one goal should be to think about (and practice trading) a variety of iron condors so a decision can be reached on which feels most comfortable to trade.[337] There is much to learn and many decisions to be made, so being comfortable with the position is important in reducing anxiety. And that leaves the trader well-suited to making intelligent decisions. When worried about the position, when queasy, when trading something that is not yet well understood, when money is on the line; that is when a trader is not in the best frame of mind to make the good decisions. And we *learn how to trade* by recognizing when our decisions were 'good' or could have been improved. For all those reasons, this discussion is primarily about the most commonly used iron condors.

A note on my personal style:[338] I currently (markets change, conditions change, and the winning trader must be flexible) prefer to buy 10-point iron condors on a broad based index (RUT, SPX) with a three-month expiration with a premium near $300.[339] Target profits and risk-management exit/adjustment points are part of the trade plan and are discussed later.

Buying iron condors: Introduction

Per the discussion on credit spreads (Chapter 17), when deciding which iron condor position to trade, consider using various expiration dates. I recommend that your very first trade be constructed with options that

---

[337] There is nothing like having money at risk, or taking a paper-trading account seriously, to locate your DISCOMFORT zone. That guides to your comfort zone.

[338] This is not to suggest this style is the best approach. Far from it. It suits my comfort zone and that is no reason to believe it suits yours. The purpose of including this discussion is to illustrate how one trader chose a trading style.

[339] In May 2013, as the final edits are being made, IV is low and there is no chance to collect a premium that high. I plan to adopt this style again, if possible. Today I prefer 10-11 week options, when the short has a delta of 10 to 12. .Note: This is not a recommendation for other traders.

expire in roughly two months (six to nine weeks). After that, I recommend trading iron condors that expire in one month and three months. That gives you some experience on how these trades differ and makes it easier to find an initial iron condor trading style. Choosing a comfortable expiration date is not a vital factor in your trading success. However, being comfortable with positions and how quickly they earn/lose money is part of your comfort zone.

Next, we choose strike prices for the short options in the iron condor. Yes, choosing the option to buy is also important, but once the short option has been chosen, we pick the option to buy based on the width of the spread. That decision comes later.[340] There are several different (and all reasonable) methods for choosing the options to sell:

- Delta
  Traditional (Delta 8 to 12 is recommended for anyone who is first learning to trade iron condors. Delta up to 15 is acceptable for aggressive traders who already have solid option-trading experience.)

  o CTM (Delta 20 to 30; not for iron-condor beginners because these can be *very* uncomfortable to manage)

  o FOTM[341] (low priced options; not recommended for anyone)

- Number of points that the option is OTM

- Percentage of stock price that the option is OTM

- Number of standard deviations[342] OTM (1.0, 1.5, and 2.0 are common choices)

Buying front-month iron condors gives traders the most rapid time decay—and that is a big advantage. After all, it is that time decay that provides our gains.[343] However, there is also extra risk due to negative gamma. This is a constant investment theme: in general, higher profits require taking extra risk. This is not always true, but it works as a guide when using option strategies.

---

[340] I recommend small spread width; 5- or 10-points.
[341] Far out of the money
[342] Stock price * volatility / (SQRT of time), where time is the number of days until the option expires divided by 360.
[343] Profits can also come from a decline in the implied volatility of the options. However, over the longer-term, theta generates profits and represents the reward for accepting the risk that the market will not move too far each day.

- Buying longer-dated iron condors is more comfortable for some traders because they generate higher premium and come with less negative gamma.[344]

- When a trader's preferred style is selling reasonably far OTM spreads, he can go further OTM and still receive good prices by choosing longer-dated options. There are two basic and conflicting needs to satisfy: the ability to earn a satisfactory return on the investment and the desire to reduce risk. There are enough iron condor variations that every trader can find a suitable position. If uncertain about how to proceed when making the first few trades, consider using a paper trading account.

More detailed definition of iron condor

To be a true iron condor, these conditions are necessary (but there is no need to trade a true iron condor):

- All options expire at the same time.

- The difference between the strike prices of the call spread (spread width) equals the difference between the strike prices of the put spread. For example, sell XYZ Jun 80/90 call spread and XYZ Jun 60/70 put spread. Both spreads are 10 points wide.

- The number of put spreads equals the number of call spreads. If trading with a market bias, you may elect to sell fewer put or call spreads, but the position is not a 'true' iron condor. The position is an iron condor plus the extra credit spreads.

- Strike prices do not overlap. By far the most common iron condors use OTM options and the calls have higher strike prices than the puts. If there is overlap and the middle strike is the same, then the position is an iron butterfly.[345] For example, an iron butterfly is selling XYZ Jun 80/90 call spread and XYZ Jun 70/80 put spread. The 80 strike is common to both spreads.

---

[344] Shorter-term options have more gamma. See Chapter 15.
[345] "Butterfly" and "condor" are examples of winged spreads. The butterfly combines a bull and bear spread such that the two spreads share a common strike price. The butterfly is a condor. The difference is that there is a separation between the strike prices of the bull and bear spreads in the condor, and there is no separation (the spreads share one strike price) in the butterfly. All options in the spread are calls OR puts. In the "iron" variety, one call spread and one put spread are sold.

- When selling both call and put spreads, the trader owns an iron condor. When buying one call (or put) spread and selling another of the same type, the trader owns a condor.

- When selling credit spreads, the more expensive (and higher delta) option is sold. For clarification: The options sold are less far OTM than the options bought. Thus, money is lost when the short option moves ITM or threatens to move ITM. When expiration arrives, OTM options are no longer a threat because they expired worthless.

.When short options expire worthless, the maximum profit is earned. That possibility is a trap. When time remains, there is still a chance for OTM options to move ITM, causing large losses. Just because options appear to be safely out of the money when the market closes Thursday of expiration week, it does not guarantee that the true closing price, or settlement price (determined at the opening Friday morning), will find these options are still OTM. We already discussed how surprising the actual settlement price can be when the markets gap at the opening. I recommend avoiding that risk by exiting the spreads no later than Thursday afternoon of expiration week.

> **NOTE:** The term, "threatens," is used throughout this chapter. When a short option is out of the money after the settlement price is determined, it has expired worthless and no longer presents any risk. But whenever the underlying (stock, ETF or index) approaches the strike price of a short option, there is imminent risk of losing serious money. In fact, the position is probably already losing money, but that depends on how much time remains before the options expire[346] and the premium collected. Doing nothing is not a viable strategy.

> When in this situation, it is prudent to take risk-reducing action. Yes, the possibility of seeing the options expire worthless is tempting. Avoid that temptation. See Chapter 17 for ideas on possible adjustments. Risk graphs and the Greeks help quantify risk. Closing or rolling all or part of the iron condor is possible. So is holding (a little longer) without an adjustment. There is never a "best" solution. But there is a 'worst' and that is doing nothing and hoping for a lucky outcome.

---

[346] The less time, the less may have been lost to this point. But in this situation, less time remaining doesn't translate into less risk (Table 17.4). It may reduce the probability of getting hurt, but the amount that can be lost grows as expiration gets nearer. Once again, see that all-important Table 17.4

Afterward, when the smoke clears, it is easy to see what would have worked best. Do not fall into the trap of letting that influence future decisions. One action may work best this time, but there is no reason to believe it will be best next time. No one likes to lock in a loss, but it is far worse to allow losing positions to run. In addition to the monetary loss, there is the psychological hurt that comes with knowing that you should have made a wiser decision.

Trading iron condors is a topic that can be approached from several different points of view, and volumes have been written on this single investment strategy. When compacting lessons on how to trade iron condors into a single chapter, some details must be omitted. The focus here is showing readers how to choose appropriate options to trade with some ideas on managing risk. Do not be concerned with trying to find the 'best possible trade.' There is no such beast. Buying iron condors is a market-neutral strategy that profits most of the time. As with all methods described in this book, your job is to be certain that the inevitable losses are not excessive.

There are two major psychological shortcomings with this strategy and it is easy to believe that iron condor trading is always profitable and investors may be tempted to take on too much risk:

- Investors often believe the odds of success are greater than they are in reality.

- Margin requirements are relatively small and it is easy for investors to sell more spreads than are appropriate for their experience and account size.

When selling 10-delta options, the likelihood that one of the options will finish in the money is 20%.[347] If you write a new iron condor every month (selling 10-delta options), you must anticipate that one of your options finishes ITM at least twice per year. There is another problem: part of the time the option may threaten to move in the money, causing the prudent trader to adjust the position. It doesn't matter if that option eventually finishes OTM, because the adjustment has already been made. This is another way of saying this strategy is not a 'gimmie.' Traders win often, but must manage risk to stay in the game and be profitable over the long term. With relatively small margin requirements, there may be a

---

[347] The two 10% probabilities are additive and one of the option is expected to finish ITM 20% of the time, or one time in five.

temptation to double or triple the number of contracts traded. Please avoid this trap.

Entering orders

This topic was thoroughly discussed in Chapter 17, but when trading iron condors there is one further consideration. Decide whether to:

- Enter the iron condor as a single order (recommended)

- Enter the call (or put) spread first, and then enter the other spread when the first spread is filled (a reasonable plan for the experienced and disciplined trader)

- There is a third choice, but I never use it. Traders may buy (or sell) one strangle[348] and then complete the iron condor by selling (or buying) the other strangle to complete the iron condor. Example: Buy Nov 200 put and 280 call. Then sell Nov210 put and 270 call.

It is far safer—and this is especially true for option rookies—to enter the whole iron condor as a single order. That eliminates the possibility of selling one spread and then discovering that an acceptable price is not available for the other half of the iron condor. If uncertain how to enter an iron condor order, ask your broker for instructions. These orders consist of four legs (individual options) but should pose no problem for any broker.

When using a live broker and you decide to sell three iron condors consisting of the XYX Jan 100/110 call spread and the Jan 80/90 put spread, and if you want a minimum premium of $405 per iron condor, tell your broker: "I want to trade 3-lots of an XYZ Jan iron condor for a net credit of $4.05 each. I'm selling both the Jan 80/90 put spread and the Jan 100/110 call spread, both to open."

Making the Trade: Strike prices

We already outlined how to select appropriate options to trade. The same general principles apply when initiating an iron condor position. The only real difference is that two spreads are sold instead of one.

Once the iron condor has been bought, the ideal situation is for the underlying asset to trade in a narrow range where the short options remain out of the money and eventually expire worthless. This pleasant scenario does happen. However, it is unreasonable to play for that result all the time. The trader can increase the likelihood that the options expire

---

[348] A strangle is one call and one put, with different strikes and same expiration. When buying the wings (outer strikes) first, then sell the two higher priced options immediately thereafter. Or, if the broker allows, sell the inner strikes first and buy the wings immediately thereafter. I say 'immediately' to minimize risk. Obviously you may wait, but it is not recommended.

worthless by selling options that are so far out-of the money that there is little chance that the underlying stock or index will move far enough for those options to move in the money.

That is a dangerous iron condor strategy. You may win almost every time, but you cannot expect to collect much premium—and that premium represents profits. If the goal is to earn a decent return on an investment, do not sell options for nickels and dimes.

As an extreme example, consider selling very far OTM call and put spreads, collecting $0.05 each. After expiration, the profit is $10, less commissions. The margin requirement is $990 and the return on investment is less than 1%. Isn't 12% a fantastic return for such small risk? Yes it is, but the true return is less and the cash at risk is large. The risk/reward parameters for this trade are terrible. If disaster strikes, up to $990 can be lost per spread. Although that is not likely, if it does happen, it wipes out 99 months of profits (and that ignores commissions). If you lose only half that amount, and if it happens once every four years, your trading is still not profitable. There is an additional problem. When it becomes necessary to reduce risk, human nature being what it is, almost every trader would refuse to adjust because the $10 reward is so small that the idea of spending $100 or $200 (or more) to salvage the position is unappealing. That is foolish thinking (adjustments should be based only on risk management), but it remains a fact. It is a poor idea to sell very cheap credit spreads.

In Chapter 17, we discussed choosing the strike prices for a put credit spread. The thought process is the same when trading iron condors, except that you must also consider your choices when selling a call spread. Many brokers offer lenient margin requirements when trading iron condors—the margin requirement covers both the call and put spreads.

Let's consider opening one iron condor position. Table 18.1 contains data for RUT, the Russell 2000 Index. RUT is priced at 790.42 and it is 42 days before the October options expire.

Making the Trade: Spread Width
Once the option to sell has been selected, the recommended course for rookies is to construct a spread with the minimum possible spread width. Refer to the discussion in Chapter 17 because the decision-making process is the same.

Table 18.1 RUT options
42-days before expiration; RUT = $790.42

Strike	Call Mid	Delta	Strike	Put Mid	Delta
			620	$2.45	-5
800	$28.45	49	630	$3.05	-6
810	$23.15	44	640	$3.65	-7
820	$18.45	38	650	$4.35	-8
830	$14.35	33	660	$5.20	-9
840	$10.80	27	670	$6.15	-11
850	$7.90	22	680	$7.20	-12
860	$5.50	17	690	$8.45	-14
870	$3.70	13	700	$9.85	-16
880	$2.45	9	710	$11.35	-18
890	$1.50	6	720	$13.05	-21
900	$1.00	4	730	$14.90	-23
			740	$17.10	-27
			750	$19.45	-30
			760	$22.05	-33
			770	$25.05	-37
			780	$28.30	-41

Mid = Midpoint between bid and ask prices

Making the Trade: Sell OTM options

Most iron condor traders prefer to write options that are not near the current market price of the underlying—with the proviso that the premium must be sufficient to provide enough profit potential to make the effort worthwhile. It is not possible to define 'sufficient' because that number depends on the nature of the underlying and the comfort zone of the individual trader. But remember, when the premium is too low, there is little money to be made. By choosing options with strike prices that are far out-of-the-money, an investor may feel safe and believe the options will expire worthless.[349] Do not get overconfident.

---

[349] The strikes may appear to be far OTM right now, but tomorrow they may be ITM!

Making the Trade: Option Delta

When trading iron condors, we use the term 'delta' in two different scenarios. The first refers to the delta of the options sold. That is a measure of how far out of the money the option is now and the probability of being in the money when expiration arrives.

There is also 'position delta,' calculated by adding the delta of each of the four options.[350] From Table 18.1: When selling 10-lots of the RUT Oct 880/890 call spread, the delta is 10 * (6-9), or -30. If selling 10-lots of the RUT Oct 660/670 put spread, the delta is 10 * [-9 - (-11)], or +20. This iron condor position begins life short 10 deltas.[351]

One point about delta: the software returns delta values out to several decimal places. The numbers are not that accurate. When an option has a delta of 19.6754, please think of it as a 20-delta option.

It is not necessary to own a position with zero deltas. 'Near zero' is good enough for our purposes. It is more important to own a position that suits your comfort zone and trade style. For rookies, I urge the sale of call and put options with deltas that are near each other.[352] There are just so many details that can concern us. The trader's comfort zone outweighs the need to begin a position with exactly zero delta.

Making the Trade: The Put spread

Let's consider which put spread to sell. The prices in Table 18.1 are unlikely to be available because these are the midpoints between the bid and the ask prices, but for this discussion, assume those represent the real-world premium.

EXAMPLE

The 620/630 put spread[353] is 160 points out-of-the-money, has a delta of +1 and is expected to finish OTM 94% of the time (i.e., the delta of the 630 put is -6). It takes a move of about 20% for these options to move ITM when the index is priced near 800 (RUT is 790.42). The premium is $60 and if this position expires worthless, the profit is 6% on the $940 margin requirement. That is a nice return for six weeks. However, we want to consider the

---

[350] When an option is sold, its delta is subtracted, i.e., selling a call or buying a put adds negative delta to your position, and buying a call or selling a put adds positive delta to the position.

[351] That is 10 deltas for 10-lots; or one delta per iron condor.

[352] To me, selling call and put options with the same delta gives us a position that feels 'more neutral' than owning an iron condor for which the position delta is zero. IV is different for every strike. Although the options we sell may have equal delta, the options buy will not.

[353] Lower strike prices are available.

274

entire trade plan, and mine calls for covering this short at $0.15. That reduces the maximum gain to $45, less commissions.

This spread is part of an iron condor, and the call spread generates additional cash with no additional margin,[354] increasing the potential return. Selling this spread is a possibility.

The 630/640 spread can be sold for $60. This is a no-brainer. If you can collect $60 for the 620/630 spread, there is no reason to accept only $60 for this spread because it is less far OTM.

The decision process involves looking at each combination of puts (and then calls) until a suitable spread is found. This tedious-sounding procedure is much easier than it appears right now. Once you have gone through this a few times, you will have a good idea of where to begin and that means most of the options can be eliminated from consideration immediately. As a new iron condor trader, you may not have any basis for making a choice. In that situation, I recommend getting started by selling a spread in which the short option has a delta of 8 to 10.

> **NOTE:** When dealing with indexes with many strikes, you may occasionally encounter a situation in which one or two of the individual options appear to be priced out of line. That happens (seldom) when an individual investor enters an order to buy or sell a few contracts at a limit price—a price that differs from the market maker price. That may be why the 620/630 spread appears to be priced so attractively, compared with the 630/640 spread. A customer may be offering to sell the 620 puts at a relatively low price.[355]

To find an appropriate put spread, consider each possibility,[356] looking for one that feels right. There is no scientifically correct method for selecting the very best spread, because there is none. Your experience and comfort level help with the decision-making process. The higher the strike, the more premium collected, but (obviously) the more likely the spread is to require an adjustment before expiration. Once again, there is no "best" spread to sell.

---

[354] Assuming it is a 10-point spread with the same expiration
[355] The exchanges are required to publish the best bid and best offer. Thus, everyone sees the price at which the customer wants to trade.
[356] In Chapter 17 we discussed how to choose between selling a 10-, 20- or 30-point spread. That discussion is valid for iron condors as well.

Keep in mind that trading an iron condor and not a credit spread means you can afford to settle for a bit less cash from the put spread because additional cash comes from the call spread.

When short an option that threatens to move in the money, sometimes it is prudent to cover that short spread,[357] accept the loss, and exit the position. As an alternative, the position can be rolled. If choosing that path, do not forget to cover the other portion[358] of the iron condor at a low price. It is probably FOTM if adjusting the other part is being considered.

Do not expect smooth sailing every time. Be prepared for the trade to require at least one risk-management decision before there is an opportunity to exit profitably. The primary reason for selling options that are far out-of-the-money is to avoid being forced to make adjustments. In this scenario, my choice is to sell the 680/690 put spread (14 delta), collecting ~$1.25. An alternative is the 670/680 spread (12 delta), collecting ~$1.05.

After trading iron condors a few times, you will have a much better idea of how to stay within *your personal* comfort zone. It is not helpful to trade according to my zone, unless you use it as a starting point with the intention of making changes. If you can treat fictional trades with respect, then begin with a paper trading account without using real money. For that to prove beneficial, you must react as if using real money. It takes time to become comfortable when adopting new strategies, so have patience. Leave your ego behind[359] and concentrate on earning money.

Making the Trade: The Call Spread

It is time to choose a call spread to go along with the put spread to complete the iron condor. The suggested put spread is reasonably far OTM. It is customary to select a similar call spread. But for variety only, let's look at call spreads from a different perspective—one that is CTM.

> **NOTE:** Do not assume that my recommendation is to pair one OTM spread with one CTM spread. It is far better to choose spreads so that the initial position is market neutral. To go along with my put choice above, I recommend the 870/880 call spread (delta 13); premium $1.25.

---

[357] If I did not make this clear, we cover the SPREAD and not only the option we are short.

[358] If rolling the calls, do not ignore the residual put position. If rolling puts, do not forget the calls. Those low-priced spreads can result in a big pain if and when the market reverses direction.

[359] No one likes to admit to trading 1- or 2-lot spreads. But it is a very intelligent thing to do. If discussing trading with friends, be honest about position size.

EXAMPLE

Sell CTM options.

> **NOTE:** This idea is not suitable for new iron condor traders. Begin with the more typical iron condor simply because it is (emotionally) easier to manage. This is one of those 'more advanced ideas' that may appeal to you the second time you go through this book. Suggestion: once you have experience with traditional iron condors, to play with the CTM strategy, use a paper-trading account. CTM positions are not for everyone.[360]

Let's define 'CTM' as an option that is closer-to-the money (about 10 deltas closer) than the options we typically trade when adopting the 'traditional iron condor' strategy.

CTM Trade 1: RUT is 790; 6 weeks before expiration

Sell 710/720 put spread @ $1.70 (delta 21)

Sell 850/860 call spread @ $2.40 (delta 22)

Net credit: $4.10

This is a typical CTM spread. The premium is at least 40% of the maximum value for the ion condor.[361]

CTM Trade 2: RUT is 790; 6 weeks before expiration

Sell 730/740 put spread @ $2.20 (delta 27)
Sell 840/850 call spread @ $2.90 (delta 27)
Net credit: $5.10

> This 27-delta iron condor is on the aggressive side, with a premium equal to more than 50% of the maximum spread value. My suggestion is to collect a premium that falls between $4.00 and $5.25 for a 10-point CTM iron condor.

I began trading CTM spreads over the last few years. It is not an easy transition for traders whose experience comes from owning iron condors

---

[360] It is better to avoid the CTM strategy than trying the difficult task of managing a position that makes you uncomfortable. Being confident that you can handle the decisions is an important part of trading.

[361] Reminder: IC cannot be worth more than the spread width, or $1,000 in this example.

where the options are far less likely to move ITM. There is a 'safer'[362] feeling when the position is not always facing an immediate risk of moving ITM. Managing CTM iron condors is very different from managing the more traditional iron condor (Chapter 19).

Making the Trade: Margin requirement

Once you understand iron condors, including the risk and reward potential and how to manage them, there is no need to trade a true iron condor.

If it suits, modify iron condors by adopting any of the following:

- Sell more call spreads than put spreads.

- Sell more put spreads than call spreads.

- Choose call and put spreads of different widths.

For example, sell the SPX 1650/1675 call spread and sell the SPX 1350/1400 put spread.

Basically any variation that comes to mind can be used, but there are advantages to using true iron condors. The primary advantage is that most brokers (sadly, not all) have lenient margin requirements for true iron condors. When the position is modified in any way, those advantages disappear, and margin is required for the call spreads *and* the put spreads.

EXAMPLE

Sell 12 10-point call spreads

Sell 8 15-point put spreads

Margin is $12,000 for the call spreads PLUS $12,000 for the put spreads

Sell 8 10-point call spreads

Sell 6 10-point put spreads

Margin is $6,000 for 6 iron condors plus $2,000 for two extra call spreads

---

[362] There may be a feeling of safety, but the traditional iron condor is not as safe as it appears. When the premium collected is much higher and the options are CTM, the maximum possible loss is less. Because I prefer to define risk as the amount that can be lost, these traditional iron condors are not all that safe.

Iron Condor Risk management

When feasible, I recommend a safer, less-aggressive approach: cover the call or the put spread (note cover the *spread*, not the individual short option) when it first becomes available @ $0.15 to $0.25.[363] The price depends on how much time remains before the options expire. Holding positions through expiration involves far too much risk for the small additional reward (Refer to Table 17.4).

Do not expect all trades to work as planned. Part of the time, there may be no opportunity to exit with an acceptable profit, even as expiration nears. That problem arises when one of the spreads (calls or puts) is not very far out of the money and the cost to exit is more than you want to pay. It is easy to be stubborn (or over-confident) and allow the position to remain open. Be very careful when this happens. The less experience you have trading iron condors, the more important it is to accept the fact that a given trade did not work well and accept the loss. If you do hold onto this risky position, it takes skill and discipline (and the ability to avoid panic) to manage the trade. Going with my belief that our first objective as traders is avoid the big loss, I encourage readers to get out of at least half, if not 100%, of the position when there are only two or three weeks remaining before the options expire. Stubbornness and being a successful trader are incompatible.

As traders, we are going to have trades with limited profit potential. Losing money on some trades is also part of the business—at least when adopting the strategies outlined in this rookie's guide.

Do not take high risk in an attempt to avoid a loss. Accept the fact that losing trades are inevitable. When safety dictates taking a loss, take it. There are many more trade opportunities in your future.[364]

Trading iron condors is not mechanical. Strategic thinking is required.

Risk management: Adjusting in stages

Each adjustment idea mentioned in the last chapter (on credit spreads) applies to iron condors as well. And that is understandable because an iron condor consists of two credit spreads. For most traders, making an adjustment is a painful process because it is associated with losing money. But not everyone feels that way. Some professional investors look at the adjustment process as an opportunity for earning additional profits.

That may occur when a new position is attached onto the original. The combined position is less risky and remains within a trader's comfort zone. Such adjustments are not always possible, and I must mention: the purpose of an adjustment is not to increase profit potential: it is to reduce

---

[363] Or a different low price that suits your trading style.
[364] Unless you blow up your account

risk. Sure, making it possible to earn more money is a plus, but it is not the primary reason for adjusting.

Why adjust in stages? A small initial adjustment is not costly, reduces the increasing risk, and allows more time for the position to work—assuming the position remains good enough to own.

With that 'small initial adjustment' in mind, let's discuss the idea of making adjustments in stages, instead of all at once. Adjusting in stages reduces account volatility (less fluctuation in the value of the account), and that is a good thing for every investor. Experienced traders know that it is more comfortable to incur smaller drawdowns (losses) and steadier gains than seeing the account fluctuating with giant gains/losses.

Another advantage is that there is less pressure when it is time to make an adjustment decision—the necessary risk-reduction takes place and the trader still has a good opportunity to exit with a profit. Adjusting in stages softens losses, and when it becomes necessary to exit the entire position, the first-stage adjustment will have cut overall losses. In other words, the first and second (depending on how many stages are used) stage each saved money.

As with other aspects of trading options, there are no hard and fast rules. I suggest adjusting in three stages, but two or four may be suitable.

One note of caution: the process of adjusting in stages is not compatible with every option strategy and should only be used when appropriate. I understand that rookie traders may not know when it is appropriate, so here is my guiding principle: Adjusting in stages is used when the trader has a pre-determined exit or adjustment point in mind, but prefers not to wait until that point is reached before taking defensive action. By making a suitable adjustment (on a portion of the position) early, the possibility of the large loss is cut significantly.

Do not adjust in stages when trading CTM credit spreads or CTM iron condors.[365]

EXAMPLE:

Stage 1. You own an XDN (fictional broad based index) iron condor position and the market moves towards the strike of one (calls) of your short options. The usual strategy is to close the entire position as soon as your trigger is reached. That trigger could be one of the following:

---

[365] The nature of the trade (large cash credit) makes it desirable to wait longer before adjusting, eliminating the need for stages. If waiting longer is not comfortable, then trade the more traditional variety, rather than the CTM.

- The delta of the short option reached a specific level

- The short strike is ATM (or is a specific distance OTM)[366]

- The maximum allowable loss (per the trade plan) has been reached

Sell 20 XDN Jun 600 calls

Buy 20 XDN Jun 610 calls

XDN has recently rallied from 500 to 570 and the 600 strike is only 30 points, or 5%, out of the money. The put portion of this iron condor is not relevant to this discussion, but I recommend entering a bid to cover at a low price.

When XDN hits 570, you decide to make a Stage I adjustment. (More conservative traders will have already made an adjustment before XDN reaches 570.)

Some alternatives (There are others):

- Cover 3 to 6 Jun 600/610 call spreads, reducing position size by 15 to 30%.

- Roll down calls to higher strike prices.

- Add protection. Buy one or two naked calls, Jun 590s or possibly Jun 600s.

- Add protection. If IV is low enough to encourage buying vega, buy July calls instead of Jun calls.

- Do not ignore the puts. Do not chase them, but if the put spreads are cheap enough (you must decide when the risk of allowing that spread to remain outstanding is too high for the potential reward), enter a bid to buy the spread at your desired price.

Stage I. If the position is a 10-delta iron condor, make a stage I adjustment when delta reaches 25 (-25 for puts). Make a Stage II adjustment at 30-delta.[367] If any position remains, a third stage (the exit) could occur at delta 35. Choose adjustment points based on keeping the amount of cash at risk, and the probability of losing that cash, at acceptable levels. It takes some time before a trader knows how to do this effectively.

---

[366] For example, 20-points OTM or 3% OTM could be your adjustment/exit trigger.

[367] If these 25- and 30-delta choices make you nervous, then adjust sooner. But please do not adjust at anything less than 20 deltas. Otherwise you would be making far too many adjustments.

Suggestion: After the Stage II adjustment, 50% of the original position should have been adjusted (or closed).

EXAMPLE

Stage II. You made an adjustment by buying 2 Jun 590 calls and the price of XDN holds steady for a few days, before resuming its upwards march. When XDN hits 585, the short option is 15-points OTM (only 2.5%), and that makes you nervous. Unless you are ready to exit the trade,[368] more protection is in order.

Having made a Stage I adjustment, Stage II may be easier because you will probably consider similar adjustment trades. The important decision is 'how much' additional protection is needed. If your plan is to exit at Stage III, I encourage using Stage II to cut the original trade size in half.

When closing part of the position, it is easy to know what represents 20%. (Cover 4-lots in this example). However, if buying extra call options, it is less obvious. The best and simplest solution is to cover 20% of the short delta and possibly some of that negative gamma. Another good choice is to pick a (higher) NDX price and own a position that loses no more than a specific sum (based on the risk graph) at that price.[369] In other words, if NDX rises 2% from its current level, see how much the predicted loss is (from risk graph). If that number is too high, choose a lower NDX price until you find one that results in an acceptable loss and make that NDX price your exit or adjustment point.

If you bought two Jun 590 calls as a stage I adjustment, it is reasonable to buy 2, 3, or 4 more as a Stage II trade. These specific numbers are not recommendations because the size of the adjustment depends primarily on the current position delta[370] and on how comfortable you are with that position.

EXAMPLE

Stage III. If the strike is breached, you may decide that the current position is acceptable—because of the two earlier adjustments. That is an independent decision. But if you decide

---

[368] That includes selling the options bought as protection
[369] Risk graphs should be easy to use. Ask your broker for help using their graphs.
[370] Not to be confused with delta of the short options. Position delta is the sum of the current delta (multiplied by number of options owned or sold) for each of the four options in the iron condor. Your broker supplies this information.

that this is now beyond your comfort zone boundaries, exit the trade. You probably have a loss, but it is much less than it would have been with no previous adjustments. And that is the key to survival. When exiting, be sure to also exit the trades made as an adjustment because they are no longer needed.

If the market reverses and never reaches Stage III, there is one more decision: whether to keep the extra options already purchased in case they are needed again, or sell them at a loss. There is a good argument for either decision. The point is not to ignore those options, but to reach a well-reasoned decision. I prefer not to sell, unless closing the whole call position.

One idea for making this decision: you own an adjusted iron condor. The call portion is now the original spread plus the adjustment trade. Is that the position you want to own as a hedge against being short the put spread? The answer may be 'yes' or 'no,' and it is your job, as risk manager, to decide which position to own. We do not know whether the market will continue lower or soon resume the rally.

Risk management: General advice

1. Most important: do not adjust solely to keep the position alive. Accepting this single sentence as the best possible advice will save you from a lot of grief. Too many traders refuse to accept a loss and make one adjustment after another, trying desperately to earn a profit. This is a trap. Quit a bad position and begin with a clean slate and a position that has a good chance to make money. Why struggle with a high-risk unsuitable position?

2. Profits spend the same, and it does not matter which specific trade earns those profits.

3. When it is time to adjust, the position has already passed beyond the borders of your comfort zone and closing is always a reasonable choice. It is very comfortable to own *only* positions that offer a good opportunity to earn money going forward. It is efficient to get out of a trade that is not going well and which cannot be easily fixed. Spend your energy on trades that you (and your skill level and experience) can manage comfortably

4. Managing risk for iron condors differs from put credit spreads in an important way: do not ignore half of the iron condor position because it appears to be safe. For example, assume the market takes an unfavorable move to the upside and you made a good adjustment to the call spread. The position is now the newly adjusted call spread plus the old put spread. Often, the remaining put spread is priced so low that it offers no good hedge.

> **NOTE:** Very Important (and worth repeating). When trading iron condors, the calls act as a hedge against being short the puts and the puts act as a hedge against being short the calls. In other words, we do not sell the call spreads to 'make money'; we do not sell the put spreads to make money. We sell both spreads, looking to earn a profit from the whole position. See Chapter 19 for more details.

When one spread no longer provides a reasonable hedge, it is time to cover. It may also be time to cover AND sell another spread[371] that is closer to the money and which generates additional cash. Be certain to cover. That cheap spread cannot produce meaningful gains, but may lead to a gigantic loss.

The most efficient method way to cover a cheap spread is to place a bid (I prefer entering the order every morning, rather than entering a good 'til canceled bid) to cover the spread at your chosen (low) price. Limit orders, only.

5. Market neutrality and the Greeks. If accepting the premise that you do not know whether the market's next big move is higher or lower, why own an unbalanced position? Iron condor traders tend to prefer market-neutral positions. When the position is no longer neutral enough for your personal comfort, an adjustment is made.

---

[371] The roll-up trade

6. One important aspect of adjusting iron condors is to consider position delta. Make a trade that cuts current delta especially when the trade adds some positive gamma[372] to further reduce risk.[373] Any time a position is adjusted, the market can reverse direction, resulting in another loss (whipsaw). For that reason, when adjusting the call spread, it is a good idea, when feasible, to make some risk reduction on the put side of the trade. This is not always possible, but one idea is to exit the puts, if the price is low enough. The same action works when it is the put spread that has been adjusted and the calls are cheap enough to cover.

When adjusting, the trader often decides to roll-up the unthreatened portion of the iron condor. That generates both cash and needed delta. However, it does introduce market reversal risk. As always, when additional profit potential is added, it is accompanied by risk.

Personal note: after being whipsawed, I am very uncomfortable—so much so that I prefer to cover the cheap puts without rolling-up the put spreads. This is not market neutral and is *not logical*. Nor is it recommended. It is merely a personal defense mechanism I use to avoid getting whipped. Overall, it has been a losing technique and I mention it in full disclosure. The emotional satisfaction of avoiding whips works for me, but it cost money over the longer-term and I do not recommend that you do the same.

7. The best possible adjustment. There is no 'best' trade. Our goal is to find a good trade and avoid mistakes. My goal is to illustrate the pros and cons of various alternatives and trust you to make a reasonable decision that suits your personal style. I offer guidance and recommend a place to begin. However, I do not believe there are rules that anyone must follow.

Decisions become natural and easier as time passes. Trade small positions until you become confident that you can make good decisions under pressure. Trading is a very personal business.

Risk management: Summary

It is worth repeating: do not roll a position just because your current position is in trouble and you feel you must do something. The 'must do something' part is important. Do something. But do not automatically

---

[372] Examples: buy single options, buy debit spreads, buy OTM calendars or butterflys. Any trade that gains in value when the underlying continues to move in the same direction is suitable.
[373] Negative gamma makes things difficult when the rally (or decline) continues. Reducing gamma is quite helpful.

select the roll, unless you truly want to own the new, post-rolling position. If no 'fix' is attractive, exit, take the loss and wait for a better opportunity.

There is little to gain by refusing to cover a spread that costs a few nickels. It is more profitable to get the position 'off your sheets'[374] and make a new trade that has a chance to contribute to future earnings.

Another method for reducing risk: do not hold positions into expiration week. It is difficult to accept this advice because it requires closing just as theta becomes most attractive. Just remember that attractive time decay is always offset by an unattractive negative gamma. I suggest closing positions no later than two or three weeks[375] before options expire. The major benefit is eliminating the risk associated with a significant market move. (Refer to Table 17.4)

When adopting this 'safety play,' the ability to maximize profits is sacrificed. For some traders, that is not a satisfactory tradeoff. For those who believe that survival comes first and profits come next, this is an easy decision. However, you know your comfort zone better than anyone else.

---

[374] Market-maker terminology for closing the position; it means removing the position from your daily statements.

[375] If you prefer to hold longer, be aware that risk increases every day. The basis of this risk reducing method is to exit as expiration nears.

QUIZ 18

1. Iron condors are the ideal strategy when very bullish. **TRUE or FALSE**

2. It is almost impossible to lose money over the long term when buying iron condors in which both spreads are very far out of the money. **TRUE or FALSE**.

3. When buying a 10-point iron condor on a European-style index, collecting a $300 premium, and holding through expiration with no adjustments, you can never lose more than $700. **TRUE or FALSE**

4. When buying a 20-point iron condor, the margin requirement is:
   a) $4,000 ($2,000 each for the call spread and put spread)
   b) $2,000
   c) It depends on the strike prices

5. 5. Do these four trades comprise a true iron condor?
   a) Sell 10 IBM Nov 90 puts
   b) Buy 10 IBM Nov 80 puts
   c) Sell 15 IBM Nov 110 calls
   d) Buy 15 IBM Nov 120 calls

6. When you initiate an iron condor position, it is possible to estimate the probability that all options expire worthless. How do you do that?

7. When selling an OTM put spread and a CTM call spread, it is not a true iron condor. **TRUE or FALSE**

Quiz 18 Answers

8. False. If anticipating a major move in either direction, iron condors are not suitable. They work best for traders who have a neutral outlook, or who have no opinion on market direction. If very bullish, buy call spreads.

9. False. The premium is so small, that a significant loss every few years is more than enough to make this a losing strategy.

10. True. When expiration arrives, the worst case scenario occurs when one of the spreads is completely ITM and worth 10 points.

11. b) $2,000. But, some brokers insist on imposing a $4,000 requirement.

12. No. A true iron condor contains an equal quantity of put spreads and call spreads.

13. Find the delta for each of the options being sold. Add those deltas (ignoring the minus sign for puts). Subtract from 100.

14. False. The distance each spread is from the underlying price is not relevant in determining whether a position is a true iron condor. If expiration, underlying asset, distance between the strikes and the quantities are identical, it is a true iron condor.

Chapter 19

Thoughts on Risk Management

This chapter is intended to get readers to think about the concept of managing risk. It is easy to believe (because it is true) that you can become a successful options trader by becoming an expert in using one or two option strategies. However, it is essential to recognize:

- Being skilled at opening and exiting the trade is not sufficient.

- The most important part of any trade strategy is the ability to recognize and manage risk.

Deciding which strategy is appropriate for a given market condition, deciding how many contracts to trade, establishing profit targets etc. are all important. However, if risk is ignored or managed carelessly, the chances are good that the trader will fail.

Every trade involves risk, and part of becoming an expert on any given strategy must include knowing how to:

- Avoid large losses. Close positions that are not worth owning

    o Too little reward for the potential loss

    o Probability of earning a profit is not adequate, considering the potential loss. There is nothing wrong with owning trades with a low probability of success. However, the reward must be large enough to justify the higher probability of incurring a loss.

- Adjust positions as needed, when losses accumulate or when the probability of losing money has increased enough to make the position uncomfortable to hold.

- Modify the trade plan as conditions change. The trade plan was not written in stone and represented your plan at the time the trade was initiated. Much of the time it is best to carry out the original plan. However, the thinking trader knows when to abandon a plan that has become obsolete.

Knowing when risk is too high and having the discipline to take defensive action are the keys to success. Option traders make money; they lose money; and your *job* is to see that losses do not overwhelm gains.

Technical Analysis (TA)

In this book, I ignore the idea that traders can find a 'best time' to enter any trade. However, if you are well versed in technical analysis, or plan to make a big study of the topic, then you will be far more confident when making trade decisions.

> **NOTE:** Being more confident does not translate into being correct. It only refers to the fact that anyone who follows the charts believes he/she is making a good trade decision, and making it at the right time. The ultimate proof is in the results. I urge readers not to use TA without taking the time to establish a record that proves you can predict market ups and downs.[376] Technical analysis skills are not as easy to develop as some would have you believe. I do not use technical analysis for my trading.

The Rookie Trader

This book's primary audience is the rookie option trader. You will not always be a rookie and when you return to these pages to further your education, you will be better placed to use more advanced trading and risk management methods. This chapter is intended for that second reading. Do not skip over this material, but if you are a very new option trader, I encourage you to gain some general trading experience using your choice of the strategies that we discussed (two additional strategies follow this chapter). Then return to this chapter for additional ideas on risk management.

Plan to manage risk, starting with your very first trade. Some begin trading when not yet sufficiently confident of being ready. That is acceptable, when the trade size is very small and little money is at risk. The plan should be very simple. For example:

- Hold the position. Avoid exiting immediately, if possible. Keep a written record of your thoughts on a daily basis. Keep a record of the 'facts': trade date; opening price of the position; daily profit/loss; price of underlying asset along with price and delta of the options.[377]

---

[376] Keep written records. Do not depend on your memory.

[377] Keeping these records allows you to return to re-examine the data and determine if you would make a different risk-management decision at that later date. It may take a little time to only be worried about something meaningful, and not becoming too uncomfortable when the trade loses $0.10. You may not have a clear idea of when to exit a losing trade, but that will come with a little experience. That is one good reason for adopting a less complicated strategy – it is easier to picture what is happening and what may happen in the marketplace.

- Are you confident that the trade is going well (so far)?

- Are you concerned about losing too much money? How much are you losing?

- Are you worried, but do not know the exact reason? Much of the time it is because trading is a new experience.

- Does your target profit still appear to be attainable?

- If truly uncomfortable, exit. Then carefully plan the next trade, trying to avoid the situation that made you uncomfortable.[378]

Keep it simple. It is more important to have a risk-management plan that to have a complex plan. Why? Get in the habit of making trade plans. More sophisticated plans can wait because that comes as your own understanding of trading grows. Many ideas about risk management represent common sense. Once introduced to an idea,[379] it will become part of your everyday *modus operandi*.

Managing Risk is the Key to Success

In general, anyone who understands how options work can adopt the basic option strategies described in this book. And that person will have many winning and losing trades. It may seem natural to keep score by the percentage of winning trades, but that is not what is important. We could choose strategies that statistically are expected to win 95% of the time. However, for traders, the bottom line is measured in dollars. Profitable trades must earn far more than we lose from our losing trades. Amazingly, this simple fact is often overlooked by the person obsessed with recordkeeping.[380]

The primary goal for any investor or trader is to avoid blowing up a trading account. If the losing trades are well managed; if losses do not exceed an 'acceptable' level for each trade; then the winning trades will more than compensate for the losing trades—if the trader understands how to use options.

Avoiding all losses is not the theme.

---

[378] That can be almost anything. Options were too close to the money, or too far out of the money; wrong stock; unlucky timing etc.

[379] Assuming the idea fits into your trading style. Just as you will not adopt every strategy, you may find that certain ideas on how to manage risk are unappealing.

[380] Keeping records is good. Spending many hours developing spreadsheets is not.

NOTE: Any trader can exit a position as soon as it is losing a total of $5.[381] That certainly prevents large losses. The problem is that would be every trade. When we understand slippage (money lost by dealing with the bid/ask spread), we can never get out of a position just entered at break even. Every trade encounters that immediate loss, plus an additional loss from paying commissions.

If you understand how to adopt a strategy; if you choose your initial trade carefully (i.e., do not make a randomly chosen trade); if you understand and follow the guidelines outlined in this Rookie's Guide; if you believe that managing risk is essential; if your personality traits do not preclude you from doing well;[382] then the chances of finding success are good. No guarantees, because options are not for everyone—more than that, trading is not for everyone.

Pre-insurance

Risk-management ideas have been mentioned throughout this book. Now let's consider something different.

The idea of making an adjustment to a brand-new position may seem strange because there is no imminent risk. The purpose of buying insurance at the moment the trade is made is to create a more conservative position, for which both profit and loss potential are reduced. I refer to this adjustment as buying protection before it is needed, or pre-insurance.

Pre-insurance is a reasonable (for the right trader; *it is not for everyone*) method for protecting an investment portfolio, and it works just as any insurance policy. When buying auto, home, or life insurance, most of the time, the insurance is 'wasted', and that is good news.[383] Keep in mind that the usual trader mindset is: 'I do not need insurance now, and I can always buy it later, if necessary.' Pre-insurance is rarely used, primarily it cuts into profits and investors seldom consider 'fixing' a problem that does not yet exist.

Pre-insurance refers to buying *extra* insurance to protect a specific position or entire portfolio. When selling credit spreads or trading iron condors, insurance is built in—it is the wing, or the option already owned

---

[381] That means five dollars in cash. It does not mean $5 per position because that translates into $500.

[382] Lack of discipline is very difficult to overcome.

[383] When you buy homeowner's insurance, are you not pleased that your house doesn't burn and you do not collect on that insurance policy? But if a disaster strikes, that insurance is badly needed.

as part of the spread. That is protection against unlimited losses. In this chapter, the discussion concerns buying extra insurance to further reduce the possibility of incurring a large, but limited loss.

If you are first starting to trade, or if your bankroll dictates owning small positions, then pre-insurance is not suitable. But, you will not always have a small bankroll, so consider this concept as food for thought.

EXAMPLES

1. Reduce position size

    Assume you decide to sell 10-lots of a credit spread and the plan is to adjust in stages. If the trade is initiated with only 8-lots instead of 10, that is equivalent to having begun with a 10-lot and making a 2-lot adjustment to both the call and put spreads at break-even prices (and with zero commission cost).

    This may seem trivial, but reducing size at the start of any trade is one way to own very cheap insurance. The only cost is a reduced profit potential.

2. Buy a spread as protection

    This idea was not previously discussed in detail. One way to adjust a position is to buy protection. Simply stated, that 'protection' is any position that earns money when the original position is losing money. Thus, the trade is a hedge, and the objective is to offset a portion[384] of any potential loss.

    If you sold a call spread and the market is rising, at some point it becomes necessary to take action to reduce the growing risk. One idea is to cover some credit spreads and reduce position size.

    Another idea is to buy a different credit spread, i.e., not cover the specific spread that was sold earlier. This spread should be closer to the money, with the same expiration as the current position. Typically the spread width is identical, but that is not a requirement. For example, if short 10 ABC Dec 200/210 call spreads, buy two[385] ABC Dec 180/190 (or 185/195 etc.) call spreads as protection.

    If you elect to buy those debit[386] spreads at the same time that the original trade is made, then it is pre-insurance. If they are

---

[384] If you prefer to hedge all potential losses, the best idea is to exit the position and not bother with protection

[385] Or the quantity that appeals right for your comfort zone. The objective is to reduce risk to an acceptable level.

[386] These spreads cost cash and are, by definition, debit spreads.

bought only when needed (when risk has increased), then it is a 'regular' adjustment. Do not let this terminology bother you. The decision is: do you want to pay for pre-insurance or wait. When waiting, much of the time, insurance is not needed. However, when needed, it will cost more.[387]

3. Buy a naked option as protection

When the underlying asset moves *substantially* higher (or lower), nothing provides protection as well as owning an extra call (or put) option. Please remember that these 'substantial' price changes do not occur often, and buying single options tends to be too expensive for most traders. At the outset of this discussion, it is   important   to   emphasize   specific   facts:

This discussion contains many details which are needed to present a clear picture of how this specific style of risk-management works. However, do not allow the length of the discussion to convince you that this is a technique that must be adopted. Please know that:

- Buying extra options is expensive and severely cuts profit potential. Most traders prefer (as I do) to avoid this method. It is included because readers should be aware of a variety of risk-management techniques.

- Buying extra options works wonders when the price of the underlying asset undergoes a huge price change. If the market gaps and you own an option (or two) that is now 10% in the money, the extra options could generate enough profit to overcome all of the loss associated with the original credit spread or iron condor.[388] Please recognize that this would be a very rare occurrence and I do not recommend buying extra options just to prepare for this contingency.

Buying extra options can present a false sense of security. Manage risk carefully. Do not count on the extra options to take care of all problems. If the market slowly moves towards the strike of your short position, that single (or two) extra options is not going to provide much help as a hedge. For example, when the 10-point credit spread is at the money, it will be

---

[387] When the spread is less far OTM, it costs more. And it is less far OTM because the underlying price changed.

[388] Think of a 10-lot iron condor that is suddenly losing the maximum of $8,000 or $9,000 coupled with one extra option being 80-points TM. This insurance, in this instance, covers the entire loss.

worth near $500, regardless of how much time remains before expiration. When time is short, the extra option will have lost most of its time premium and because it is only 10- or 20- points in the money, it does not provide enough gain to offset the losses.[389]

Even worse, the credit spread (now priced near $500) can lose another $500 ($5,000 for a 10-lot) when owning an extra one-lot gains only $1,000.[390] This is a limited-help adjustment—unless the price change is big.[391]

Selecting the option to buy

When buying options as insurance, there are important considerations. Options come with a variety of expirations and numerous strikes. To keep this discussion to a reasonable length, let's only consider a few possibilities.[392] Once you become a more experienced trader, generate your own ideas and feel free to modify any suggestions made in this book.

> **NOTE:** In the following discussion we repeatedly mention the number of days remaining in the lifetime of the options. Thus, instead of using a specific month, the three-letter symbol for the month has been replaced by the number of days. For example, instead of referring to IBM Oct 90 calls, we refer to IBM 36-day 90 calls (when the 3rd Friday of Oct arrives in 36 days). One week later, those become the IBM 29-day 90 calls.

To get a clear picture of pre-insurance and what it can (and cannot) do, let's examine three scenarios in which options with different expirations are bought.

> **Scenario 1**: Buy insurance that expires one month later than the credit spread.

> **Scenario 2**: Buy insurance expiring at the same time.

---

[389] It may not be profitable. If the original price was $2,400 and it is only worth $2,000 now, it may have provided insurance against a gigantic market move, but because that move did not occur, it did not produce any profit.

[390] If the stock rises another 10-points by expiration, the 10-lot of call spread loses another $5,000, becoming worth the maximum $10,000, and each extra call increases by only $1,000.

[391] The credit spread cannot move beyond $10, but the extra call can increase in value indefinitely.

[392] In theory, any option can be used as insurance. In reality, as time goes by, options with strike pricthan the position being protected become ineffective. Thus, when owning (for example) a position with a 1000 strike price, do not consider buying puts struck at 800 (800 strike price) as insurance.

   Scenario 3: Buy insurance that expires one month earlier[393] than the credit spread.

Figures 19.1 through 19.4 show profit and loss (risk) for the initial trades. The options chosen are representative of the available choices and are based on cost. Each graph represents a single point in time and does not show the importance of the passage of time (that discussion follows).

How to read the profit/loss graph

If plots such as those in Figure 19.1 are unfamiliar, here's how the data are presented. The price of the underlying asset (RUT in this example) is plotted along the horizontal (x) axis and the change in the value of the position is plotted along the vertical (y) axis.

- On the y-axis, 0.0 represents the break-even point, assuming that the position is opened the same day the graph is created.

- In the upper left hand corner, the scale is listed. In Figure 19.1, it is "x10^4." That means the numbers on the vertical axis must be multiplied by 10,000.

- In the lower right hand corner, the scale is listed. In Figure 19.1, it is "x10^3." That means the numbers on the horizontal axis must be multiplied by 1,000.

The value (y axis) of the portfolio is set zero when the position was opened (the y-axis reads 0.0 at the vertical line on the x-axis, which represents the current RUT price).

Comparing the graphs

Table 19.1
Strike Prices of Insurance Options
Protect 65-day 740/750P; 900/910C IC

Figure #	Call Strike	Put Strike
19.1	none	none
19.2	920	690
19.3	910	720
19.4	770	880

Strike prices of insurance options

---

[393] For this discussion, the possibility of trading Weeklys options is ignored.

Table 19.1 is presented to make it easier to compare the graphs by emphasizing strike prices of the options bought as insurance. The iron condor uses 900 calls and 750 puts as the short options.

Notice that the positions illustrated in figures 19.2 and 19.3 use options that are more distant OTM than the position being protected. The position represented in figure 19.4 uses options that are closer to the money than the iron condor shorts. When comparing the figures, the benefit of owning those CTM options becomes clear.

- Figure 19.1 is that of the uninsured iron condor.

- Figure 19.2 represents the same IC, with protection that expires 4-weeks **later**.

- Figure 19.3 shows the risk profile when all options expire **simultaneously**.

- Figure 19.4 shows risk when insurance expires 5-weeks **earlier** than IC.

Points of Interest

Be certain to look at the P/L scale at the left because *the graphs are not drawn on the same scale.*

1. Short-term options are far less expensive and allow us to own closer-to-the-money options for the same[394] cost. See Figure 19.4. However, once they expire, the original trade becomes unhedged. This is not a problem for traders who plan to exit the iron condor one month prior to expiration. For everyone else, the choice becomes: buy another round of short-term options or hold the position without insurance.

---

[394] The cost of buying protection is essentially identical for each scenario.

2. The 93-day options (Figure 19.2) are farther OTM than the options being protected (690 puts to protect 650s and 920 calls to protect 900s). This is necessary to keep the cost of those extra options at a reasonable level. Options with better strikes are far more expensive. If that is not obvious, or if you prefer to see real numbers, look at any RUT or SPX option chain (for ~93 day options) to see typical numbers. As mentioned previously, these farther OTM options are undesirable to own *as insurance*.[395]

3. The 65-day options (Figure 19.3) provide intermediate protection (as expected). The extra options are only slightly farther OTM than the position being protected.

4. The 30-day options (Figure 19.4) were each 20-points closer to the money than the options being protected. That offers *powerful* protection, albeit for a limited time. The P/L graph shows that risk of incurring a significant loss is absent. Below we will discover whether that holds true as time passes.

---

[395] Owning them as a separate, directional play is another matter. I do not recommend that trade idea, but it is much better than buying these options as insurance.

Figure 19.1
Buy 40 RUT 65-day 740/750 900/910 Iron Condors; RUT Price = $823.35
No Insurance

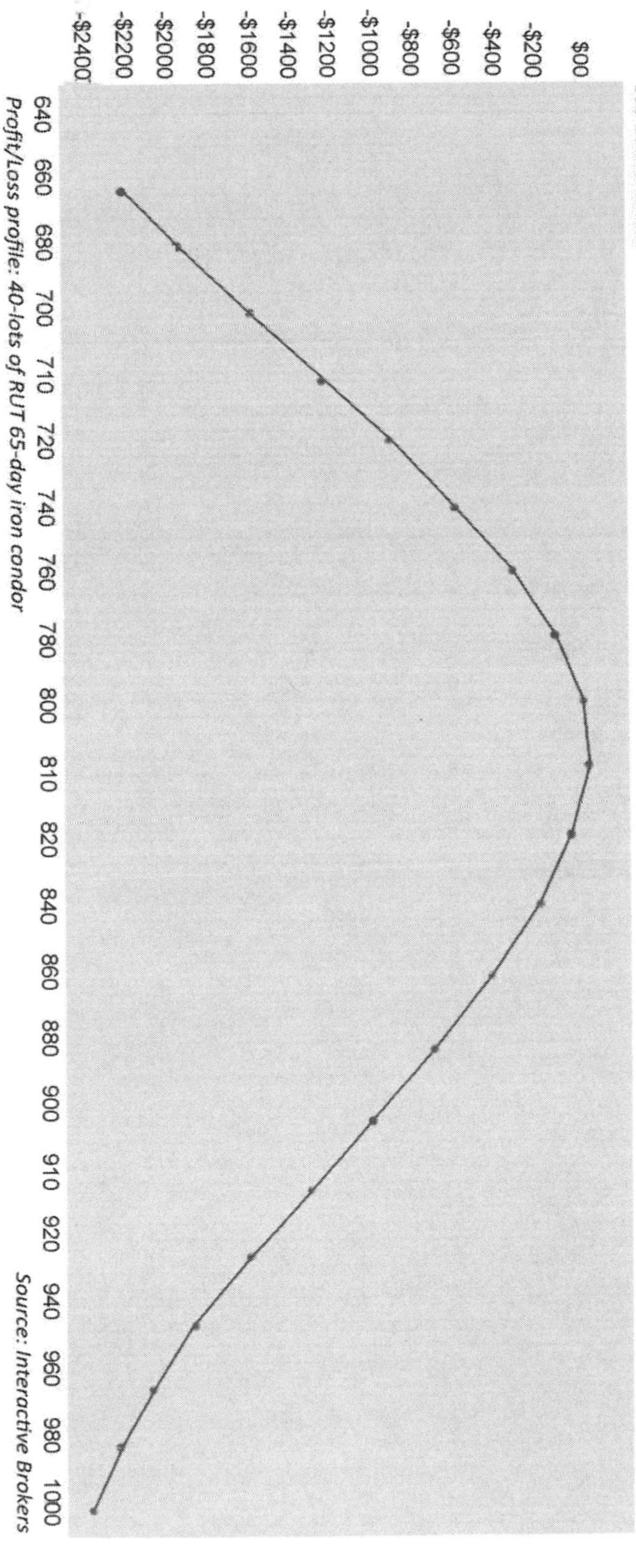

Profit/Loss profile: 40-lots of RUT 65-day iron condor

Source: Interactive Brokers

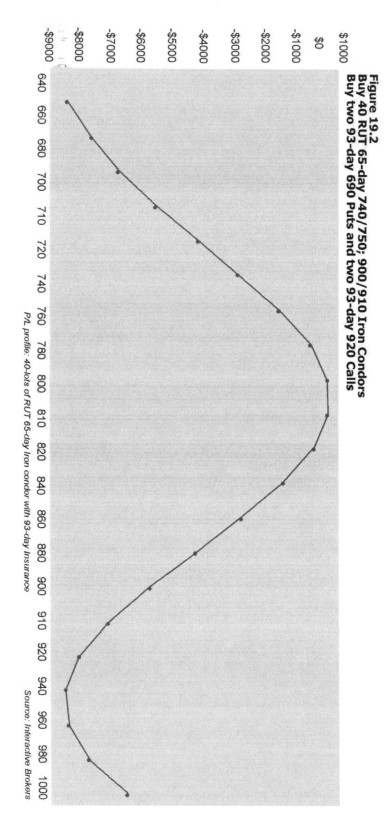

Figure 19.2
Buy 40 RUT 65-day 740/750; 900/910 Iron Condors
Buy two 93-day 690 Puts and two 93-day 920 Calls

P/L profile: 40-lots of RUT 65-day Iron condor with 93-day Insurance

Source: Interactive Brokers

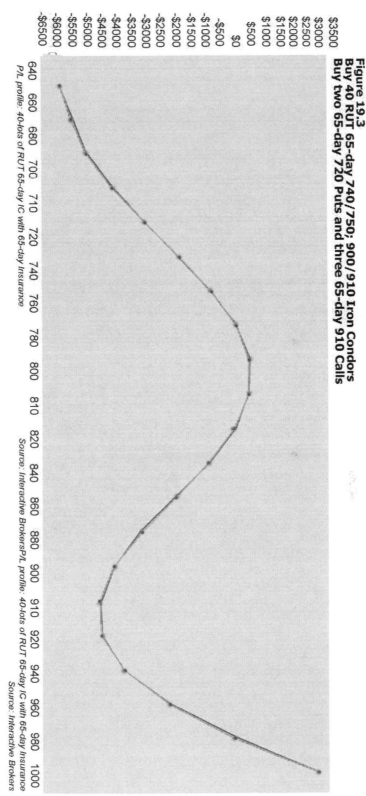

Figure 19.3
Buy 40 RUT 65-day 740/750; 900/910 Iron Condors
Buy two 65-day 720 Puts and three 65-day 910 Calls

P/L profile: 40-lots of RUT 65-day IC with 65-day Insurance

Source: Interactive BrokersP/L profile: 40-lots of RUT 65-day IC with 65-day Insurance

Source: Interactive Brokers

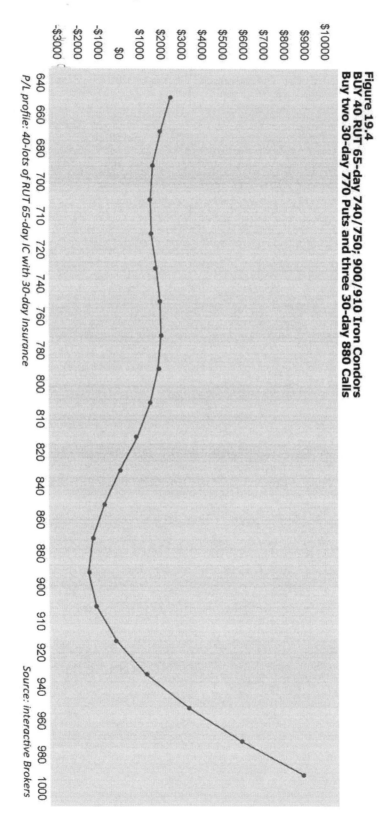

Figure 19.4
BUY 40 RUT 65-day 740/750; 900/910 Iron Condors
Buy two 30-day 770 Puts and three 30-day 880 Calls

P/L profile: 40-lots of RUT 65-day IC with 30-day Insurance

Source: interactive Brokers

Next, let's look at the same graphs after time has passed.

Traders who plan to exit their iron condor at the same time that insurance expires, and who are willing to pay the daily theta cost, can buy front-month options with their very helpful strike prices. These provide the best protection (figure 19.4), and that protection, although reduced, is still very effective[396] as expiration approaches (figure 19.8).

Do not jump to the conclusion that buying near-term options as insurance is enough to declare that the risk-management battle has been won. That strategy is only for traders willing to pay for insurance and who exit their iron condor positions no later than when the insurance options expire.[397]

Traders who do not exit their iron condors already spent up to 25% of the original premium on insurance and may want to buy front-month insurance again. That doubles the cost of insurance, and does not leave much profit potential.

Remember that most traders choose *not* to own insurance. Do not let these graphs convince you to buy insurance. This discussion is offered to help traders decide whether to consider buying insurance.

Time

The passage of time hurts the value of options bought as insurance. This is where the situation can get tricky. Time has also been an ally because the iron condor loses value when time passes. However, as noted earlier, being short any credit spread is extra risky when two conditions are true: expiration is near and the options are not very far out of the money (Table 17.4).

The important question becomes: how valuable (as protection) are the farther OTM options as time passes. To allow harvesting of the needed information, these graphs show risk (P/L potential) when *the insurance options* expire in two days. [When insurance expires after the iron condor, the best we can do is examine the position two days prior to the *iron condor expiration*.]

---

[396] Farther OTM options become almost worthless as expiration nears. They remain effective for giant market moves.

[397] That means no later than the opening of the market on the 3rd Friday for AM settled options. Closing the previous day is recommended. When the options are PM settled, exiting any time Friday is acceptable.

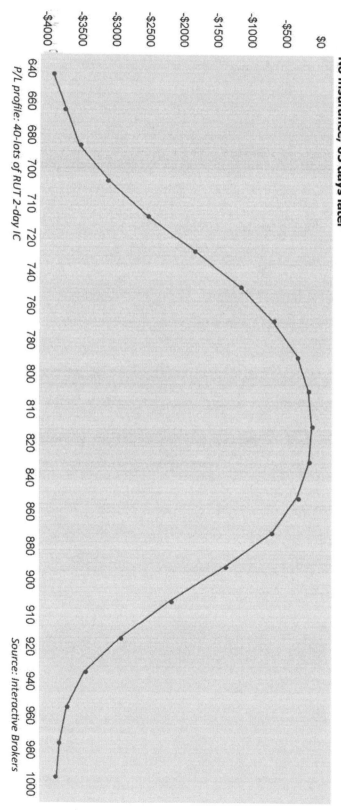

Figure 19.5
Buy 40 RUT 65-day 740/750 900/910 Iron Condors.
No insurance; 63 days later

P/L profile: 40-lots of RUT 2-day IC

Source: Interactive Brokers

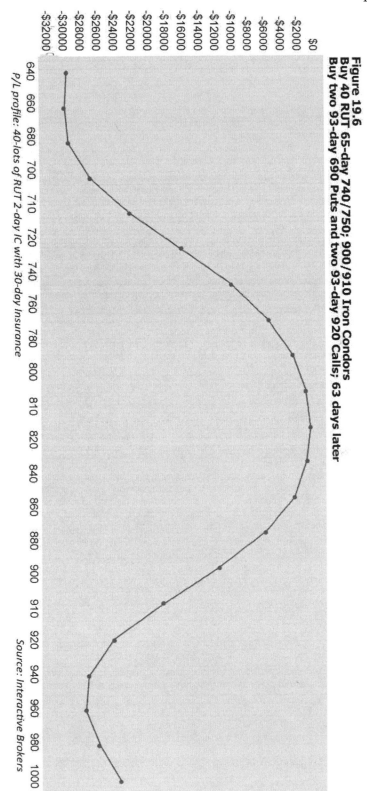

Figure 19.6
Buy 40 RUT 65-day 740/750; 900/910 Iron Condors
Buy two 93-day 690 Puts and two 93-day 920 Calls; 63 days later

P/L profile: 40-lots of RUT 2-day IC with 30-day Insurance

Source: Interactive Brokers

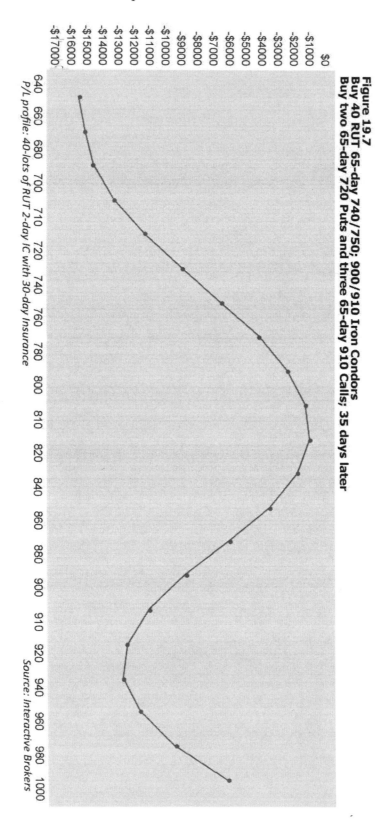

Figure 19.7
Buy 40 RUT 65-day 740/750; 900/910 Iron Condors
Buy two 65-day 720 Puts and three 65-day 910 Calls; 35 days later

P/L profile: 40-lots of RUT 2-day IC with 30-day Insurance

Source: Interactive Brokers

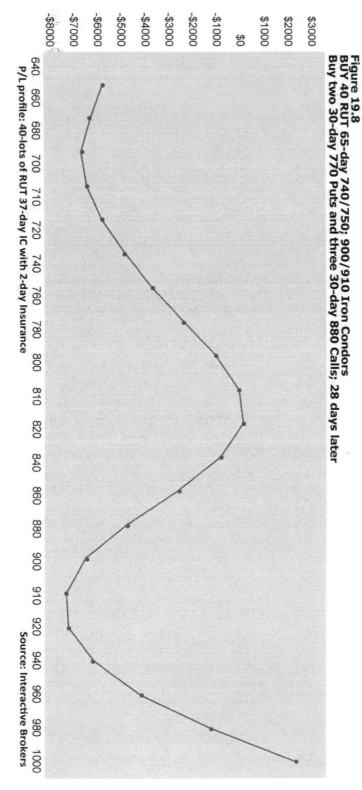

Figure 19.8
BUY 40 RUT 65-day 740/750; 900/910 Iron Condors
Buy two 30-day 770 Puts and three 30-day 880 Calls; 28 days later
P/L profile: 40-lots of RUT 37-day IC with 2-day Insurance

Source: Interactive Brokers

Scenario 0. The uninsured position (Figures 19.1 and 19.5

Figure 19.1 shows the profit/loss profile when buying 40-lots of the RUT 65-day 740/750 put, 900/910 call iron condor. $3.00 ($12,000 cash) premium is collected, making the maximum loss $28,000.[398] The position is slightly bearish (because a profit is earned when RUT declines from 823 to ~805. Typical of iron condors, losses increase as RUT moves away from the sweet spot (either delta neutral price or midpoint between strike prices).

Figure 19.5 makes it clear that holding a position into expiration increases the danger of a huge loss. Portfolio value approaches its worst possible level (-$40,000) when RUT is just under 640. If RUT were to decline to that price on trade day, the loss would be only ~$20,000. **Clarification**: the maximum loss for the trade remains $28,000. If that decline were to occur two days prior to expiration, the cost to exit would be nearly $40,000 (resulting in a $28,000 loss).

Scenario 1. 93-day insurance (Figures 19.2 and 19.6)

Figure 19.2 illustrates the effect of buying two calls and two puts. The calls cost $640 and the puts $860, or $3,000 total. 25% of the proceeds from the sale of the iron condors were invested to buy insurance.

Has the insurance helped? Is the value of the portfolio protected? Yes and no. If RUT undergoes a major, unexpected, decline (approximately 20% to 660) the insured position loses less money (compared with uninsured position, figure 19.1). The savings are approximately $8,000.[399] Similarly, the resulting loss when RUT soars 17% to 960, is reduced by ~$11,000. The question a trader must ask is whether it is worthwhile to invest $3,000 to acquire this protection. In my opinion, the cost of this protection is too high.

True, if the market tumbled 20% tomorrow, any trader would be pleased to own those two extra puts. However, when looking at the bigger picture (Figure 19.6), once two months go by, that 20% decline leaves the trade with a cost of $30,000 to exit, only $10,000 worse than for the unprotected iron condor. That does not feel like protection to me.

You may ask whether it is reasonable to consider such large changes (20%) in the price of the underlying. Isn't it more practical to consider what happens when RUT moves 5%? Yes it is. Looking at the graphs (figures 19.1 and 19.2), we see that when RUT moves ~5% to 780 or 860, insurance provides only a small benefit. Again, insurance is not worth the cost. Insurance can always be bought once needed, although at a higher cost.

Pre-insurance is not effective in this scenario.

Scenario 2. 65-day insurance (Figures 19.3 and 19.7)

---

[398] The maximum value of 40 10-point iron condors is $40,000. Subtracting the $12,000 premium, the maximum loss is $28,000.
[399] From $17,000 to about $9,000

Reminder: options are a wasting asset and lose considerable value as time passes. In addition, as expiration nears, the iron condor position involves greater risk (Table 17.4). That combination suggests that insurance may be even less effective as time passes. We can see the truth of this reminder by comparing figures 19.3 and 19.7 (same position, 35 days later).

Three extra 910 calls and two 720 puts[400] cost $2,980.

The general shape of the curve remains the same. When the underlying moves far enough, the rate at which money is lost deceases, and then reverses.

As expected, insurance becomes less effective and the potential loss is significantly greater (figure 19.7) than it was 35 days ago (figure 19.3). This effect is even more obvious on the right-hand portion of the graph. If a huge rally (RUT to $1,000) were to occur immediately, the position would earn a profit (figure 19.3). However, just five weeks later (figure 19.7, the rally would leave the position underwater as RUT approaches $1,000.[401]

Looking at scenarios 1 and 2, I am convinced that buying options *as insurance* is ineffective when the options are farther out of the money than the position being protected. For this insurance to become worth owning there must be a very quick and very large change in market conditions.[402]

Compare figures 19.2 and 19.3. Then compare 19.6 with 19.7. The same situation (better protection) obtains even after time passes.[403]

This is an interesting result. It turns out that owning three puts instead of two and owning options with strike prices that are closer to the money offers better risk-reduction than owning more expensive options with longer lifetimes.[404] These 'better' options cost less than the longer-term options with farther OTM strikes.

Because scenario 2 provides better insurance than scenario 1, let's take this idea one step further and consider the purchase of insurance that expires even sooner: one month before the iron condor expires. Many traders find it uncomfortable own insurance that expires earlier than the insured item.[405] That does not deter us from looking at that scenario.

---

[400] It is not necessary to buy an equal number of puts and calls. Puts trade with a higher implied volatility and are more expensive when equally far OTM. In this example, calls are $420 and puts cost $860. The strikes chosen are illustrative and alternatives are available.

[401] And that happens even when owning three calls that are 90 points ITM, and worth $9,000 each.

[402] A big (big) move or a surge in IV would be beneficial to the portfolio.

[403] The number of days that passed is different, but the trend remains: Time decay hurts the ability of the extra options to protect against loss.

[404] Many traders have a tendency to prefer longer-dated options, never bothering to consider alternatives.

[405] When the options bought as insurance expire, the iron condor still has a one-month lifetime. There are two choices: close the position or buy more insurance. If you agree with the earlier idea (Chapters 17, 18) that it is worthwhile to open positions in the 2nd and 3rd months and exit when they become front-month options, then these methods are consistent. When owning front-month options as insurance, close the iron condor position when the insurance lapses (expires).

Scenario 3. 30-day insurance (Figures 19.4 and 19.8)

In this scenario, the 40-lot of 65-day iron condors is protected by insurance that expires in 30 days. Because these options are so much less expensive than longer-term options, we can buy options with very desirable strikes. The two 30-day 770 puts cost $6.90 each and three 30-day 880 calls are $3.40. Net insurance cost: $2,400.[406]

To protect against the 900/910 call spread, buy 880 calls. Compare figures 19.2, 19.3, and 19.4 to see how much better the risk graph looks. In scenarios 1 and 2, the 880 calls were prohibitively costly.[407]

Similarly, 770 puts are bought as protection against being short the 740/750 put spreads. Comparing those same three risk graphs makes it clear that 30-day, closer-to-the-money options provide far better protection against loss (at the same or lower cost).

When looking at the effect of time on the ability of the near-term options to protect the position from big loses (compare figures 19.4 and 19.8), we can see that once again the passage of time lessens the value of insurance. However, insurance does its job. The near-term options not only cost less ($2,400 vs. $3,000), but with only two days of lifetime before they expire, the position is still well protected against a catastrophe (compare figures 19.6, 19.7, 19.8).

Pre-Insurance bottom line

The major conclusion is clear: near-term options are far more effective *as pre-insurance* than longer-term options because they cost far less, making it possible to own insurance options with better[408] strike prices.

However, this type of insurance does not work for every trader. When using any form of pre-insurance as part of a risk-management plan, it is still important to remember that the risk-management plan and the trade plan have to be consistent with each other.

Clarification: You must be comfortable with the idea of exiting the iron condor position when insurance lapses,[409] or buying additional insurance. It is important to mention again: just because I gave much space to this discussion, it does not suggest that it is recommended. This information is offered to traders who like the idea of owning pre-insurance. Consider it as

---

[406] At that price you could buy another put or two more calls. I see no reason to spend the full $3,000.

[407] Using up too much of the original iron condor premium

[408] Closer to the money

[409] When the short options (in the iron condor) are both pretty far OTM, it is very tempting to hold longer, even without insurance. In today's world, the possibility of a terror attack/political assassination or a sudden announcement of huge importance from Europe/U.S. Federal Reserve can move markets.

another option strategy for managing risk. No trader adopts every possible strategy. Utilize those ideas which fit into your comfort zone.

Another big decision is: do you buy insurance for every position? The answer depends on how comfortable you are with uninsured positions and where you stand as a conservative/ aggressive trader. The rationale for buying iron condors is based on collecting theta, or the daily time decay.[410] Owning front-month options cancels much of that positive theta. Emphasis: this insurance is expensive and not for everyone.

Pre-Insurance Summary:

1. Near-term options provide the best protection for any iron condor position, even those that expire later. These options are cheaper than longer-dated options, and you can afford to buy options with attractive strikes.

2. 2nd month options are appropriate as insurance against an iron condor position that expire in the 3rd month, but these options are expensive and this insurance does not provide the same protection as near-term vs. 2nd or 3rd month iron condors.

3. It is more effective to own calls and puts with better strike prices than to buy a larger quantity of farther OTM options.[411]

4. It is acceptable to wait to buy protection until it is needed. It is more expensive, but does not have to be purchased for every position. The downside is that a big gap opening leaves the trader unprotected.[412]

5. If pre-insurance is for you, I recommend using short-term options.

To gain insight I encourage paper trading. Dull markets may convince you that insurance is a waste of money, but volatile markets may convince you otherwise.

I do not specifically recommend pre-insurance. What I do recommend is being aware that it is available for those times when you prefer to own it.

Most risk management decisions are made in the heat of battle, and not as pre-insurance.

---

[410] In other words, theta is our reward for taking the risk of a big market move.
[411] Owning more options, each further OTM, only pays off in the event of a big disaster (or huge rally).
[412] This unpleasant event is not a big disaster when your trades are sized properly.

Risk Reduction

After this discussion on pre-insurance, it is time to talk about protecting at-risk positions when that protection is needed. One important point: the words 'adjustment' and 'protection' express the same idea—a position has moved outside the trader's comfort zone and action must be taken to reduce risk.

Most traders manage risk as needed. When it comes to selecting a specific method for 'fixing' a position—reducing risk coupled with being certain the position is still worth owning—the choices are almost unlimited. There is no single best strategy to adopt when making adjustments, but after a little experimentation, we traders tend to find one or two ideas that best suit our individual investing style. There is some psychological boost that comes with using a method that feels right, suits our personality,[413] and produces the required results.

1. Rolling

The idea of rolling a position has been covered in Chapters 11, 18, and 19. Rolling is a two-trade decision. The trader exits all (or part) of an existing position and simultaneously (or shortly thereafter) opens a new, similar position. The key decision is being certain that the new position is one that you want to own. I repeat this so often because 'rollers' want to get out of the current 'mess' and substitute something new. They often ignore the quality of the newly-rolled position because their focus is on the wrong problem.

There are two basic rolling categories: Maintaining the same expiration for the position (rolling down, or rolling up)[414] or moving the expiration to a more distant expiration (rolling out). Traders can roll 'down and out' or 'up and out.'

Do not roll just to get out of trouble. Do not limit choices by requiring a cash credit when rolling. Substitute a new position for the old (that is rolling) only when the new position is good. It is far better to exit the 'mess' and when ready, open a brand new position. Yes, that means locking in the loss. Please do not be afraid to accept the fact that many trades are going to lose money. Your job is to avoid the poor roll—a decision that is likely to cost additional money.

---

[413] For traders who 'hate' the idea of adjusting positions, managing risk is a difficult proposition. When we believe the adjustment is both necessary and financially sound, our outlook is better. Make no mistake, feeling good about your positions is a big part of becoming successful—and that is the reason for adjusting only when the new position is something you honestly want to own.

[414] Rolling down refers to moving the position to one with strikes that are farther OTM. That costs cash. Rolling up refers to collecting cash and moving the position less far OTM.

One key point often overlooked: when a trader rolls a bad position into one that is less bad, sometimes the result is positive. In other words, after much stress, time and effort, the original loss can be overcome. That feels good and the trader tends to forget the numerous trades that continued to bleed money. However, the overlooked issue is that with the same time and effort, and with no stress, the trader could have opened a fresh position and earned as much, if not more, money.

My advice: Your job is to earn money from good positions. It does not matter whether a new position produces that cash or it is 'recovered' from a trade that is currently losing money.

2. Buying a debit spread

Risk is reduced any time the new trade earns money at the same time that the original trade is losing money. When making an adjustment (or buying protection), the goal is to reduce, not eliminate losses. The best method for eliminating future losses is to exit the position.

Similarly, when a position is threatening to violate your comfort zone, covering part (20% to 50%) of the position represents an intelligent adjustment. Sometimes traders prefer to make a very similar adjustment instead of covering. For example, assume you sold a put spread that was nicely out of the money, but the market has declined and the position is no longer comfortable to own.

EXAMPLE

Sold 10 XYZ 450/460 put spreads when XYZ was $540

Current XYZ price is $495

Expiration arrives in 6 weeks

Instead of covering some of the 450/460P spreads, the trader may buy a different debit spread—with one specific condition: the new spread must be less far OTM than the position being protected.

Buy two[415] (same expiration) 470/480P spreads.[416] Note that the spread does not have to be the same width. Instead of buying two 10-point spreads, it is equally effective to buy four 5-point spreads (470/475 or 465/470).

The debit spread is more expensive than covering one of the original spreads. It is a tempting strategy because it avoids locking in a loss. That is not an acceptable rationale for choosing one trade over another. Buying

---

[415] The quantity is not locked in stone. I suggest two or three (as a Stage 1 adjustment) when protecting a 10-lot.
[416] A few alternatives: 475/485; 480/490; 475/480.

two 450/460 spreads in a closing transaction is not very different from buying two 470/480 spreads as protection. Note the warning below.

Warning: The debit spread is a limited-profit trade and a 10-point spread can never be worth more than $10. Thus, there has to be a limit for the price paid.[417] I recommend paying no more than 40% of the maximum spread value. That means $4.00 or less for a 10-point spread. When the cost is higher, there is too little to gain and thus, not enough to offset additional losses which will accrue if the market continues to fall (or rise when dealing with call spreads).

Do not adopt buy debit spreads when your rationale is refusing to cover some of the current position at a loss. Do it *only* when the debit spread is attractively priced (compared with covering some of the original spread) and the newly adjusted position is one you feel comfortable owning.

Also consider market reversal risk. When the market stops falling, that is good for your entire position. However, buying debit spreads cost more than covering an equal number of the existing spreads—and that means the adjustment cost more than it had to cost.

Do not think of this trade as a chance for a miracle finish and extra profits. In our example,, if the position is held to expiration (high risk) and if the settlement price is in the sweet spot (between 460 and 470), extra profits would be earned. The original spread expires worthless and the debit spread moves to its maximum value. Sure, that is a great result, however if you would hold onto the adjusted position longer, based on the hope of achieving that miracle, I urge you to avoid adding debit spreads as an adjustment. You do not want to own *any trade* (including the prospect of a very lucky result) when that trade encourages you to take on more risk.

3. Buy an OTM calendar or butterfly

This idea is mentioned for completeness, I recommend that new option traders avoid this idea for now. Why? You do not want to become overwhelmed with too many new ideas at one time, especially because this strategy makes it more difficult to manage the whole position.

Please accept the truth of this sentence: all else being equal, both the butterfly[418] and calendar spreads[419] (Chapter 21) earn money when time passes and the underlying asset moves towards the strike price.[420]

---

[417] If paying $900 for a 10-point spread, the maximum gain is $100 and that is essentially no protection. Worse than that, if the market reverses, up to $900 may be lost.
[418] The butterfly is a condor with zero distance between the call and put spreads.
[419] Two options with the same strike; buy the longer-term option, sell the shorter-term option.
[420] That is the simple idea. It is more complicated than that because this strategy is very dependent on vega and the IV of the options.

The idea is to buy a position that gains money as the underlying moves towards a specific strike price. That is exactly how these two spreads work. However, once the underlying reaches that strike and continues to move, then the positions begin to lose value. Thus, when adopting this adjustment method, it is essential to unload the calendar or butterfly once it reaches the point of maximum protection.

These strategies offer *limited profits* and are not viable in volatile markets. The ideal situation occurs when you believe the market will continue to move towards the area of major pain, but not much farther. Adding a calendar with a strike near your high-risk point may soften the loss, but only when the market moves slowly. Calendars are too expensive when markets are volatile.[421]

4. Any strategy that gains while original trade loses

Most trades that help neutralize the Greeks should be effective as a risk-reducing adjustment. Translation: when the position has negative delta, adding positive delta reduces risk. When the position has positive delta, adding negative delta reduces risk.

> **NOTE:** There are important exceptions. As mentioned previously, do not buy options that are farther OTM than the options being protected

The strategies recommended in this book come with negative gamma. When reducing risk, be careful to avoid adding more negative gamma. It may not be easy to find an acceptable trade that adds positive gamma, but adding more negative gamma adds to overall risk.

EXAMPLE

When you sold a call spread and the underlying asset moved dangerously[422] near the strike of your short option, it may be tempting to sell put spreads[423] to gain positive delta. Please be aware that such a trade adds more negative gamma. Over the longer-term, that strategy is going to cost money. First the sale of put spreads introduces downside risk where there was none. Second, the upside protection is limited to the cash collected for

---

[421] Because the positions have + vega
[422] A term defined by your individual comfort zone
[423] Many people recommend selling these puts. It is attractive to collect cash and increase the potential reward. This is an illusion. Selling 'more' of anything increases risk and is the same as trading larger position size. I urge you to avoid this trap.

the puts. That is inadequate protection when the market continues higher.

Summation

The objective in preparing this book is to provide the information needed for readers to use options effectively. Experienced traders know it is essential to manage risk carefully. Thus, the inclusion of this chapter represents only the tip of the iceberg where risk management is concerned. By presenting a few ideas, I hope to convince you that managing risk is not difficult and the prospect of undertaking that task should not frighten you. In fact, I hope that my repeated warnings are understood as my way of telling you that I was not a careful risk manager when trading as a market maker. And trust me when I tell you that I wish I had been as careful then as I am now. Risk management is the key to success.

If you are not yet ready to trade credit spreads or iron condors—that is OK. Take your time. It is more important to gain hands-on experience with methods that are well understood and which are compatible with your investment philosophy. You have your entire future to trade options, so be patient and take time to understand how options really work. (That is something that most beginners avoid. They'd rather jump right in and take their chances.)

When comfortable with any of the basic strategies discussed in Part II, it is not difficult to switch to the sale of put spreads—and you may even decide to adopt that as your primary option strategy. It is after all, the way most investors approach the stock market—with a bullish bias.

When selling put spreads, the portfolio is hedged and has limited downside risk. The traditional investor who owns stocks and mutual funds does not know what limited risk means. Although those bullish investors have unlimited upside potential, you have enough upside potential to earn a very good return on your investment. And if those earnings are compounded (perhaps in a retirement account), they may provide for your future financial security. Isn't sacrificing some of that upside potential in exchange for extra downside security an intelligent tradeoff?[424]

One advantage of selling credit spreads is that the trader can choose to be 'market neutral' rather than always bullish. That is accomplished by selling call spreads along with put spreads. Do not forget the bottom line: if trading the three basic conservative strategies feels right for your comfort zone, there may be no reason to go any further (at least for now and years to come).

---

[424] To this author, the answer is 'yes.' But, not everyone agrees.

No strategy is guaranteed to bring profits. Sometimes there are many consecutive trades with nary a problem and profits accumulate. At others times, markets are turbulent and you may be forced to adjust and/or exit positions frequently. Skilled risk management is needed for survival during those turbulent times. Please remember that sitting on the sidelines is an acceptable risk-management technique—one that is not used often enough.

> **NOTE:** Pre-insurance may be right for the conservative trader. However, most option rookies are better off postponing the use of pre-insurance. That does not apply to standard risk-management practices. Those are necessary.

You may thoroughly grasp the concepts of pre-insurance, but there is no substitute for hands-on trading before knowing which of several risk-management ideas make you more comfortable and confident when trading.

Plan to re-read this chapter after a few months of trading. If you decide that pre-insurance is not for you, don't fret. It is too costly for many traders.

QUIZ 19

1. If selling a put spread and collecting a cash credit, should you buy puts or calls as pre-insurance (assuming you elect to own insurance)?

2. When owning puts as pre-insurance, you will probably earn a quick profit on that insurance policy when
   a) The Federal Reserve cuts interest rates by 0.25%.
   b) The President of the United States undergoes minor surgery.
   c) Terrorists simultaneously blow up the Eifel Tower and Washington monument.
   d) A definitive cancer cure is announced.

3. When buying a one-lot iron condor, also buy pre-insurance. True or false.

4. Investors who believe pre-insurance is too expensive and decline to own it are making a big mistake. **TRUE or FALSE**

5. Which of these are true? Near-term options provide better insurance for iron condor positions because:
   a) The options are less expensive
   b) You can afford to buy more options
   c) Options with better strike prices are available at the same cost per option
   d) They have a much slower rate of daily time decay

6. Closing a position is a good method for managing risk. **TRUE or FALSE**

QUIZ 19 Answers

1. Puts. This spread cannot lose money if the underlying rallies. The only time insurance is needed occurs when the underlying declines.

2. c. These events would cause panic.

3. False. When buying an iron condor, those puts and calls you own (the wings) act as an insurance policy. For very small positions, there is no appropriate option to buy as extra insurance.

4. False. Pre-insurance is not for everyone.

5. a,b,c.

6. True. It is not always the best choice, but it is always effective in reducing risk.

Chapter 20

Calendar Spreads

Let's begin with a definition: a calendar spread (sometimes referred to as a 'time spread') consists of two options—one is bought and the other sold. Both options are of the same type (both are calls or both are puts), have the same underlying and strike price, but different expiration dates. When buying the option that expires later, you own the calendar spread. When buying the option that expires first, you sell the calendar spread.

For practical reasons,[425] we will only refer to situations in which we buy calendar spreads.[426]

Many individual investors trade calendar spreads, and it is one of the most popular option strategies. Calendars are typically used to place a low-cost bet on where the underlying stock will be trading in the not-too-distant future. Thus, the calendar is a directional play. In turn, that allows calendar spreads to be utilized as a risk-management tool that provides limited protection (as discussed in Chapter 19).[427]

In this Rookie's Guide, we will cover the most basic use of calendar spreads. This is a simple-looking strategy, but one with enough complexities that a complete discussion is beyond the scope of this book. Because the position involves two different expiration dates, some considerations that we have not previously discussed come into play. In simple terms, the trader has to pay attention to the relationship between two different sets of options simultaneously. Options expiring on one date comprise the first set, while the second set consists of options expiring on the second date.

Previously, we chose option spreads with a single expiration date based on simple factors, such as which position appealed to our comfort zone. When simultaneously using options with different expirations, traders must avoid buying options that are unfavorably priced when compared with the set of options being sold. Understanding how to take advantage of

---

[425] For reasons that do not make sense to me, the powers that be established high margin requirements when the option owned expires before the option sold. In fact, the sold option is considered to be a naked short when calculating margin.

[426] Obviously, when exiting a position, we have to sell our calendar spreads. What we will not be discussing is the strategy of selling calendars spreads as a new position.

[427] If you own a calendar spread that makes money when the market declines, then the calendar acts as a hedge against positions that lose money on a decline. But please note: This protection is limited. As you will learn later in this chapter, if the market moves too far (past the strike price of the calendar), then any accrued profit can disappear in a hurry.

subtle differences to find a trading edge is a topic for more advanced traders. [428]

The majority of investors/traders prefer to make directional plays, and if you are in that group, calendar spreads add another strategy to your investment arsenal. Our two primary reasons for learning about the calendar are:

- To use it as a risk-management tool.

- To increase your understanding of how to adopt another strategy, the diagonal (or double diagonal) spread (Chapter 21). That strategy combines the credit spread with a calendar spread (or an iron condor with two calendar spreads).

If you gain nothing else from this chapter except for a better understanding of how to use the Greeks, then consider it to be time well spent. The three primary Greeks that play a role in trading calendars are theta gamma, and vega. The objective when buying (very few investors sell these spreads[429]) a calendar spread is to take advantage of your ability to make a good estimate of where the underlying stock (or index) is headed between the time of purchase and the time of exit. Lacking that predictive ability limits the use of calendars. However, as with the iron condor, you can buy an at-the-money calendar spread, playing for the stock to remain in a narrow trading range.[430]

Calendars and the Greeks

All else being equal (and it never is in the real trading world), the spread trades at its maximum value—and thus earns the maximum profit—when the underlying stock is very near the strike price[431] as expiration arrives.

As the stock moves farther away from the strike, the calendar spread loses value because the near-term option has a higher **gamma** than the longer-term option. That means delta of the near-term option changes more rapidly as the stock moves. Thus:

---

[428] For example, IV for the longer-dated options tends to be lower than that of the nearer-term options. If that IV difference becomes too large or too small, or reverses, that may offer an opportunity to buy one expiration date and sell the other. However, we cannot devote the space to discussing when and how to make this decision. In this Rookie's Guide, our objective is to teach the general concept of using calendar spreads at a basic level.

[429] It is a trade where seasoned investors own an ATM position with positive gamma.

[430] I strongly prefer the iron condor for the same wager. However, at times you may prefer the calendar spread.

[431] The long and short options share the same strike, and this is the only spread we discussed for which this is true.

- As the stock moves beyond (above the strike for calls; below for puts) the strike price, delta of the near-term option *increases* faster than that of the longer term option. Consequently, the near-term (we sold this one) option increases in value more rapidly than the longer-term option (we own this one), and the spread loses value.

- As the stock moves away (lower for calls; higher for puts) from the strike price, each option loses value. Delta for the near-term option *decreases* faster and loses value more slowly.[432] Thus, the calendar spread loses value.

As time passes and expiration nears, the spread increases in value because the near-term option has a higher **theta** and loses value more rapidly than the longer-term option.

Combining the effects of both theta and gamma: The spread has the highest value when the underlying is near the strike price, and very little time remains before the near-term option expires. This is the reason that calendar spreads require a bit of market prognostication. If you are correct in selecting the strike price, there is a nice profit to be earned. However, if the stock is far removed from that strike price, the calendar spread is likely to show a substantial loss.[433]

It is true that the spread attains maximum value when you own it late in the day on expiration Friday (for American style equity options) and the stock is priced within a couple of pennies of the strike. But, as with other negative-gamma situations, gamma increases rapidly.[434] When holding the position, a trader is in a familiar position of betting that time will pass without an unfavorable price change. In other words, the trader accepts a high risk for the chance to gain a big reward.

When the near-term option is nearly worthless (or has been covered at a very low price), the longer-term option has to be sold. Its value depends on time remaining and implied volatility. Holding is a pure gamble

If you recall the discussion on the theoretical value of an option in Chapter 6, the implied volatility (IV) of an option plays a major role in determining its value.

A calendar spread comes with positive vega (longer-term option has more vega than shorter-term option). Thus, the price of the longer-term option is more sensitive to a change in the implied volatility than the shorter-term option.

---

[432] Do not get confused. Just think of it this way. As the stock moves higher through the strike, short-term call delta moves towards 100 more quickly. That means it picks up value faster. As the stock falls, the delta of the front-month option moves towards zero more quickly. That means it loses value more slowly.

[433] That loss is limited to the premium paid for the spread.

[434] Delta can go from 0 to 100 when the stock moves from 49.99 to 50.01 at 3:59:50 pm ET on expiration Friday.

As IV increases, the longer-term option increases in value by more dollars than the shorter-term option and the calendar spread gains in value. One rationale for buying a calendar spread is an expectation that market volatility and implied volatility will increase.[435] However, that volatility increase has to be gentle and not gigantic. There are two potential complications:

- Large IV increases often occur after a significant market decline and those almost always result in a much larger IV increase for the front-month options. For example, the longer-term IV may increase from 35 to 50 while IV for the front-month option moves from 37 to 65. Even though the longer-term option has a higher vega, the 15-point increase is not enough to offset the 28-point increase in the front-month vega, and the calendar owner loses money.

- If IV increased due to a stock price change, and if the stock is now priced farther from the calendar's strike, then any profit from an IV increase may not be sufficient to overcome the loss resulting from the calendar being farther OTM.

Warnings:

- When the stock finishes near the strike, if IV is low, the premium of the longer-term option may prove to be a disappointment.

- If IV is too high when the trade is initiated, the trader pays too much for the calendar spread.

- If IV is too low when the trade ends, the trader collects too little when selling the position.

Opening and managing calendar spreads helps a trader gain an understanding of how to select an expiration date when opening any option position.

Example of a calendar spread

Some brokers do not allow customers to sell calendars as a new position—but when they do, the margin requirement is steep. If you have an account that uses 'portfolio margin' rather than 'Reg T' margin, this limitation does not apply to you.[436]

---

[435] *Just as traders get long when expecting a rally, option traders can buy vega when anticipating an IV increase.*

[436] Brokers require a minimum account value of $100,000 before allowing portfolio margin. Regulation T describes 'normal' margin requirements imposed on investors by the brokerage industry. Note: brokers do not set margin rules, the SEC does. But brokers are allowed to impose stricter margin requirements on their customers.

Here's an example of buying a calendar spread:

Buy 10 IBM Jan 200 calls
Sell 10 IBM Dec 200 calls

> **NOTE:** The options can expire on any date, and the number of days, weeks or months between expiration dates is immaterial. It is a calendar spread when both options share the same strike but have different expirations.

Why buy a calendar spread? How does it earn a profit?

The idea behind buying the calendar spread is to take advantage of the fact that the near-term option decays faster than the long-term option. But, it is not that simple. If the rate of time decay were the only factor, this type of spread would almost always be profitable. Calendars can lose money because other factors come into play.

Our example position (Long 10 Jan/Dec IBM 100 call spreads) earns the highest profit (ignoring implied volatility for the moment) when December expiration arrives and IBM is trading @ 100.00. Under those conditions, IBM Dec 100 calls expire worthless (but, do not forget about pin risk;[437] see page 188) and the spread owner sells the Jan100 calls. Except on rare occasions (see below), you can expect to collect more for the January calls than the original cost of the spread. That difference is the profit.

When IV is elevated, the profit is higher (more cash when selling the Jan calls). When IV and profits are depressed, I encourage you to accept that less-than-hoped-for profit and sell the Jan calls.

Exiting the calendar spread

If expiration has come and gone, and you still own your IBM Jan 100 calls, the question is: why? You are naked long those calls and it is a gamble to hold them. You have a choice between selling to eliminate the entire position, or hedging by creating a new spread.[438] It is more common (and recommended) to exit the trade no later than the afternoon of expiration Friday, rather than holding over the weekend.

- If IBM is above $100 per share, to close the calendar spread position, buy back (cover) IBM Dec 100 calls at the same time that

---

[437] Covering the Dec 100 call is a prudent method for eliminating that risk. In fact, the best method for exiting the trade is to enter an order to sell the calendar spread. That is less risky than using separate orders to buy Dec calls and sell Jan calls.

[438] Perhaps by selling 10 Jan 95 calls to create a bear call spread, or by selling the Jan 105 calls to create a bull call spread.

the IBM Jan calls are sold. In other words, sell the IBM Jan/Dec 100 call calendar spread.

- If IBM is less than $100, the December calls expired[439] worthless and your task is to sell the January calls and thereby exit the position. WARNING: If it is 10 minutes before the market closes on the 3rd Friday and the stock is anywhere near the strike price ($99, for example), do not assume that the December calls will expire worthless. It is good risk management to cover those December calls for a few pennies before selling the Jan calls. [In fact, it is even better risk management to exit earlier.] Remember, margin rules prevent selling the Jan options before the Dec options are covered.

When selling the IBM Jan 100 calls. Several factors are in play in determining the value of those calls, with IV being #1. IV for Dec calls is far less important. With so little time remaining, the effect of implied volatility on this option is small.

Let's see how IV plays a major role in determining the final profit or loss.

EXAMPLE

If IBM closes at 100 on the 3rd Friday of December, then the price you can collect for the IBM Jan 100 call depends on IV). See Table 20.1.

If you owned the Feb/Dec spread instead of a Jan/Dec spread, the effect of IV is even greater because longer-term options have more vega.

NOTE: The trade may have been initiated as a prediction of future stock price, but the profit (or loss) may hinge on IV, rather than on the stock price.

If you decide to hold until the near-term option expires, the settlement price of the underlying stock, or index, plays a vital role in determining the profitability of the calendar spread. Table 20.2 shows the value of IBM Jan/Dec 100 call spread when the position is closed at the end of the day on expiration Friday. Volatility is assumed to be 45 (as good a guess as any):

---

[439] Or will soon expire worthless. If there is any reasonable chance that this call may move ITM, please pay a few pennies to cover.

Table 20.1
Value of IBM calls as Implied Volatility Changes
Stock price = 100; 28 days before expiration

IV		35	40	45	50	55
Call Value		$4.02	$4.57	$5.12	$5.67	$6.22

ATM calendar spreads increase as implied volatility increases

Table 20.2
Value of IBM Jan/Dec 100 call spread as settlement price changes.
28 days before January expiration; Implied Volatility 45

IBM Price	88	92	96	100	104	108	112
Dec 100 C	$0.00	$0.00	$0.00	$0.00	$4.00	$8.00	$12.00
Jan 100 C	$0.98	$1.89	$3.26	$5.12	$7.47	$10.38	$13.58
Spread	$0.98	$1.89	$3.26	$5.12	$3.47	$2.38	$1.58

Calendar spread loses value as the underlying moves away from strike price

NOTE: When IBM is 100 or less, the December 100 call expires worthless and the value of the Jan 100 call is the value of the calendar spread. When IBM is higher than 100, the December call is in the money. For table 20.2, the assumption is made that the IBM Dec 100 call is bought at parity (intrinsic value) and the IBM Jan 100 call is sold at its value.

As can be seen from the data (Table 20.2), the value of the spread is highest when the stock is near the strike price and steadily decreases as the stock moves away from the strike.

Do not forget to exit

One way to make a low cost directional play is to buy an OTM calendar spread. If you are correct, and the stock moves towards the strike, you not only gain as time passes, but you gain as the stock moves towards the strike.

There are two variables at work to minimize or eliminate profits. Be aware of these possibilities when trading calendar spreads.

- If implied volatility decreases as the stock rises—a frequent occurrence—then the value of your spread may decline when the effect of IV is greater than the effect of positive gamma and positive delta. NOTE: When bearish and trading an OTM put spread, this is not an issue. In fact, it is likely that IV is increasing (as it tends to do when markets decline) and the calendar can provide bonus profits.

- If the stock rises too far and moves beyond the strike price, the spread begins to lose value. Thus, it is important to consider exiting a calendar spread when the stock moves near its strike price. Even though time is on your side, once the stock reaches the strike, a stock move in either direction hurts.

There is a problem with purchasing an at-the-money calendar spread when your outlook for the stock is neutral. The calendar costs more when the stock is near the strike. If the stock price is steady (as predicted), IV will probably decline, thereby reducing the value of the calendar. Buying an iron condor may be a better choice.

Versatility of options

The true versatility of options becomes apparent when you realize there are alternative strategies for similar market outlooks. Thus, there are numerous bullish strategies, but they differ in subtle ways that affect the risk, reward, and probability of earning a profit. Some allow for unlimited profits (buying calls) while others represent reduced risk with limited gains and losses (buy call spreads, sell put spreads, buy OTM call calendar). Table 20.3 provides a list of the strategies discussed in this book and the applicability for investors with bullish, bearish, or neutral outlooks. This is not a complete list of option strategies. There is always a good strategy available that suits your outlook for the stock market (or a specific stock or index). Most investors/traders prefer to trade options based on their market outlook, and it is a good idea to understand which methods are appropriate to suit that outlook. Some traders never try to outguess the market, but if you trade with a bias, it is to your advantage to know which strategies are suitable.[440]

Table 20.3 lists calendar, and other spreads we discussed, and indicates which can be used as bullish, neutral, or bearish plays.

My choice for bullish or bearish plays is the sale of a credit spread because they can constructed with a high probability of success. If you are a talented stock picker, then you should prefer a play that gives you the opportunity for larger gains. But knowing that it is difficult to pick direction on a consistent basis, I prefer to win more often—even when gains are limited.

---

[440] Selecting a strategy is important. Do not trade positions/strategies that make you uncomfortable or which are not well understood. My basic premise: risk-management is far more important that strategy selection in determining your future success.

Table 20.3 Directional Option Strategies

Strategy	Direction
Buy call	Bullish
Write covered call	Bullish
Write naked put	Bullish
Buy collar	Bullish
Buy call spread	Bullish
Sell put spread	Bullish
Buy OTM call calendar spread	Bullish
Buy iron condor	Neutral
Buy/sell straddle	Neutral
Buy/sell strangle	Neutral
Buy ATM calendar spread	Neutral
Buy put	Bearish
Sell naked call (avoid)	Bearish
Buy put spread	Bearish
Sell call spread	Bearish
But OTM put calendar spread	Bearish

Bullish, neutral, and bearish strategies

I recommend iron condors for market neutral strategies.

This is an area in which your individual personality helps determine which methods are suitable. Find strategies that suit your trading style and philosophy.

With the exception of buying puts or calls, these methods all benefit from the passage of time. Even market neutral strategies involve some predicting[441] of market movement—higher, lower, or range-bound.

Bottom Line: This chapter does not provide a comprehensive study of how to trade calendar spreads. It is intended to help the options rookie gain an understanding of this popular strategy. Here are a few ideas about using the calendar:

- When bullish on volatility, the calendar offers an opportunity to earn a profit when IV increases. With no belief that volatility will increase, there are alternatives to the calendar spread.

---

[441] You may prefer to use one of the following terms: hoping, praying...

- Use at-the-money calendar when you believe the market will trade in a narrow range, but only when not concerned with a decline in implied volatility.

- The major difference between the calendar and other strategies[442] that profit from a range-bound market is vega. The calendar contains a built-in bet on IV moving higher.

- Buy out-of-the-money calendars when believing the market will move higher or lower, *towards a specific price*. This works both as limited protection for a credit spread and an inexpensive directional play. But, it remains a vega play.

- If bullish with no opinion on volatility, consider selling an OTM put spread instead of buying the OTM call calendar spread.

- If bearish with no opinion on volatility, consider selling an OTM call spread instead of buying the OTM put calendar spread. However, most market declines come with an increase in IV, making the OTM put calendar a good (limited-profit) choice when bearish.

- Remember: sell calendar when that OTM strike becomes ATM.

To trade iron condors and/or credit spreads (at least part of the time), it is to your advantage to learn how to combine them with calendar spreads. That is next when we look at diagonal spreads.

---

[442] Iron condor; butterfly when middle strike is same as calendar strike

QUIZ 20

1. You sold the INDX Nov 850/860 call spread, with INDX trading at $760. It is appropriate to buy some INDX Dec/Nov 950 call calendar spreads as pre-insurance. **TRUE or FALSE**

2. IV for XXX options has been rising and you want to make a trade that makes money under these conditions. **It is mid-July**:

   - IV has reached its peak and is declining.

   - XXX will drift from its current price ($180) to $200 over the next few weeks.

   Which of these trades work well for those market opinions?
   Is one a much better choice than the others?
   Is one a much poorer choice than the others?

   a) Buy XXX call Sep/Aug 200 call calendar spread
   b) Buy XXX Aug 190/200/210 call butterfly
   c) Buy XXX Aug 190/200/210 put butterfly
   d) Buy XXX Aug 180/190P; 210/220C iron condor

QUIZ 20 ANSWERS

1. True. OTM calendar spreads offer some protection. When far enough OTM, they can be used as very inexpensive protection.

2. Trades b, c, and d would work well
Best choice: The two butterfly spreads are equally as good. They represent the top choices.

The iron condor offers a higher probability for earning a profit (XXX has to be between 190 and 210 at expiration), but the butterfly is less expensive and is a better choice when you want to bet on that $200 number being accurate.

Poorest choice is (a): Buying a calendar spread when believing IV will decline is a poor choice.

Chapter 21

Double Diagonals

Under certain market conditions there are advantages to owning positions with options that expire at different times. The most often used such strategy is the calendar spread (Chapter 20).

When the strike price is identical, the position is a calendar (or time) spread. When the strike prices differ, the position is referred to as a diagonal spread. In theory a trader may own the option that expires first or the option that expires later. For practical reasons, we'll only discuss diagonal (and calendar) spreads when you own the option that expires later.[443] As with credit spreads, either calls or puts are used to create diagonal spreads. For the purposes of our discussion, we sell the diagonal spread—that means:

- We sell the near-term call and/or the near-term put

- We buy the longer-term call and/or put

- We buy options that are farther out of the money than the options sold.[444]

EXAMPLE

Buy SPX Dec 1550 call; Sell SPX Nov 1525 call

Buy MSFT Apr 35 puts; Sell MSFT Feb 40 puts

The rest of the nomenclature remains the same. The above spreads are referred to as a 25-point SPX diagonal call spread and a 5-point Microsoft diagonal put spread.

---

[443] As mentioned in Chapter 20, margin rules stipulate that the option owned must expire at the same time, or later than, the option sold. Otherwise the short option is considered to be "naked," with a larger margin requirement.

[444] In contrast with same-month credit spreads, when selling the diagonal you do not always sell the higher priced option—but you still buy the 'wings'—or options that are farther out of the money. Traditional option terminology stipulates that buying a spread means buying the lower strike call, or the higher strike put. However, when dealing with different expirations, buying the spread refers to owning the longer-dated option.

When simultaneously buying a diagonal call spread and a diagonal put spread, the position is called a double diagonal. Any expiration months may be chosen, but the most common strategy is to buy and sell options that expire in adjacent months.[445] These double diagonals are very similar to iron condors. The only difference is that the options bought expire later. Thus, the double diagonal is equivalent to owning an iron condor and two calendar (Chapter 20) spreads. Do not make all these trades, but think of a double diagonal as buying an iron condor and then buying two calendar spreads. Each calendar sells the near-term option previously purchased (as part of the iron condor) and replaces it with a longer-dated option (same strike).

EXAMPLE

DD spread is equivalent to Iron Condor + 2 Calendar spreads

Iron Condor:
Sell 15 IBM Nov 105 calls
Buy 15 IBM Nov 110 calls

Sell 15 IBM Nov 85 puts
Buy 15 IBM Nov 80 puts

Double Diagonal:
Sell 15 IBM Nov 105 calls
Buy 15 IBM Dec 110 calls

Sell 15 IBM Nov 85 puts
Buy 15 IBM Dec 80 puts

Stating the obvious to avoid confusion: when you buy the wings of any spread, the objective is to limit losses. This insurance is not to be confused with buying *extra* options as insurance (Chapter 19).

The idea behind trading the double diagonal *instead of* the iron condor is:

- When it is time to close the position, the expectation is that the Dec options will have lost *less time value* than the Nov options. Thus, the DD is often more profitable.

---

[445] Weeklys options offer more alternatives, yet a 4- or 5-week difference in expiration dates remains a comfortable choice.

o If the December options lose more total value[446] than the November options would have lost, then the double diagonal turns out be less profitable than the IC.

- Both strategies use the same Nov options (105C and 85P). Thus, the difference in profitability depends on the relative performance of the Nov or Dec wing[447] option.

Why consider diagonals?

Let's continue the discussion of double diagonal spreads by looking at the profit potential. After all, that is the main reason for adopting any investment strategy.

When selling a typical credit spread, sometimes the underlying approaches the strike price of the short option as expiration nears. As previously discussed, that is a risky proposition, and the prudent action is to close, or otherwise adjust, the position to reduce/eliminate that risk.

Would it not be better if, instead of holding positions that become more risky as expiration nears, you owned positions that become more profitable? Diagonal spreads do just that. But before deciding that this is an ideal situation, please recognize that diagonals have their own risky situations. There is a good chance that you will elect to adopt both strategies, depending on market conditions at the time a new trade is made.

When trading diagonal spreads, there is an additional factor to consider. As mentioned, when buying a calendar spread (Chapter 20), a debit is paid. When opening an iron condor position, a cash credit is collected. Depending on market conditions and the volatility environment, as well as which strike prices are chosen, the double diagonal may require a cash payment (making it a debit spread) when initiating the trade. For many iron condor buyers, that is an anathema—something they cannot tolerate. I *prefer* collecting cash, but when trading double diagonals, that is not always possible. Your comfort zone will dictate your actions, but it is far more important to trade the position you prefer to own, rather than force a trade, just because it provides a cash credit.

The calendar spread trader expects to see the value of the calendar spread widen (increase) as time passes.[448] That is also the consideration of diagonal (or double diagonal) spread traders. Paying extra cash for one or

---

[446] If you do not believe that is possible, consider what happens when implied volatility gets crushed—it kills the value of those December options (Nov options are about to expire). There is also the possibility that risk management was ignored and the underlying moved far beyond the strike of the short option. When that happens the Nov/Dec calendar spread shrinks in value.
[447] The option owned
[448] If that is not the expectation, then there is no reason to own the calendar spread.

two embedded (part of the diagonal) calendar spreads allows for the possibility of offsetting losses. If the underlying moves towards a danger point,[449] owning the longer-term option instead of the shorter-term option may be sufficient to offset a significant part of the loss resulting from the unfavorable price change. **Clarification**:

- The credit spread loses money when the underlying nears the short strike.

- When owning a diagonal, an embedded calendar spread is part of the position.

- That calendar will widen[450] as time passes and the short strike is approached.

- The widening calendar provides an offset to the loss from the credit spread.

- If the IV increase is large, the calendar spread may provide enough gains to more than offset the credit spread loss. In other words, the diagonal spread may be profitable as risk increases.

- Warning: That possibility tempts traders to hold positions too long.[451]

EXAMPLE

As either a standalone trade, or as part of an iron condor, you sold the YYZ Oct 100/110 call spread. If YYZ is moving toward 100 as expiration nears, that call spread is losing money and threatening to become a significant loss (if the stock continues to rise).

When owning the Nov 110 call instead of the Oct 110 call, the picture is very different. Your long call is no longer facing imminent extinction, and the Nov 110 call—depending on IV— may be worth enough to offset the loss from the 100/110 call spread.

This possibility demonstrates that there is much to gain from a diagonal spread. But, as always, there are inherent risks that must be considered,

---

[449] The short strike of the diagonal
[450] Earn money
[451] Holding near expiration is just as risky as always. However, the chance to make some good money tempts traders to accept more risk that they ought to accept. Be alert to this possibility.

Trading style

In the example that follows, we sell the S&P500 Index (SPX) March 1350 puts. Then we find a put to buy. If choosing Apr 1300 puts, an SPX 50-point diagonal put spread is opened. If the decision is to buy Apr 1275 puts, a 75-point diagonal put spread is created. Based on what you learned when selling credit spreads, the maximum value for the spread is the difference between the strikes (x 100), which is $7,500 for the 75-point spread and $5,000 for the 50-point spread. In reality, that maximum value is less because the Apr put retains some time premium when March expiration arrives, even when it is deep in the money.

On the other hand, buying April 1300 puts costs more, (the higher strike put is more expensive than the lower strike put). That could result in the trade becoming a debit spread. There is nothing wrong with paying cash for these positions, but some investors have a style that demands collecting cash (credit spread only; no debit spreads) to remain within their comfort zones. The choice is between collecting more cash upfront vs. having a smaller maximum loss. The intelligent trader (after gaining some experience) understands how to make this choice.

When selling call spreads, the choice is made in a similar manner. Choose a March call that is comfortable to sell and find an appropriate April call option to buy. When buying an iron condor, it is customary to sell an equal number of put and call spreads, and for each spread to be equally wide (difference between strikes). Many brokers do *not* give their customers the same margin break for double diagonals as they do with iron condors,[452] so the incentive to have put and call spreads of equal width is eliminated.

One big decision is always: how far out-of-the-money are the options? Those of you who prefer CTM options when trading iron condors or put credit spreads will probably feel comfortable selling CTM options for double diagonal spreads. Once again, I caution against using options that are very far OTM and which trade at relatively low prices.

EXAMPLE

Let's assume SPX is trading near 1501, March expiration is seven weeks from today, and

April expiration is four weeks later. Choosing the strike prices to sell is important because it establishes how far the underlying index (or stock) must move before the position is no longer comfortable to hold. Thus, you choose strike prices as usual when

---

[452] Thus, the margin requirement for the double diagonal is the margin for the call spread plus the margin for the put spread.

trading credit spreads, creating positions that allow you to remain within your comfort zone.

Assume four Mar 1350 puts at $12.10 each[453] are sold. To complete the diagonal spread, let's consider the possibility of buying either of two April puts:

- Apr 1300 put at $13.60[454]

- Apr 1275 put at 11.70[455]

Let's assume the Apr 1300 puts are bought. The debit for the put spread is $1.50. Buying Apr 1275 puts would generate a $0.40 credit. When looking at the calls, notice that calls trade with a much lower implied volatility (~17 vs. ~30), because calls that are equally far OTM are much less expensive than puts. This phenomenon has been true since the market crash of October 1987, which made the world aware that markets decline faster than they rise. In turn, that generated a permanent need for some investors to own puts, which resulted in greater demand and higher prices for puts than calls.[456]

The trade decision is made: sell four Mar 1600 calls at $9.00[457] and buy four Apr 1625 calls, paying $11.80[458]. Paying cash may not be suitable for all traders, but when the maximum loss is only $2,780[459] (compared with $5,150[459] for the put spread) that may compensate for any disappointment.

The total debit for the double diagonal is $4.30. Another big decision (discussed later in this chapter) is deciding just how much debit a trader can afford to pay for a diagonal spread.

In the following tables, the value of the double diagonal spread is calculated under various conditions. Because we are beginning the discussion with reasons for opening such a position, let's consider the most favorable outcome first. In Table 21.1 the potential profit when expiration is only one day away is identified. (i.e., it is Thursday and time to decide whether to close or hold and accept settlement risk.) You already know

---

[453] IV = 29, delta = -14, vega = $125/point, theta = $38/day.
[454] IV = 30, delta = -12, vega = $177/point, theta = $25/day.
[455] IV = 31.5, delta = -11, vega = $168/point, theta = $19/day.
[456] For equity options that are equally far OTM, the put is priced higher.
[457] IV = 17, delta = 18, vega = $150/point, theta = $27/day.
[458] IV = 17, delta = 19, vega = $192/point, theta = $23/day.
[459] Spread width, plus the debit paid.

that I strongly recommend not taking that risk, especially when the short option is anywhere near being ATM.

This spread is long vega and the profit or loss is *very* dependent on the implied volatility.

If you find yourself in this pleasant (but high risk) situation (index price near strike of the short option a day or two before expiration), be aware that if IV is on the low end of expectations, there may barely be any profit (Table 21.1).

Table 21.1
Value of double diagonal spread as IV varies; SPX = $1,350
One day prior to Mar expiration; 29 days before Apr expiration

Put IV	Mar 1350 P	Apr 1300 P	Credit	Apr 1625 C	Call IV
20	$5.70	$10.33	$4.63	$0.00	10
25	$7.11	$16.29	$9.18	$0.00	15
30	$8.52	$22.85	$14.33	$0.01	20
35	$9.93	$29.58	$19.65	$0.14	25
40	$11.34	$36.47	$25.13	$0.60	30
45	$12.75	$43.45	$30.70		

When owing a double diagonal spread, if the underlying index is near the strike of the near-term short when expiration is near, the practical[460] maximum profit is earned. Note that profits increase dramatically as IV increases. Value = price of Apr 1300 put less price of Mar 1350 put, minus $430. Value of call is ignored, but any value is a bonus.

Double Diagonals

As IV nears 40, each spread earns more than $2,000. That is an exceptional reward. However, there is a trap: are you willing to pay more than $1,100 (Table 21.1) to cover the March option that will cease to exist as soon as the market opens tomorrow?[461] Isn't that a lot of money to pay when there is so little time remaining?

Yes, it *is* a very high price to pay. Do not allow that to get in the way of intelligent risk management. Look at the market price of the Apr 1300 put. It is worth almost $3,650. To safely sell this expensive option, you must

---

[460] The theoretical maximum profit is earned when the settlement price equals the strike price of the short option, but it is very poor strategy to hold overnight, waiting for settlement to be determined Friday morning (Chapter 17). If you held the position this long, do not be greedy.
[460] The theoretical maximum profit is earned when the settlement price equals the strike price of the short option, but it is very poor strategy to hold overnight, waiting for settlement to be determined Friday morning (Chapter 17). If you held the position this long, do not be greedy.
[461] Reminder: SPX options are sometimes settled at the opening (when it is the 3rd Friday of the month) and at other times at Friday's close. This is a **very** significant difference.

cover the Mar 1350 put[462] to lock in profits. If you hold this position overnight and the market opens significantly higher, you will save the entire cost of covering the March put. However, if IV shrinks—as is likely on a rally—you may find that the Apr put declines by far more than you saved. That is too much risk for me.

Table 21.2
Double diagonal spread value as IV varies; SPX = $1,600
One day before Mar expiration; 29 days before Apr expiration

Call IV	Mar 1600 C	Apr 1625 C	Value	Apr 1300 P	Put IV
10	$3.42	$9.62	$6.20	$0.00	20
15	$5.09	$18.06	$12.97	$0.03	25
20	$6.76	$26.79	$20.03	$0.24	30
25	$8.43	$56.25	$47.82	$0.82	35
				$1.86	40

When owing a DD and the short option is ATM near expiration, the profit is very dependent on IV.

In Table 21.2, we consider a similar situation. This time SPX is trading at $1,600, the strike price of the March calls. Note that profits are even higher for the call spread than they were for the puts. That may be surprising because IV is significantly lower after a rally.

The reason the calls fared better in this specific trade is because the April calls are only 25 points farther OTM than the calls sold. That difference was 50-points for the put spread. This scenario (SPX at strike price the day before expiration) is illustrative of an ideal situation. If you own a double diagonal, it is very difficult to hold as expiration nears because the risk of turning a good-sized profit into a large loss is real—and that possibility becomes more acute with each passing day.[463] Deciding when to exit is a true measure of your ability to manage risk.

---

[462] An experienced trader may look for an alternative. Perhaps selling the April put and buying a far less expensive put to hedge the short Mar 1350 put overnight (perhaps the March 1340 put?). Do not gamble by selling the April put and remaining naked short the March put. Settlement risk is real. The high IV suggests that the market anticipates a gap opening. The safest thing to do is exit the position and be pleased with the result.
[463] In Table 17.4, we showed how the high gamma of the front-month option increases risk as time passes. The diagonal spread is less risky than the put credit spread in this situation, but the risk of holding into expiration still exists.

Risk of holding into expiration

- It is tempting to collect that large positive theta. However, while waiting, negative gamma may result in the loss of accumulated profits. This is especially true when the calls are ATM because a continuing rally usually results in a lower IV for the long calls.

- A sudden decrease in implied volatility may kill accumulated profits, especially when the put side is ATM and IV is high due to a recent market decline. The rally may result in an IV crush.

- When the front-month option moves ITM, losses accumulate quickly because higher gamma causes delta to get out of line.

- Settlement risk. Each of the above problems is enhanced when the market gaps on Settlement Friday[464]—especially when the market reverses direction immediately after the market opens.

Of course, there are scenarios in which you earn even more money by holding through settlement, and that makes it tempting to hold. Just remember that potential losses exceed any potential gains. Miracle finishes (settlement right at the strike) are pleasant, but unlucky finishes (settlement far away from the previous night's close) are destructive.

If you hold the position, despite this advice, be certain that you understand: once the market opens on settlement Friday, the price for the expiring option is set (the value is not yet known, and will be calculated hours later) and you are naked long those (expensive) April options. That is not a risk you want to take. Sell, or hedge those April options immediately. And hope it is not too late.

What should you do with the other long option—the call or put that is now FOTM but has one month of remaining lifetime? You can sell and collect a few nickels. Or you can hold and keep those options as an inexpensive insurance policy against other positions in your portfolio. It is not a clear decision, but I keep my FOTM options because they are too inexpensive to sell, and insurance is always worthwhile. These FOTM options are likely to expire worthless, but they are worth very little right now and may become more valuable later.

It is unlikely that your position will perform as described above. If the underlying moves too far in either direction, then the position behaves similarly to iron condors. They lose money and require adjustments to maintain acceptable risk.

---

[464] All expirations for NDX and RUT and the 3rd Friday for SPX options

It is tempting to believe the calendar spread as not needing such adjustments. The truth is that they need adjustments even more than iron condors. The two top reasons:

- The spread width is usually wider for the diagonal spread, increasing the maximum theoretical loss.

- When the underlying zips through the strike, the embedded calendar loses money, worsening the situation.

The good news is that the passage of time is more helpful when you own double diagonals, compared with iron condors. In Table 17.3 we noticed that the passage of time was profitable for iron condor owners, but when the short strike price is threatened, it is a money-losing situation. Continuing to hold the position added to risk. The situation is much better with double diagonals.

In Table 21.3 the effect of time on the double diagonal is indicated for an ATM put. In this table, assume that IV remains constant. This may not be a position you want to hold (due to risk), but it is necessary to understand how the value of the position changes with time. This spread was initiated seven weeks before March expiration @ $4.30 per double diagonal. If the market drops suddenly, you have a loss because it costs more than $4.30 to exit. Note that loss declines as time passes (Table 21.3), and the position becomes profitable if enough days go by (It costs only $3.87 to close 28 days before expiration). When trading iron condors (or put credit spreads), the passage of time helps, but a decline through the strike price results in a loss.

That is the main difference between these spreads. In return for accepting the risk that comes with positive vega positions, you are compensated by a more profitable time decay and the *possibility* of making money if the short strike is threatened.[465]

Implied volatility

Double diagonal spreads are not always a good idea. The time decay makes these positions look good, but the fact that you must be long vega to own them is important. When implied volatility is high, you must pay a relatively high price for the options you purchase. When IV is relatively low, you buy your long options at a much more favorable price.

One benefit of lower implied volatility is the ability to open diagonal spreads and collect a cash credit. It is not important to collect a cash credit,

---

[465] "Short strike is threatened" means that the underlying is poised to drive through the strike price of your short option.

but if that credit is essential for your comfort zone, then you must wait for times when IV is low enough to provide that credit.

The data in Table 21.4 shows the same situation when the *call* strike price is threatened.

**Table 21.3
Value of DD as IV varies; SPX = $1,350
IV = 29 for Mar Puts; 30 for Apr Puts**

Time	Mar 1350P	Apr 1300P	Value
49days	$53.94	$46.54	($7.40)
35 days	$46.04	$40.72	($5.32)
28 days	$41.41	$37.54	($3.87)
21 days	$36.09	$34.15	($1.94)
10 days	$25.21	$28.29	$3.08
3 days	$13.97	$24.12	$10.15
2 days	$11.44	$23.49	$12.05
1 day	$8.11	$22.85	$14.74

As time passes, the diagonal increases in value. If the short put is near ATM, it may be possible to exit and collect cash, depending on how much time passed. Compare with data in Table 17.3. In that situation (put credit spreads and iron condors), exiting always requires a cash payment.

**Table 21.4 Value of DD as IV varies
SPX = $1,600; IV = 17**

Time	Mar 1600 C	Apr 1625 C	Value
49 days	$43.31	$43.46	$0.15
35 days	$36.15	$37.85	$1.70
28 days	$32.10	$34.86	$2.76
21 days	$27.56	$31.71	$4.15
10 days	$18.70	$26.37	$7.67
3 days	$10.06	$22.65	$12.59
2 days	$8.18	$22.10	$13.92
1 day	$5.75	$21.53	$15.78

As time passes, diagonal spread increases in value. If the short call is threatened, you may be able to exit and collect cash – depending on how much time has passed.

In Chapter 6 we showed how increasing the implied volatility of an option plays a vital role in determining the market price of that option. That idea is reinforced in Tables 21.1 and 21.2, where you see how the price of an individual option changes as IV changes. For example, when IV moves from 35 to 40, the value of the Apr 1300 put moves higher by almost $700. Because you are buying vega when you open a double diagonal position, it is to your advantage to own diagonal spreads when IV is going to be increasing. You have a better chance of owning a position for which IV rises when you open these positions when IV is relatively low, rather than relatively high. As rookies, you may not have a good idea how to determine whether IV is high or low, based on its historical levels. By looking at the VIX (CBOE volatility index graph), you can get a good idea of how current IV levels compare with historic levels.[466]

Risk

With either iron condors or double diagonals, you purchase an OTM call and an OTM put. When the strike prices (both calls or both puts) are near each other, the maximum loss is less than when they are further apart.

With the iron condor trade, you truly hope that both your short options expire worthless (or that the entire position is closed for a decent profit before expiration arrives) and that no adjustments are necessary. Your profit depends on the cost of covering your short options. The value of the wings is less important – but you must own them to limit risk.

With the double diagonal spread, your long options are not going to be worthless when the front-month options expire and the premium you collect when selling them has a significant effect on your total profit or loss. This is the reason implied volatility plays such a big role when trading diagonal spreads. When you decide to exit the trade, the higher IV, the more cash you receive when selling those longer-term calls. If IV decreases during the lifetime of the diagonal spread, selling your options is going to produce less cash than you may have anticipated. Perhaps enough less to turn the entire trade into a loser. Double diagonals 'look' so much more profitable than iron condors because you know your long options will retain some residual value. But, there is danger in that thought process because the residual cash may be very small when IV gets crushed. Thus, diagonal spreads are not just a bet against the underlying asset making a large move – it is also a bet on the future level of implied volatility.

There is nothing wrong with paying a cash debit to open a diagonal spread. The problem occurs only when the debit is large. Think of it this way. If you open a diagonal spread and pay $1,000 more for the Sep put than you collect for the Aug put, and if the market moves higher, it is possible that your Sep put is going to be worth far less than $1,000 when the Aug options expire. Thus, you not only had downside risk when owning

---

[466] VIX graphs are available on the Internet at sites such as cboe.com.

this put diagonal spread, but you can also lose money when the market rises. That is not possible when you own a put credit spread or an iron condo position because you always collect a cash credit. To minimize the possibility of this undesirable result, I recommend not paying 'much' cash to own a diagonal spread. This point is discussed in the next example below.

Sometimes you must pay a small debit to make the spread fit into your comfort zone. And that is very important. If the position makes you nervous from the time you make the trade, you are going to have a difficult time managing risk. Do not force the trade. If you are not comfortable paying a debit, that is fine. Only open diagonal spreads when you can find one that suits your needs. If you buy Sep options that are too many strike prices removed from the Aug options that you sell, then a big market move places you in jeopardy of a large loss—something to be avoided.

You want to own a position that you believe can earn a nice profit, but risk must be reasonable. If you are comfortable trading iron condors on a broad based index when the strike prices are 10-points apart, you will probably feel comfortable trading diagonal spreads when the strikes are 20 or perhaps 30 points apart (I choose 30 points most of the time). But do not buy options that are 50 or 100 points further out of the money than your short. That involves too much risk.

Because it is undesirable to pay a big debit for a diagonal (or DD) spread (as mentioned above, it is because you can lose on each spread, rather than on only one, when the market makes a large move), these spreads are difficult to trade when implied volatilities are elevated. That higher IV translates into higher prices for the options you buy. It also affects the options you sell, but to a much lesser extent (Remember longer-term options have more vega than near-term options). Unless you pay a significant cash debit for the double diagonal position, the strike prices will have to be further apart than they are when trading iron condors—and the further apart, the greater the maximum loss. Thus, choosing strike prices that are near each other produces a less risky position, but you must often pay a large debit to acquire that diagonal. And a high IV environment practically guarantees the debit will be large. If you love the idea of DD spreads, then go for it. But, my personal comfort zone requires a low IV environment.

EXAMPLE

Assume you choose an NDX Mar - Feb double diagonal spread and the put half costs $1,000. For this discussion, strike prices are not important. The greatest risk when owning any diagonal spread is a quick market move through the strike.

When paying a significant debit for the put spread,[467] there is an additional risk—one that is easy for newer diagonal traders to overlook. If the market moves higher and threatens the call strike (of the double diagonal position), not only must risk be managed for the call portion of the trade, but the diagonal put spread is threatened. How is that possible? This cannot occur with an iron condor. When one side of the IC gets into trouble, the other always produces some gains to offset part of the loss.

The rally can push the puts far OTM. Sure, it is great when the Feb put heads to zero, but if the March put declines to $4 or $5, then the put diagonal is worth only $400 to $500 when you paid $1,000. Thus, both halves of the DD can lose money at the same time. If that is not bad enough, when the rally is accompanied (as expected) by a declining implied volatility, the price of the March put options can truly collapse.

This is a risk associated with double diagonals, and the best way to avoid that risk is to open diagonal positions for which the debit for each portion of the trade is small (or a credit).

As time passes, the diagonal spread increases in value. If the short call is threatened, it is possible to close the position and earn a profit—depending on how much time has passed. Once again, this profit is not possible with iron condors (unless the initial credit was very high).

If you prefer to trade as simply as possible, you do not have to pay attention to actual implied volatility. All you have to do is try to find a double diagonal that suits your comfort zone. That includes opening the position for a credit or reasonable debit, *and* keeping the strike prices relatively near each other.[468] If IV is low enough, such spreads are available. When IV is high, it is better to buy iron condors because higher credits are collected. When IV is low, double diagonal spreads can be advantageous because cash credits are available when money at risk is reduced (strikes can be less far apart).

---

[467] The discussion is also applicable when paying a large debit for the call spread.

[468] It is difficult to agree on distance between strike prices for double diagonals. For me, RUT calls should be 20 to 30 points apart—and puts no more than 40. For SPX, 30 to 40 points is my maximum. For NDX, I prefer 50 points but have used 75-point differences. This is my comfort zone. Choose your own based on market conditions.

Additional thoughts

1. When trading double diagonals it is always tempting to allow more time to pass, because profits can increase much more quickly than they can for iron condors. However, recognize that profits can disappear in two ways:

   - If the market moves to threaten one of the short options, a further move will be costly. It is prudent to close (or roll) to prevent large losses (and preventing those losses remains the name of the game for long-term success).

   - When the underlying suddenly reverses direction and moves away from the strike, it is often a good plan to exit diagonal positions once they moved near the strike and enough time has passed to generate good profits.[469] This path to profitability is absent when trading iron condors.

2. I recommend trading double diagonals by selling front-month options and buying second month options.[470] If you prefer less negative gamma, you can sell options that expire in the second month and buy options that expire in the third month. As with iron condors, this strategy encourages traders to exit positions well before expiration arrives—not only to eliminate negative gamma, but also to lock in good-sized profits.

3. For the non-beginner: when your portfolio has negative vega risk[471]— enough to make you uncomfortable—the addition of a few diagonal spreads reduces that risk.[472] If the short vega comes from iron condors, do not sell more of the same front-month option when adding diagonals (or double diagonals). That strike is already a danger point, and increasing current jeopardy is not the best plan when trying to reduce risk.

Consider selling further OTM options and buying appropriate long options as a diagonal adjustment. For example, in Chapter 19 we bought RUT Nov 740/750 put, 900/910 call iron condors. A suitable diagonal that adds protection[473] involves selling Nov 730 puts and buying an appropriate Dec put. I suggest no specific put, because market conditions (implied volatility, index price) affect the selection process. Just remember when

---

[469] To play for larger profits, consider scaling out of the position in stages.
[470] Weeklys are available, but I recommend using options with expirations about 4-weeks apart.
[471] From other positions
[472] This is a good example of how one specific risk factor (referred to as the Greeks) can be adjusted.
[473] If time passes, this spread provides protection, but not if the decline comes quickly.

strikes are near each other, the spread costs more, but the ultimate risk is less.

If you can find a suitable spread,[474] consider selling the November 920 calls and buying an appropriate December call.

4. As with iron condors, a few additional calls and/or puts can be bought as pre-insurance.

5. Margin requirements are much larger for double diagonals than for iron condors. The typical iron condor may be 10 points wide, requiring margin of $1,000. The double diagonal spread is almost always wider. Even when 20-points wide, the call and put spread each require $2,000 margin.

It is not your imagination—this chapter contains less detail than others. The decision to trade double diagonals can be made on its own merits. This spread is most commonly used by iron condor traders—but only when conditions are right—and that means when you believe it is a good environment for owning calendar spreads (Chapter 20).

Those conditions include a relatively low IV environment and either:

- An expectation that IV will increase.

- As insurance (because the portfolio is already short vega) against an IV increase.

When you understand how and why to use credit spreads, iron condors, and calendar spreads, it is not necessary to provide all the details of using them together.

Do not build a double diagonal spread by buying the iron condor and then buying the calendar spread. It is too costly to make so many trades (and pay extra commissions and encounter extra bid/ask slippage) when you can open the position in a single spread transaction.

Double diagonals represent an additional strategy for your investment arsenal. They work best when IV is low, but can be used to add positive vega to any portfolio to reduce risk associated with a surge in implied volatility.

---

[474] The Nov 920 call may be priced too low to allow building a good diagonal call spread. That is ok. Do not force the trade just to get protection. If the call is priced that low, you probably do not need protection.

QUIZ 21

1. Double diagonal spreads are not subject to settlement risk.
   TRUE or FALSE

2. You own a double diagonal position. The market trades in a small range over the next four weeks and the short-term options expire worthless. Is this a good result?

3. With one week remaining before expiration, if the market makes an unfavorable move and is heading toward the strike price of your short call option, would you rather own an iron condor or a double diagonal?

4. Margin requirements are essentially the same for iron condors and double diagonals. **TRUE or FALSE**

5. The implied volatility for an actively traded stock has ranged between 40 and 70 over the past three years. IV is currently 75. Are you better off with iron condors or double diagonals?

6. When collecting a cash credit for a double diagonal, a profit is guaranteed. **TRUE or FALSE**

Quiz 21 Answers

1. False when the option is AM-settled in cash and European style. True for options on individual stocks and PM-settled European style options.

2. Probably. If you collected a credit when opening the position, you can collect another credit now to exit.

   a) If you paid a debit, it is almost certain that you can sell your options for more than the original debit.

   b) However, if you paid a relatively high debit, and if IV has dropped significantly, the value of your long options has been hurt by the IV decrease and by the passage of time. Thus, it is *possible* that you have a loss because the value of your options is less than the original debit.

3. Double diagonal. This position is probably profitable and you can still collect that profit and remove all risk by closing. The iron condor position is losing money and becoming more and more risky to hold.

4. False. Iron condors require much less margin.

5. Iron condors are better when IV is high. But be aware that this is a very volatile stock. This is not a good time for trading CTM positions.

6. False. There are no guaranteed profits when trading double diagonals. However, if both short-term options expire worthless, then a profit is guaranteed when the initial trade was made for a cash credit.

Chapter 22

Exercising an Option

One interesting aspect of working with new traders is discovering which basic concepts of trading are immediately obvious and which require careful explanations. The very simple idea of whether it is a good plan to exercise an option is one of those. One of the very first things that someone learns is the definition of call and put options. Part of that definition is the *right* but not the obligation to exercise. And that is where the discussion ends.

For the 2nd edition, this chapter is included to be certain that all readers avoid common misconceptions.

Here are the two basic truths:

- You can exercise an option only when you currently own it. If you owned an option and sold it, you may not exercise.

- Traders and investors should probably *never* exercise any options. Yes, there are exceptions (discussed later in this chapter), but when buying options, the general trade plan should be to sell those options when they are no longer needed.

  o When buying options as a *directional play*, sell that option once the target profit has been earned. Or, sell long[475] options when you change your mind and no longer want to own them.

  o When buying options *as part of a spread*, it is important to maintain ownership of the entire spread— until the whole spread is no longer needed.

  NOTE: On occasion, you may be assigned an exercise notice on an option that is part of a spread. When that happens, do not automatically exercise the option you own (to offset being assigned). Only do so when <u>that option is ITM and expiration has arrived</u>. If it is not in the money, offset the assignment by buying or selling stock and then sell your long option or allow it

---

[475] Options you own

to expire worthless (when there is no bid). If it is not yet expiration, you have alternatives.[476]

How to Exercise

Prior to expiration: For the rare instance when this matters, instruct your broker to exercise. Each broker has a preferred method for being notified. Some prefer a telephone call and others require submission of a notice via a direct link from your online trading account. (Choose this option when it is available.) It is your obligation to learn your broker's requirements, so ask. Keep the information readily accessible because there is a cut-off time each afternoon—shortly after the market closes for the day.

At expiration: If you own an option that is in-the-money (ITM) and for some reason you failed to sell that option,[477] you probably want to exercise, rather than allow the option to expire worthless. Note that this is not always true.

If an option is only worth one dollar (that means $.01 per share), it is often not worthwhile to exercise. Most brokers charge a commission to exercise. For example, if you exercise a call option—converting it into a long stock position—many brokers charge a fee. Then you are forced to pay another commission to sell the stock (unless you plan to hold the shares). Those combined commissions easily cost more than the penny or two per share earned by exercising.

However, if you are short another ITM option and know you will be assigned on that call or put, then DO exercise your option to offset the assignment.

Do not overlook the risk of holding unhedged stock (long or short) over the weekend. You must pay three day's interest on the cash required to buy the shares—if you borrow that cash from your broker. The stock may open significantly higher or lower next Monday compared with where it last traded on expiration Friday. All things considered, it is far better for you, the individual investor, to let an option expire worthless when it is in-the-money by only one or two pennies and you are unable to sell it.[478] But

---

[476] Cover the stock and sell the option or hold when there is no margin call.

[477] Often it cannot be sold because it is needed as protection or insurance. Example: when short one ITM option and long another as part of a spread. This is one time when it is best to keep the option and exercise if it is ITM at expiration.

[478] But this is not true for professional market makers. They almost always exercise an option AT EXPIRATION even when in-the-money by one cent. They do that because their positions are hedged and there is a tiny profit to be made by exercising options that are slightly ITM. Thus, if you find yourself short such an option, you won't know if the option is going to expire worthless or be exercised by its owner until your broker notifies you Sunday (online) or Monday (before the market opens).

please—do try to sell it, and do not wait until the last few minutes of the trading day to enter that sell order.

> **Important NOTE:** If the long option is part of a spread and the other side of the spread is ITM (you will be assigned an exercise notice) then DO exercise the long option at expiration, but only when it is ITM. The conversation about not exercising applies only when you own the option outright, with no offsetting position.

- **Automatic exercise**. When expiration arrives, if you own an option that is in-the-money by $0.01 or more, the powers that be decided that you are better off by exercising this option—and they automatically exercise it. I think this is a terrible idea, but that is the rule. The option owner is supposed to have the right, but not the obligation, to exercise, but somehow the rules change at expiration and the obligation to exercise is forced upon the option owner.

- When you do not want to exercise, and were unable to sell that option, then you must notify your broker of that decision before the cutoff time.

The process is identical to the process by which you notify your broker that you do want to exercise, but this time you must notify the broker that you do not want to exercise. It is best not to find yourself in this situation, and it can be avoided, if you remember to sell, or at least attempt to sell, any option before the markets close on expiration Friday.

- **Automatic assignment**. When expiration arrives and you are short (sold without covering) an ITM option, expect to be assigned an exercise notice. You *may not be assigned* per the discussion above, but anticipate receiving that exercise notice.

Clarification: The term 'automatic assignment' is a misnomer. Assignment is never automatic. The 'automatic' part is the exercise. When every long option is exercised, then everyone who is short that option will be assigned an exercise notice. When some options are not exercised, there is a random selection of which specific account holder will 'slide' and not be assigned. You may NOT request an assignment. You, as the option seller, have no rights and must wait.

More advanced discussion of exercise/assignment

The last portion of this chapter may not be readily understood by option rookies the *first* time the book is read. It refers to situations with which you are not yet familiar. However, this discussion on whether an option owner should exercise an option logically belongs here.

I've discovered that too many beginners fail to grasp the importance of the following information. To understand the entire concept behind options and the rationale for traders who buy them, it is necessary to know why an option owner must not exercise options *any earlier than necessary*.

This information is important and I encourage reading it now, but be prepared to read this chapter again[479] if it is not clear.

Now that you understand how to exercise a put or call option, the question arises as to *when* you should do so. In the vast majority of cases, your best action is to sell the option and not bother with the exercise. Nearly all exercises occur at expiration, but there are three situations in which you may decide to exercise an option prior to expiration.

Exercising an option early – prior to expiration

- **Exercising** for the dividend: discussed in detail on pp. 120-1. **The married put.** This is a rare situation. If you own one put and 100 shares of stock, and if the stock drops very far below the strike price, the put option is said to be 'deep in the money' (DITM). Sometimes it is a good idea to exercise the DITM put, thereby closing both the put position (cancelled via the exercise) and the stock position (exercising the put results in the stock being sold). The *only* benefit from taking this action is to eliminate the paying of interest on the cash used to own the put and stock. Unless interest rates are high, *there is no good reason to take this action* because it sacrifices the possibility of earning a big profit if the stock reverses direction and moves well above the put strike price before expiration arrives.[480]

- **Bid below parity**. When you own an option with significant intrinsic value, and time to expiration is short, it is common for market makers to bid less than the option is worth. For example, if you own a put struck at 50 and the stock is $43, the put has an intrinsic

---

[479] In a couple of months
[480] If the stock runs past the put strike price, then you will eventually sell stock at that higher price. Once the put is exercised, that possibility is lost because the stock was sold at the strike

354

value of $7.[481] If the best bid for the option is $6.80 or $6.90, it is better to buy stock at $43, and exercise the put (to sell stock at $50). This is equivalent to selling the put at $7 (but do not ignore the extra commissions).

Why Exercising is often a poor choice

There are very good reasons for selling rather than exercising options.

- Commissions. Most brokers charge higher fees to exercise an option that they do for other transactions, and it is better to avoid that fee. If you exercise a call option and plan to sell stock immediately, it is better to sell the option. That avoids paying the exercise fee plus the commission to sell stock. Instead, pay a single commission to sell the option.

- Time premium. An option's value is the sum of the option's intrinsic value[482] and it is time value (time premium). Time premium is described on p 68. When you exercise an option, that option is converted into stock (long or short) and the only remaining value from that option is the intrinsic value. Time value is lost. **Never exercise an option that has time value.** It is better to sell the option and collect that time value in cash than to throw it away via an exercise.

EXAMPLE

You bought 10 YZY Mar 40 calls when YZY was $38 per share. You paid $2 for each option, for a total investment of $2,000. Let's assume time passes, three weeks remain before the Mar 40 calls expire, and YZY has rallied to $44. The call options are trading at $5 ($4 of that is intrinsic value and $1 represents the time value). By selling the options, you receive $500 for each, netting a $300 profit[483] per option, or $3,000.

If you exercise the calls, the options are cancelled and you buy stock at the strike price, or $40 per share. That is $40,000 cash for 1,000 shares. When you sell stock at its current price of $44, you have a $2,000 profit. Why isn't the profit $4,000? You collect $44,000 when selling the stock, but the total investment cost is the $40,000 paid for stock plus $2,000 paid for the options. Total cost: $42,000. Thus, the profit is $2,000.

---

[481] If you buy stock at $43 and exercise the put, you come out with $700 cash (pay $43, sell @ $50).
[482] The amount by which the stock price is above the strike price of a call; or the amount by which the stock price is below the strike price of a put
[483] Paid $200; sold at $500

If you sell the calls, you earn $3,000. But, if you exercise the calls and immediately sell stock, your profit is only $2,000. Where is the missing $1,000?

Answer: From your perspective, the $1,000 is in the trash. You threw it away by exercising the calls when they had time premium remaining as part of their value. Upon exercise, all remaining time premium is lost.

The money is not really in the trash. You gave it as a gift to the person who was assigned an exercise notice. That investor thanks you and has the opportunity to go after that $1,000 by buying stock and selling that call (again). The person assigned the exercise notice owns the same covered call position that was held earlier, but also has that $1,000 premium.

Bottom line: When selling an option, you collect both the intrinsic value *and* the time value. When exercising an option, you sacrifice all residual time value. Thus, when an option owner decides it is time to exit the position, it is more convenient and profitable to sell rather than exercise.

- Risk. The following example is crucial to your understanding. If you 'get' this, then you understand why trading options is advantageous compared with trading stock. If you find it 'obvious' then congratulations. Let me assure you that too many traders cannot understand (at this early stage of their education) why this works.

This explanation represents another 'more advanced' concept. If this remains vague, please take the time to think about it again. It may be helpful to review covered call writing (Chapters 9 to 11) and why a trader writes calls. The major reason for adopting that strategy is to collect time premium. Imagine how profitable that strategy would be if the option owners exercised those call several weeks before expiration.

NOTE: Option owners have limited risk. The worst that can happen is for the option to expire worthless. The maximum loss is the cost of the option. But once an option is exercised and converted to stock, both risk and margin requirements increase dramatically. There are no more limits on losses. The stock could go bankrupt after a call has been exercised, or may double in value after a put has been exercised.

EXAMPLE

Let's return to an example used earlier. You own Mar 40 calls when they are trading at $5. If this stock suddenly releases bad news and the stock tumbles to $33, you will lose all (or almost all) of the $500 that each option had been worth before the news release. The original cost of those calls was $2,000 (for 10 calls) and your net loss is $2,000.

That is a tough loss, but there is nothing to do about that now. It serves no purpose to dwell on why you chose not to sell the calls yesterday. Now look at what would happen if you had exercised the calls. You would own 1,000 shares of stock @ $40 per share. When the stock declined to $33, your investment would be worth only $33,000. Not only has that $7 per share been lost[484] on the stock price (bought @ $40; current price $33), but the option cost of $2 per share is also gone. Total loss: $9 per share, or $9,000.

You paid $2,000 (limiting losses) for those calls. By exercising, you not only *had nothing to gain*, but the potential loss became much larger. Repeat: you had nothing to gain by exercising. One reason for buying options is to avoid owning expensive stock that may tumble in price.

Bottom line: There is little reason to exercise an option prior to expiration. It is more efficient to own the option, rather than stock. If you plan to exercise and immediately sell stock, why bother? Just sell the options.

> **NOTE:** The trade plan should be to buy and eventually sell options. Profit occurs when the trader's expectations come true. There is no reason to convert options to shares via exercise.

The arguments are identical for put options. Once exercised (stock sold short), upside losses become unlimited. When holding options, the worst result is to see the puts expire worthless.

Exercising an option when expiration arrives
The same arguments can be made when it is expiration time. The only reason for exercising an ITM option is because you *want* to own a position in the underlying stock, or to offset an already existing position.[485] That includes taking on all risk associated with stock ownership. Unless the trade plan involves exercise (which would be unusual), sell the options.

---

[484] If your mindset is that nothing has been lost because the position is still open, it is time for a serious mindset change. The money is gone. It may be worthwhile to hold this stock now; it may produce a gain in the future, but for now, you have only $33,000 worth of stock.

[485] For example, if you own stock plus a put option, when that put is ITM at expiration you can sell the put to collect some cash or exercise the put to sell stock at the strike price.

NOTE: You may decide to buy an option as insurance. When expiration arrives and that option is ITM, it may be preferable to maintain the original stock position and sell the option.

When you own stock and buy one put option per 100 shares, the position is protected. The concept is simple: if the stock is below the strike price when expiration arrives, you can exercise the option and sell shares at the strike—regardless of its current market price. For example, assume you own stock currently priced at $42. You also own a put option that is struck at 50. Your original plan may have been to exercise and get rid of the stock. However, you can keep the shares (assuming you truly want to own them at $42 per share) and sell the put, collecting $800 in cash.

It is fine to exercise. However, there are few situations where exercising represents the most efficient choice.

Afterword

I am frequently asked the same question: "Can anyone make money consistently when trading options?"

Options are tools that provide help in the completion of a task. It is not 'option trading' that makes money. It is the trader and his/her decisions, strategy selection, stock selection, and especially, risk management technique and demonstrating good discipline.

Yes you can make money with options. But no one is handing it to you. As with anything else in life, it requires an effort to learn to use options effectively. If you are diligent and careful when managing risk, you can make money with options. My part of the deal is to teach you how to adopt various strategies, offer suggestions and guidelines for initiating, managing and exiting trades, and offer guidance in developing a winning mindset.

Your part of the deal is to think about your alternatives and try to decide which best fit your comfort zone. Do not expect to get it right with your first trade. It takes some experience to recognize when a position is too risky or too unrewarding. You will find you way. All I ask is that you do not rush through the lessons. There is a time to every purpose, and at first, reading, thinking, paper-trading should be at the top of your priority list.

Options allow investors to pursue investment alternatives that are not otherwise available. The investor can:

- Write covered calls to collect the equivalent of extra dividends.

- Buy puts or collars to protect the value of an investment portfolio.

- Adopt conservative strategies with limited gains and/or limited losses.

- Gamble with high risk/high reward trades - something I believe is best avoided.

I trust that you felt welcome entering the options universe and that your journey (to this point) has been satisfying. The ideas presented here have been developed over the course of 38 years of trading options. If you understand the principles behind options and *understand* how they work, you are well placed to make money by adopting one or more of the strategies outlined in this book.

Every method discussed has been selected because of its compatibility with a generally conservative investing philosophy. In my experience, the major downfall of many new option traders is their tendency to trade more than their financial capacity (and trading experience) allows. Do not be in a hurry—you have the rest of your lifetime to make money with options. Get familiar with options by paper trading or using real money with small positions. When confident that you understand what you are doing, then you will be ready to trade with real money. Have patience. You now have the tools to become a successful, long-term options trader.

Options are investment tools. Use them wisely.

Options are versatile. Use them to reduce risk.

If you have questions (Please understand that I cannot offer specific investment advice), I'll try to respond: rookies (at) mdwoptions (dot) com.

Mark D. Wolfinger
Evanston, Illinois
Aug 2014

Appendix A

Symbology

Identifying an option by its symbol

Options are fungible, meaning they are interchangeable. Fungibility allows any trader to sell a position that was purchased earlier ('closing' transaction). For that to be possible, each option must be identifiable and unambiguously different from all other options.

That must seem trivial, but some people use the term 'options' when they really mean 'calls' or 'call options'. That can be very confusing to the person who hears or reads those words, but when making a trade, no confusion is allowed.

Four pieces of information are necessary to identify any option:

For example: GOOG Sep '13 830C or GOOG Sep 20 '13 830C

- Stock or index symbol

- Strike Price

- Expiration date.

- Option Type: Put or Call

Option symbology was given a facelift in 2010. The current *formal method* for identifying an option is used by exchanges, clearing houses, and OCC (Options Clearing Corporation). You and I can use much more simplified symbols, as described above.

For the sake of completeness, below is the current symbology for any option. It contains all possible details, avoiding misunderstandings.

GOOG150918C00830000, where

- GOOG is the ticker symbol of the underlying asset.

- The next six numbers (150918) represent the *last day of trading* for the option

  o 15 is the year.

  o 09 is the month.

  o 18 is the last day of trading. Expiration date is Sat, Sep 21.

  o Thus, Sep20, 2013.

- C identifies the option as a call (C) or put (P).
- The final eight digits represent the strike price.
  - The first five digits are the whole dollars.
  - The strike price in this example is 830.000
  - The final three digits represent pennies.

Appendix B

Adding New Strike Prices

There is a protocol for listing[486] new options with additional strike prices.

For example, if Feb options for XYZ with strike prices ranging from 90 through 115 are already listed for trading, options with new strike prices are added for trading when:

- XYZ trades as high as 115 (the current highest available strike price). The 120s (and probably 125s) are added the next day. This is true for all expiration dates other than LEAPS[487], and all options whose remaining lifetime is fewer than five business days.

- If XYZ trades as low as 90 (the lowest available strike price), then 85s (and probably 80s) are listed for trading the next day.

- Upon request (call 1-800-options to make the request). New strike prices are added when exchanges honor requests from customers or market makers. Requests may be denied.

  NOTE: When new options are added, the strike prices are not chosen at random. Intervals are 1, 2½, or 5 points. Higher priced stocks tend to have options with strikes every 5 points. Many lower-priced stocks and some exchange traded funds (ETFs) have options with strike prices every point.

EXAMPLE

Assume CHEM, a manufacturer of specialty chemicals used for academic research, is priced at $41 per share and has the following listed options (Table B1):

- If CHEM trades as high as 45, options with a 50-strike are added for all expirations.

- If CHEM trades as low as 35, options with a 30- strike price are added for Mar, Apr and Sep (Jun 30 is already listed for trading).

---

[486] Listing for trading on an exchange

[487] LEAPS are options with more distant expiration dates. I pretty much ignored LEAPS in this book.

363

Table B1
CHEM Options

Exp	Strike
Mar	35
Mar	40
Mar	45
Apr	35
Apr	40
Apr	45
Jun	30
Jun	35
Jun	40
Jun	45
Sep	35
Sep	40
Sep	45

CHEM options
After Expiration

After expiration, options with a new expiration date are added (Appendix C). There is a protocol for adding these options. There must be at least one OTM call and put option. Other options are added as deemed necessary. **Translation**: Extra strikes are listed for the more volatile stocks. Thus, GOOG may close at $500 on expiration Friday, but new options will have many more than three different strikes.

When stocks are less volatile, the number of strikes is more limited.

The idea is to list options that will attract interest from customers. There is no need to list a $350 strike for a very, very non-volatile stock when the price is $300 per share. However, for GOOG, it may be appropriate to list options from $700 to $900.

Once an option is listed for trading, and has any open interest,[488] it remains available until the option expires.[489] The only time an option can be delisted occurs when both the calls and puts have no open interest.

---

[488] The number of options in existence; in other words, the number of options sold that have not yet been covered

[489] Options are almost never delisted, but when the open interest remains at zero for a while, it is possible for the market makers to request a delisting.

Appendix C

Adding New Expiration Dates

There is a standard protocol for adding new expiration dates. These rules apply to options that expire on the standard 3rd Friday. Weeklys[490] options are added every week.[491]

1. Each stock is assigned to an expiration cycle. Those cycles are:

    - Jan, Apr, Jul, Oct

    - Feb, May, Aug, Nov

    - Mar, Jun, Sep, Dec

2. Monday following expiration, every underlying asset gets options with a new monthly expiration. The two nearest calendar months are always available. For example, if February options expired last Friday, the following Monday, each stock, index and ETF offers monthly options that expire in Mar and Apr.

3. Each underlying asset has options that expire in two additional months, with the proviso that each of those months comes from its expiration cycle. From the cycle, the two nearest months (that are not already trading) are added. That results in the following:

    - **Jan cycle**: Mar, Apr, Jul, Oct
      Mar and Apr are the two front months. Jul and Oct are from the Jan cycle. These stocks already have Jul options. Thus, Oct is the newly listed month.

    - **Feb cycle:** Mar, Apr, May, Aug
      Mar and Apr are the two front months. May and Aug are from the Feb cycle, with Aug as the new addition

    - **Mar cycle:** Mar, Apr, Jun, Sep
      Mar and Apr are the two front months. Jun and Sep are from the Mar cycle (Sep is new)

---

[490] The unusual spelling (Weeklys) is a result of the CBOE choosing this spelling as a trademark.
[491] But not for the week with the 3rd Friday; there is no reason to add an option that already exists.

Many stocks list LEAPS options (<u>L</u>ong <u>T</u>erm <u>E</u>quity <u>A</u>ntici<u>p</u>ation <u>S</u>ecurities).[492] LEAPS eventually change symbols and become 'regular' January options when it is time to add Jan via the above protocol.

Special Note

As of Feb 15, 2015, the official options expiration date will change

- From: Saturday, following "expiration Friday"

- To: Friday

This change alleviates any confusion in options terminology. Expiration has been on Saturday ever since options began trading on an exchange (1973). Expiration will soon be the Friday specified in the option contract.

---

[492] The final "S" is part of the acronym. These are LEAPS and never 'leap options'.) LEAPS expire in Jan and may be as far as three years in the future.

Appendix D

Stock Splits and other Adjustments

For most readers, there is nothing in Appendix D that you must know. Once again this material is included for traders who want to have a more complete understanding of the options world.

When a stock splits, the options are treated just like the shares. In other words, if you own 10 IBM Jul 200 call options, and if the company splits its stock 2 for 1, you now own 20 IBM Jul 100 calls.

Here's how to think about such a split: you own calls, each of which gives you the right to buy 100 shares of stock at $200 per share. Thus, each option represents the right to buy $20,000 worth of IBM stock. If the stock splits, your rights as an option owner are not affected. You still have the right to buy $20,000 worth of IBM stock for each option owned. Because the stock split cuts the stock price in half, the exercise price of the options is also cut in half. The right to pay $200 per share for a stock trading at only $100 per share is not worth very much, and it doesn't make sense for the options suddenly to become worthless. Thus, each option now gives you the right to buy 100 shares of IBM stock at $100 per share, or $10,000 worth of stock. To restore your previous position, you also receive one extra option for each option held originally. This means you now own twice as many call options, each of which gives you the right to buy $10,000 worth of stock. You are right back where you began: you own IBM call options (20 Jul 100 calls), which gives you the right to buy the same $20,000 value in IBM stock as you previously had the right to buy.

That was a lengthy way of telling you that the options split just as the stock does. In the case of a 2 for 1 split, you now own options with the right to buy twice as many shares at one-half the price. Put owners now have the right to sell twice as many shares at one-half the price. The expiration date is unchanged.

In the event of a 4 for 1 stock split, you would own four times as many options and the strike price would be one-quarter the original strike price.

Unless the split is 2 for 1 or 4 for 1, the deal is more complicated and a different protocol is used. There are two situations to consider:

An Even Split (i.e., 3 for 1)

- The strike price is unchanged.

- The number of contracts remains the same.

- The deliverable[493] changes to reflect the split.

- The option symbol changes to differentiate these options from the new options ('regular' options, representing 100 shares) which are listed once the stock split is effective.

EXAMPLE

- Yesterday you owned five ABC Aug 40 calls. Each call gave its owner the right to buy 100 shares of ABC at a cost of $4,000, or $40 per share. The market price was $2.10. The value of each option is 100 x $2.10, or $210.

- Today the 3 for 1 split is effective and the stock is priced at ~$13.33. You still own five ABC Aug 40 calls. Each call represents the right to buy 300 shares of ABC at a total cost of $4,000 (i.e., exercising gives you the same number of shares that the holder of 100 pre-split shares received when the stock split, and at the same total cost). The option premium is $0.70 and each option is worth $0.70 x 300, or the same $210 as it was worth yesterday. **Warning:** Again, this is confusing. An option may appear to be far out of the money and vastly overpriced.[494]

An Uneven Split (i.e., 3 for 2)

- The strike price is unchanged.

- The number of shares is different.

You own five ABC Aug 40 calls and the company announces a 3 for 2 stock split. Once the split becomes effective, you still own five ABC Aug 40 call options (with a new option symbol), but each call is an option on 150 shares (the deliverable) of ABC stock. If the stock were trading at $45 yesterday, it is trading at $30 today, after the 3 for 2 split.

Here is the tricky part. And it is tricky. It appears that the Aug 40 calls are out-of-the money by 10 points (40 strike vs. 30 stock price), but with this type of stock split, you must multiply the underlying (that is ABC stock price) by the effective split ratio. In other words, the stock price (as far as determining whether your options are in- or out-of-the-money) is 30

---

[493] The deliverable is the same items that a call option owner has the right to receive (or a put owner has the right to sell). In this example, that is 300 shares per option

[494] ABC closed at $42 yesterday, and the Aug 40 call was $3.00. Today, after the 3:1 split, the stock is $14, the strike is still $40 and the option is $1.00. That option appears to be very far OTM (40 strike) when it is really ITM. The $1.00 premium appears to be very high, and almost free money for sellers. This can be a trap for the unwary.

x 1.5, or 45. Thus, the calls are five points in the money (with an intrinsic value of $500 each). They are not out of the money.

This methodology will cause problems for some investors (in my opinion). Today, you can look at the strike price and look at the stock price and know whether the option is in the money. With this new (since 2010) scheme, the underlying price must be multiplied by the correct factor (1.5 in this example) to determine whether the option is in the money.

Avoid trading these options. After the split, there will be new options with normal strike prices: 25, 30, 35, etc.

Bottom line: When a stock splits, the option owner is unaffected[495] and maintains the right to buy (or sell) the same dollar amount of the underlying security at the same total cost.

Adjustments

ZZX is a company that acquires other companies. Let's say that ZZX decides to make a tender offer to buy all outstanding shares of MYCO (my company) and that you have an option position in MYCO. What happens to your options if the deal is finalized?

You have the same rights or obligations you had before the takeover. If we assume that ZZX pays $28 cash for each share of MYCO, then:

- If you own five Nov 25 call options, you will have the right to buy the deliverable ($2,800 cash) by paying $2,500 (100 x the $25 strike price).

  o Once the deal is final, MYCO shares no longer exist. Each call is worth $300.

  o Before the deal is final, the value of the calls fluctuates. Why? Because the deal may fall through and the calls could become near worthless. Also because another suitor may come along and bid more than $28 per share. Oct 30 calls are worthless if the deal goes through, but will be worth $200 if another company offers to buy MYCO at $32 per share.

- If you sold five Nov 25 calls, you will be assigned an exercise notice, and must sell the new deliverable ($2,800) for $2,500. Thus, once assigned, your account will be $300 lighter for each of the five options, and those options will no longer exist.

---

[495] Obviously, if the price of the underlying stock rallies when the split is announced, then the call owner profits and the put owner loses. But that gain or loss is a result of a change in the price of the stock and is not directly the result of the announced split.

- If you are the owner of Dec 22.5 puts, you still have the right to sell $2,800 and get $2,250 in return. This is not a good idea and all puts with a strike price below $28 are worthless.

- If you are short (i.e., you sold) Dec 25 puts, they are worthless (unless the deal falls apart and MYCO shares tumble). No one is going to exercise and they will expire worthless in December.

- Call options with lower strike prices are worth their individual intrinsic values. Do not be surprised if you are assigned an exercise notice immediately.[496]

- Put options with higher (>$28) strike prices will be worth their intrinsic values once the deal is finalized. Thus, the Jan $30 put will be worth $200. Before the deal is final, the put prices fluctuate just like the call prices.

Non-cash takeover

Sometimes a takeover involves only shares of stock or cash. Sometimes it is a combination. For example, assume ZZX buys MYCO by paying $20 cash plus 0.20 shares of ZZX stock for each share of MYCO. That complicates matters for option traders, but it is not difficult to understand the situation.

If you own one MYCO call option, once the merger is finalized, you have the right to exercise, pay 100 x strike price, and receive the same package that the owner of 100 MYCO shares received. Before the merger, the option owner had the right to buy 100 shares of MYCO. Now the option owner has the right to buy $2,000 plus 20 ZZX shares.[497]

The MYCO option represented 100 shares of MYCO. The post-split option represents cash plus only 20 shares of ZZX. Add to that the fact that ZZX is a much larger, much less volatile, company. The new options are for 20 shares (plus cash, which has no volatility) of a non-volatile stock. From an option buyer's perspective, these options have very little appeal and these options do not carry much time premium. ITM options will trade near intrinsic value[498] and OTM options will be very low-priced.

The good news for call owners (and bad news for put owners) is that ZZX probably had to bid significantly above market price to complete the takeover, and that means MYCO shares probably jumped in price. The bad

---

[496] After the deal is finalized—not when the deal is announced. There is NO RISK when the call owner exercises and takes the $2,800 in cash.
[497] $20 per share plus 0.20 shares of ZZX translates to $2,000 plus 20 ZZX shares per option.
[498] Options are usually worth more than their intrinsic value. We refer to that extra value as the time premium. In this case, the option is worth the $2,000 cash plus 20 shares of a non-volatile stock. The time value is very small.

news for call owners is that the value of the option above its intrinsic value is almost zero.

EXAMPLE

Calculating the intrinsic value of MYCO options, assuming ZZX is trading at $40 per share. One share of MYCO is worth:

- $20 cash, plus

- 0.20 shares at $40 per share or $8

- Total current value of one MYCO share is $20 + $8, or $28.

- Total value for MYCO 25 calls: Intrinsic value is $3; time value is probably less than $0.25.[499]

- Total value for MYCO 30 puts: Intrinsic value is $2; time value is probably less than $0.25.

- MYCO 30 calls are out of the money and will expire worthless unless ZZX rises above $50[500] (unlikely) before the MYCO options expire.

Bottom line: When a merger involves cash, the call owner has the right to exercise the option and receive the same cash payment as the owner of 100 shares. When a merger involves a complex mix of cash, stock, bonds or anything else, the call owner has the right to exercise the option and receive the same mix as received by the owner of 100 shares.[501] The option owner's right to exercise is protected.

When the trader is fortunate enough to own calls *before* the takeover is announced, that trader is likely to have a good-sized gain depending on the terms of the takeover.[502]

After the merger is final, no new MYCO options are listed for trade and all outstanding MYCO options get a new symbol and a new deliverable—as described above.

---

[499] Time value is small and depends on implied volatility for ZZX options and time remaining.

[500] When ZZX is $50, the value of the takeover deal is $30 ($20 cash plus .20 ZZX shares worth $10). If ZZX trades any higher, the MYCO 30 calls go in the money and accumulate intrinsic value.

[501] And the put owner has the right to sell that same mix and receive the strike price x 100.

[502] Call owners usually gain, because takeovers occur at a price substantially higher than current market price. Put owners tend to lose.

Appendix E

The Options Clearing Corporation (OCC)

In 1973 the Chicago Board Options Exchange (CBOE) became the first exchange to list options for trading. At the same time, the Options Clearing Corporation (OCC) came into being. Today the name has been changed to OCC.[503] The existence of a clearing firm is necessary because it is responsible for the matching of all buys and sells that occur in the marketplace.

Clearing provides smoother and more efficient markets because each party in a transaction makes transfers directly to the clearing corporation, rather than to the other individual with whom the trade occurs. Thus, OCC acts as an intermediary and assumes the role of both buyer and seller in order to reconcile orders between transacting parties. An option buyer never has to be concerned with whether the option seller has the financial wherewithal to meet the obligations imposed by the contract. And that is important. Imagine what would happen if you owned a call option and were required to find, and notify, the seller before you were allowed to exercise an option. And if that other party refused to sell stock at the strike price (assuming you exercised a call option), what would you do? Sue? That takes time and money. Fortunately, OCC makes sure that is never a problem. OCC assumes responsibility and guarantees that all obligations are met.

OCC began as a clearinghouse for listed equity options and has grown into a global entity that clears a multitude of sophisticated products. Today, OCC is the world's largest equity derivatives clearing organization and operates under the jurisdiction of both the Securities and Exchange Commission (SEC) and the Commodities Futures Trading Commission (CFTC). It clears transactions for options on common stocks, stock indexes, ETFs, foreign currencies, interest rate composites, single-stock futures, futures and options on futures.

Exercise and Assignment

As an investor who buys or sells options, you never have to be concerned with the workings of OCC. But, for those who are interested in details, OCC plays a vital role when someone exercises a put or a call. The first step taken by OCC is to verify that the person who exercises an option owns that option and has the right to exercise. Mistakes occur and

---

[503] *Not 'the OCC'—just OCC*

someone could easily make an error and exercise (for example) XYX Nov 80 calls when the investor owns the Nov 70 calls instead.

Once verified that the customer has the right to exercise, OCC randomly chooses one of its customers (a broker, for example). That broker chooses (randomly or FIFO[504]) one of its clients who has a short position in that specific option. That customer is assigned an exercise notice and must honor the terms of the option contract. The process is a bit more detailed than this simple explanation, but if you are assigned such a notice, it is a done deal and there is nothing you can do about it.

Being assigned an exercise notice is something that many new option traders fear. But, there is no reason for that. One of the most popular option strategies (covered call writing) involves selling call options. If people who adopt this strategy are assigned an exercise notice, it is a good result. It affords the investor the maximum possible profit. You cannot do better than that, and being assigned an exercise notice should be a rewarding experience, not something to dread.

That does not mean it is always good be assigned an exercise notice.[505]

> **NOTE:** The assignment process occurs overnight, when the markets are closed. Thus, if you have a short position in a specific option, but cover those options in a closing transaction, you have no remaining position at the end of the trading day. Under such circumstances, you cannot be assigned an exercise notice. Similarly, once you receive that assignment notice, it is too late to cover the short option[506] in an attempt to cancel the assignment.

Modernization of the options industry

Some standards have been in place since options first began trading on an exchange. The industry has grown enormously since 1973 and some changes have been necessary.

New Symbology

The method used to assign a symbol to each option series had been in place since options first began trading on an exchange in April 1973.

The new system is described in Appendix A.

Stock splits and adjustments

How options are affected by stock splits and adjustments was discussed in Appendix D.

---

[504] First in; first out; the customer who sold first is assigned that exercise notice.
[505] The terms are interchangeable: exercise notice and assignment notice.
[506] You are no longer short. The assignment eliminated your position.

Appendix F

Calculating the volatility of an individual stock

When a measurement is repeated, the nearer each one is to the average, the more confidence you have in the average. If the 'average' of a series of measurements is 35, the average is a more reliable number when the measurements are 33, 34, 34, 35, 37 and 37 than when the measurements are 20, 25, 30, 40, 45 and 50.

The standard deviation is the most commonly used measure of how much the values in a set of numbers vary from the mean. If the data points (the daily closing stock prices) are near each other, then the standard deviation is small. If many data points are distant from each other, then the standard deviation is higher.

When it comes to stock prices, we know each data point is accurate because it is the closing price for the stock. We use the standard deviation to calculate how volatile the stock has been. When the standard deviation is small (for example, when the average daily price change is 3 cents per day for a $30 stock, then the volatility is low. When the standard deviation is large (another $30 stock moves an average of 25 cents per day), then the volatility is higher.

Definition

When a stock is described as having a volatility of 30 that means:

- ~68% of the time, the price of the stock will be within 30 percent (one standard deviation) of its starting price after one year.

- ~95% of the time, the stock will move less than 60 percent (two standard deviations) in one year.

From the opposite point of view, 5 percent of the time, or once every 20 years, on average, a stock whose volatility is 30 can be expected to move (in one year) more than two standard deviations, or 60%.

Standard deviation can be calculated for any given period. It does not have to be for one year. When trading an option with T days to expiration, the standard deviation is calculated by using the formula:

SD = S * V/[SQRT (T)]

Where:

SD is the standard deviation

S is the stock price

V is the volatility of the underlying stock (as a decimal)

T = # of days divided by the # of days in one year

Glossary

1256 contracts—IRS Code Section 1256 states that any gains or losses from the sale of options on broad based indexes (for example, SPX, NDX, RUT) are subject to the 60/40 rule (60% of gains and losses are long—term and 40% are short—term, regardless of how long securities are held). Bottom line: tax advantages when you earn profits trading these indexes.

1—lot—Refers to the trade of a single option or option spread. Thus, 20—lots refers to a trade of 20 contracts or spreads.

A

American style—An option that may be exercised *any time* after it is purchased, providing the exercise occurs before the option expires.

Ask—The price at which an option (or stock) is offered for sale.

Assignment notice—The method used to inform an investor than an option he/she sold has been exercised by its owner. The more formal terminology to describe this process is—"you have been assigned an exercise notice." Once the notice has been received, it cannot be reversed and the assignee is obligated to fulfill the conditions of the option contract.

At the money (ATM)—An option whose strike price equals (or very nearly equals) the price of the underlying asset.

B

Bear spread–A spread designed to profit when the underlying declines. A put debit spread or a call credit spread.

Beta—A term that is not used when discussion options. Beta represents the relative volatility of one stock compared with the volatility of a large group of stocks (S&P 500 Index).

Bid—Price buyers are willing to pay for an option or stock.

Bid/Ask spread—The difference between the bid and ask prices. When this spread is narrow, the markets are said to be 'tight' and that is beneficial to the investor. When the markets are 'wide' it is more difficult for the investor to get a satisfactory price when entering an order.

Box spread—A riskless position with a known payout. It is composed of one call spread and one put spread (both bought or both sold) with the same strike prices and expiration date.

Bull spread—A spread designed to profit when the underlying rallies. A call debit spread or a put credit spread.

Butterfly spread—A winged spread built by buying one bullish spread and one bearish spread (equal distance between the strikes) when both spreads are calls or both are puts. The strike prices overlap such that each spread has one strike price in common.

C

Call—An option that gives its owner the right, but not the obligation, to buy 100 shares of the underlying asset at the strike price any time before the option expires.

Carry, Cost of—The cost of owning a long position. It is the interest paid by using cash to purchase an asset *or* the interest not earned because cash is tied up in the asset rather than earning interest.

Cash settled—An option that doesn't require the delivery of a physical asset (such as shares of stock) when exercised. Instead, the intrinsic value (in cash) of the option is transferred from the account of the investor who received an assignment notice and delivered to the account of the exerciser.

Class—The term used to describe all the puts *or* all the calls of a specific underlying asset. Example—'IBM calls' represents an option class.

Closing transaction—The purchase or sale of an option that offsets all or part of an existing position. Example, when you sell options you previously bought, it is a closing transaction.

Collar—A conservative investment strategy consisting of three parts—long stock, long put, short call. This position has limited profit potential and limited loss potential. The collar is composed of a covered call position with a long put option.

Condor—A winged spread, built by buying one bullish call spread and one bearish put spread, with the condition that each put option has a lower strike price than each call option. In addition, each spread must be of equal width (distance between the strike prices).

Credit—The cash collected from an option transaction.

Credit Spread—A spread whose seller collects cash.

D

Debit—The cash paid to complete an option transaction.

Debit spread—A spread whose buyer pays cash.

Delta—a) The expected change in an option's price when the underlying asset moves one point; b) The probability that an option finishes in the money.

Derivative—An asset whose value is based on the value of another asset.

Diagonal spread—Similar to a credit spread, with the exception that the long option expires in a different month than the short option.

Deliverable—The items received when a call owner exercises the call and pays the strike price; or the items sold when a put owner exercises the put and collects the strike price. Usually 100 shares of the underlying stock, but when there is corporate action, such as a merger or spinoff, the deliverable may involve stock, cash, bonds etc.

Dividend—A taxable distribution of the earnings of a corporation to its shareholders.

Dividend, exercise for—The process of exercising a call option one (or more) day before a stock goes ex—dividend for the purpose of collecting the dividend. (Shareholders, but not option owners collect the dividend.)

Dividend, risk of losing—The possibility that a covered call writer is assigned an exercise notice before the stock goes ex—dividend. When that occurs, the covered call writer no longer owns the stock and does not collect the dividend.

Dollar delta—The delta of a position, multiplied by its share price.

E

Equivalent position— A position with the same risk/reward profile as another. The positions appear to differ, but are essentially identical. Example—Covered call and naked put.

ETF – Exchange traded fund. A group of stocks constructed to mimic the performance of a specific index. The modern version of the mutual fund with very low management fees, ETFs can be bought or sold whenever the markets are open

European style— An option that cannot be exercised, except for a brief period shortly before the option expires.

Exercise –The process by which an option owner implements the rights granted by the option contract. The call exerciser buys (or the put owner sells) 100 shares of the underlying asset at the strike price.

Expiration—The time, after which, an option is no longer a valid contract.

Expire worthless—To be out of the money when expiration arrives. When an option expires without being exercised, it becomes worthless.

Extrinsic value—The portion of an option's price that is not intrinsic value. An option's time value.

F

Fill—The completion of an order to buy or sell options (or stock).

Front month (or week)—Next set of options to expire.

Fungible—Interchangeable.

G

Gamma—The expected change in an option's delta when the underlying asset moves one point.

Gap opening – The first trade of the day (opening) that occurs at a price that differs significantly (the gap) from the previous trade.

H

Hedge—A position that completely, or partially, offsets the risk of holding another position.

I

In the money (ITM)—An option with an intrinsic value. A call is ITM when the strike price is below the asset price. A put is ITM when the strike price is above the asset price.

Inside market—The tightest market. Often an individual investor only sees the outside market for spreads and is unaware of the true highest bid or lowest offer.

Intrinsic value—The amount by which an option is in the money. When added to the time value, the sum represents the option premium.

Iron butterfly—A combination built by selling one call credit spread and one put credit spread with the same expiration, with the additional requirements that the call options are equally far apart from each other as the two put options and each spread has one strike price in common. Example— Sell GE Jun 40/45 call spread and 35/40 put spread.

Iron condor— A combination built by selling one call credit spread and one put credit spread with the same expiration and four different strike prices, with the additional requirement that the call options are equally far apart from each other as the two put options. Example— Sell GE Jun 40/45 call spread and 30/35 put spread.

L

Leg – As a noun: one part of a spread or one part of a position. As a verb: to open one part of a spread at a time, as in "He legged into the trade." Thus, not entering the order as a spread.

Limit order—An order to buy or sell with restrictions. The order establishes a minimum price (when selling) or a maximum price (when buying) at which the order may be filled.

Locked market—A situation occurs when the bid price equals the ask price. This occurs when one (or two) customer orders are sent to a designated exchange and the broker refuses to send it to an exchange where it can be filled. When the market is locked, the option can only trade at that 'locked' price until either the bid or offer disappears.

Long – A situation in which the investor owns an asset, as in: "She is long 300 shares of IBM." A bullish bias. An option position that profits when the underlying asset increases in value.

M

Market maker—A professional trader who stands in a trading pit on the floor of an options exchange and continuously displays bids and offers for all options trading in that pit. In today's electronic environment, the market maker may be represented by a computer that displays bids and offers.

Market order – An order to buy or sell that is to be executed as quickly as possible at the best price available when the order reaches the trading pit. Electronic market orders are filled instantly.

N

NBBO – Acronym for National Best Bid or Offer. That quote takes the highest published (displayed for all to see) bid, and the lowest published offer on any of options exchange and combines them into one bid/ask quote.

O

Obligations (of an option seller) – If (and only if) assigned an exercise notice, the option seller must honor the conditions of the option contract. Thus, the call seller must deliver 100 shares of stock in exchange for being paid the strike price. The put seller must buy 100 shares at the strike price.

OCC – Options Clearing Corporation. The organization that handles the clearing of all option trades and regulates the listing of new options.

Open Interest – The number of outstanding option contracts. It is the number of option that have been sold 'to open' that have not yet expired or been repurchased in a closing transaction. The OI is recalculated daily, after the market closes for the day.

Opening transaction – The purchase or sale on an option that initiates a new position, or adds to an existing position.

Option – A contract that:

- Grants to the buyer, the right to buy or sell a specific asset at a specific price for a specified period of time.

- Potentially (only if assigned an exercise notice) obligates the seller to buy (or sell) a specific asset at a specified price for a specified period of time

Out of the money (OTM) – An option with zero intrinsic value. A call option whose strike price is higher than the price of the underlying; a put option whose strike price is below that of the underlying.

Outside market – The widest possible market, i.e., the published bid and offer. Most of the time, there is a tighter, or inside market.

P

Parity – The price of an option equal to its intrinsic value; an option with no time premium. When an option trades at its intrinsic value, it is said to trade at parity.

Pin Risk – The risk associated with being short options when the underlying stock closes at the strike price on expiration Friday. The investor never knows whether the options will expire worthless of if an assignment notice is on its way.

Pre—insurance – Buying puts and calls as insurance before an adverse market moves increases risk to an unacceptable level. Usually used when an investor sells credit spreads and/or iron condors.

Premium – The price of an option in the marketplace.

Put—An option that gives its owner the right, but not the obligation, to sell 100 shares of the underlying asset at the strike price any time before the option expires.

R

Resistance—A price level at which a stock's rising trend was previously halted.

Rho – The change in the value of an option when the interest rate changes by one percent.

Rights (of an option owner) – The ability to exercise an option, demanding that the seller fulfill the conditions of the contract.

Roll (a position) – A transaction in which an existing position is closed and an appropriate new position is opened. Rolling is often used as a risk reducing strategy, but can be used to lock in profits.

S

Scalping – Repeated buying and selling of securities in an attempt to earn small profits.

Series –All options of the same class having the same strike price and expiration date.

Settlement price – The price of a security on which the value of all expiring options is based. The settlement price for European style, cash—settled index options is calculated from opening prices on the 3rd Friday of the month. The settlement price for all stock options is the underlying's last trade at the close of business on the 3rd Friday of the month.

Settlement risk – The risk associated with holding positions (long or short) in European style index options after those options cease trading on Thursday afternoon, one day before the settlement price is calculated. The risk is that a substantial market move can significantly change the value of those options.

Short – The condition of having sold an asset the investor doesn't own. A bearish bias. A position that profits when the asset decreases in value.

Slide – Escape, as in not being assigned an exercise notice at expiration, despite the fact that the option you are short is ITM by a few pennies. The term is also used when you are not assigned an exercise notice on an ITM option and thereby collect a significant dividend.

Spread – A simultaneous transaction involving two or more options. Also an order submitted in an attempt to execute such a transaction.

Standard deviation—A measure of the dispersion (how far apart) of a set of data.

Standardized – Options became standardized when they were first listed for trading on an exchange. That means strike prices and expiration dates were placed at regular and predictable intervals.

Straddle – One call plus one put with the same strike price, expiration date, and underlying security. An investor can buy or sell straddles.

Strangle – One call and put with *different* strike prices, but the same expiration date and underlying security. An investor can buy or sell strangles.

Strike price – The price at which the owner of an option has the right to buy or sell the underlying.

Support – A price level at which a stock's declining tread was previously halted.

Synthetic equivalent – An option position that behaves exactly the same as a different option position. Example: a covered call and a naked put are equivalent positions when the strike price and expiration date are identical.

T

Theta – The rate at which the value of an option decays in one day.

Threat – The increasing likelihood that the underlying moves beyond the strike price of an option the investor is short.

Time Premium – The portion of an option's price due to volatility, time, and interest rates. Option premium minus intrinsic value.

Time Value – See time premium.

U

Underlying – The asset from which the value of an option is derived. Also the asset received when a call owner (or that must be delivered when a put owner) exercises the option.

V

Vega – The change in the value of an option when the implied volatility changes by one point.

Volatility – The tendency of an asset to undergo price changes.

Volatility, estimated – Also called forecast volatility. An educated guess as to how volatile the underlying will be between the current time and the option's expiration.

Volatility, historical – An exact measurement of how volatile the underlying has been over a specified period of time.

Volatility, implied – The future volatility (from the current time until the option expires) of the underlying as predicted by the option premium. Also, the volatility, plugged into an option calculator that makes the actual option price equal to its theoretical (fair) value.

W

Wasting asset – A security whose value erodes as time passes.

INDEX

Thank you for buying The Rookie's Guide to Options

Join my e-mail list for occasional updates:
http://blog.mdwoptions.com/sign-email-list/

Visit my blog: http://blog.mdwoptions.com/

For 1,000 great articles about trading options.

Special promotions and discounts.

Information on new books.

Ask questions: rookies (at) mdwoptions (dot) com

Other Books by Mark D Wolfinger

My Dead-Tree Books
The Rookies Guide to Options, 2nd Edition (2013)
Create your own Hedge Fund (2005)
The Short Book on Options (2002)

The Best Option Strategies Series of eBooks
Book One. (Volume 0) Intro to Options: The Basics (2014).
Book Two. (Volume 1) Writing Naked Puts (2014).
Book Three (Volume 2) Iron Condors (2014).

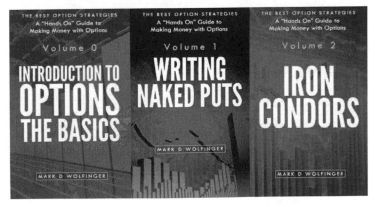

My other eBooks:

The Short Book on Options (2002, 2014)
The Option Trader's Mindset: Think like a Winner (2012)
Lessons of a Lifetime: My 33 years as an Option Trader (2010)

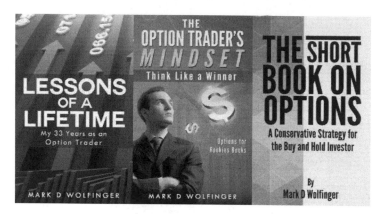

Available at your favorite bookseller.

About the Author

Mark Wolfinger has been in the options business since 1977, starting as a market maker on the trading floor of the Chicago Board Options Exchange. He is now an author and educator of individual investors, specializing in the conservative use stock options.

Born in Brooklyn, New York in 1942, he resides in Evanston, Illinois with his life partner Penny.

He received a BS degree from Brooklyn College and a PhD from Northwestern University (Chemistry).

His blog: http://blog.mdwoptions.com
He writes on options for about.com: http://options.about.com

Made in the USA
San Bernardino, CA
28 March 2015